FREE RADICALS

McGRAW-HILL SERIES IN ADVANCED CHEMISTRY

William A. Pryor

Associate Professor of Chemistry
Louisiana State University

FREE
RADICALS

McGraw-Hill Book Company

New York
St. Louis
San Francisco
Toronto
London
Sydney

541.224
P95f
62414
August 1968

Free Radicals

Copyright © 1966 by McGraw-Hill, Inc. All Rights
Reserved. Printed in the United States of America.
This book, or parts thereof, may not be reproduced in
any form without permission of the publishers.

Library of Congress Catalog Card Number 64-8731

50901

1234567890 HD 7321069876

For the CBP

"I am convinced that the universe is connected by a truly simple law and that if we can only do things well enough, everyone will see the kind of understandable world we live in."

Professor Werner Heisenberg, *The New Yorker* Magazine,
October 15, 1960, p. 34.

Preface

This text is designed to introduce the subject of radical chemistry to students who have had one year of organic chemistry and who are taking or have had the year course in physical chemistry. The average text for the first-year course in organic chemistry includes very little material on radical reactions. On the other hand, the field is a very active one for current research. This book attempts to provide a bridge between the numerous advanced research publications appearing on radical chemistry and the traditional one-year course in organic chemistry.

Although the modern history of radical chemistry is only some thirty years old, the fruits of research in this field are already of enormous value. Radicals are involved in many reactions which are of industrial importance, including thermal cracking of petroleum and many of the processes by which plastics are produced. Many vital life processes, including respiration and photosynthesis, involve radical intermediates.

In this text an attempt has been made to outline the entire field at an introductory level. Experiments in both the gas and the liquid phase are discussed, as are results from both rate and product studies. The approach is that of physical organic chemistry with an emphasis on the mechanism and kinetics of radical reactions. A large number of problems are given, and most include a literature citation to encourage the student to compare his answers with those of the original investigators. Further readings are listed at the ends of chapters, and key references to the original literature are given in the text. These are meant to stimulate the student to do further reading rather than to provide a complete review.

A word is in order concerning the currentness of the literature cited. The first draft of this manuscript was completed in 1963; it was revised during 1964, and most of the literature was updated through September 1964 during the revision. For example, it was during this period that newer mechanistic suggestions for NBS brominations (pages 196–197) and halogen-bridged free radicals (pages 36–37) were published, and these were incorporated into the text. With the cooperation of the publisher, a limited amount of rewriting and a few new references were added to the galley proofs; in this way some references from late 1964 and early 1965 could be included.

It is a pleasure to express thanks to my friends and colleagues who took time from their busy schedules to read, criticize, and help edit various sections of this text.   I am particularly indebted to Professors Cheves Walling, Robert E. Davis, Robert C. Fahey, Kenneth L. Rinehart, James G. Traynham, Richard Sneen, Philip S. Skell, James N. Pitts, Glen A. Russell, Gary W. Griffin, Sean P. McGlynn, and Dr. Ennio Ciuffarin.   Michael Griffith and Dr. James Schreck helped read the galley proofs.   Professors D. F. DeTar, E. A. Kosower, G. A. Russell, P. S. Skell, and Dr. M. L. Poutsma generously allowed me to read certain of their manuscripts prior to publication.

William A. Pryor

Contents

part
one THE NATURE
OF RADICALS

chapter one Introduction

A two-electron chemical bond can cleave either symmetrically or unsymmetrically:

$$X-Y \longrightarrow X\cdot + \cdot Y$$
$$X-Y \longrightarrow X^+ + {}^-\!:Y$$

In the first case, radicals result, and in the second, ions. This text is devoted to the study of reactions that involve radicals as intermediates.

Radical reactions are widespread in occurrence and extremely important. Most reactions initiated by light, including photosynthesis, involve radicals. Explosions, combustions, most halogenations, many polymerizations, and most pyrolyses are radical reactions. Many of the reactions involving oxygen, including respiration, have radical mechanisms.

HISTORY

Today, the term radical can mean either a distinguishable group of atoms in a molecule or a species with an odd number of electrons, i.e., a "free" radical. This duality arose during the last century, when the nature and existence of radicals were shrouded in mystery.

In the early 1800s the term radical meant a part of a molecule, and most chemists believed these parts to be capable of independent, separate existence. However, as the valence theory was developed and it was recognized that carbon is normally tetravalent, and as methods of molecular weight measurement were made more accurate, it became clear that species assumed to be radicals were actually molecules. For example, reactions that had been thought to yield stable methyl radicals $CH_3\cdot$ were found actually to have produced ethane CH_3-CH_3. The counterswing was so violent that near the end of the last century it was concluded that there were no organic "free" radicals. Although iodine atoms, sodium atoms, and certain other elements were known to exist as radicals in the gas phase, organic radicals were believed not to be stable enough to be isolated. Two discoveries upset this extreme view.

In 1900, Gomberg attempted to prepare hexaphenylethane by treating solutions of triphenylmethyl chloride with silver or zinc. Instead of the stable compounds he expected, he obtained yellow solutions that were decolorized very rapidly by air, iodine, and a number of other materials now known to react rapidly with radicals. Gomberg correctly concluded that he was dealing with solutions of the colored triphenylmethyl (trityl) radical.

$$\phi_3C—Cl + Ag \longrightarrow \phi_3C\cdot + \underline{AgCl}$$
$$2\phi_3C\cdot \rightleftharpoons \phi_3C—C\phi_3$$

The decoloration reactions observed by Gomberg are typical of the reactions of radical scavengers with radicals; iodine, for example, reacts with radicals to produce iodine atoms:

$$\phi_3C\cdot + I_2 \longrightarrow \phi_3C—I + I\cdot$$

Colored   Colorless

In 1929, Paneth reported elaborate and elegant evidence which unambiguously established that radicals can exist in the gas phase. Figure 1-1 is a diagram of his apparatus. Nitrogen at 1 to 2 mm pressure was passed down a tube and saturated with tetramethyllead vapor. The vapor was then allowed to pass through a section of the reactor which was heated to 450°C by a movable furnace, and a lead mirror was deposited from the decomposition of the tetramethyllead. The gaseous products from the decomposition flowed down the tube for a distance of 5 to 30 cm and then were passed over a previously deposited mirror which was heated to 100°C. Paneth observed that the second mirror, which could be zinc or antimony as well as lead, was gradually removed. These experiments indicated that tetramethyllead decomposes at 450°C to form methyl radicals:

$$(CH_3)_4Pb \xrightarrow{450°C} 4CH_3\cdot + Pb$$

These radicals then flow down the tube and react with a second metallic mirror to regenerate a metal alkyl:

$$4CH_3\cdot + Pb \longrightarrow (CH_3)_4Pb$$
$$2CH_3\cdot + Zn \longrightarrow (CH_3)_2Zn$$

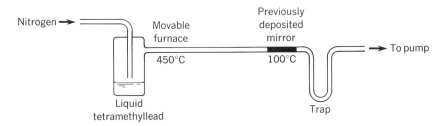

Figure 1-1   Diagram of the apparatus used by Paneth.

After this elegant work, other radical reactions were recognized and identified. In 1937, Hey and Waters in England and Kharasch, Engelmann, and Mayo in America published detailed mechanisms for some reactions which until then had been difficult to explain. Most notably, the radical mechanism was identified for the anti-Markovnikov addition of hydrogen bromide to olefins and for the homolytic aromatic substitution reaction. In the same year, Flory first suggested the now accepted radical mechanism for addition polymerization. Therefore, the modern history of radical chemistry can be dated from 1937.

The Second World War forced many nations to develop synthetic sources for what had been natural products; many of these synthetic materials were produced by radical polymerization processes. An example is the production of synthetic rubber from styrene and butadiene. The polymerization of styrene grew from a curiosity to a multimillion-dollar industry, on which the fate of nations might literally be said to turn. With the invention of Neoprene, polyethylene, and other plastics, radical chemistry achieved industrial significance and became a field of enormous research investment and interest.

DEFINITIONS

Today, a radical can be defined as an atom or group of atoms with an unpaired electron. A diradical is a species with two unpaired electrons. In this definition, chlorine atoms, sodium atoms, nitric oxide, and methyl ($CH_3\cdot$) are all radicals. Methylene, $CH_2\colon$, has two unshared electrons that may be either paired or unpaired; if the electrons are unpaired, it is a diradical. This definition, while so broad as to be occasionally clumsy, is necessary for accuracy. Thus, in their hydrogen abstraction reaction with hydrocarbons, methyl radicals and chlorine atoms react similarly.[†]

$$CH_3\cdot + R—H \longrightarrow CH_4 + R\cdot$$
$$Cl\cdot + R—H \longrightarrow HCl + R\cdot$$

The reaction of alkali metals with organic compounds can produce radicals. For example, ketones undergo a one-electron reduction to a radical ion which subsequently dimerizes.

[†] Notice the convention of showing only the odd electron in chlorine atoms and methyl radicals. Note also that the terms methyl, methyl radical, and methyl free radical can all be used to describe the species $CH_3\cdot$.

$$R-\overset{\overset{\displaystyle O}{\|}}{C}-R \;+\; Na\cdot \;\longrightarrow\; R-\overset{\overset{\displaystyle O^-}{|}}{\underset{\underset{\displaystyle R}{|}}{C}}\cdot \;+\; Na^+$$

$$2\,R-\overset{\overset{\displaystyle O^-}{|}}{\underset{\underset{\displaystyle R}{|}}{C}}\cdot \;\longrightarrow\; R-\overset{\overset{\displaystyle O^-}{|}}{\underset{\underset{\displaystyle R}{|}}{C}}-\overset{\overset{\displaystyle O^-}{|}}{\underset{\underset{\displaystyle R}{|}}{C}}-R \;\xrightarrow{\;H_2O\;}\; R-\overset{\overset{\displaystyle OH}{|}}{\underset{\underset{\displaystyle R}{|}}{C}}-\overset{\overset{\displaystyle OH}{|}}{\underset{\underset{\displaystyle R}{|}}{C}}-R$$

As is shown in the example above, radicals need not be neutral. The one-electron reduction of ketones gives negative radical ions. Positive radical ions are produced in the chamber of a mass spectrograph when electrons collide with organic molecules to knock out valence electrons.

$$R\!:\!R + e^- \longrightarrow R\!\cdot\!R^+ + 2e^-$$

Naphthalene also reacts with sodium; the product is the colored naphthalene radical ion.

MAIN TYPES OF RADICAL REACTIONS

Radical reactions may be divided into three main types: reactions in which radicals are formed, those in which the site of the radical is transferred, and those in which radicals are destroyed. It will be helpful at this point to examine a few examples of each of these types of processes.

Radical-forming processes and radical-destroying processes are conceptually quite simple. Radical centers are formed in pairs by the cleavage of two-electron bonds;† examples include peroxide dissociations,

$$ROOR \longrightarrow 2RO\cdot$$

photolysis of halogens,

$$Cl_2 \xrightarrow{\;Light\;} 2Cl\cdot$$

† Radicals can be formed individually in certain electrode processes.

or decomposition of azo compounds,

$$CH_3-N=N-CH_3 \longrightarrow 2CH_3\bullet + N_2$$

Radicals also are destroyed in pairs. For atoms, these reactions are combination processes. For example, a termination step in chlorination reactions is the combination of two chlorine atoms:

$$2Cl\bullet \longrightarrow Cl_2$$

Methyl radicals also terminate by combination, in this case to form ethane:

$$2CH_3\bullet \longrightarrow CH_3-CH_3$$

However, higher alkyl radicals terminate by two competitive processes that occur simultaneously: combination and disproportionation. In disproportionation, a hydrogen atom is transferred from one radical to the other. The ethyl radical, for example, terminates as shown below.

$$2CH_3-CH_2\bullet \xrightarrow{\text{Combination}} CH_3-CH_2-CH_2-CH_3$$
$$2CH_3-CH_2\bullet \xrightarrow{\text{Disproportionation}} CH_3-CH_3 + CH_2=CH_2$$

For the isopropyl radical, the termination reactions are

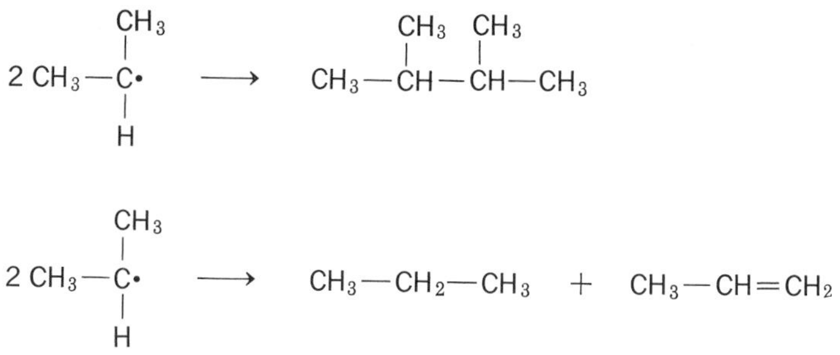

$$2\ \underset{\underset{H}{|}}{\overset{\overset{CH_3}{|}}{CH_3-C}}\bullet \longrightarrow \underset{\overset{|}{CH_3}}{CH_3-\overset{CH_3}{\underset{|}{CH}}}-\underset{\overset{|}{CH_3}}{\overset{CH_3}{\underset{|}{CH}}}-CH_3$$

$$2\ \underset{\underset{H}{|}}{\overset{\overset{CH_3}{|}}{CH_3-C}}\bullet \longrightarrow CH_3-CH_2-CH_3 \ + \ CH_3-CH=CH_2$$

Radical reaction sequences are complicated by the fact that most radical reactions are chain processes. A reactive radical is generated in a radical-forming reaction, and then products are formed through a chain sequence until termination ends the chain. An example is the chlorination of a hydrocarbon, RH.

Initiation

$$Cl_2 \xrightarrow{\text{Light}} 2Cl\bullet \tag{1-1}$$

Propagation

$$Cl\bullet + RH \longrightarrow R\bullet + HCl \tag{1-2}$$
$$R\bullet + Cl_2 \longrightarrow R{-}Cl + Cl\bullet \tag{1-3}$$

Termination

$$2Cl\bullet \longrightarrow Cl_2 \tag{1-4}$$
$$2R\bullet \longrightarrow R{-}R \tag{1-5}$$
$$Cl\bullet + R\bullet \longrightarrow R{-}Cl \tag{1-6}$$

Chlorine molecules absorb light and become activated sufficiently to break the Cl—Cl bond. The chain is propagated by a combination of two transfer steps: The first is a displacement by a chlorine atom on hydrogen to give the alkyl radical; the second is a displacement by an alkyl radical on a chlorine molecule. Note that the *sum* of reactions (1-2) and (1-3) is

$$R{-}H + Cl_2 \longrightarrow R{-}Cl + HCl \tag{1-7}$$

Both reactions (1-2) and (1-3) are substitution reactions analogous to ionic substitution reactions. Therefore, it is convenient to regard reactions (1-2) and (1-3) as homolytic substitution reactions and to use the symbol S_H2 (substitution, homolytic, bimolecular). This symbolism suggests an analogy between the nucleophilic displacement reaction, which is usually referred to as the S_N2 or Walden inversion process, and the S_H2 process. The S_N2 process

$$R{-}X + Cl^- \longrightarrow R{-}Cl + X^- \tag{1-8}$$

has been thoroughly studied and is known to involve an attack by the nucleophile on the back side of the central carbon atom; this mechanism involves an inversion of configuration of the central carbon ("Walden inversion") and a characteristic rate profile as the R group is varied.[†] However, most of the known S_H2 reactions occur on univalent atoms, and inversion of an optically active center cannot be used to probe the stereo-

[†] See A. Streitwieser, Jr., "Solvolytic Displacement Reactions," McGraw-Hill Book Company, New York, 1962, p. 5.

chemistry of the reaction. Thus, in reaction (1-2) the S_H2 reaction involves displacement on the hydrogen atom rather than on the nucleus of the carbon atom, and reaction (1-3) involves a displacement on a chlorine. For this reason, the stereochemistry of the S_H2 reaction has been very difficult to determine experimentally. At present, it is not known with certainty whether a radical displacement at a multivalent atom would involve back-side attack and a Walden inversion or front-side attack and retention of configuration. However, as we shall see in Chap. 12, the available evidence suggests that the radical S_H2 reaction very probably involves a back-side attack mechanism similar to that known to apply to the ionic S_N2 reaction.

NATURE OF PROPAGATION STEPS

We have seen that radical chain reactions involve an initiation step in which radicals are produced, propagation steps in which products are formed, and termination steps which end the chain. The propagation steps are of great interest since they are usually the key to understanding the nature of the products formed. In propagation reactions the site of the odd electron changes but the number of radical sites is not changed.†

Propagation reactions are of four main types: (1) atom transfer reactions, (2) addition reactions, (3) fragmentation reactions, and (4) rearrangements.

1. *Atom transfer reactions.* These reactions are usually hydrogen or halogen abstractions. Examples are

$R\cdot + R'H \longrightarrow RH + R'\cdot$ $R\cdot + R'Cl \longrightarrow RCl + R'\cdot$

$Cl\cdot + RH \longrightarrow HCl + R\cdot$ $R\cdot + CCl_4 \longrightarrow RCl + \cdot CCl_3$

$R\cdot + HCl \longrightarrow RH + Cl\cdot$

---

† In some radical processes, the numbers of radicals may *increase* in one of the propagation steps in the chain sequence. Such reactions are called branching reactions, and they occur in flames and explosions. For example, under some conditions, hydrogen-oxygen flames involve the step

$H\cdot + O_2 \longrightarrow HO\cdot + O\cdot$

We shall not consider such branching chains in this text, and the reader should refer to more advanced books for their description. See, for example, S. W. Benson, "Foundations of Chemical Kinetics," McGraw-Hill Book Company, 1960, pp. 427–489. Branching chains are discussed very briefly in W. J. Moore, "Physical Chemistry," Prentice-Hall, Inc., Englewood Cliffs, N.J., 3d ed., 1962, pp. 289–291.

2. *Addition reactions.* These include the addition of radicals to ordinary olefins, as in the two examples below.

$$Cl\cdot + RCH{=}CH_2 \longrightarrow R\overset{\bullet}{C}H{-}CH_2Cl$$

$$CH_3\cdot + RCH{=}CH_2 \longrightarrow R\overset{\bullet}{C}H{-}CH_2{-}CH_3$$

Addition occurs so as to form the more stable radical; in the above examples, a secondary radical is formed in preference to a primary radical. For aliphatic radicals, stability increases in the sequence primary $<$ secondary $<$ tertiary.

The chain propagation step in the radical polymerization of olefins is also an addition reaction. In this case, a polymeric radical containing n olefin units adds one more unit of the olefin to grow to a chain containing $n + 1$ units. This addition can be symbolized† as shown below for the olefin $CH_2{=}CHR$.

$$R'{-}(CH_2{-}\overset{\overset{\textstyle R}{|}}{C}H)_n{}^{\bullet} + CH_2{=}CHR \longrightarrow R'{-}(CH_2{-}\overset{\overset{\textstyle R}{|}}{C}H)_n{-}CH_2{-}\overset{\overset{\textstyle R}{|}}{C}H\cdot$$

Here, also, the direction of addition is such as to form the more stable secondary radical rather than the less stable primary radical. The reaction above can be abbreviated as

$$M_n\cdot + M \longrightarrow M_{n+1}^{\bullet}$$

where M is a molecule of the polymerizable olefin (called the monomer) and $M_n\cdot$ is a polymeric chain containing n monomer units. Alternatively, the end unit can be shown, and the rest of the polymeric chain can be indicated by a heavy, wavy line:

$$\sim\overset{\bullet}{C}HR + CH_2{=}CHR \longrightarrow \sim CHR{-}CH_2{-}\overset{\bullet}{C}HR$$

The condensation step in aromatic substitution reactions is also an addition reaction:

† The nature of the R′ group need not be considered at this point. We shall return to this topic on pp. 232–233.

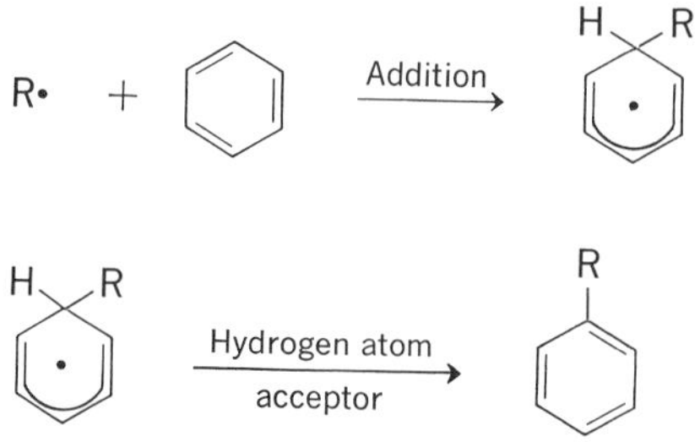

3. *Fragmentation reactions.* The most common fragmentation reaction is a β-scission, in which the pair of electrons beta to the odd electron splits up and a radical fragment is ejected:

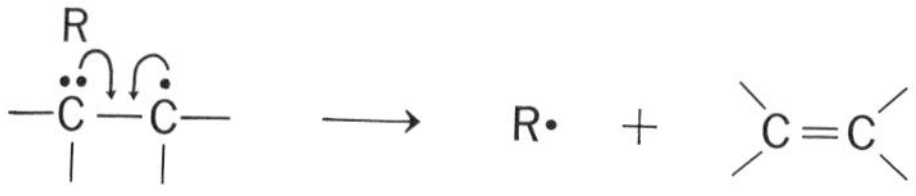

This reaction is the reverse of an addition reaction. Generally, there are three possible electron pairs which could take part in the β-scission. Experimentally it is found that the β-scission predominates which gives rise to the most stable radical. For example, the alkoxy radical below can undergo three different β-scissions, resulting in three different sets of products.

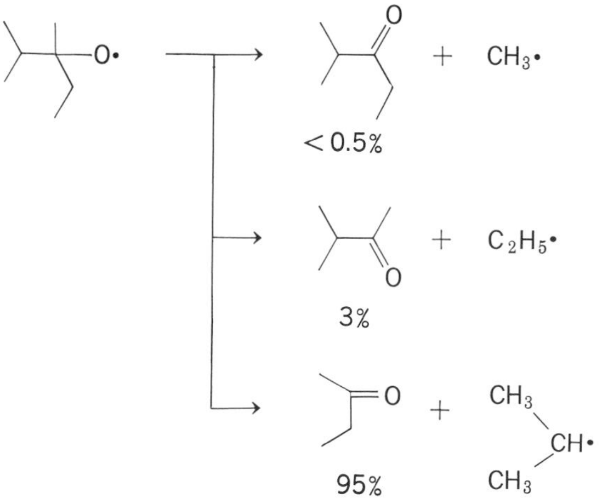

As shown, the amounts of the products† parallel the stability of the radicals formed: i-Pr• $>$ Et• $>$ Me•.

4. *Rearrangements.* Sometimes the propagation step is a radical rearrangement, for example,‡

$$Cl• \; + \; CH_3-\underset{\underset{H}{|}}{\overset{\overset{H}{|}}{C}}-CH_2Cl \; \longrightarrow \; CH_3-\underset{\underset{H}{|}}{\overset{•}{C}}-CH_2Cl \; + \; HCl$$

$$CH_3-\underset{\underset{H}{|}}{\overset{•}{C}}-CH_2Cl \; \xrightarrow{\text{Rearrangement}} \; CH_3-\underset{\underset{H}{|}}{\overset{\overset{Cl}{|}}{C}}-\overset{•}{C}H_2$$

$$CH_3-\underset{\underset{H}{|}}{\overset{\overset{Cl}{|}}{C}}-CH_2• \; + \; HCl \; \longrightarrow \; CH_3-\underset{\underset{H}{|}}{\overset{\overset{Cl}{|}}{C}}-CH_3 \; + \; Cl•$$

POLAR CHARACTERISTICS OF RADICALS

A naïve view of radicals might indicate that, since they are electrically neutral, they are not subject to the same kinds of polar influences that affect the reactions of ions. In this view, radical reactions would show little or no solvent effects and would not be influenced by the electronic nature of the reactants. Sometimes this simple view is realized, but frequently radical reactions are markedly affected by polar influences.

An example of *insensitivity* to polar influences in radical reactions is provided by the contrast between the radical dissociation of *t*-butyl peroxide and the ionic dissociation of alkyl halides. *t*-Butyl peroxide dissociates at the same rate in the gas phase and in solutions of benzene, cumene, amines, and most other solvents.

$$ROOR \; \longrightarrow \; \underset{\substack{\text{Transition} \\ \text{state}}}{[RO\cdots\cdots OR]} \; \longrightarrow \; 2RO•$$

$R = t\text{-Bu}$

† F. D. Greene, M. L. Savitz, F. D. Osterholtz, H. H. Lau, W. N. Smith, and P. M. Zanet, *J. Org. Chem.*, **28**, 55 (1963).

‡ H. L. Benson and J. E. Willard, *J. Am. Chem. Soc.*, **83**, 4672 (1961).

Apparently there is very little charge separation in the transition state, and solvation by polar solvent molecules plays only a small role in aiding the dissociation. This contrasts strongly with the ionic dissociation of alkyl halides, where dissociation occurs only in solvents that can solvate the ions being formed.

$$R—Cl \longrightarrow [R^{\delta+} \cdots \cdots Cl^{\delta-}] \longrightarrow R^+(\text{Solvated}) + Cl^-(\text{Solvated})$$

The dissociation of t-butyl chloride is calculated to occur 10^{100}-fold faster in aqueous solution than in the gas phase. Lack of sensitivity to the nature of the solvent is so typical of radical reactions that it is frequently used as a test to prove that a new reaction is radical rather than ionic.

Many radical reactions, however, show polar influences not unlike those in ionic reactions. As might be expected, these polar influences usually occur in the reactions of species of differing electronegativities. Perhaps the simplest example is the preference for the combination of two radicals that differ in polar type. When two different radicals are present in the same reaction system, three different combination reactions are possible. For example, if radicals A• and B• are both present, the following reactions can occur:

$$2A• \xrightarrow{k_{aa}} AA$$

$$2B• \xrightarrow{k_{bb}} BB$$

$$A• + B• \xrightarrow{k_{ab}} AB$$

The ratio of rate constants shown below is called ϕ.

$$\phi = \frac{k_{ab}}{(k_{aa}k_{bb})^{1/2}}$$

Statistically, ϕ would be expected to be equal to 2.† In agreement with

† The fact that this ratio is statistically equal to 2 can be seen most easily by considering the case where the concentrations of A• and B• are equal, although it is true under all conditions. The rates of formation of AA, BB, and AB are defined as shown below.

$$R_{AA} = \frac{d(AA)}{dt} = k_{aa}(A•)(A•)$$

$$R_{BB} = \frac{d(BB)}{dt} = k_{bb}(B•)(B•)$$

(Footnote continued on p. 15)

this statistical expectation, the value of ϕ is found to be 2 for combinations between radicals of similar polarity.   For example, ϕ is 2 when one radical is ethyl and one is propyl.   However, in combination reactions between two radicals that differ in electronegativity, ϕ is frequently found to be larger than 2.   In the oxidation of compounds by molecular oxygen, both R• and ROO• radicals are present.   The propagation reactions are

R• + O_2 $\longrightarrow$ ROO•
ROO• + RH $\longrightarrow$ ROOH + R•

and three termination reactions can occur:

2R• $\longrightarrow$ Nonradical products
2ROO• $\longrightarrow$ Nonradical products
R• + ROO• $\longrightarrow$ Nonradical products

Values of ϕ larger than 2 are frequently found in these oxidation systems. A preference for the cross-termination reaction occurs, since the alkyl and peroxy radicals differ in electronegativity; the transition state for the cross-termination reaction is stabilized by polar resonance forms in which the peroxy radical bears a negative charge.

$$R_{AB} = \frac{d(AB)}{dt} = k_{ab}(A\bullet)(B\bullet)$$

A given number of A• radicals have the same probability of colliding with either A• or B•.   If we assume that all collisions are equally effective, then these A• radicals produce identical amounts of AA and AB per unit time.   By the same reasoning, if all collisions are equally effective, a given number of B• radicals will form the same amount of BB and AB per unit time.   Therefore, in the entire reacting system, AB is formed at a rate twice that of either AA or BB:

$$R_{AB} = 2R_{AA} = 2R_{BB}$$

Therefore,

$$\frac{R_{AB}}{(R_{AA} R_{BB})^{1/2}} = 2$$

and, using the definitions above,

$$\frac{R_{AB}}{(R_{AA} R_{BB})^{1/2}} = \frac{k_{ab}(A\bullet)(B\bullet)}{[k_{aa}(A\bullet)(A\bullet)k_{bb}(B\bullet)(B\bullet)]^{1/2}} = \frac{k_{ab}}{(k_{aa}k_{bb})^{1/2}} = \phi$$

Thus, if all collisions are equally effective and statistics alone determine the ratios of products, ϕ should be equal to 2.

$$[ROO\cdot \quad \cdot R \longleftrightarrow ROO\colon \quad {}^{+}R]$$

Transition state for the
cross-termination reaction

Cross-termination reactions frequently are favored over homo-termination reactions in the radical copolymerization of two olefins. In the copolymerization of styrene $CH_2{=}CH\phi$ with butyl acrylate

$$CH_2{=}CH{-}\overset{\overset{\displaystyle O}{\|}}{C}{-}OBu,$$ the radical with a styrene unit on the end prefers to cross-terminate with a radical having an acrylate end group.†

In fact, in the styrene–butyl acrylate copolymerization, ϕ has the very large value of 150. This large preference for cross-termination arises because the styryl radical is relatively electron-donating and the acrylate radical is electron-accepting. The transition state for the cross-termination reaction is stabilized by resonance forms in which an electron is transferred from one radical to the other.

Polar effects also frequently influence radical substitution reactions. The data below give the relative rates at which a chlorine atom abstracts a hydrogen from the various positions in butane and 1-fluorobutane.

	$CH_3{-}CH_2{-}CH_2{-}CH_3$				$CH_2F{-}CH_2{-}CH_2{-}CH_3$			
Relative rates:	1.0	3.7	3.7	1.0	0.9	1.7	3.7	1.0

† It is assumed that only the nature of the terminal olefin unit affects the reactivity of the polymeric radical.

The data for butane illustrate the usual preference for abstraction of secondary rather than primary hydrogen atoms. This selectivity is due to the fact that secondary C—H bonds are weaker than primary, and secondary hydrogens are therefore more labile. In 1-fluorobutane, this normal selectivity for secondary hydrogens is evident from the relative rates for attack on the hydrogens furthest from the fluorine substituent. However, the rate of abstraction of the hydrogens on the carbon β to the fluorine substituent is reduced to 1.7/3.7, or 46%, of the expected value, and the rate of abstraction of the α hydrogens is 0.9/1.0, or 90%, of the expected value. Since hydrogen and fluorine atoms are close to the same size, it is unlikely that these rate reductions are due to steric effects. A more likely explanation is that the electronegative chlorine atom has electron-seeking (electrophilic) properties; that is, it has a greater tendency to attack hydrogen atoms which are relatively electron-rich. The fluorine substituent in 1-fluorobutane, with its large electron-withdrawing inductive effect, decreases the electron density on nearby hydrogen atoms and makes them less susceptible to attack by the electrophilic chlorine atom.

PROBLEMS

1-1 Show the chain steps in the photobromination of methane.

1-2 Give all possible products from β-scission of the radicals shown below. Which products would be expected to predominate?

a. $CH_3—CH_2—\overset{\bullet}{\underset{\underset{CH_2—CH(CH_3)_2}{|}}{C}}—CH_2—CH_2—CH_3$

b. $CH_3—CH_2—O\bullet$

c. $\phi CH_2—CH_2—\overset{\bullet}{C}H—CH_2—CH_3$

1-3 In the oxidation of hydrocarbons, a preference for a cross-termination reaction is sometimes found. For example [L. Bateman, *Quart. Rev. (London)*, **8**, 152 (1954)], in the oxidation of ethyl linoleate, ϕ is 3. Representing the two radicals present as R• and ROO•, draw the transition states for the three termination reactions. Explain the preference for the cross-termination reaction.

1-4 Draw structures for 1-fluorobutane which illustrate the electron-withdrawing properties of the fluorine atom. Draw the transition state for the reaction of a chlorine atom with a β hydrogen in 1-fluorobutane; show electronic structures for the transition state which illustrate the rate-retarding effect of the fluorine substituent. Suggest a possible reason why the rate retardation is greater for β hydrogens than for α hydrogens. [I. Galiba, J. M. Tedder, and R. A. Watson, *J. Chem. Soc.*, 1321 (1964).]

chapter two Detection of Radicals

The question may be asked: What evidence is there that species with an odd number of electrons really exist? For some stable radicals, for example, NO_2, ordinary chemical evidence can be adduced. For more reactive radicals, as we have seen in the work of Gomberg and Paneth, indirect reasoning must be used. However, *direct* evidence for the presence of an odd electron can sometimes be obtained from the magnetic properties due to the unpaired electron.

MAGNETIC SUSCEPTIBILITY

Most substances are diamagnetic; that is, they exert a force to move out of a magnetic field when they are placed between the poles of a powerful magnet. This force is due to the fact that all the paired electrons in the molecule align themselves so as to oppose the external magnetic field. Substances with unpaired electrons, however, are paramagnetic and are drawn into a magnetic field. In these substances, the paramagnetic contribution by the odd electron opposes the diamagnetic contribution of all the paired electrons.

The total magnetic susceptibility of substances can be measured by the force exerted on them when they are in a magnetic field. The oldest device able to accomplish this is the Gouy balance, developed in 1889. In 1910, Pascal deduced that the diamagnetism of molecules is a simple additive function of the elements present. Therefore, if the actual magnetic susceptibility of a substance is found to be less than that predicted from Pascal's additivity rules, a canceling paramagnetic contribution due to an unpaired electron is known to be present. For example,[†] by this method, hexaphenylethane was shown to dissociate to radicals to the extent of 2% in benzene at 20°C. The actual calculation is

	cgs units
Molar susceptibility of 5% solution of ϕ_6C_2 in benzene	-272×10^{-6}
Susceptibility calculated using Pascal's constants	$-(-325 \times 10^{-6})$
Paramagnetic contribution	$+53 \times 10^{-6}$

The solution has a less negative susceptibility than calculated because of the positive, paramagnetic contribution of the radicals. At 20°C, a mole of radicals is known to have a susceptibility equal to $1{,}270 \times 10^{-6}$ cgs units. Since each molecule that dissociates produces two radicals, the ethane is

[†] M. F. Roy and C. S. Marvel, *J. Am. Chem. Soc.*, **59**, 2622 (1937).

dissociated to the extent of $53/(2 \times 1{,}270) = 2.1\%$ at $20°C$. Notice that the method has an inherent lack of accuracy because the positive paramagnetic contribution is obtained as a difference between two numbers that are of a similar order of magnitude.

ELECTRON PARAMAGNETIC RESONANCE (EPR)

A technique was developed in 1945 which measures the paramagnetism due to an unpaired electron directly. The method is called either electron paramagnetic resonance or electron spin resonance. Measurements by EPR are extremely sensitive to radicals; concentrations as low as 10^{-8} M can be measured at present, and the method is constantly being made more sensitive.

The electronic instruments used for measuring EPR spectra are complex and will not be described here. Since the theory is difficult and requires some understanding of quantum mechanics, only a simplified and introductory description will be given.

The EPR spectra arise because an electron has spin, and this spin has an associated magnetic moment. When an external magnetic field is applied, the electron magnetic moment can be oriented with or against the field, and, therefore, the electron can exist in either of two energy levels.

Figure 2-1 shows the transition that occurs when the single energy level for an electron is split by a magnetic field into two levels. Transitions between these two levels produce a line in the EPR spectrum. The frequency ν at which this line occurs is given by

$$\nu = \frac{g\beta H}{h} \tag{2-1}$$

where h is Planck's constant, β is a conversion factor called the Bohr

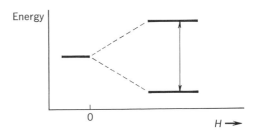

Figure 2-1 Transition for an electron in a magnetic field H.

magneton which converts angular momentum to magnetic moment units, H is the strength of the external field, and g is a proportionality constant called the gyromagnetic ratio. For a free electron, g has the value of 2.0023; in organic radicals, g varies from 2.002 to 2.006. Inserting values for the constants into Eq. (2-1) gives

$$\nu = 2.8026H \qquad (2\text{-}2)$$

where H is the field, in gauss, and ν is megacycles per second (Mc/sec). As Eqs. (2-1) and (2-2) show, higher-frequency (higher-energy) transitions occur as the magnetic field H is increased. For practical reasons, fields of about 3,000 gauss are usually used, and transitions occur at about 9,000 Mc/sec. This is a wavelength of about 3 cm, which is in the microwave region.

So far, we have considered a free electron in a magnetic field and have seen that the EPR spectrum obtained is a single line. However, almost all free radicals give spectra consisting of more than one line. This results from so-called hyperfine splitting. If the odd electron in a radical is located on an atom that has a nucleus with a magnetic moment, this magnetic moment interacts with the electron and splits its energy levels further. Examples of nuclei with magnetic moments are H, F^{19}, N^{15}, C^{13}, and P^{31}.

In the case in which an odd electron interacts with one proton, the magnetic field of the proton produces a small additional field which adds to or subtracts from the external magnetic field. Each level in Fig. 2-1 is then split in two by interaction with a proton, as is shown in Fig. 2-2. Nuclear spins do not change when the electron changes levels, and, therefore, transitions occur between half the levels in Fig. 2-2, i.e., those having the same nuclear spin. Thus, two transitions occur, and the electron that

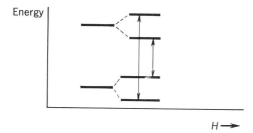

Figure 2-2 Transitions for an electron interacting with one proton in a magnetic field H.

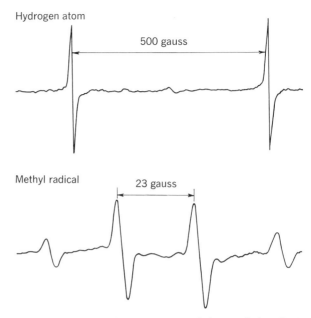

Hydrogen atom

500 gauss

Methyl radical   23 gauss

Figure 2-3   The EPR spectra of the hydrogen atom and the methyl radical. (*Varian Associates.*)

produced the single EPR line in Fig. 2-1 now produces a pair of lines. Examples of radicals that would be predicted to give a two-line spectrum are H• and •CHCl$_2$.

In general, a nucleus splits an EPR line into $2I + 1$ lines, where I is the nuclear spin. For hydrogen, where I is ½, a single proton produces two lines. When n equivalent protons interact with the electron, the spectrum consists of $n + 1$ lines. For example, the methyl radical with three protons should give a spectrum of four lines. Figure 2-3 shows the spectra of H• and CH$_3$•; they contain two and four lines, respectively, as predicted. Note that the amount of splitting is greater for H• than for CH$_3$•. In the hydrogen atom, the electron is actually on the atom with a nuclear spin. In the methyl radical, the electron is on the carbon, and the atom with nuclear spin is the adjacent atom, giving less interaction and a smaller amount of splitting.†

The semiquinones are series of compounds which illustrate these phenomena. Quinones can be reduced in a one-electron step to the semiquinone radical ion.

† For further examples of EPR spectra of hydrocarbon radicals, see R. W. Fessenden and R. H. Schuler, *J. Chem. Phys.*, **39**, 2147 (1963).

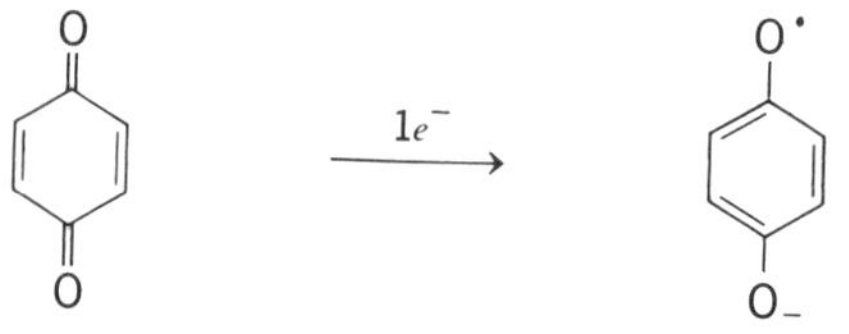

These semiquinones are moderately stable and can be obtained in high concentrations. Their stability is explained by resonance forms in which the odd electron is placed on the ring carbon atoms as well as on both oxygens.

Since the electron can be placed on the ring carbons, the EPR spectrum should be split if there are protons on these carbons. This is observed, and the number of lines found is that predicted by the $n + 1$ rule. For example, tetrachlorosemiquinone gives only one line. As the chlorine is replaced with hydrogens, the number of lines increases, as shown below.

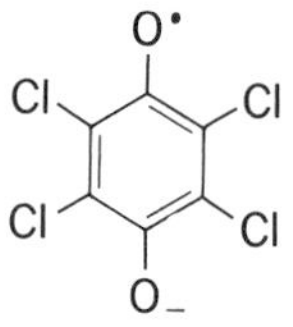

1 line 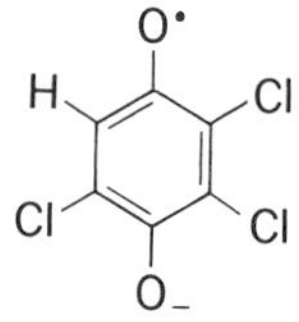   2 lines 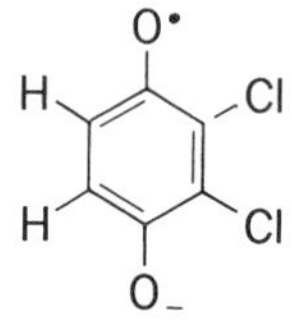   3 lines

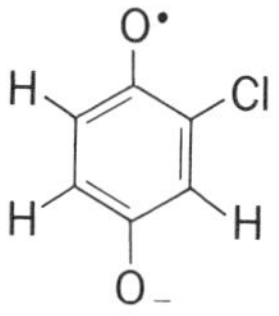

4 lines 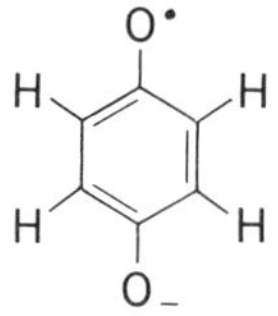   5 lines

A similar set of EPR spectra can be observed in the enzymatic oxidation of olefins by peroxidase–hydrogen peroxide. Oxidation of dihydroxyfumaric acid, ascorbic acid, and reductic acid gives the radicals shown below as (I), (II), and (III).

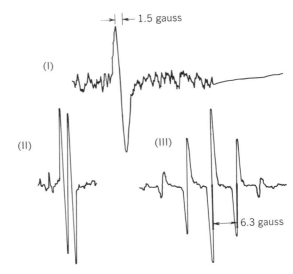

The EPR spectra of these three radicals would be predicted to show one, two, and five lines, respectively. The three spectra are shown in Fig. 2-4, and the predicted number of lines are observed.

The amount of splitting (or "hyperfine interaction") that would be produced if an electron spent all its time on an atom can be calculated from theoretical principles. The actual splitting found for a particular atom, therefore, can be correlated with the fraction of the odd electron density occurring on that atom. This allows experimental measurement of the resonance distribution of the odd electron. The amount of splitting, in gauss, is called the hyperfine splitting constant, a_H. [Equation (2-2)

Figure 2-4   The EPR spectra of radicals I, II, and III. (*Varian Associates.*)

shows that 2.80 times a_H gives the frequency of separation of the lines, in megacycles per second.] The benzene radical ion can be obtained by reduction of benzene with potassium:

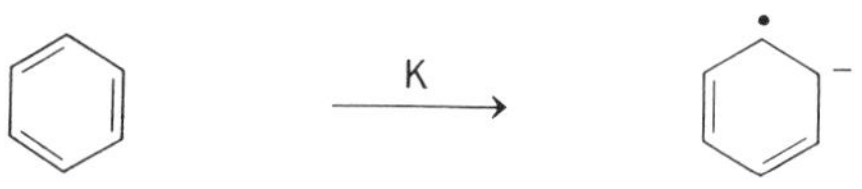

The spectrum of this radical ion consists of seven equally spaced lines with an a_H equal to 3.75 gauss. By symmetry, one-sixth of the odd electron density must occur on each carbon, and, therefore, the splitting constant for the benzene radical ion might be expected to be approximately one-sixth of the value for methyl, or $(\frac{1}{6})(23) = 3.8$ gauss, very close to that observed.

SPECTRA

In many cases, optical spectra can be used to identify free radicals. The triphenylmethyl radical is yellow in solution.

$$\phi_3C-C\phi_3 \quad = \quad 2\phi_3C\cdot$$

Colorless and   Yellow and
diamagnetic   paramagnetic

If iodine or oxygen is present, the yellow color fades:

$$\phi_3C\cdot + O_2 \longrightarrow \phi_3C-O-O\cdot$$
Colorless

Diphenylpicrylhydrazine can be oxidized to the hydrazyl radical:

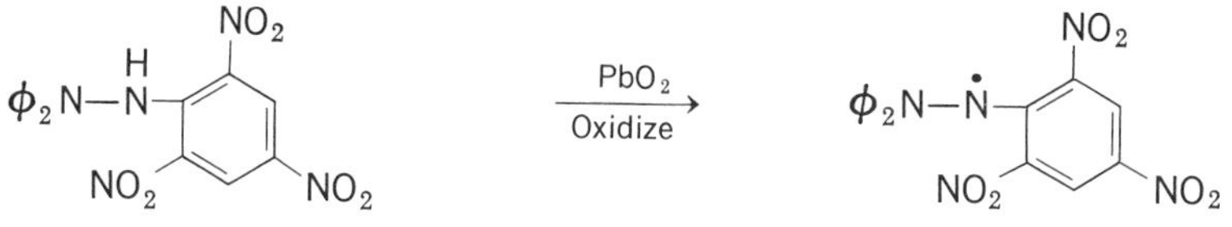

Diphenylpicrylhydrazine   Diphenylpicrylhydrazyl (DPPH)

The DPPH radical is deep violet, and it is stable in the solid form for years. Even 10^{-5} M solutions of it are colored, and it can be used as an "indicator" to detect the presence of radicals, much as an acid-base indicator might be used in a titration.   A complication arises, however, since the products of the reaction of DPPH with radicals often are not known.   In the few cases where they are known, they are not those which would result from simple coupling reactions at the nitrogen where the electron is shown above.

TRAPPING

If species known to react rapidly with radicals affect the rate of a reaction, the conclusion is that radicals are involved.   For example, DPPH inhibits polymerization of monomeric olefins such as styrene.   The conclusion is that the polymerization involves radical intermediates, and these are trapped by the DPPH.   In solution, iodine, quinones, oxygen, sulfur, and many other substances have been used as radical scavengers.   In the gas phase, butadiene has been used; the radicals add to the diene to form a product that dimerizes, and the dimer can be isolated and identified.

SUGGESTIONS FOR FURTHER READING

Electron paramagnetic resonance

Carrington, A.: *Quart. Rev. (London)*, **17**, 67 (1963).
Ingram, D. J. E.: "Free Radicals as Studied by Electron Spin Resonance," Butterworth Scientific Publications, London, 1958.
Symons, M. C. R.: "Identification of Organic Free Radicals by Electron Spin Resonance," in V. Gold (ed.), "Advances in Physical Organic Chemistry," vol. I, Academic Press Inc., New York, 1963, p. 284.

Magnetic susceptibility

Michaelis, L.: in A. Weissberger (ed.), "Technique of Organic Chemistry," vol. I, pt. II, Interscience Publishers, Inc., New York, 1st ed., 1946.

General

Trotman-Dickenson, A. F.: "Free Radicals," Methuen & Co., Ltd., London, 1959, pp. 1–24.

Walling, C.: "Free Radicals in Solution," John Wiley & Sons, Inc., New York, 1957, pp. 1–24.

Waters, W. A.: "Chemistry of Free Radicals," Oxford University Press, London, 2d ed., 1948, pp. 1–34.

chapter three Conformation of Radicals

There are three possibilities for the most stable conformation for a free radical. The carbon atom bearing an odd electron could be planar (like a carbonium ion), or tetrahedral, or a shallow pyramid which is neither planar nor tetrahedral. Figure 3-1 shows these three possible conformations. Although this subject is still under investigation, at present it seems most likely that organic radicals are very nearly, but probably not exactly, planar and have the geometry of a very shallow pyramid. However, the energy required to convert this shallow pyramid to a planar or to a tetrahedral conformation is apparently very low.

If a radical were planar, the hybridization of the bonds would be sp^2, just as in a carbonium ion, and the remaining p orbital would contain the odd electron (Fig. 3-1a). If the radical were pyramidal, the p orbital containing the electron would contain some s character—i.e., it would be some hybrid between pure p and sp^3—and there would be a dissymmetric distribution of electron density in any one conformation of the radical. Figure 3-2 shows the two enantiomorphic conformations of a pyramidal radical.

It would seem that the conformation of radicals could be most directly investigated by those physical and spectral methods which give bond lengths and angles of stable molecular species. However, even the most sophisticated techniques have not indicated unambiguously whether typical organic radicals are planar or are slightly pyramidal. For the methyl radical, which has been studied in the most detail, the ultraviolet, infrared, Raman, and EPR spectra have all been obtained and have been analyzed to determine the conformation of the radical.[†] The conclusion from all these studies is that $CH_3\cdot$ is either planar or is very nearly planar. Unfortunately, none of the methods can distinguish between a planar conformation and one in which there is a 10 to 15° deviation from planarity. These techniques do show that the energy barrier between the planar conformation for $CH_3\cdot$ and a shallow pyramid is very low.

Part of the difficulty in obtaining the spectra of radicals is that most radicals are so reactive that they can only be studied in frozen glasses at very low temperatures. However, the EPR spectra of several alkyl and cycloalkyl radicals have been observed by a novel experimental technique in which the liquid hydrocarbons are irradiated with high-energy electrons while in the cavity of an EPR instrument and the spectra are

[†] The optical spectra are discussed by G. Herzberg, *Proc. Roy. Soc. (London)*, **262A**, 291 (1961), and *Ann. Rev. Phys. Chem.*, **9**, 327 (1958). The EPR spectrum is discussed by M. Karplus, *J. Chem. Phys.*, **30**, 15 (1959), and M. Karplus and G. K. Fraenkel, *ibid.*, **35**, 1312 (1961).

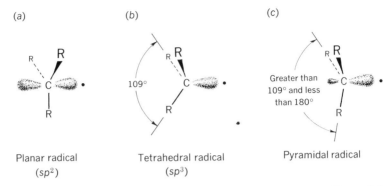

(a)

R
R
C   •
R

Planar radical
(sp^2)

(b)

109°
R
R
C   •
R

Tetrahedral radical
(sp^3)

(c)

Greater than
109° and less
than 180°
R
R
C   •
R

Pyramidal radical

Figure 3-1

recorded during irradiation.† In this way, concentrations of radicals high enough to give EPR signals can be produced at ordinary temperatures. Unfortunately, the spectra usually do not indicate whether the radical center is planar or pyramidal. A discussion of the cyclohexyl radical will illustrate the difficulties. The EPR spectrum of the cyclohexyl radical either in the liquid at 10°C or in the solid at −10°C shows that the pair of β hydrogens on the carbon next to the radical center are not equivalent. One β hydrogen interacts with the odd electron more strongly than does the other, and the two splitting constants are 41 and 5 gauss. Cyclohexane, of course, exists in a chair conformation, and has hydrogens which are either axial or equatorial. Models show that the axial and equatorial hydrogens would not appear identical in the EPR spectrum of the cyclohexyl radical regardless of whether the radical center were planar or pyramidal. Figure 3-3 shows the cyclohexyl radical assuming that the radical center is planar. The bond to the equatorial hydrogen lies near the nodal plane of the p orbital containing the odd electron, and therefore the equatorial hydrogen should couple relatively weakly with the odd

† R. W. Fessenden and R. H. Shuler, *J. Chem. Phys.*, **39**, 2147 (1963); S. Ogawa and R. W. Fessenden, *ibid.*, **41**, 994 (1964).

R'
R
C   •
R''

⇌

R   R'
•   C
R''

Figure 3-2

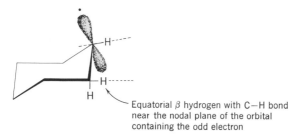

Equatorial β hydrogen with C—H bond
near the nodal plane of the orbital
containing the odd electron

Figure 3-3 Cyclohexyl radical shown with a planar radical center.

electron. The axial hydrogen should couple more strongly. Figure 3-4 shows the cyclohexyl radical assuming that the radical center is pyramidal. The odd electron can then be either axial or equatorial. When the odd electron is axial, it again couples strongly with the axial and more weakly with the equatorial hydrogen; when the odd electron is equatorial, it couples approximately equally with both β hydrogens. The net result is that the odd electron should couple more strongly with the axial hydrogen whether the radical center is planar or pyramidal.†

In connection with the question of the geometry of trigonal carbon atoms, it is interesting to examine the geometry of other atoms which contain an odd electron. Of particular interest is the series of nitrogen compounds shown below.

$$O \overset{\overset{\displaystyle ..}{N}}{\diagdown} O^{-} \qquad O \overset{\overset{\displaystyle .}{N}}{\diagdown} O \qquad O = \overset{+}{N} = O$$
$$\quad 115° \qquad\qquad\quad 134° \qquad\qquad\quad 180°$$

Nitrite ion   Nitrogen dioxide   Nitronium ion

In this series, the nitrite ion is bent almost to a tetrahedral angle; nitrogen dioxide, which is a stable free radical, has a slightly bent conformation; and the nitronium ion is linear. Comparison of these three compounds with the three carbon species shown below would suggest conformations

---

† Cyclohexyl and other saturated hydrocarbon radicals have splitting constants for the α hydrogen which are quite different from those for the vinyl and cyclopropyl radicals. However, it does not necessarily follow from this that normal hydrocarbon radicals are exactly planar or that both the vinyl and cyclopropyl radicals are nonplanar. The detailed arguments on the cyclohexyl radical are complex, and the article by S. Ogawa and R. W. Fessenden, *J. Chem. Phys.*, **41**, 994 (1964), should be consulted.

Figure 3-4 Cyclohexyl radical shown with a pyramidal radical center. (*a*) Odd electron axial; (*b*) odd electron equatorial.

in which the radical is a shallow pyramid and the carbanion is a deeper pyramid or is tetrahedral.†

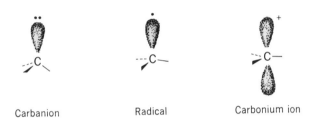

If radicals were planar, they would have a plane of symmetry and could not exist in optically active forms. Therefore, one approach used to determine whether or not they are planar has been to prepare radicals from optically active starting materials. However, no experiment of this type has indicated the preferred geometry of radicals. For example, the chlorination of optically active 1-chloro-2-methylbutane gives reaction products that do not retain any of the optical activity.‡

$$\underset{\text{Optically active}}{C_2H_5-\overset{\displaystyle H}{\underset{\displaystyle CH_3}{C}}-CH_2Cl} \xrightarrow{\text{Cl·}} \left[C_2H_5-\overset{\displaystyle \bullet}{\underset{\displaystyle CH_3}{C}}-CH_2Cl \right] \xrightarrow{Cl_2} \underset{\text{Racemic}}{C_2H_5-\overset{\displaystyle Cl}{\underset{\displaystyle CH_3}{C}}-CH_2Cl}$$

This result, however, can be explained in two ways. In the first, the loss

† A brief discussion of inorganic oxyanions and the suggestion that their geometry may not resemble hydrogen-substituted compounds is given by P. W. Atkins, N. Keen, and M. C. R. Symons, *J. Chem. Soc.*, 250 (1963).

‡ H. C. Brown, M. S. Kharasch, and T. H. Chao, *J. Am. Chem. Soc.*, **62**, 3435 (1940).

of optical activity in the products is explained as due to the fact that the radicals are planar and cannot exist in optically active forms.

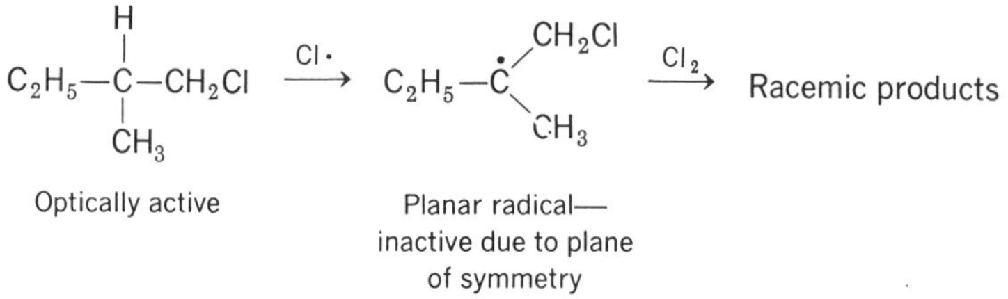

$$C_2H_5-\overset{\overset{\displaystyle H}{|}}{\underset{\underset{\displaystyle CH_3}{|}}{C}}-CH_2Cl \quad \overset{Cl\cdot}{\longrightarrow} \quad C_2H_5-\overset{\cdot}{C}\overset{\displaystyle CH_2Cl}{\underset{\displaystyle CH_3}{\diagdown}} \quad \overset{Cl_2}{\longrightarrow} \quad \text{Racemic products}$$

Optically active   Planar radical— inactive due to plane of symmetry

In the second explanation, the loss of optical activity is ascribed to the fact that the inversion of the radicals is more rapid than the transfer reaction with chlorine molecules. For example, consider the reaction of D molecules to give D radicals.

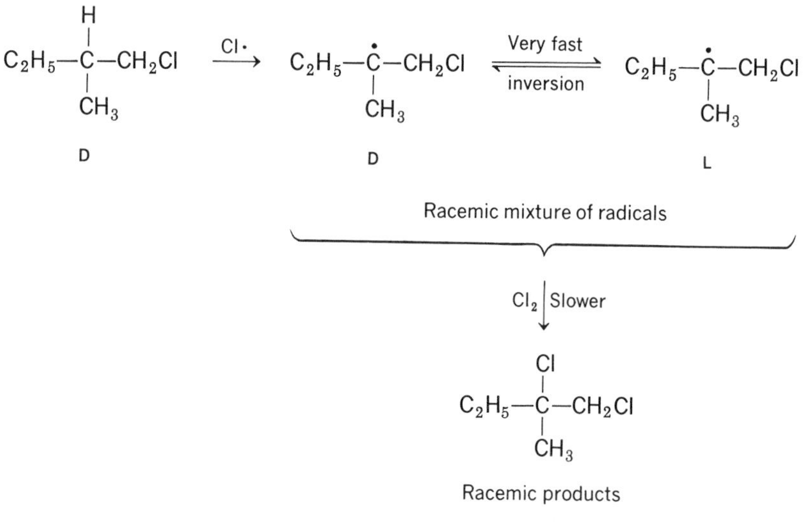

$$C_2H_5-\overset{\overset{\displaystyle H}{|}}{\underset{\underset{\displaystyle CH_3}{|}}{C}}-CH_2Cl \xrightarrow{Cl\cdot} C_2H_5-\overset{\overset{\displaystyle \cdot}{}}{\underset{\underset{\displaystyle CH_3}{|}}{C}}-CH_2Cl \underset{\text{inversion}}{\overset{\text{Very fast}}{\rightleftharpoons}} C_2H_5-\overset{\overset{\displaystyle \cdot}{}}{\underset{\underset{\displaystyle CH_3}{|}}{C}}-CH_2Cl$$

D   D   L

Racemic mixture of radicals

Cl_2 | Slower

$$C_2H_5-\overset{\overset{\displaystyle Cl}{|}}{\underset{\underset{\displaystyle CH_3}{|}}{C}}-CH_2Cl$$

Racemic products

The conversion of D to L radicals shown above is a simple inversion process.

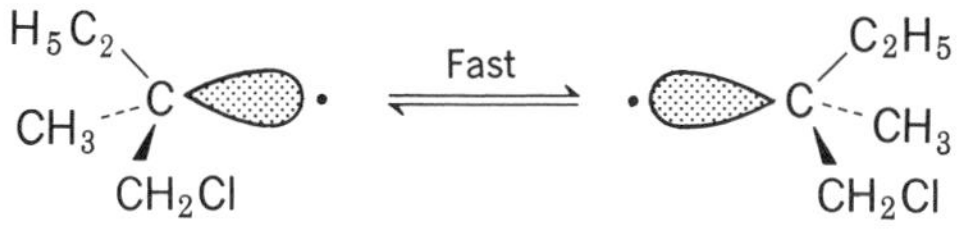

$$\underset{CH_3}{\overset{H_5C_2}{\diagdown}}C\overset{\text{Fast}}{\rightleftharpoons}C\underset{CH_2Cl}{\overset{C_2H_5}{\diagup}}$$

Since it is known that amines invert rapidly, it is quite reasonable to suppose that radicals would invert very rapidly if they had pyramidal structure.

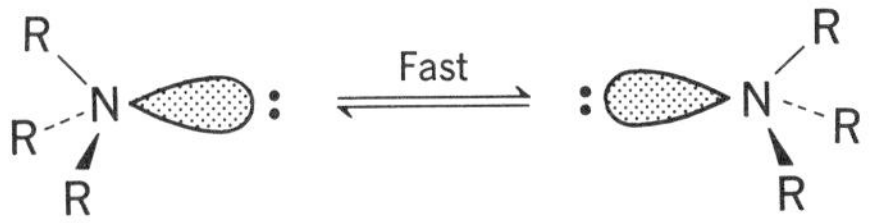

Even where optically active products are obtained, the results are not subject to clear-cut explanation. The bromination of optically active 1-chloro- or 1-bromo-2-methylbutane leads to optically active products.† The most straightforward explanation of these results is that bromine molecules trap the optically active radicals before they can racemize by inversion. For example, the D molecules might react as shown below.

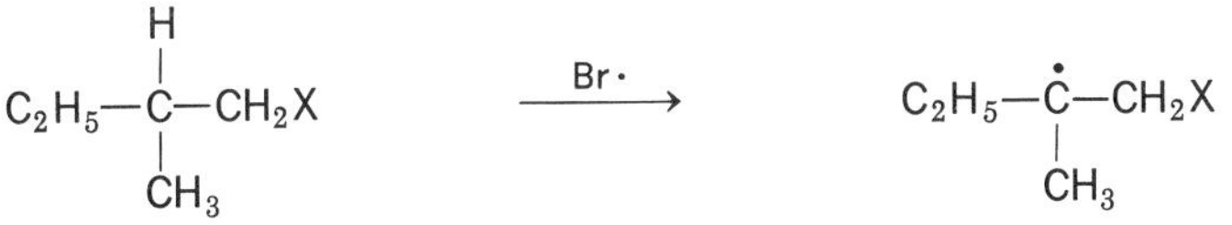

Since bromine is a better transfer agent than chlorine, it is possible that bromination could give optically active products and chlorination give racemic products.

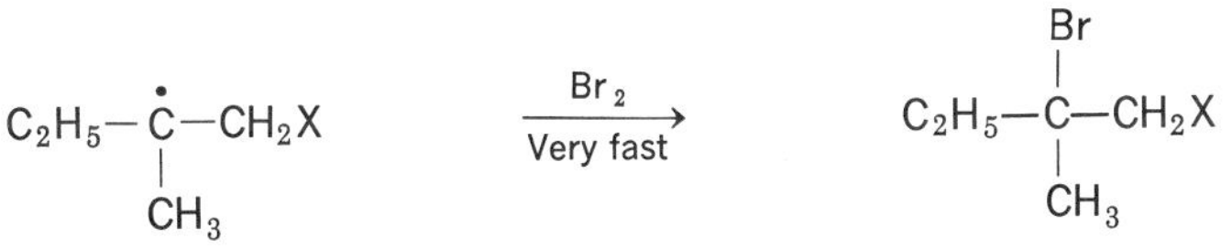

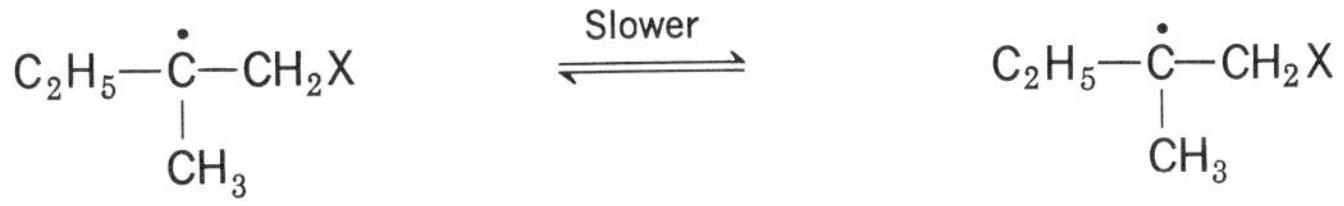

However, there is the possibility that optically active products are obtained from these α-halo radicals because the halogen atom is able to bridge to form a triangular radical that cannot invert and racemize. This is shown below.

† P. S. Skell, D. L. Tuleen, and P. D. Readio, *J. Am. Chem. Soc.*, **85**, 2849 (1963).

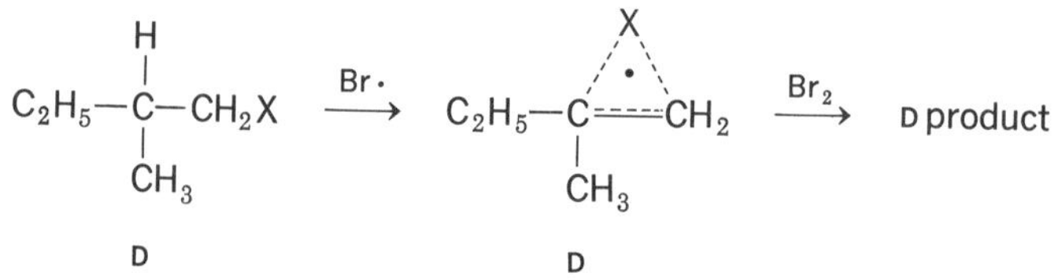

$$C_2H_5-\overset{\overset{\displaystyle H}{|}}{\underset{\underset{\displaystyle CH_3}{|}}{C}}-CH_2X \quad \xrightarrow{\;Br\cdot\;} \quad C_2H_5-\overset{\overset{\displaystyle X}{\triangle}}{\underset{\underset{\displaystyle CH_3}{|}}{C}}\!\!=\!\!=\!\!=\!\!CH_2 \quad \xrightarrow{\;Br_2\;} \quad D\;product$$

D   D

This possibility cannot be ignored, since both chlorine and bromine atoms are known to migrate to adjacent atoms in radical processes, and this rearrangement must involve a transition state in which the halogen atom is partly bonded to each carbon atom (e.g., see page 13). In the reaction shown above, the starting materials are postulated to form the bridged radical directly *without ever proceeding through an open-chain radical*. If this is the case, then the retention of optical activity in the products of these brominations has no bearing on the problem of the conformation of open-chain radicals.

Another possibility also exists: Bridged radicals could be formed from the open-chain radicals.

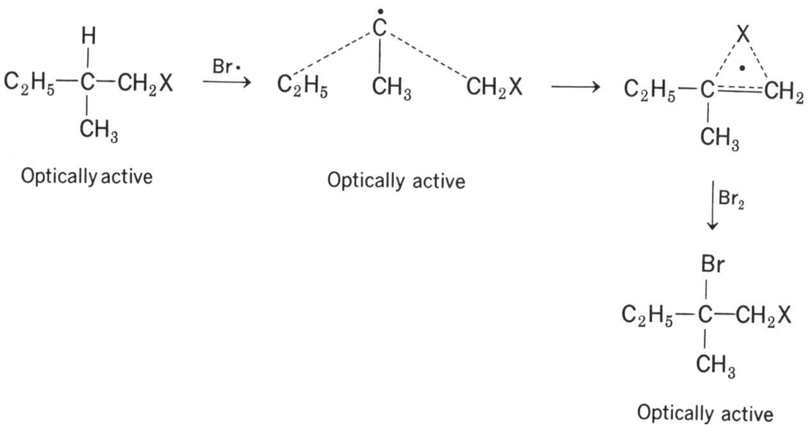

$$C_2H_5-\overset{\overset{\displaystyle H}{|}}{\underset{\underset{\displaystyle CH_3}{|}}{C}}-CH_2X \quad \xrightarrow{\;Br\cdot\;} \quad \overset{\displaystyle \dot{C}}{C_2H_5 \quad CH_3 \quad CH_2X} \quad \longrightarrow \quad C_2H_5-\overset{\overset{\displaystyle X}{\triangle}}{\underset{\underset{\displaystyle CH_3}{|}}{C}}\!\!=\!\!=\!\!=\!\!CH_2$$

Optically active   Optically active

$\Big\downarrow Br_2$

$$C_2H_5-\overset{\overset{\displaystyle Br}{|}}{\underset{\underset{\displaystyle CH_3}{|}}{C}}-CH_2X$$

Optically active

Clearly, if this is correct, the bridged radical is simply another intermediate in the reaction scheme, and open-chain radicals must be capable of existence in optically active conformations.†

† An explanation for stereospecificity in the halogenation of 2-halobutanes has been given which invokes conformational effects rather than bridged radicals. See P. S. Fredricks and J. M. Tedder, *J. Chem. Soc.*, 3520 (1961). Bridged radicals will remain speculative until more concrete evidence for their existence is obtained. This controversy has its counterpart in ionic chemistry. See D. J. Cram, *J. Am. Chem. Soc.*, **86**, 3767 (1964), and H. C. Brown, K. J. Morgan, and F. J. Chloupek, *ibid.*, **87**, 2137 (1965).

The problem of whether bridged radicals or open-chain radicals are the more stable is the subject of intensive current research, and a definitive answer is not available. However, strong evidence exists in one system that bromine substituents bridge to form radicals with lower energy than the analogous open-chain radicals.† In *cis*-1-bromo-4-*t*-butylcyclohexane (I), the bulky *t*-butyl group holds the molecule in a conformation in which the bromide is axial. This compound is brominated to give the 1,2-*trans* dibromide (II) as the major product:

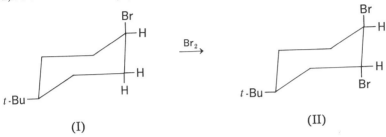

(I)   (II)

Two lines of evidence suggest that *only bridged radicals are involved in this reaction*. Firstly, the open radical (III) would be expected to react to form major amounts of both (II) and the product in which the two bromines are *cis*:

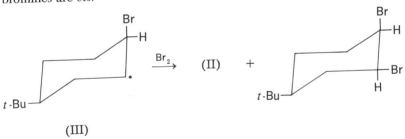

(III)

On the other hand, a bridged radical such as (IV) would explain the predominance of the *trans* product:

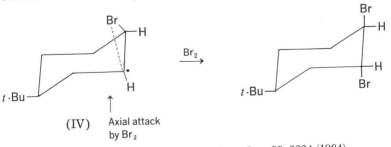

(IV)   Axial attack
        by Br$_2$

† P. S. Skell and P. D. Readio, *J. Am. Chem. Soc.*, **86**, 3334 (1964).

Attack by bromine on (IV) from the axial direction must be postulated, but this is known to be the preferred direction for attack in ionic reactions.

The second line of evidence suggesting that the bridged radical (IV) is formed directly from (I) involves kinetic data. It is known that halogenation is usually retarded by an α halogen substituent. (See, for example, the data in Table 13-6.) Therefore, *the formation of the α-halogenation product (II)* as the *predominant product* cannot be explained without postulating some special effect. The most reasonable explanation for preferential bromination of (I) at the α position is a *neighboring effect* by the α bromide substituent.†

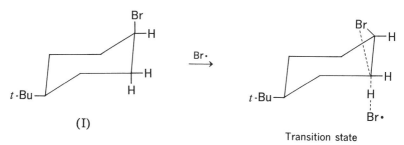

(I)

Transition state

In this explanation, the neighboring bromide bridges to stabilize the transition state in which the α C—H bond is stretched. One of the steric requirements for such bridging is that the bromide substituent be axial. Therefore, this mechanism is confirmed by the fact that the epimeric compound (V), which has an equatorial bromide substituent, is brominated less than one-fifteenth as rapidly as (I):

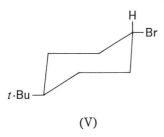

(V)

It is clear that an axial bromine adjacent to a C—H bond in cyclohexane produces *an enhanced rate of hydrogen abstraction* through a neighboring-group effect.‡ The complete reaction scheme is

† We shall discuss the neighboring-group effect of an iodide substituent on perester O—O bond homolysis on p. 124.

‡ B. Capon, *Quart. Rev.* (*London*), **28**, 45 (1964), gives a discussion of the neighboring-group effect. Most of the examples concern ionic reactions, but radical reactions are briefly covered on p. 104.

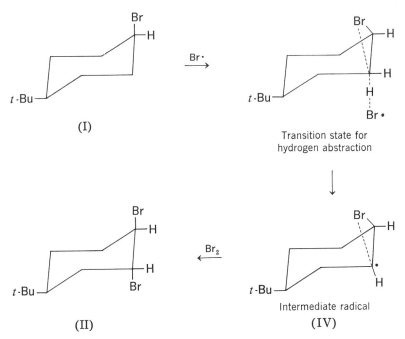

Transition state for
hydrogen abstraction

(I)

(II)

(IV)

Intermediate radical

We shall return to further consideration of bridged radicals in Chap. 14.

Evidence on the preferred conformation of radicals can be derived from studies of the rate at which radicals are formed from substances of known geometry. These studies show that radicals are formed in ordinary unstrained systems at about the same rates as they are in systems held in either a planar or a nonplanar configuration. This would again indicate that the difference in energy between a planar and a nonplanar radical is small.

Bicyclic compounds cannot become planar at the bridgehead position because of the constraining forces in the bridge. For example, carbonium ions, which prefer to be planar, are formed extremely slowly at bridgehead positions.

However, the comparable radical reactions proceed with nearly normal rates. For example, the analogous peroxide, apocamphoyl peroxide, dissociates in carbon tetrachloride to give normal products:†

† M. S. Kharasch, F. Engelmann, and W. H. Urry, *J. Am. Chem. Soc.*, **65**, 2428 (1943).

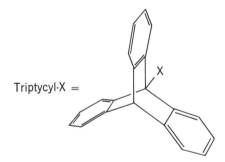

It is apparent that the bridgehead radical was formed in this reaction and that it is not of especially high energy.

Similarly, the silver salt of apocamphoric acid undergoes normal radical bromination in carbon tetrachloride:†

Derivatives of triptycene with bridgehead substituents offer another example of the same phenomenon:

Triptycyl-X =

† P. Wilder and A. Winston, *J. Am. Chem. Soc.*, **75**, 5370 (1953).

Triptycyl cations are formed very slowly since the ion cannot become planar:

$$Tr—X \xrightarrow{\text{Very slow}} Tr^+ + X^-$$

(Tr = triptycyl)

Triptoyl peroxide, on the other hand, reacts as shown below.†

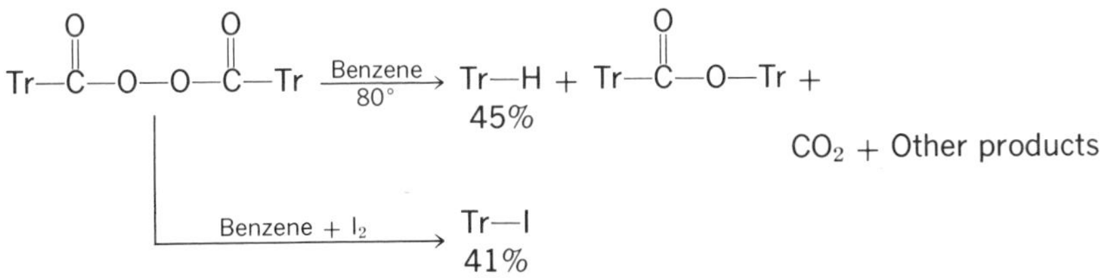

The trapping of the triptycyl radicals as the iodide, Tr—I, indicates that triptycyl radicals are involved in these reactions. The fact that the triptycyl radical abstracts hydrogen from benzene, which is a very unreactive hydrogen donor, indicates that it has somewhat higher energy than an ordinary radical.

A further example is shown on page 42.‡ The bridgehead hypohalite photolyzes to produce the corresponding alkoxy radical. This radical undergoes a β-scission reaction in two major ways: by elimination of a

† P. D. Bartlett and F. D. Greene, *J. Am. Chem. Soc.*, **76**, 1088 (1954).

‡ F. D. Greene, M. L. Savitz, F. D. Osterholtz, H. H. Lau, W. N. Smith, and P. M. Zanet, *J. Org. Chem.*, **28**, 55 (1963).

methyl radical [reaction (3-1)] or by elimination of a bicyclic radical [reaction (3-2)]. The interesting feature is that the bicyclic radical is split off more often than is methyl and that the bicyclic radical remains intact and forms a bicyclic product.

PROBLEMS

3-1 In the experiment shown in reactions (3-1) and (3-2), very different products are obtained if cyclohexene is used as a solvent. In cyclohexene, the main products are dimethyl-(1-norbornyl)carbinol $\left[\vphantom{\rule{0pt}{3em}}\right.$ ⬡—C(CH$_3$)$_2$OH $\left.\vphantom{\rule{0pt}{3em}}\right]$ and 3-chlorocyclohexene in 94% yield. Explain this result.

3-2 The rate constants for the formation of radicals from acetyl peroxide, benzoyl peroxide, triptoyl peroxide, and apocamphoryl peroxide $\left(\vphantom{\rule{0pt}{2em}}\right.$⬡$-\!\overset{\overset{\displaystyle O}{\|}}{C}\!-\!O\left.\right)_2$ differ by less than a factor of 10 at 80°C. [P. D. Bartlett and F. D. Greene, *J. Am. Chem. Soc.*, **76**, 1088 (1954).] What statements can you make about the stability of radicals at (nonplanar) bridgehead positions from this information? Note: Consider carefully which bonds are breaking at the transition state.

3-3 Bromination of optically active 1-bromo-2-methylbutane by *t*-butyl hypobromite gives some 1,2-dibromo-2-methylbutane which is optically active, plus other products. *t*-Butyl hypohalite gives chlorination products that are all inactive. [P. S. Skell, D. L. Tuleen, and P. D. Readio, *J. Am. Chem. Soc.*, **85**, 2849 (1963).] Explain these facts.

3-4 Carbonium ions prefer to be planar. Carbanions are isoelectronic with ammonia, which is known to be pyramidal but with an activation energy for inversion of only 6 to 8 kcal/mole. [J. F. Kincaid and F. C. Henriques, *J. Am. Chem. Soc.*, **62**, 1474 (1940).] Would you expect the activation energy for inversion of a radical to be higher or lower than that for a carbanion?

3-5 Draw structures for the cyclopentyl radical assuming (*a*) a planar ring and a planar radical; (*b*) a planar ring and a nonplanar radical; (*c*) a nonplanar ring and a planar radical; (*d*) a nonplanar ring and a nonplanar radical. Mark the structures in which β hydrogens are equivalent. The EPR spectrum of the cyclopentyl radical indicates that the β hydrogens are equivalent at −40°C but begin to become nonequivalent at −80°C. Does this fact allow a choice to be made for the geometry of the radical? Explain.

SUGGESTION FOR FURTHER READING

Eliel, E. L.: "Stereochemistry of Carbon Compounds," McGraw-Hill Book Company, New York, 1962, chap. 13.

chapter four Energetics and
Rates

RATES

Radicals are reactive species that usually react with other materials very rapidly. However, a single radical isolated in a total vacuum obviously would be stable indefinitely, regardless of its reactivity. The rate at which radicals disappear depends both on the inherent stability (or, conversely, the reactivity) of the radicals and their concentration and also on the reactivity and concentration of the other substances present.

It will be helpful at this point to review the expression for reaction rates. The rate of the reaction

$$a\text{A} \longrightarrow b\text{B}$$

is given by

$$\text{Rate} = \frac{1}{a}\frac{-d(\text{A})}{dt} = \frac{1}{b}\frac{+d(\text{B})}{dt} = k(\text{A})^n$$

where parentheses indicate concentration (moles per liter for work in solution) and the fractions $1/a$ and $1/b$ are statistical corrections based on the stoichiometry of the reaction. The reaction rate depends on the concentration of A raised to the nth power and is said to be of the order n. Texts on reaction kinetics should be consulted for the experimental techniques used to obtain reaction orders.

The amount of energy that a molecule must possess in order to react is called the activation energy E. Figure 4-1 shows this energy and also shows the activation energy necessary for the reverse reaction, E'. Note that the heat of reaction, ΔH, is equal to the difference between the two activation energies:

$$\Delta H = E - E' \tag{4-1}$$

(The energy levels shown in Fig. 4-1 are above the energy minima because of the zero-point energy of vibration.)

A knowledge of activation energies is of great importance in understanding the driving forces behind chemical reactions. Quantities approximating the activation energy can be obtained by studying the variation of reaction rate with temperature. The most commonly used equation to express this variation is the Arrhenius equation:

$$k = Ae^{-E_a/RT} \tag{4-2}$$

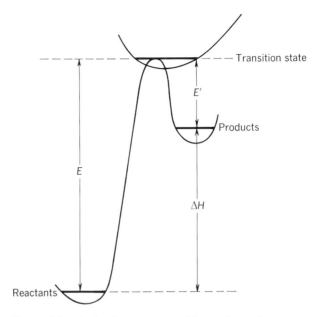

Figure 4-1 Activation energy and heat of reaction.

Most reactions are found to obey this equation; that is, the rate constant can be expressed in terms of two parameters, an Arrhenius activation energy E_a and a pre-exponential term A which is related to the probability of the reaction occurring at any given temperature. The Arrhenius activation energy is a good approximation to E.

Transition-state theory gives another formulation for the rate constant. In this treatment, the reactants are assumed to be in equilibrium with an "activated complex" or "transition state," and the rate constant is given as

$$k = \frac{\kappa T}{h} e^{-\Delta F^{\ddagger}/RT} \qquad (4\text{-}3)$$

$$k = \frac{\kappa T}{h} e^{\Delta S^{\ddagger}/R} e^{-\Delta H^{\ddagger}/RT} \qquad (4\text{-}4)$$

where κ is the Boltzmann constant, h is Planck's constant, T is the absolute temperature, $\Delta S^{\ddagger}$ is the entropy of activation, and $\Delta H^{\ddagger}$ is the enthalpy (heat) of activation. The Arrhenius activation energy and $\Delta H^{\ddagger}$ for a gas-phase reaction are related by the equation

$$\Delta H^{\ddagger} = E_a - nRT$$

where n is the molecularity, or order, of the reaction. For a reaction in solution,

$$\Delta H^{\ddagger} = E_a - RT$$

For a unimolecular reaction, Eqs. (4-2) and (4-4) can be combined to give

$$A = \frac{e\kappa T}{h} e^{\Delta S^{\ddagger}/R}$$

The value of $e\kappa T/h$ at $25°C$ is 1.7×10^{13} sec^{-1}, and if the value of ΔS is near zero, the approximation shown below can be written.

$$k \cong 10^{13} e^{-E_a/RT} \qquad \text{sec}^{-1} \qquad (4-5)$$

For many unimolecular reactions the pre-exponential term A has been found to be close to this value of 10^{13} sec^{-1}.

To return now to the reactivity of radicals and the speed of radical reactions, the rate constant for the dimerization of methyl radicals has been measured by techniques to be discussed in Chap. 15. The rate constant is given by

$$k = 2 \times 10^{10} \text{ sec}^{-1}$$

If this is compared with Eq. (4-2), it can be seen that the activation energy for the dimerization of methyl radicals is zero, A has the value of 2×10^{10} sec^{-1}, and the rate constant is independent of temperature. The implication is that methyl radicals are reactive enough to form ethane every time they collide.†

The lifetime of radicals in the gas phase can be obtained from experiments of the type done by Paneth (see page 5). In these experiments, radicals are generated, flow down a tube, and remove a previously deposited metallic mirror placed downstream. The mirror is not removed if it is too far downstream from the site of generation of the radicals, implying that the radicals have been destroyed by termination reactions before they reach the mirror. If the rate of flow and the distance between the site of generation of the radicals and the mirror are known, the lifetime

---

† Since bond formation between two radicals is very exothermic, radicals may collide elastically without forming a bond unless an inert body or a wall is present to accept the excess energy. This "third-body" effect is discussed in Chap. 20.

of the radicals can be calculated.   At flow rates of about 10 meters/sec, methyl radicals are found to exist for about 0.1 meter; that is, their lifetime is about 0.01 sec.   Even very reactive radicals, therefore, exist for finite times if termination reactions are slow.

BOND DISSOCIATION ENERGIES

There are several methods for obtaining bond energies; an elementary text on physical chemistry should be consulted for complete details.   Two methods in particular have applications to radical chemistry.   In one, the Arrhenius activation energy for a unimolecular dissociation reaction is identified with the bond dissociation energy.   In the reaction,

$$AB \longrightarrow A\bullet + B\bullet$$

The bond dissociation energy $D(A—B)$ is equal to the heat of reaction:

$$D(A—B) = \Delta H$$

If the activation energy for the reverse reaction (i.e., the recombination of the radicals) is zero and if the radicals are formed in their ground vibrational states, then, from Eq. (4-1),

$$E_a = \Delta H$$

and $\quad D(A—B) = E_a = \Delta H$ $\hspace{4cm}$ (4-6)

As an example of this method, consider the dissociation of t-butyl peroxide:

$$t\text{-BuO—OBu-}t \longrightarrow t\text{-BuO}\bullet + \bullet\text{OBu-}t$$

The bond dissociation energy of the O—O bond, $D(t\text{-BuO—OBu-}t)$, can be identified as the activation energy obtained for this reaction from kinetic studies, 37 kcal/mole.

The second method for obtaining bond energies involves use of Hess's law.   This law states that ΔH for a reaction is independent of the pathway postulated as the mechanism for the reaction.   (A more detailed description of Hess's law may be found in physical chemistry texts; see the references at the end of this chapter.)   For example, the bond dissociation energy for the breaking of one of the C—H bonds in methane can be obtained as follows: The activation energy for the forward and reverse reactions has been measured for the reaction below.

$$CH_4 + Br\bullet \underset{E_a = 2}{\overset{E_a = 17}{\rightleftarrows}} CH_3\bullet + HBr$$

Then, from Eq. (4-1), $\Delta H = 15$ kcal/mole. The value of $D(\text{H—Br})$ is found to be 87 kcal/mole from spectroscopic measurements. Therefore, the cycle shown below can give the energy of the CH_3—H bond.

$$\begin{matrix} & & & & \Delta H, \\ & & & & \text{kcal/mole} \end{matrix}$$

$$\begin{array}{llr} CH_4 + Br\bullet \longrightarrow & CH_3\bullet + HBr & 15 \\ HBr \longrightarrow & H\bullet \ + Br\bullet & 87 \\ \hline \text{Sum:} \ CH_4 \longrightarrow & H\bullet \ + CH_3\bullet & 102 \end{array}$$

HEATS OF FORMATION

Heats of formation can be calculated from bond-energy data, and a knowledge of some heats of formation allows prediction of the energetics of other reactions. The heat of formation, ΔH_f°, is defined as the energy change when a substance is formed from the elements in their normal states at 25°C and 1 atm. An example of the calculation of heat of formation is that of the hydrogen atom from the dissociation of hydrogen gas:

$$H_2 \longrightarrow 2H\bullet \qquad \Delta H = 103.4 \text{ kcal/mole}$$

The heat of reaction is equal to the sum of the heats of formation of all the products minus the sum of the heats of formation of all the reactants:

$$\Delta H = \Sigma \Delta H_f^\circ \ (\text{Products}) - \Sigma \Delta H_f^\circ \ (\text{Reactants})$$

Therefore, for hydrogen,

$$\Delta H = 103.4 = 2\Delta H_f^\circ(\text{H}\bullet) - \Delta H_f^\circ(\text{H}_2)$$

$$\Delta H_f^\circ(\text{H}\bullet) = \frac{103.4 + 0}{2} = 52 \text{ kcal/mole}$$

Next, consider the calculation of the heat of formation of a t-butoxy radical. The heat of formation of t-butyl alcohol can be calculated from its measured heat of combustion to be -77 kcal/mole. The bond dissociation energy of the O—H bond has been measured by various methods and is found to be 102 to 104 kcal/mole. Therefore,

$$t\text{-BuO—H} \longrightarrow t\text{-BuO}\bullet + \text{H}\bullet \qquad \Delta H = 104 \text{ kcal/mole}$$

and, then,

$$\Delta H_f^\circ(\text{H}\bullet) + \Delta H_f^\circ(t\text{-BuO}\bullet) - \Delta H_f^\circ(t\text{-BuOH}) = 104 \text{ kcal/mole}$$

$$\Delta H_f^\circ(t\text{-BuO}\bullet) = 104 - 52 + (-77) = -25 \text{ kcal/mole}$$

The heat of formation of the t-butoxy radical just calculated can be used to predict the activation energy for the reaction

$$t\text{-BuO—OBu-}t \longrightarrow 2t\text{-BuO}\bullet$$

The heat of formation for t-butyl peroxide (TBP) can be calculated from its measured heat of combustion; it is found to be -85 kcal/mole. Therefore, the activation energy for the dissociation of the peroxide, which should be equal to the bond energy of the O—O bond, is

$$\Delta H = E_a = 2\Delta H_f^\circ(t\text{-BuO}\bullet) - \Delta H_f^\circ(\text{TBP})$$

$$= 2(-25) - (-85) = 35 \text{ kcal/mole}$$

Notice that this prediction is within 2 kcal/mole of the bond dissociation energy obtained experimentally (page 49).

The heat of reaction can be calculated from bond dissociation energies. For example, consider the reactions

$$\text{A—B} \longrightarrow \text{A} + \text{B} \qquad\qquad (4\text{-}7)$$
$$\underline{\text{B—C} \longrightarrow \text{B} + \text{C}} \qquad\qquad (4\text{-}8)$$
$$\text{Difference:} \quad \text{A—B} + \text{C} \longrightarrow \text{B—C} + \text{A} \qquad\qquad (4\text{-}9)$$

Reaction (4-9) is obtained by subtracting reaction (4-8) from (4-7). If the heats of these reactions are ΔH_7, ΔH_8, and ΔH_9, then, from Hess's law,

$$\Delta H_9 = \Delta H_7 - \Delta H_8$$

If the assumptions necessary for Eq. (4-6) to apply are met, then

$$\Delta H_7 = D(\text{A—B})$$
$$\Delta H_8 = D(\text{B—C})$$

and, therefore,

$$\Delta H_9 = D(\text{A—B}) - D(\text{B—C})$$

Thus the heat of reaction is simply the difference in the bond dissociation energies of the bonds that are broken and those which are formed. For example, the heat of reaction of chlorine atoms with methane can be calculated as

$$CH_4 + Cl\cdot \longrightarrow HCl + \cdot CH_3$$
$$\Delta H = D(CH_3\text{—H}) - D(\text{H—Cl}) = 101 - 102 = -1 \text{ kcal/mole}$$

The reaction is about 1 kcal/mole exothermic, since a slightly stronger bond is formed than is broken.

PROBLEMS

4-1 For a unimolecular reaction in the gas phase, assume that A is 10^{13} sec^{-1}. Calculate the half-life at 100°C, assuming that the activation energy is (a) 15.0 kcal/mole and (b) 30.0 kcal/mole.

4-2 Using the bond energies given in this chapter, predict ΔH for the reaction

$$CH_3\cdot + t\text{-BuOH} \longrightarrow CH_4 + t\text{-BuO}\cdot$$

SUGGESTIONS FOR FURTHER READING

Kinetics

Benson, S. W.: "Foundations of Chemical Kinetics," McGraw-Hill Book Company, New York, 1960, particularly chaps. 12 and 13.

Frost, A. A., and R. G. Pearson: "Kinetics and Mechanism," John Wiley & Sons, Inc., New York, 1961.

Moore, W. J.: "Physical Chemistry," Prentice-Hall, Inc., Englewood Cliffs, N.J., 3d ed., 1963, pp. 253–305.

Bond energies and heats of formation

Cottrell, T. L.: "Strengths of Chemical Bonds," Academic Press Inc., New York, 1958.

Gray, P., and A. Williams: *Chem. Rev.*, **59**, 239 (1959).   (On alkoxy radicals.)

Moore, W. J.: "Physical Chemistry," Prentice-Hall, Inc., Englewood Cliffs, N.J., 3d ed., 1963, pp. 50–59.

Natl. Bur. Standards, Circ. 500, Washington, D.C.

THE PRODUCTION
OF RADICALS

chapter five Introduction:
Methods of
Producing Radicals

Radicals can be formed in three types of processes: irradiation, thermal homolysis, and oxidation-reduction reactions. A general description of these processes is given in this chapter; succeeding chapters take up each of them in turn.

IRRADIATION

In irradiative processes, the energy necessary to form radicals can be supplied by any of the forms of electromagnetic radiation (ultraviolet or visible light, x-rays, etc.) or by corpuscular radiation (high-energy electrons; α, β, γ particles; neutrons; protons; etc.). In this text we shall limit our attention to processes involving the absorption of light, a subdivision of radiation chemistry called photochemistry. Absorption of very-high-energy particles frequently produces ionization and reactions beyond the scope of this text.

THERMAL HOMOLYSIS

The normal carbon-carbon bond energy is about 90 kcal/mole, and thermal excitation of molecules becomes sufficient to break these bonds at temperatures of 350 to 550°C. For example, thermal cracking of petroleum is carried out in this temperature range. However, some compounds have exceptionally weak bonds and therefore decompose to form radicals at lower temperatures. These compounds can be used to initiate radical processes at temperatures of 50 to 150°C.

Equation (4-5) gives the rate constant for a unimolecular reaction as

$$k = 10^{13}e^{-E_a/RT} \qquad \text{sec}^{-1}$$

This equation predicts that a molecule containing a bond with a dissociation energy of 25 kcal/mole will dissociate with a 1-hour half-life at 50°C; a compound containing a bond energy of 32 kcal/mole would be predicted to dissociate with a 1-hour half-life at 150°C.

Thus molecules with bond energies of 25 to 35 kcal/mole should be useful radical initiators at 50 to 150°C. Several types of compounds have bonds with strengths in this range, but by far the most commonly used are those containing the peroxide O—O bond. Table 5-1 lists some commercially available peroxides that are used as initiators. The table gives the activation energy for the dissociation reaction and the temperature at which the peroxide produces radicals with a 1-hour half-life. It can be

Table 5-1   Frequently used initiators

Name	Structure	Arrhenius activation energy, kcal/mole	°C for 1-hr half-life
t-Butyl peroxide	t-BuO—OBu-t	37	150
t-Butyl perbenzoate	t-BuO—O—$\overset{\displaystyle O}{\overset{\|\|}{C}}$—$\phi$	34	125
Benzoyl peroxide	ϕ—$\overset{\displaystyle O}{\overset{\|\|}{C}}$—O—O—$\overset{\displaystyle O}{\overset{\|\|}{C}}$—$\phi$	30	95†
Acetyl peroxide	CH_3—$\overset{\displaystyle O}{\overset{\|\|}{C}}$—O—O—$\overset{\displaystyle O}{\overset{\|\|}{C}}$—$CH_3$	30–32†	85‡
Azoisobutyronitrile	$(CH_3)_2\overset{\displaystyle CN}{\overset{\|}{C}}$—N=N—$\overset{\displaystyle CN}{\overset{\|}{C}}(CH_3)_2$	30	85

† Solvent dependent; data given for inert solvents.
‡ In the gas phase.

seen that the prediction based on the Arrhenius equation is borne out. Table 5-1 also lists azoisobutyronitrile (AIBN), a common initiator which dissociates because of the driving force to form the stable N_2 molecule.

$$CH_3-\underset{\underset{CH_3}{|}}{\overset{\overset{CN}{|}}{C}}-N=N-\underset{\underset{CH_3}{|}}{\overset{\overset{CN}{|}}{C}}-CH_3 \longrightarrow 2CH_3-\underset{\underset{CH_3}{|}}{\overset{\overset{CN}{|}}{C}}\cdot \ + N_2$$

AIBN

The compounds listed in Table 5-1 are useful because they are stable enough to be synthesized at ordinary temperatures and they can be stored for long periods in a refrigerator. They can be used as initiators at temperatures at which most bonds do not undergo thermal homolysis.

REDOX SOURCES OF RADICALS

Often an oxidation-reduction reaction is useful as a source of radicals. For example, the polymerization of styrene-butadiene mixtures to make synthetic rubber produces materials with better physical properties if the polymerization is done at 0 to 10°C rather than at higher temperatures. It would be difficult to find an easily synthesized initiator that would decompose at this low temperature, but the redox pair ferrous ion–cumene hydroperoxide can be used:

$$Fe^{++} + \phi-\underset{\underset{CH_3}{|}}{\overset{\overset{CH_3}{|}}{C}}-OOH \longrightarrow Fe^{3+} + \phi-\underset{\underset{CH_3}{|}}{\overset{\overset{CH_3}{|}}{C}}-O\bullet + OH^-$$

This reaction has an activation energy of only 12 kcal/mole. In Chap. 11 we shall consider other examples of metal-ion redox reactions of this type.

chapter *six* Photochemistry

Light can be transmitted, refracted, scattered, or absorbed by a system. It is a fundamental tenet of photochemistry that only the light absorbed can produce a chemical or physical change. In general, each quantum of light that is absorbed activates a single molecule.

A quantum of light of frequency ν has an energy given by

$$E = h\nu$$

where h is Planck's constant. A mole of quanta is called an einstein and has energy equal to $Nh\nu$, where N is Avogadro's number. The relation between the wavelength or frequency of light and the energy associated with 1 einstein of the light, therefore, is

$$Nh\nu = \frac{Nhc}{\lambda} = \frac{2.859 \times 10^5}{\lambda \text{ (in A)}} \qquad \text{kcal/einstein}$$

Thus, light of 7500 A wavelength represents 38 kcal/einstein; light of 3130 A wavelength represents 91 kcal/einstein, enough to cause the scission of carbon-carbon bonds.

Intense light sources must be used in photochemical experiments. For example, a 1,000-watt ordinary light bulb delivers only about 0.05 watt of its energy as visible light in a given direction in a 10 A band. At 4000 A, 0.05 watt corresponds to 10^{17} quanta/sec, and at this rate it would take 6×10^6 sec, or about 10 weeks, to deliver one einstein of light. However, special light sources and reactors with carefully designated geometries are now available in which light in the region of 2000 to 4000 A can be delivered at rates up to 1 einstein in 8 to 24 hours.

POSSIBLE REACTIONS OF PHOTOACTIVATED SPECIES

When a molecule absorbs a quantum of light and becomes excited, it can lose this energy in any of the following ways:

Physical processes:
    Thermal quenching
    Fluorescence
    Phosphorescence
    Internal conversion
    Intersystem crossing

Chemical processes:
    Radical reactions
    Nonradical reactions

We shall mainly be interested in the chemical processes which follow light absorption. However, before we discuss examples of these chemical reactions, it is necessary to consider the physical processes because, as we shall see, they may occur in competition with chemical processes and also because they lead to a better understanding of the nature of photoexcited states.

The most obvious physical process by which molecules can become deactivated is by transfer of their excitation energy to other molecules present in the system. This is called energy transfer to the solvent molecules, or quenching. It occurs in both the gas and liquid phases, and different solvent molecules show differing efficiencies as quenchers. For example, in the gas phase, mercury atoms can be raised to an excited state, $Hg°$, and various gaseous diluents M can quench this excitation:

$$Hg + h\nu \longrightarrow Hg^*$$
$$Hg^* + M \longrightarrow Hg + M$$

Methane is relatively ineffective, hydrogen is more effective, and higher hydrocarbon molecules are still more so. Hydrogen and the higher hydrocarbons are particularly effective quenchers because they can lose the excitation energy in dissociative processes:

$$Hg^* + H_2 \longrightarrow Hg + 2H\cdot$$
$$Hg^* + RH \longrightarrow Hg + R\cdot + H\cdot$$

Quenching is also observed in the recombination of iodine atoms. When molecular iodine is photolyzed, the iodine atoms produced have too much excess energy to recombine. Solvent molecules can quench this excess energy and aid recombination reactions. The efficiencies of various solvents have been measured in both the gas and liquid phases.† It is observed that the yield of free iodine atoms is lower in solution than in the gas phase. In solution, iodine dissociates to form two excited iodine atoms which are held in close proximity by a "cage" of solvent molecules. (We shall discuss the nature of this cage in more detail in Chap. 7.) The

---

† G. Porter and J. A. Smith, *Proc. Royal Soc. (London)*, Ser. A, **261**, 28 (1961); F. W. Lampe and R. M. Noyes, *J. Am. Chem. Soc.*, **76**, 2140 (1954).

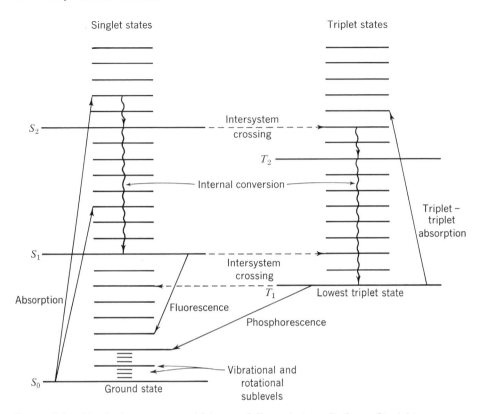

Figure 6-1   Physical processes which can follow photoexcitation.   Straight arrows represent radiative processes; wavy arrows, nonradiative processes; and dashed arrows, intersystem crossing.

iodine atoms can lose their excess energy to the solvent cage and then recombine.   Since solvent molecules are present at a higher concentration in solution, this recombination reaction has a much higher probability in solution than in the gas phase.

The other physical processes for de-excitation of a molecule can best be illustrated using Fig. 6-1.   This figure schematically shows several electronic levels and some of the vibrational and rotational sublevels of a typical organic molecule.   Singlet electronic levels are on the left of the figure and triplet levels on the right.†   First, let us consider only the singlet states:

† In spectroscopy, the multiplicity of a species is given by $2S + 1$, where S is the total electron spin.   If only paired electrons are present, all spins cancel, $S = 0$, and the species is a singlet.   If two electrons have parallel spins, each with the value of ½, $S = 1$, and the state is a triplet.

absorption can be followed by radiationless processes. This is shown at the left of the figure as wavy arrows representing cascades down vibrational sublevels and internal conversion to lower singlet electronic levels; the energy lost in these processes is quenched by other molecules in the system. Absorption can also be followed by a transition which produces an emission of radiation; such transitions are shown as solid arrows in the figure. Radiative transitions between two states of the same multiplicity are called fluorescence. Since the lifetime of species in excited states is very short, fluorescence occurs within 10^{-9} to 10^{-6} sec after absorption.

Now consider the triplet states shown at the right of Fig. 6-1. Some molecules can decay from an excited singlet to a metastable triplet state. A radiationless transition between states of different multiplicities is called intersystem crossing; these transitions are shown as dashed arrows in Fig. 6-1. Notice that intersystem crossing occurs from one electronic level to a vibrational level at the same energy in the other manifold; that is, it occurs adiabatically. In theory, transitions between states of different multiplicities are forbidden; however, real states are not pure triplet or singlet, and intersystem crossing occurs but with a lower probability than ordinary internal conversions. The lifetime of a species in the triplet state may be longer than in an excited singlet state, and radiative decay or intersystem crossing from the triplet back to the singlet state may be delayed by 10^{-3} sec or even longer. Any radiative transition between states of different multiplicities is called phosphorescence. In organic molecules, the usual phosphorescence involves that shown in Fig. 6-1 from the lowest excited triplet to a vibrational level of the ground electronic state.

The definitions which have been given are summarized below.

1. *Internal conversion:* nonradiative transition between states of like multiplicity.
2. *Fluorescence:* radiative transition between states of like multiplicity.
3. *Intersystem crossing:* nonradiative transition between states of different multiplicities.
4. *Phosphorescence:* radiative transition between states of different multiplicities.
5. *Quenching:* any deactivation of an excited species by other components of the system.

Before we turn to examples of various chemical reactions which can follow absorption of light, it is of interest to consider how light quanta can be measured.

ACTINOMETRY

Measurement of the total amount of radiation incident on a system is called actinometry. One type of actinometer is a thermopile; this is a group of thermocouples with their ends imbedded in a black surface. The radiation absorbed by a system is determined by placing a thermopile behind the reaction vessel and measuring the difference in the intensity of the light with the vessel full and empty. Thermopiles can be calibrated by using lamps of known intensity. (Standard lamps are available from the National Bureau of Standards.)

It is also possible to use a chemical reaction of known quantum yield to determine the light intensity. The quantum yield Φ is the number of product molecules formed per quantum of light absorbed. A more useful definition can be given in terms of moles: The quantum yield is the number of moles of product per einstein of light absorbed. Since the absorbed energy can be lost in physical processes that do not involve chemical reaction, the quantum yield can be very small. On the other extreme, products may be formed by a chain reaction initiated by the primary photochemical process, and Φ can be very large.

A chemical reaction frequently used in actinometry is the decomposition of oxalic acid photosensitized by uranyl salts. The uranyl ion UO_2^{++} absorbs light in the region of 2500 to 4500 A. The excited uranyl ion $(UO_2^{++})^*$ is able to transfer its excess energy to an oxalic acid molecule and produce its decomposition:

$$UO_2^{++} + h\nu \longrightarrow (UO_2^{++})^*$$
$$(UO_2^{++})^* + CO_2H\text{---}CO_2H \longrightarrow UO_2^{++} + CO_2 + CO + H_2O$$

The quantum yield of CO and CO_2 has been measured for a variety of experimental conditions, and the reaction is sensitive enough to allow detection of 7×10^{13} quanta of light.[†]

EXAMPLES OF PHOTOCHEMICAL REACTIONS

In some cases, irradiation of a molecule leads to both physical and chemical processes occurring in competition. For example, when anthracene is exposed to light in benzene solution, it either dimerizes or fluoresces. As the benzene solutions are made more concentrated, the quantum yield

[†] D. H. Volman and J. R. Seed, *J. Am. Chem. Soc.*, **86**, 5095 (1964).

of the dimer product increases and the intensity of the fluorescence decreases. The equations for these reactions are given below.

$$A \; + \; h\nu \; \longrightarrow \; A^* \tag{6-1}$$

$$A^* \; + \; A \; \xrightarrow{\;k_2\;} \tag{6-2}$$

Dimer

$$A^* \; \xrightarrow{\;k_3\;} \; A \; + \; h\nu' \tag{6-3}$$

where A is anthracene, A^* is a molecule of photoexcited anthracene, ν is
the frequency of the irradiation, and ν' is the frequency of the fluorescence.
Activated molecules are produced by reaction (6-1) and are destroyed in
(6-2) and (6-3). Since the excited species A^* is present in very small concentrations, it is reasonable to assume that its concentration will reach a
steady value very early in the reaction. This is called the *steady-state
assumption* and is valid for any very reactive species. It is approximately
true because reactive species are present at low concentrations. Since
their concentrations are small, the rate of change in their concentrations
also will be small and can be set approximately equal to zero. At the
steady state, the rate of change in the concentration of A^* is zero, and its
rate of formation equals its rate of destruction:

Rate of formation of A^* = Rate of destruction of A^*

The rate of formation of A^* is given by ϕI_{abs}, where ϕ is the fraction of A
molecules that become activated upon absorption of light and I_{abs} is the
rate of absorption of light by A, frequently called the intensity of absorbed
light. The rate of destruction of A^* is given by $k_2(A)(A^*) + k_3(A^*)$.
Therefore, at the steady state in the concentration of A^*,

$$\phi I_{abs} = k_2(A)(A^*) + k_3(A^*)$$

and $\qquad (A°) = \dfrac{\phi I_{abs}}{k_2(A) + k_3}$

The rate of formation of dimer is

$$\frac{d(\text{dimer})}{dt} = k_2(A)(A°)$$

$$= k_2(A)\frac{\phi I_{abs}}{k_2(A) + k_3} = \frac{\phi I_{abs}(A)}{(A) + k_3/k_2}$$

The quantum yield of dimer is then given by

$$\frac{d(\text{dimer})/dt}{I_{abs}} = \Phi_{dimer} = \frac{\phi(A)}{(A) + k_3/k_2}$$

At low concentrations, $k_3/k_2 > (A)$, and $\Phi_{dimer} = (\phi k_2/k_3)(A)$, and the yield of dimer increases as the anthracene concentration is increased. At high concentrations, $(A) > k_3/k_2$, $\Phi_{dimer} = \phi$, and a limiting value of the quantum yield of dimer is reached.

In some cases, irradiation leads to the occurrence of both radical and nonradical reactions occurring in competition. For example, irradiation of butyraldehyde in the gas phase produces two decomposition reactions; one gives propyl and formyl free radicals, and the other gives ethylene and acetaldehyde.†

$CH_3-CH_2-CH_2-CHO + h\nu \longrightarrow (CH_3-CH_2-CH_2-CHO)^*$
$(CH_3-CH_2-CH_2-CHO)^* \longrightarrow CH_3-CH_2-CH_2\bullet + \bullet CHO$
$(CH_3-CH_2-CH_2-CHO)^* \longrightarrow H_2C{=}CH_2 + CH_3-CHO$

A photochemical process which has been studied in considerable detail is the reaction of chlorine and hydrogen. The mechanism is

$Cl_2 + h\nu \longrightarrow 2Cl\bullet$ $\qquad\qquad\qquad\qquad\qquad$ (6-4)

$Cl\bullet + H_2 \xrightarrow{k_5} HCl + H\bullet$ $\qquad\qquad\qquad\qquad$ (6-5)

$H\bullet + Cl_2 \xrightarrow{k_6} HCl + Cl\bullet$ $\qquad\qquad\qquad\qquad$ (6-6)

$2Cl\bullet \xrightarrow{k_7} Cl_2$ $\qquad\qquad\qquad\qquad\qquad\qquad$ (6-7)

The rate of formation of chlorine atoms is $2\phi I_{abs}$, and their rate of disappearance is $2k_7(Cl\bullet)^2$. At the steady state,

† F. E. Blacet and J. G. Calvert, *J. Am. Chem. Soc.*, **73**, 661 (1951).

$$2\phi I_{abs} = 2k_7(\text{Cl}\cdot)^2$$

$$(\text{Cl}\cdot) = \left(\frac{\phi I_{abs}}{k_7}\right)^{1/2}$$

The rate of formation of hydrogen chloride is

$$\frac{d(\text{HCl})}{dt} = k_5(\text{Cl}\cdot)(\text{H}_2) + k_6(\text{H}\cdot)(\text{Cl}_2)$$

At the steady state in the concentration of hydrogen atoms, reactions (6-5) and (6-6) must have equal rates. Therefore,

$$\frac{d(\text{HCl})}{dt} = 2k_5(\text{Cl}\cdot)(\text{H}_2)$$

$$= \frac{2k_5}{k_7^{1/2}}(\phi I_{abs})^{1/2}(\text{H}_2)$$

The quantum yield of hydrogen chloride, Φ_{HCl}, for this process is 10^4 to 10^6. Each chlorine atom formed in (6-4) initiates many thousands of chain sequences (6-5) and (6-6) before reaction (6-7) destroys the active chlorine atom.†

It is convenient to distinguish between the quantum yield of the primary photochemical process ϕ and the quantum yield of an ultimate product Φ. The primary photochemical yield ϕ is defined as the fraction of the absorbing molecules that react per photon absorbed; the value of ϕ must lie between zero and unity. The quantum yield Φ of a given product of the photochemical system is the number of product molecules formed per photon absorbed. Values of Φ range from zero to a million or more, as we have seen. In the photolysis of chlorine discussed above, the quantum yield for the primary photochemical process [reaction (6-4)] cannot be larger than unity, since each photon can produce the dissociation of only one chlorine molecule. The quantum yield for the formation of hydrogen chloride, Φ_{HCl}, can be as large as 10^6, because of the chain length of the reaction sequence.‡

† For a more detailed treatment of the related reaction of hydrogen with bromine, see A. A. Frost and R. G. Pearson, "Kinetics and Mechanism," John Wiley & Sons, Inc., New York, 2d ed., 1953, pp. 236–241.

‡ The difference between the terms *yield* and *quantum yield* should be noted. The *yield* of a process usually is defined as the number of moles of product formed per mole of starting materials consumed. The *quantum yield* is moles of product formed per mole of photons absorbed.

CARBONYL COMPOUNDS

For photochemical reactions to occur, either the substrate must absorb the wavelength of light used, or a photosensitizer must be present which can absorb the radiant energy and transfer it to the substrate. Many of the early studies† of photochemical reactions were on carbonyl compounds, since these compounds have an absorption band near 3200 A and Pyrex glass is transparent to light of this wavelength. Furthermore, commercial mercury arcs deliver about 5 percent of their energy at 3130 A, and carbonyl compounds therefore can be photoexcited using relatively simple equipment.

The long wavelength band of carbonyl compounds corresponds to excitation of a nonbonding (n) electron to an antibonding π orbital (written as $\pi°$). This n-$\pi°$ excitation process can be represented as shown in Fig. 6-2. The nature of the molecular orbitals can best be seen in the representation of the n-$\pi°$ process shown in Fig. 6-2a. The π bond has a high electronic density between the carbon and oxygen atoms; the $\pi°$ orbital has a node there and has zero electron density between these atoms. The n-$\pi°$ excitation process involves promoting one of the unshared electrons on oxygen to the $\pi°$ orbital. This electron is shown as partially $(\delta\cdot)$ on both oxygen and carbon in Fig. 6-2a. The $\pi°$ orbital has its center of gravity displaced toward the carbon, however, and for this reason the lobes on carbon are shown as being larger. In Fig. 6-2b this is represented by two resonance structures for the excited state. It is clear from Fig. 6-2b that the carbon atom has a higher electron density in the excited state than in the ground state. This places a highly localized site of photochemical reactivity at the n orbital on oxygen. Furthermore, the oxygen is electron-deficient and reacts not unlike an electrophilic alkoxy radical. For example, n-$\pi°$ states may abstract hydrogen atoms:

$$\text{>C=O:} \xrightarrow{h\nu} \text{>C=O}\cdot \xrightarrow{RH} \text{>C-O-H} + R\cdot$$

If a reagent fails to approach the oxygen atom during the lifetime of the n-$\pi°$ excited state, the molecule returns to the ground state either by a radiative transition or by intersystem crossing.

So far we have not considered whether the n-$\pi°$ excited state is a

† J. N. Pitts, *J. Chem. Educ.*, **34**, 112 (1957); C. R. Masson, V. Boekelheide, and W. A. Noyes in A. Weissberger (ed.), "Technique of Organic Chemistry," vol. II, Interscience Publishers, Inc., New York, 2d ed., 1956, pp. 307–322.

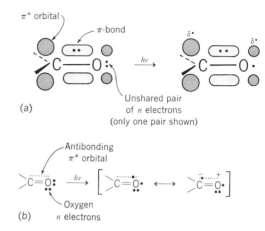

Figure 6-2 Two representations of the n-π^* excitation process.

triplet or a singlet. It is certainly not surprising that triplet states show radical-like reactions such as hydrogen abstraction. However, it is perhaps less expected that singlet excited states may also. Both the singlet and the triplet excited states involve some separation of the electron pair; in the singlet the electron pair retains antiparallel spins, and in the triplet one spin flips over during intersystem crossing. However, the spatial distribution of the pair may be very similar in the two states. Thus the odd electron pair may not be any further separated in the triplet than in the singlet state in some molecules.

A more detailed treatment† indicates that an important consideration is the difference in the energies of the singlet and triplet states. If the difference is small, both states tend to have the same electron distribution and the singlet state may also undergo radical-like reactions. If the energy difference is large, the two odd electrons are further apart in the triplet, it behaves like a diradical, and the singlet state would not be expected to show radical-like reactivity. In either case, the triplet state is paramagnetic and the singlet state is not.‡

---

† S. P. McGlynn, F. J. Smith, and G. Cilento, Some Aspects of the Triplet State, in "Photochemistry and Photobiology," vol. 3, Pergamon Press, New York, 1964, pp. 269–294. P. J. Wagner and G. S. Hammond, *J. Am. Chem. Soc.*, **87**, 4010 (1965).

‡ The difference in reactivity patterns of triplet and singlet states is not completely known at present. However, in the case of these photoexcited states, kinetic considerations indicate that the triplet state probably is responsible for typical hydrogen abstractions. As we have seen, singlet excited states usually decay to the ground

With this background we can consider the photochemical reactions of the carbonyl compounds in more detail. When aldehydes are excited by light, they can undergo four different types of chemical reactions; the reaction which predominates depends on the structure of the aldehyde and the wavelength of the light used. The four reactions are shown below for a generalized straight-chain aldehyde.

$R-CH_2-CH_2-CHO \longrightarrow R-CH_2-CH_2\cdot + \cdot CHO$
$R-CH_2-CH_2-CHO \longrightarrow R-CH_2-CH_3 + CO$
$R-CH_2-CH_2-CHO \longrightarrow R-CH=CH_2 + HCHO$
$R-CH_2-CH_2-CHO \longrightarrow R-CH_2\cdot + \cdot CH_2-CHO$

Ketones also can undergo a variety of photochemical decompositions. Acetone photolyzes to give acetyl and methyl radicals. The acetyl radicals subsequently undergo β-scission to produce another methyl radical and a molecule of carbon monoxide. The ultimate products are ethane and carbon monoxide, as shown below.

$$C_3H_6O + h\nu \longrightarrow C_3H_6O^*$$

$$C_3H_6O^* \longrightarrow CH_3\cdot + CH_3-\overset{\overset{\textstyle O}{\|}}{C}\cdot$$

$$CH_3-\overset{\overset{\textstyle O}{\|}}{C}\cdot \longrightarrow CH_3\cdot + CO$$

$$2CH_3\cdot \longrightarrow C_2H_6$$

where $C_3H_6O^\circ$ is an acetone molecule that has absorbed a quantum of light and is in a photoexcited state. The quantum yield for carbon monoxide, Φ_{CO}, is found to be 1.0 at 2537 A, and 0.7 at 3130 A. The photolysis of acetone has been studied thoroughly, and the production of carbon monoxide is frequently used as an actinometer. This reaction also is used as a source of methyl radicals in gas-phase studies.

state within about 10^{-8} sec. Hydrogen abstraction, which typically has an activation energy of 7 kcal/mole, would not be expected to compete with these fast physical de-excitation processes. Triplets, however, often have lifetimes of 10^{-3} sec or longer, and hydrogen abstraction may be fast enough to compete with intersystem crossing or phosphorescence. We shall consider the difference in singlet and triplet reactivities again in Chap. 19 when we discuss diradicals.

Ketones containing one alkyl group at least three carbon atoms long decompose by an intramolecular mechanism that does not involve free radicals. For example, methyl butyl ketone gives acetone and propylene:

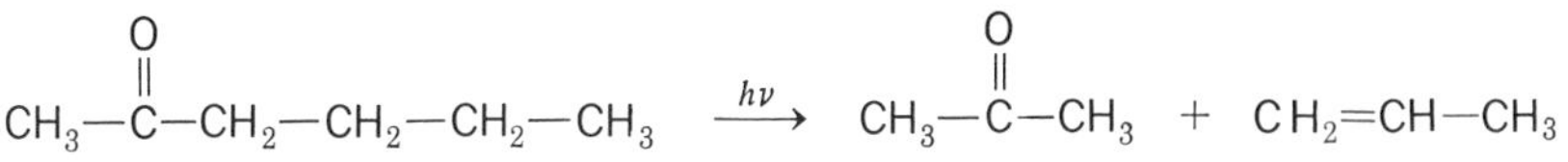

$$CH_3-\overset{\overset{\displaystyle O}{\|}}{C}-CH_2-CH_2-CH_2-CH_3 \xrightarrow{\ h\nu\ } CH_3-\overset{\overset{\displaystyle O}{\|}}{C}-CH_3 \ + \ CH_2{=}CH-CH_3$$

The quantum yields of olefin and acetone are almost equal under all experimental conditions, and so it is concluded that they are formed in the same primary photochemical process. The most likely mechanism for this decomposition involves the transfer of a γ hydrogen atom to form the enol of acetone and an olefin. This is illustrated below.

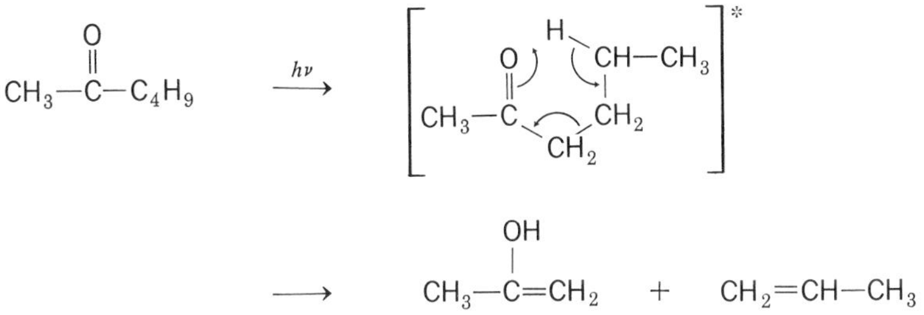

$$CH_3-\overset{\overset{\displaystyle O}{\|}}{C}-C_4H_9 \xrightarrow{\ h\nu\ }$$

$$\longrightarrow \quad CH_3-\overset{\overset{\displaystyle OH}{|}}{C}{=}CH_2 \quad + \quad CH_2{=}CH-CH_3$$

This mechanism is supported by the following observations: (1) Methyl pentyl ketone gives acetone and 1-butene; (2) methyl isopropyl ketone and di-isopropyl ketone, which do not have γ hydrogen atoms, do not decompose by an intramolecular path; (3) methyl sec-butyl ketone gives ethylene and methyl ethyl ketone, as shown below.

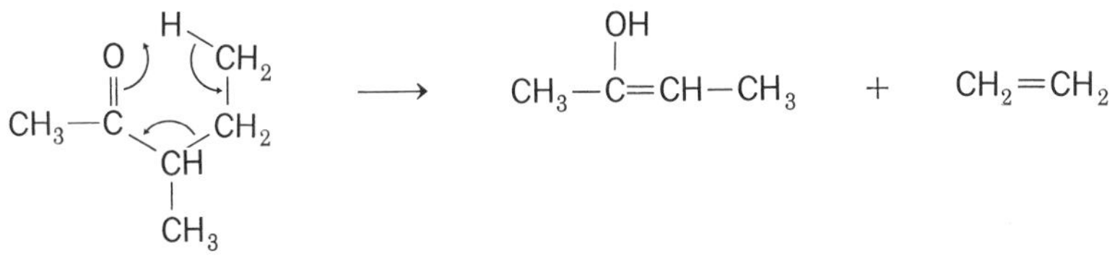

$$\longrightarrow \quad CH_3-\overset{\overset{\displaystyle OH}{|}}{C}{=}CH-CH_3 \quad + \quad CH_2{=}CH_2$$

Other ketones that decompose by this intramolecular process include di-propyl ketone, methyl propyl ketone, methyl pentyl ketone, methyl hexyl ketone, and methyl neopentyl ketone.

Energy transfer can sometimes be used to produce a desired excited molecule that is difficult to produce directly. For example, cyclopentadiene, when irradiated, does not give good yields of the triplet because of a low probability for intersystem crossing. However, the triplet state of benzophenone is produced in high quantum yield. If a mixture of these two species is irradiated, the triplet state of the ketone is produced; it then transfers its excitation to the diene, producing the triplet state. The triplet of cyclopentadiene then reacts as shown below.†

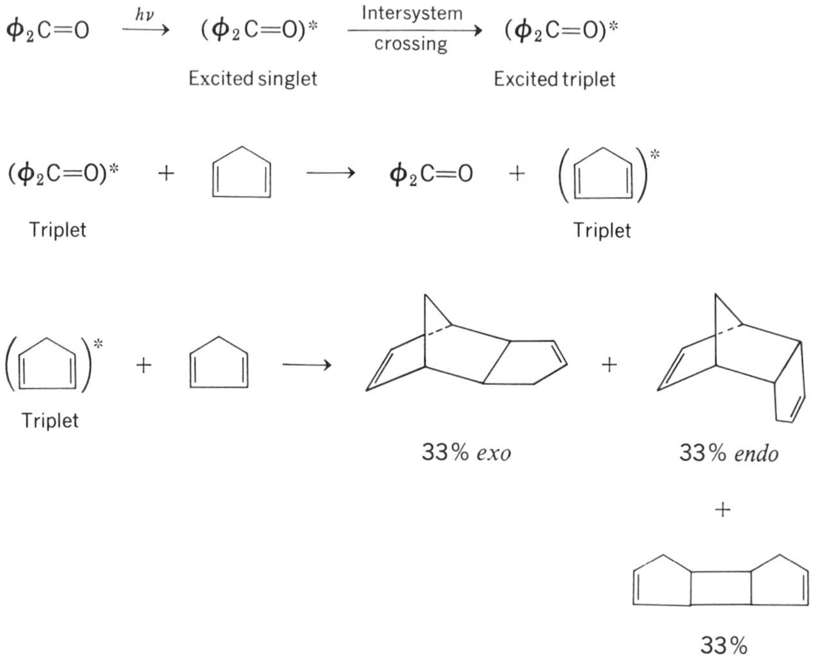

33% *exo*   33% *endo*

+

33%

This result is particularly useful since the direct thermal dimerization of cyclopentadiene by the usual Diels-Alder mechanism leads to a 100% yield of the *endo* product.

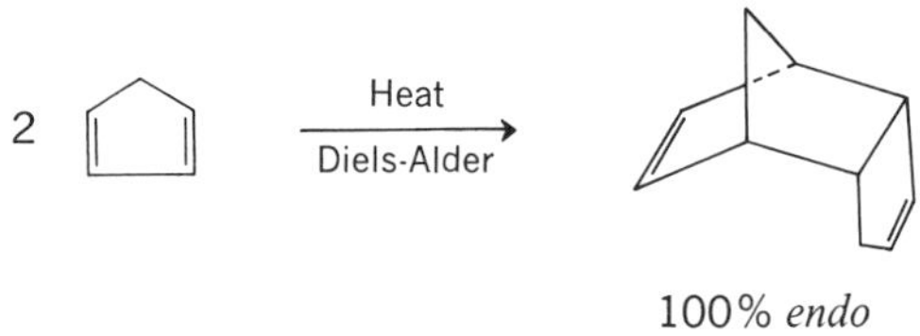

100% *endo*

† N. J. Turro and G. S. Hammond, *J. Am. Chem. Soc.*, **84**, 2841 (1962). Other examples of useful reactions which can be effected by triplet energy transfer are cited by P. A. Leermakers and G. F. Vesley, *J. Chem. Ed.*, **41**, 535 (1964).

Table 6-1   Relative rates of hydrogen abstraction by the triplet state of benzophenone compared with t-butoxy radicals†

Hydrogen donor	Relative rates	
	$\phi_2\overset{\bullet}{C}$—O•	t-BuO•
Toluene	1	1
Mesitylene	5.5	4.1
m-Xylene	3.0	2.3
p-Chlorotoluene	0.97	0.71
Cyclohexane	2.1	6.0

† C. Walling and M. J. Gibian, *J. Am. Chem. Soc.*, **86**, 3902 (1964).

In view of the ability of most radicals to abstract hydrogen atoms, it is not surprising that triplets also can react by this path. Hydrogen abstraction by the triplet of a carbonyl compound would be expected to be particularly facile since the oxygen atom in a carbonyl triplet is electron deficient and should behave much like an electrophilic alkoxy radical. Irradiation of benzophenone in the presence of various hydrogen donors gives relative rates of hydrogen abstraction that parallel the rates obtained for the t-butoxy radical. The data in Table 6-1 illustrate this.

It is not surprising that the t-butoxy radical and the benzophenone triplet abstract hydrogen atoms at similar relative rates since they both form bonds to hydrogen of similar bond energies. The bond dissociation energy of the O—H bond in t-BuO—H is 104 kcal/mole. The thermodynamic cycle below shows that the O—H bond energy in $\phi_2\overset{\bullet}{C}$—O—H is approximately 102 kcal/mole.

Reaction	ΔH(kcal/mole)
ϕ_2CH—OH $\longrightarrow$ ϕ_2C=O + H$_2$	9[a]
ϕ_2C=O $\longrightarrow$ $\phi_2\overset{\bullet}{C}$—$\overset{\bullet}{O}$	69[b]
H• + $\phi_2\overset{\bullet}{C}$—OH $\longrightarrow$ ϕ_2CH—OH	−80[c]
H$_2$ $\longrightarrow$ 2H•	104[a]
Sum: $\phi_2\overset{\bullet}{C}$—OH $\longrightarrow$ $\phi_2\overset{\bullet}{C}$—$\overset{\bullet}{O}$ + H•	102

[a] From bond energies.
[b] From spectroscopy. See W. G Herkstroeter, A. A. Lamola, and G. S. Hammond, *J. Am. Chem. Soc.*, **86**, 4537 (1964).
[c] Assumed to be an ordinary benzyl C—H bond.

One further feature of photochemical reactions is worth pointing out. The Franck-Condon principle states that the absorption of radiant energy by molecules occurs so rapidly that rearrangements of the atoms cannot occur during the absorption process. Therefore, the structure of the first excited species must be that of the substrate. For example, if acetone is photolyzed with 3130 A light, absorption by the carbonyl group occurs.

$$CH_3-\underset{\underset{O}{\parallel}}{C}-CH_3 \quad + \quad h\nu \quad \longrightarrow \quad (CH_3-\underset{\underset{O}{\parallel}}{C}-CH_3)*$$

However, the carbon-oxygen double bond is very strong, and absorption is followed by a distribution of the extra energy into the other vibrational modes of the molecule, a process requiring 10^{-12} to 10^{-8} sec. When sufficient energy becomes concentrated in a carbon-carbon bond, scission occurs.

$$(CH_3-\underset{\underset{O}{\parallel}}{C}-CH_3)* \quad \longrightarrow \quad CH_3-\underset{\underset{O}{\parallel}}{C} \cdot \quad + \quad CH_3 \cdot$$

Although the scission follows the excitation step itself, the two occur much faster than the chemical reactions that follow and occasionally are written as one step in photolysis schemes:

$$CH_3-\underset{\underset{O}{\parallel}}{C}-CH_3 \quad \xrightarrow{h\nu} \quad CH_3CO \cdot \quad + \quad CH_3 \cdot$$

PROBLEMS

6-1 A reaction has a primary photochemical yield ϕ of 0.05, and a quantum yield of product, Φ_P, of 10^4. How many hours will it take to prepare 1 mole of product P at a delivered light intensity of 10^{17} quanta/sec? How many hours if $\Phi_P = 10$?

6-2 In a typical photolysis experiment, a mercury arc equipped with filters supplies 3130 A light at the rate of 1.0×10^5 ergs/sec for 10 hours as measured by a thermopile. How many kilocalories per einstein are supplied by 3130 A light? How many total kilocalories of energy are delivered? (Use 2.39×10^{-11} kcal/erg.) How many einsteins are delivered? How many moles of product will be formed if the quantum yield is 0.25?

6-3 Irradiation of benzophenone $\phi_2C{=}O$ at $25°C$ in isopropyl alcohol using 3660 A light gives benzopinacol $\phi_2C(OH){-}C(OH)\phi_2$ with a quantum yield of 0.93 and acetone with a quantum yield of 0.92. If dissolved oxygen is present, the quantum yield of acetone is unchanged but that of benzopinacol drops to zero. Suggest a mechanism for this reaction. [J. N. Pitts, R. L. Letsinger, R. P. Taylor, J. M. Patterson, G. Recktenwald, and R. B. Martin, *J. Am. Chem. Soc.*, **81**, 1068 (1959).] Hint: The benzophenone is excited to a species capable of abstracting hydrogen. Note that one molecule of acetone is produced for each *two* molecules of benzophenone used. Be sure your mechanism accounts for this. It is also found that if optically active 2-butanol is used instead of isopropyl alcohol the recovered 2-butanol is not racemized. Does your mechanism accommodate this fact? [For further data on this reaction, see W. M. Moore, G. S. Hammond, and R. P. Foss, *J. Am. Chem. Soc.*, **83**, 2789 (1961); W. M. Moore and M. D. Ketchum, *J. Phys. Chem.*, **68**, 214 (1964).]

6-4 In experiments designed to measure the primary photochemical process in the photolysis of aldehydes, acetaldehyde was irradiated using 3130 A light at $60°C$ in the gas phase in the presence of varying pressures of iodine. The iodine acted as a scavenger for radicals, and quantum yields were lowered in its presence. The quantum yield for carbon monoxide decreased from 0.34 in the absence of iodine to 0.21 at iodine pressures from 1 to 3 mm. Simultaneously, the methane quantum yield decreased from 0.32 to 0.013. As iodine pressure increased, methyl iodide began to be an important product, finally reaching a quantum yield of 0.20 in the 1 to 3 mm iodine pressure range. Using these facts, choose between these two reactions for the primary photochemical act:

$$CH_3{-}CHO + h\nu \longrightarrow CH_4 + CO$$

$$CH_3{-}CHO + h\nu \longrightarrow CH_3{\cdot} + H\overset{\cdot}{C}O$$

Explain the fact that Φ_{CO} in the presence of iodine becomes equal to Φ_{CH_3I}. [F. E. Blacet and J. D. Heldman, *J. Am. Chem. Soc.*, **64**, 889 (1942).]

6-5 Aldehydes undergo a rapid chain decarbonylation

$$R{\cdot} + R{-}CHO \longrightarrow RH + R{-}\overset{\cdot}{C}O$$

$$R{-}\overset{\cdot}{C}O \longrightarrow R{\cdot} + CO$$

Thiols increase the chain length of this reaction by a series of hydrogen transfer steps. It has been found that benzophenone can photosensitize the decarbonylation of aldehydes and that best results are obtained if very low concentrations of both benzophenone and a thiol are simultaneously present. Write a mechanism for the decarbonylation under these conditions. [J. D. Berman, J. H. Stanley, W. V. Sherman, and S. G. Cohen, *J. Am. Chem. Soc.*, **85**, 4010 (1963).]

6-6 Irradiation of 5,9-dimethyl-2-decanone (optically active at the 5-position) with a mercury arc gives 1,2-dimethyl-2-(4-methylpentyl)-1-cyclobutanol, which has retained at least 16% of the optical activity.

Explain these results, assuming that the first step is the formation of a triplet n-$\pi°$ state. [I. Orban, K. Schaffner, and O. Jeger, *J. Am. Chem. Soc.*, **85**, 3033 (1963).]

6-7 If acetone is photolyzed in the gas phase, the ratio of the yield of methane divided by the square root of the yield of ethane is proportional to the acetone pressure. Suggest a mechanism to explain this result.

6-8 Irradiation of 5 g of 5,5-dimethyl-3-hexen-2-one in 400 ml of ether led to slow formation of an isomeric ketone which reached a maximum yield of 38% in 46 hr. The NMR spectrum of the product shows 3 hydrogens near 0 p.p.m. (characteristic of hydrogens on cyclopropane rings). Write a mechanism for the reaction and suggest a structure for the product. [M. J. Jorgenson and N. C. Yang, *J. Am. Chem. Soc.*, **85**, 1698 (1963).]

SUGGESTIONS FOR FURTHER READING

Hammond, G. S., and N. J. Turro: *Science*, **142**, 1541–1553 (1963). A brief review of the types of organic reactions which are initiated by light.

Kasha, M.: Paths of Molecular Excitation, in "Radiation Research," Supp. 2, Academic Press Inc., New York, 1960, pp. 243–275.

Kasha, M.: Chap. 5, in M. Burton, J. S. Kirby-Smith, and J. L. Magee (eds.), "Comparative Effects of Radiation," John Wiley & Sons, Inc., New York, 1960. This article and the one above describe the n-$\pi°$ and π-$\pi°$ excitation processes and discuss the electronic nature of these states.

Leermakers, P. A., and G. F. Vesley: *J. Chem. Ed.*, **41**, 535 (1964). An elementary review of the utility of photochemical reactions in organic chemistry.

Masson, C. R., V. Boekelheide, and W. A. Noyes: in A. Weissberger (ed.), "Technique of Organic Chemistry," vol. II, Interscience Publishers, Inc., New York, 2d ed., 1956, pp. 257–384. A good introduction, stressing the techniques involved and giving many examples of organic photolysis reactions.

McGlynn, S. P., F. J. Smith, and G. Cilento: Some Aspects of the Triplet State, in "Photochemistry and Photobiology," vol. 3, Pergamon Press, New York, 1964, pp. 269–294. Discusses the nature of the triplet and singlet excited states, distinctions between them, and their relation to radical-like reactivities.

Moore, W. J.: "Physical Chemistry," Prentice-Hall, Inc., Englewood Cliffs, N.J., 3d ed., 1962, chap. 21. A brief description of the physical principles of radiation chemistry at an elementary level.

Noyes, W. A., and P. A. Leighton: "Photochemistry of Gases," Reinhold Publishing Corporation, New York, 1941. A classic in the field, but examples are now dated.

Walling, C.: "Free Radicals in Solution," John Wiley & Sons, Inc., New York, 1957, pp. 539–563. Gives many examples of organic photolyses.

A series of helpful articles will be found in W. A. Noyes, G. S. Hammond, and J. N. Pitts (eds.), "Advances in Photochemistry," vol. I, Interscience Publishers, Inc., New York, 1963. Of particular interest are the articles below.

The Vocabulary of Photochemistry, by J. N. Pitts, F. Wilkinson, and G. S. Hammond. (On terminology.)

A New Approach to Mechanistic Organic Photochemistry, by H. E. Zimmerman. (A detailed analysis of a few reaction mechanisms.)

Photochemical Rearrangements of Organic Molecules, by O. L. Chapman. (An outline of a large number of light-initiated rearrangements.)

Thermal Homolysis:
Peroxides

We shall now consider the reactions involved in radical production from some of the common types of initiators. This chapter takes up the chemistry of peroxides; Chap. 8 that of peresters and peracids; Chap. 9 that of hydrogen peroxide and hydroperoxides; and Chap. 10 the chemistry of azo compounds.

Before discussing the chemistry of peroxides, it will be helpful to summarize the nomenclature used for peroxidic compounds. Table 7-1 gives generic names for peroxides and some of the most common radicals derived from them.

Peroxides decompose by at least three different mechanisms. In the first, a unimolecular homolytic scission of the peroxidic bond occurs:

$$RO-OR \longrightarrow 2RO\cdot$$

The radicals produced by this dissociation can either decompose further (for example, by a β-scission) or attack other molecules present in the system and initiate radical processes.

The second decomposition mechanism of peroxides is a bimolecular process called induced decomposition. In this process radicals attack the peroxide and cause its decomposition. The attacking radicals can be produced directly from the peroxide itself or by some subsequent reaction. The mechanism of the induced decomposition depends on the structure of the peroxide. For simple alkyl peroxides, it is thought to be hydrogen abstraction from the α carbon atom.

$$R\cdot + R_2'CH-O-O-CHR_2' \longrightarrow RH + R_2'\overset{\cdot}{C}-O-O-CHR_2'$$

For benzoyl peroxide it is an S_H2 attack on the peroxidic O—O bond.

$$R\cdot \ + \ \phi-\overset{\overset{O}{\|}}{C}-O-O-\overset{\overset{O}{\|}}{C}-\phi \ \longrightarrow \ \phi-CO_2\cdot \ + \ R-O-\overset{\overset{O}{\|}}{C}-\phi$$

The induced decomposition reaction wastes initiator since it destroys a molecule of peroxide without increasing the number of radicals.

The third decomposition of peroxides is a little-understood detonation which makes all peroxidic compounds hazardous to handle. Peroxides differ in their susceptibility to explosion. In general, the lower the molecular weight, the more dangerous is the peroxide. Of the alkyl peroxides, methyl peroxide is extremely hazardous, whereas t-butyl peroxide is unusually stable and is sold commercially. Among acyl peroxides, acetyl

Table 7-1   Nomenclature for peroxide compounds

Generic names of compounds	
Alkyl peroxide	ROOR
Acyl peroxide	$R-\overset{\overset{\displaystyle O}{\|\|}}{C}-OO-\overset{\overset{\displaystyle O}{\|\|}}{C}-R$
Hydroperoxide	ROOH
Peracid or peroxyacid	$R-\overset{\overset{\displaystyle O}{\|\|}}{C}-O-OH$
Perester or peroxyester	$R-\overset{\overset{\displaystyle O}{\|\|}}{C}-O-OR'$
Percarbonate or peroxycarbonate	$R-O-O-\overset{\overset{\displaystyle O}{\|\|}}{C}-O-O-R$
Peroxalate or peroxyoxalate	$R-O-O-\overset{\overset{\displaystyle O}{\|\|}}{C}-\overset{\overset{\displaystyle O}{\|\|}}{C}-O-O-R$

Generic names of radicals	
Alkoxy radical	RO•
Alkyl peroxy radical	ROO•
Acyl radical	$R-\overset{\overset{\displaystyle O}{\|\|}}{C}•$
Acyloxy radical	$R-\overset{\overset{\displaystyle O}{\|\|}}{C}-O•$
Acylperoxy radical	$R-\overset{\overset{\displaystyle O}{\|\|}}{C}-O-O•$

Names of specific radicals	
Methoxy	$CH_3O•$
Acetyl	$CH_3-\overset{\overset{\displaystyle O}{\|\|}}{C}•$
Acetoxy *or* acetate	$CH_3-CO_2•$
Peracetate *or* acetylperoxy	$CH_3-\overset{\overset{\displaystyle O}{\|\|}}{C}-OO•$
Benzoate *or* benzoyloxy	$\phi-CO_2•$
Perbenzoate *or* benzoylperoxy	$\phi-\overset{\overset{\displaystyle O}{\|\|}}{C}-OO•$

peroxide is very hazardous, whereas benzoyl peroxide is much less so. However, any peroxide is potentially dangerous and should not be ground or jarred or heated under conditions not known to be safe.

DIALKYL PEROXIDES

All the alkyl peroxides† undergo unimolecular decomposition reactions at similar rates. The activation energies are 34 to 37 kcal/mole for the series ethyl peroxide through t-butyl peroxide.‡

$$RO—OR \longrightarrow 2RO\cdot$$

The products from the subsequent reactions of the alkoxy radicals are not known in most cases. For ethyl peroxide, they have been reported to be ethanol and acetaldehyde. These products could result from a disproportionation between ethoxy radicals:

$$2CH_3—CH_2O\cdot \longrightarrow CH_3—CH_2—OH + CH_3—CHO$$

They could also result from a chain process in which an ethoxy radical abstracts an α hydrogen from a peroxide molecule which subsequently decomposes by β-scission.

$$CH_3CH_2OOCH_2CH_3 + CH_3CH_2O\cdot \longrightarrow CH_3\overset{\bullet}{C}HOOCH_2CH_3 + CH_3CH_2OH$$

$$CH_3\overset{\bullet}{C}HOOCH_2CH_3 \xrightarrow{\beta\text{-scission}} CH_3CHO + CH_3CH_2O\cdot$$

Because of its exceptional stability, t-butyl peroxide has been studied in more detail than have the other alkyl peroxides. It has a rate constant for decomposition given by

$$k = 10^{16}e^{-37,000/RT} \qquad sec^{-1}$$

The half-life is 11 years at 60°C and 35 sec at 180°C. The rate is almost the same in concentrated solution and in the dilute gas phase, from which it can be concluded that the majority of the peroxide decomposes by a unimolecular, nonchain path. If much of the peroxide reacted in a chain

---

† In the names of symmetrical dialkyl peroxides, the prefix *di* can be omitted. Thus, CH_3OOCH_3, for example, is correctly named methyl peroxide.

‡ W. A. Pryor, D. M. Huston, T. R. Fiske, T. L. Pickering, and E. Ciuffarin, *J. Am. Chem. Soc.*, **86**, 4237 (1964).

path of high chain length, the rate would appear to be higher in solution than in the gas phase, since radical concentrations are higher in the more concentrated solution phase. The mechanism of the decomposition in the dilute gas phase is shown below; the methyl radicals dimerize nearly quantitatively, and the main products are acetone and ethane.

t-BuO—OBu-t $\longrightarrow$ $2t$-BuO• (7-1)

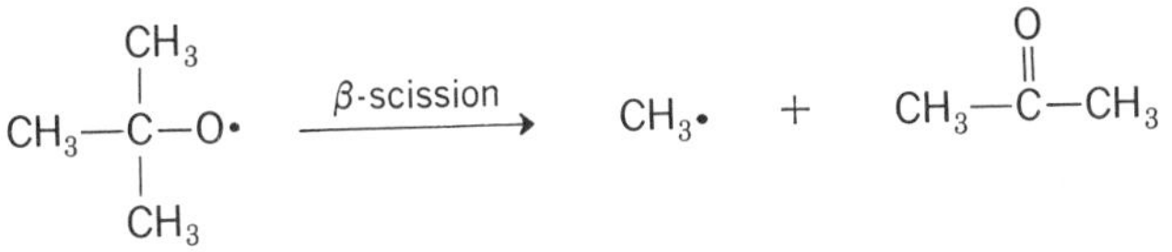

(7-2)

$2CH_3$• $\longrightarrow$ C_2H_6 (7-3)

In pure liquid peroxide as solvent, the products are

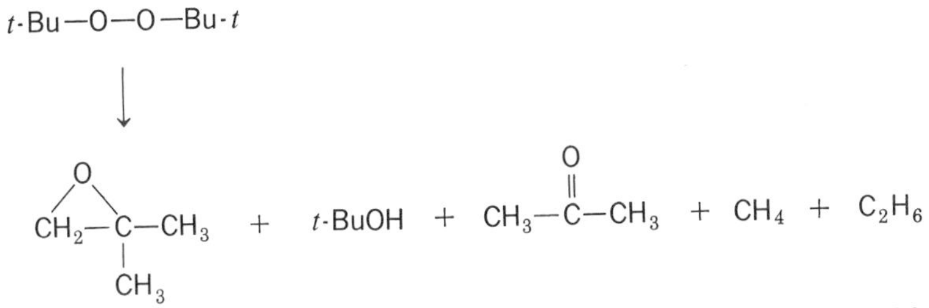

t-Bu—O—O—Bu-t

where the numbers under the compounds give moles formed per mole of peroxide. These products can be explained by the following reactions. Acetone and ethane result from reactions (7-2) and (7-3). Methane arises from hydrogen abstraction from the peroxide by methyl radicals.

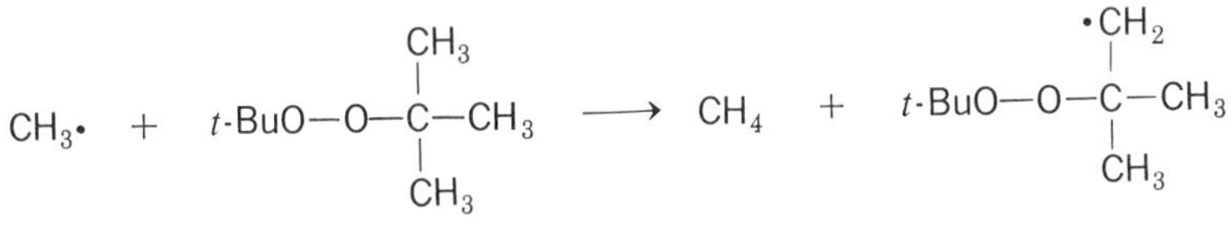

(I)

t-Butyl alcohol is formed by a similar hydrogen abstraction by the t-butoxy radical.

$$t\text{-BuO}\cdot \; + \; t\text{-BuO}-\text{O}-\underset{\underset{\text{CH}_3}{|}}{\overset{\overset{\text{CH}_3}{|}}{\text{C}}}-\text{CH}_3 \; \longrightarrow \; t\text{-BuOH} \; + \; t\text{-BuO}-\text{O}-\underset{\underset{\text{CH}_3}{|}}{\overset{\overset{\cdot\text{CH}_2}{|}}{\text{C}}}-\text{CH}_3$$

(I)

The formation of isobutylene oxide is best explained as an internal S_H2 reaction on the O—O bond in radical (I):

$$t\text{-Bu}-\text{O}-\text{O}-\underset{\underset{\text{CH}_3}{|}}{\overset{\overset{\cdot\text{CH}_2}{|}}{\text{C}}}-\text{CH}_3 \; \longrightarrow \; t\text{-BuO}\cdot \; + \; \text{O}-\underset{\underset{\text{CH}_3}{|}}{\overset{\overset{\text{CH}_2}{|}}{\text{C}}}-\text{CH}_3 \qquad (7\text{-}4)$$
(I)

A careful examination of the products from the gas-phase decomposition shows that isobutylene oxide is formed in about 3% yield under these dilute conditions also.† Therefore, some chain decomposition occurs even in the gas phase, the mechanism being

$$\left\{ \begin{matrix} \text{CH}_3\cdot \\ t\text{-BuO}\cdot \end{matrix} \right\} + t\text{-BuO}-\text{OBu-}t \longrightarrow \left\{ \begin{matrix} \text{CH}_4 \\ t\text{-BuOH} \end{matrix} \right\} + \text{(I)}$$

$$\text{(I)} \longrightarrow t\text{-BuO}\cdot + \text{Isobutylene oxide}$$

$$t\text{-BuO}\cdot \longrightarrow \text{CH}_3-\overset{\overset{\text{O}}{\|}}{\text{C}}-\text{CH}_3 + \text{CH}_3\cdot$$

If t-butyl peroxide is decomposed in the presence of an active hydrogen donor RH, the methyl and t-butoxy radicals can react by abstracting hydrogen from RH. Under these circumstances, the yields of methane and of t-butyl alcohol are greatly increased.

$$t\text{-BuO}\cdot \longrightarrow \text{CH}_3-\overset{\overset{\text{O}}{\|}}{\text{C}}-\text{CH}_3 + \text{CH}_3\cdot \qquad (7\text{-}5)$$

$$t\text{-BuO}\cdot + \text{RH} \longrightarrow t\text{-BuOH} + \text{R}\cdot \qquad (7\text{-}6)$$

$$\text{CH}_3\cdot + \text{RH} \longrightarrow \text{CH}_4 + \text{R}\cdot \qquad (7\text{-}7)$$

$$2\text{CH}_3\cdot \longrightarrow \text{C}_2\text{H}_6 \qquad (7\text{-}8)$$

† J. H. Raley, F. F. Rust, and W. E. Vaughan, *J. Am. Chem. Soc.*, **70**, 88, 1336, 2767 (1948); L. Batt and S. W. Benson, *J. Chem. Phys.*, **36**, 895 (1962).

These reactions have been used to compare the hydrogen-donating abilities of various solvents. If the yields of t-butyl alcohol and acetone are compared, the ratio of the rates of reactions (7-6) and (7-5) may be determined. Similarly, the ratio of methane to ethane gives the ratio of the rates of reactions (7-7) and (7-8). Qualitatively, the alcohol/acetone and methane/ethane ratios increase as the solvent RH becomes a better hydrogen donor.

ACETYL PEROXIDE

The reactions of acetyl peroxide can be rationalized in terms of the following mechanism:

$$CH_3\overset{\displaystyle O}{\overset{\|}{-C}}-O-O-\overset{\displaystyle O}{\overset{\|}{C}}-CH_3 \left\langle \begin{array}{l} \longrightarrow 2CH_3\bullet + 2CO_2 \quad\quad (7\text{-}9a) \\ \\ \longrightarrow [CH_3-CO_2\bullet \quad \bullet O_2C-CH_3] \quad (7\text{-}9b) \\ \quad\quad\quad\quad\quad \text{Cage} \end{array} \right.$$

$$[2CH_3-CO_2\bullet] \longrightarrow 2CH_3-CO_2\bullet \quad\quad\quad\quad (7\text{-}10)$$

$$CH_3-CO_2\bullet \longrightarrow CH_3\bullet + CO_2 \quad\quad\quad\quad (7\text{-}11)$$

$$CH_3\bullet + RH \longrightarrow CH_4 + R\bullet \quad\quad\quad\quad (7\text{-}12)$$

$$2CH_3\bullet \longrightarrow C_2H_6 \quad\quad\quad\quad\quad\quad\quad (7\text{-}13)$$

$$[2CH_3-CO_2\bullet] \longrightarrow CH_3-\overset{\displaystyle O}{\overset{\|}{C}}-O-CH_3 + CO_2 \quad (7\text{-}14)$$

$$[2CH_3-CO_2\bullet] \longrightarrow C_2H_6 + 2CO_2 \quad\quad\quad (7\text{-}15)$$

where RH is any hydrogen donor, radicals in brackets are cage radicals (see below), and other radicals are separated from one another. In the gas phase, the peroxide dissociates directly to methyl radicals and carbon dioxide [reaction (7-9a)]. However, in solution it dissociates to form two acetate radicals which are held in close proximity to each other by a solvent cage [reaction (7-9b)]. This concept of a solvent cage, first proposed by Franck and Rabinowitch in 1934 and extended and elaborated by R. M. Noyes,† gives the following picture for dissociation: In the gas phase, an excited molecule fragments into parts, and the chance of the two original parts recombining is extremely small. In solution, however, solvent molecules slow the diffusion of the original pair, and the two

---

† R. M. Noyes, *J. Chem. Phys.*, **18**, 999 (1950); **22**, 1349 (1954); *J. Phys. Chem.*, **65**, 763 (1961).

partners remain proximate for about 10^{-10} sec. During this time they may react (geminate reaction). However, once the geminate pair diffuse apart, they have an extremely small chance of recombining. The two operational tests of cage reactions are:

1. They do not occur in the gas phase.
2. Geminate reactions are not retarded or eliminated by radical scavengers (which can only trap free radicals).†

Table 7-2 gives the yields of products formed from the decomposition of acetyl peroxide in the liquid and the gas phase under comparable conditions. Much more ethane is formed in the gas phase than in solution. The ethane formed in the gas phase would be expected to be the result of a combination of free, noncaged methyl radicals, and, in agreement with this, ethane is almost eliminated if iodine vapor is present to trap free methyl radicals. On the other hand, most of the ethane formed in solution is the result of cage recombination. This follows because the liquid toluene solvent is about as good as a trap for free methyl radicals as is iodine vapor. Since iodine vapor suppresses the formation of ethane from noncage reactions in the gas phase, it would be expected that toluene would act similarly in solution. Therefore, the ethane formed in solution must result from cage reaction (7-15). Practically no methyl acetate is formed in the gas phase. Therefore, that formed in solution is the result either of cage reactions or of nonradical processes. (A nonradical process can be written with a six-membered ring as a transition state.)

The study of the decomposition of acetyl peroxide in isooctane solvent supports these conclusions. The yield of carbon dioxide per mole of

† The complete theory of cage reactions is more complex than is indicated here. Geminate recombinations are of two types: *Primary recombinations* are between radicals that have not moved from the positions they occupied at the time of the bond scission. *Secondary recombinations* occur between radical pairs that diffuse together again after diffusion has separated them by one or more molecular displacements. Both types of recombinations occur. For example, when iodine is irradiated with 5780 A light in hexane at 25°C, about 35% of the iodine atoms escape the cage completely, about 30% become separated by one molecular diameter but then recombine by diffusion, and about 35% either fail to dissociate or recombine without escaping from the cage of solvent molecules in which they are formed. [R. M. Noyes, *J. Chem. Phys.*, **18**, 999 (1950); also see H. P. Watts and G. S. Hammond, *J. Am. Chem. Soc.*, **86**, 1911 (1964).] Cage recombinations also may occur in the gas phase at very high vapor densities, although at ordinary pressures in the gas phase cage recombinations can be ignored. [R. K. Lyon, *J. Am. Chem. Soc.*, **86**, 1907 (1964).] A detailed theoretical treatment of the cage effect is given by R. M. Noyes in G. Porter (ed.), "Progress in Reaction Kinetics," vol. I, Pergamon Press, New York, 1961, pp. 131–160.

Table 7-2   Decomposition of acetyl peroxide in the gas phase and in toluene solution at 65°C†

	Gas	Solution
Reaction volume, ml	5,000	10
Peroxide, moles	3.8×10^{-5}	19×10^{-5}
Toluene, moles	0.018	0.094
Peroxide/toluene mole ratio	2.0×10^{-3}	2.0×10^{-3}
Yield products (moles per mole of peroxide decomposed)		
CH_4	0.95	0.48
C_2H_6	0.23	0.05
$CH_3-\overset{\overset{\displaystyle O}{\|}}{C}-OCH_3$	<0.005	0.15
CO_2	1.90	0.72

† L. Herk, M. Field, and M. Szwarc, *J. Am. Chem. Soc.*, **83**, 2998 (1961).

peroxide decomposed is 1.81 for a $1.3 \times 10^{-3} M$ solution of peroxide. This ratio is not changed if iodine, quinone, or styrene is added as a radical scavenger. Obviously, this ratio would be 2.0 if reaction (7-9a) were the only one occurring. The missing carbon dioxide implies that a 20% yield of ester is produced; since the yield of ester is not affected by scavengers, we again conclude that ester is formed entirely in cage or in nonradical reactions. The yield of methane is large (0.82 mole per mole of CO_2 formed) but is reduced to almost zero by 7 M styrene. Thus, methane is largely produced from scavengeable free radicals outside the cage and must result from the reaction of free methyl radicals with the solvent [reaction (7-12)]. The yield of ethane is small (0.02 mole per mole of CO_2 formed) but is not decreased by the addition of styrene. Therefore, most of the ethane must be formed in cage reaction (7-15). These conclusions, namely, that ester and ethane are formed in cage reactions but that methane is not, agree with the conclusions reached from the data in Table 7-2.

It is theoretically possible for geminate acetate radicals to combine in a cage to re-form the acetyl peroxide. This reaction has been demonstrated to be slow by a tracer experiment using acetyl peroxide in which the carbonyl oxygen is labeled with O-18. The labeled peroxide is allowed to decompose partially in solution, and then the undecomposed peroxide is reisolated. Since the recovered peroxide does not contain any material in which the O-18 has become scrambled between the carbonyl and peroxy oxygens, it is clear that recombination of acetate radicals has not occurred.[†] These reactions are shown below.

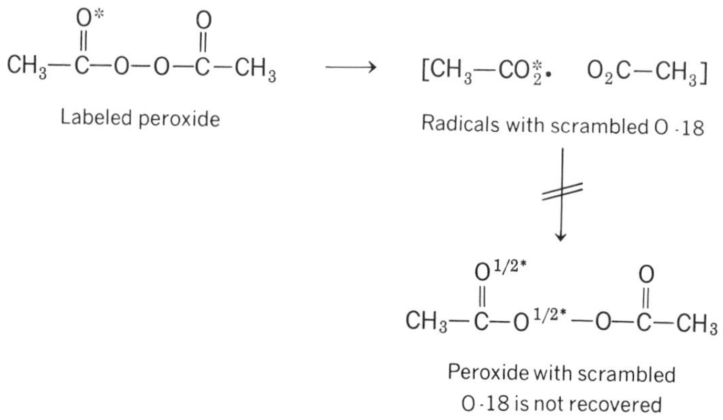

$$CH_3-\overset{\overset{\displaystyle O^*}{\|}}{C}-O-O-\overset{\overset{\displaystyle O}{\|}}{C}-CH_3 \quad \longrightarrow \quad [CH_3-CO_2^* \cdot \quad O_2C-CH_3]$$

Labeled peroxide   Radicals with scrambled O -18

$$CH_3-\overset{\overset{\displaystyle O^{1/2*}}{\|}}{C}-O^{1/2*}-O-\overset{\overset{\displaystyle O}{\|}}{C}-CH_3$$

Peroxide with scrambled
O -18 is not recovered

When methyl radicals generated from *t*-butyl peroxide, acetyl peroxide, or azomethane are allowed to react with ethylbenzene-*d*, the same ratio of CH_3D/CH_4 is produced, regardless of the source of the methyl radicals.[‡]

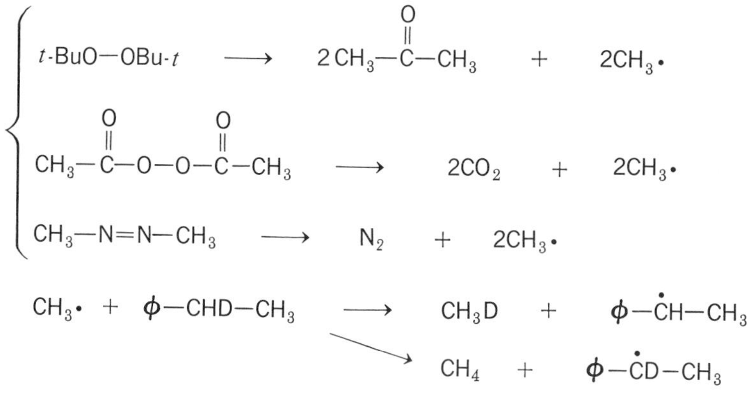

$$\begin{cases} t\text{-BuO}-\text{OBu-}t \longrightarrow 2\,CH_3-\overset{\overset{\displaystyle O}{\|}}{C}-CH_3 \quad + \quad 2CH_3\cdot \\[2em] CH_3-\overset{\overset{\displaystyle O}{\|}}{C}-O-O-\overset{\overset{\displaystyle O}{\|}}{C}-CH_3 \longrightarrow \quad 2CO_2 \quad + \quad 2CH_3\cdot \\[2em] CH_3-N{=}N-CH_3 \longrightarrow \quad N_2 \quad + \quad 2CH_3\cdot \end{cases}$$

$$CH_3\cdot \; + \; \phi-CHD-CH_3 \longrightarrow CH_3D \; + \; \phi-\overset{\displaystyle \cdot}{C}H-CH_3$$
$$\longrightarrow CH_4 \; + \; \phi-\overset{\displaystyle \cdot}{C}D-CH_3$$

Since azomethane certainly yields methyl radicals, this test identifies the radical from acetyl peroxide as a free methyl radical and not a methyl radical complexed with a molecule of carbon dioxide or a partially decomposed acetate radical.

The rate of decomposition of acetyl peroxide shows a dependence on

[†] L. Herk, M. Field, and M. Szwarc, *J. Am. Chem. Soc.*, **83**, 2998 (1961).
[‡] L. Herk and M. Szwarc, *J. Am. Chem. Soc.*, **82**, 3558 (1960).

solvent. It is faster in primary and secondary alcohols than in hydro-carbons. If deuterium-labeled isopropyl alcohol, i-PrOD, is used, none of the deuterium appears in the methane that is formed.[†] Therefore, hydrogen is abstracted from the carbon atom and not from the O—H group.

$$CH_3-\overset{\overset{\displaystyle O}{\|}}{C}-O-O-\overset{\overset{\displaystyle O}{\|}}{C}-CH_3 \longrightarrow 2CO_2 + 2CH_3\cdot$$

$$CH_3\cdot + CH_3-\overset{\overset{\displaystyle OD}{|}}{CH}-CH_3 \longrightarrow CH_4 + CH_3-\overset{\overset{\displaystyle OD}{|}}{\underset{\displaystyle \cdot}{C}}-CH_3$$

The increased rate of decomposition of acetyl peroxide in secondary alcohol solvents probably results from an induced decomposition of the peroxide caused by these radicals from the solvent.[‡]

BENZOYL PEROXIDE

Benzoyl peroxide is perhaps the most commonly used peroxide. It decomposes with a 30-min half-life at $100°C$ and has an activation energy of $30\,kcal/mole$. In inert solvents, the rate of peroxide disappearance appears to be first order in any one run, but larger constants are obtained in concentrated than in dilute solutions.[§] This indicates that some induced decomposition occurs, since more induced decomposition would be expected in concentrated solutions where the concentration of radicals is higher.

The decomposition is somewhat complicated by the fact that both phenyl and benzoyloxy radicals can be produced.

$$\phi-\overset{\overset{\displaystyle O}{\|}}{C}-O-O-\overset{\overset{\displaystyle O}{\|}}{C}-\phi \longrightarrow 2\phi-CO_2\cdot$$

$$\phi-CO_2\cdot \longrightarrow \phi\cdot + CO_2$$

[†] M. S. Kharasch, J. L. Rowe, and W. H. Urry, *J. Org. Chem.*, **16**, 905 (1951).

[‡] The mechanism of the decomposition of t-butyl peroxide in secondary alcohol solvents has been studied in detail. E. S. Huyser and C. J. Bredeweg, *J. Am. Chem. Soc.*, **86**, 2401 (1964).

[§] K. Nozaki and P. D. Bartlett, *J. Am. Chem. Soc.*, **68**, 1686 (1946).

The benzoyloxy radicals are known to be a first intermediate since, in wet carbon tetrachloride containing iodine, benzoic acid is formed.[†]

$$\phi-CO_2\cdot \ + \ I_2 \ \longrightarrow \ [\phi-\overset{\overset{\displaystyle O}{\|}}{C}-OI] \ \xrightarrow[\text{Hydrolysis}]{H_2O} \ \phi-CO_2H$$

In the pure peroxide, the products of decomposition are carbon dioxide and biphenyl, with small amounts of phenyl benzoate and benzene.[‡] At high dilution in benzene, the main products remain carbon dioxide and biphenyl, but other products resulting from the attack of phenyl radicals on the solvent also are found.[§] For example, decomposition of an 0.025 M solution of benzoyl peroxide in benzene at 80°C gives products such as those shown below.

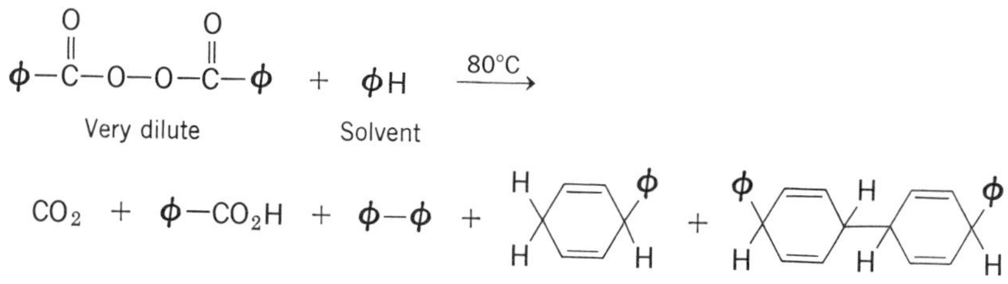

Reactions such as these, in which an organic group is substituted into an aromatic ring, are called homolytic aromatic substitution reactions. We shall return to a more complete discussion of them in Chap. 16.

The mechanism for the decomposition of benzoyl peroxide can be abbreviated as

$$P \xrightarrow{k_1} 2R\cdot \tag{7-16}$$

$$R\cdot + S \xrightarrow{k_2} S\cdot + \text{Nonradical products} \tag{7-17}$$

$$R\cdot + P \xrightarrow{k_3} R\cdot + \text{Nonradical products} \tag{7-18}$$

$$S\cdot + P \xrightarrow{k_4} R\cdot + \text{Nonradical products} \tag{7-19}$$

[†] G. S. Hammond and L. M. Soffer, *J. Am. Chem. Soc.*, **72**, 4711 (1951); H. J. Shine, J. A. Waters, and D. M. Hoffman, *ibid.*, **85**, 3613 (1963).

[‡] H. Erlenmeyer and W. Schoenaur, *Helv. Chim. Acta*, **19**, 338 (1936).

[§] D. F. DeTar and R. A. J. Long, *J. Am. Chem. Soc.*, **80**, 4742 (1958); D. H. Hey, M. J. Perkins, and G. H. Williams, *J. Chem. Soc.*, 3412 (1964); G. B. Gill and G. H. Williams, *J. Chem Soc.*, 995 (1965).

Table 7-3 Calculated kinetic order for the induced decomposition†

	Induced decomposition	
Termination reaction	Reaction (7-18) R• + P	Reaction (7-19) S• + P
R• + R•	1.5	0.5
R• + S•	2.0	1.0
S• + S•	2.0	1.5
R• + inhibitor	2.0	1.0
S• + inhibitor	2.0	2.0

† P is the peroxide, S is a molecule of solvent, R• is a radical produced from the peroxide, and S• is a radical produced from the solvent.

where P is the peroxide, S is a molecule of solvent, R• is a phenyl or benzoyloxy radical, and S• is any radical derived from the solvent.† Reactions (7-18) and (7-19) are induced decompositions; a possible mechanism for these reactions is shown on page 82. The kinetic order of the induced decomposition depends on the source of the radicals that effect the induced decomposition and on which type of termination occurs. Table 7-3 shows the kinetic order that should be observed under 10 sets of conditions. For example, if solvent molecules are not involved, the mechanism is

$$P \xrightarrow{k_1} 2R• \tag{7-16}$$

$$R• + P \xrightarrow{k_3} R• + \text{Nonradical products} \tag{7-18}$$

$$2R• \xrightarrow{k_5} \text{Nonradical products}$$

The rate of disappearance of peroxide is

$$\frac{-d(P)}{dt} = k_1(P) + k_3(R•)(P) \tag{7-20}$$

Since radicals are very reactive, it is reasonable to assume that their concentration reaches a steady value very early in the reaction. The rate of formation of radicals is

$$R_f = 2k_1(P)$$

† C. G. Swain, W. H. Stockmayer, and J. T. Clarke, *J. Am. Chem. Soc.*, **72**, 5426 (1950).

and the rate of their disappearance is

$$R_d = 2k_5(R\cdot)^2$$

Note that both expressions contain a factor of 2 since two radicals are involved in each process. At the steady state, these two rates are equal:

$$R_f = R_d$$

$$2k_1(P) = 2k_5(R\cdot)^2$$

Therefore, $\qquad (R\cdot) = \left(\dfrac{k_1}{k_5}\right)^{1/2}(P)^{1/2}$ $\hfill$ (7-21)

Substitution of Eq. (7-21) into Eq. (7-20) gives

$$\frac{-d(P)}{dt} = k_1(P) + \frac{k_3 k_1^{1/2}}{k_5^{1/2}}(P)^{1.5}$$

The second term on the right side of this equation arises because of reaction (7-18), which is an induced decomposition, and the order of this induced step in peroxide is 1.5, as shown in the first entry of Table 7-3.

Since both a unimolecular and an induced decomposition can occur, the observed rate can be a sum due to both these processes. The most convenient way of isolating the unimolecular decomposition for study is to allow the peroxide to decompose in the presence of inhibitors that suppress the induced decomposition. In inert solvents, benzoyl peroxide decomposes at a first-order rate.† However, in solvents giving radicals that can attack the peroxide, increased rates of decomposition and orders higher than 1.0 often occur. The decomposition in dioxane, for example, has a half-life of 23 min at 80°C and is not first order. However, if iodine, styrene, trinitrobenzene, or any of several other inhibitors is added to the dioxane, the decomposition becomes first order and slows to a half-life of 270 min. It is clear that in dioxane the induced decomposition is suppressed by effective inhibitors. The rates of decomposition of a series of ring-substituted benzoyl peroxides, therefore, were measured in dioxane containing 3,4-dichlorostyrene. In the presence of this inhibitor, the effect of substituents on the unimolecular decomposition could be measured without complications arising from the induced decomposition. It

---

† Note in Table 7-3 that the order of the induced step *can* be 1.0; therefore, the overall kinetic order *by itself* cannot be used as a test for an induced decomposition.

was found that the rates of these unimolecular decompositions obey the Hammett equation:†

$$\log \frac{k}{k_0} = \sigma\rho$$

In this equation, k_0 is the rate of decomposition of benzoyl peroxide itself, k is the rate constant for a substituted benzoyl peroxide, σ is an empirical constant for each substituent, and ρ is a constant characteristic of the reaction. In this case, ρ was found to be -0.4, implying that electron-donating substituents increase the rate of decomposition. Also, since a substituent could be present in each ring, an effective σ constant was used; it is the sum of the σ constants for the substituents in each ring.‡ Figure 7-1 shows these data plotted as the Hammett equation; the rate constant k_{XY} is for a benzoyl peroxide containing substituents X and Y, and σ_X and σ_Y are the sigma constants for these substituents.

Since the rate of addition of radicals to olefins is fast, the rate of initiation of styrene polymerization by radicals from benzoyl peroxide should be related to the rate of decomposition of the peroxide:§

$$\text{Peroxide} \xrightarrow{\text{Slow}} \text{Radicals} \xrightarrow[\text{fast}]{\text{Styrene}} M_n\cdot \xrightarrow{\text{Termination}} \text{Polymer}$$

In agreement with this, the effect of substituents on the initiation of styrene polymerization also obeys the Hammett equation, and ρ is -0.4 at $70°C$, the same value as found for the dissociation of benzoyl peroxide.¶

† This equation, which was first proposed by Hammett in 1937, has proved to be the most useful relation for correlating the effects of substituents on organic reactions. For further descriptions, see L. P. Hammett, "Physical Organic Chemistry," McGraw-Hill Book Company, 1940, chap. 7; also J. E. Leffler and E. Grunwald, "Rates and Equilibria of Organic Reactions," John Wiley & Sons, Inc., New York, 1963, pp. 171–262. It is interesting that this equation, which was first developed for ionic reactions, also correlates rate effects in some radical processes. This is another example of a polar effect on the rates of radical processes. The applicability of the Hammett equation to radical reactions has been reviewed by J. A. Howard and K. U. Ingold, *Can. J. Chem.*, **41**, 1744 (1963).

‡ Actually, the data fit the Hammett equation better if σ^+ values are used rather than the normal σ values. However, for present purposes, this is not an important distinction. We shall consider the application of σ^+ values in radical reactions further on p. 237.

§ As will be seen on p. 172, the rate of polymerization is proportional to the square root of the rate decomposition of the peroxide.

¶ W. Cooper, *J. Chem. Soc.*, 3106 (1951); 2408 (1952).

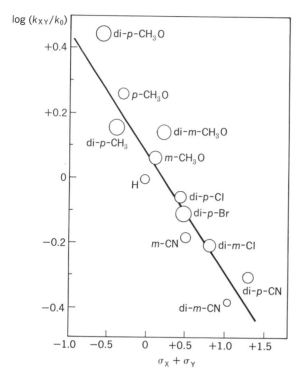

Figure 7-1 Graph of the Hammett equation for the dissociation of benzoyl peroxides in the presence of dichlorostyrene to inhibit the induced decomposition. [C. G. Swain, W. H. Stockmayer, and J. T. Clarke, J. Am. Chem. Soc., **72**, 5426 (1950).]

In the polymerization of styrene by benzoyl peroxide, the growing polystyryl radical frequently attacks the peroxide to cause an induced decomposition. The rate of this process, which can be measured by polymerization techniques to be discussed in Chap. 15, is conveniently expressed as the transfer constant C, which is the ratio of the rate of attack on the peroxide to attack on the monomer.

$$M_n\cdot \ + \ M \ \xrightarrow{k_p} \ M_{n+1}^{\cdot}$$

$$M_n\cdot \ + \ \phi-\overset{O}{\overset{\|}{C}}-O-O-\overset{O}{\overset{\|}{C}}-\phi \ \xrightarrow{k_{tr}} \ M_n-O-\overset{O}{\overset{\|}{C}}-\phi \ + \ \phi-CO_2\cdot$$

$$C = k_{tr}/k_p$$

Table 7-4 gives some transfer constants for a number of substituted benzoyl peroxides toward the radical from styrene. Notice that, in the induced step, electron-donating substituents slow the rate. This is just the reverse of their effect on the first-order decomposition shown in Fig. 7-1.

The effect of substituents on the unimolecular dissociation of benzoyl peroxide can be explained as follows: Electron-donating groups increase the first-order dissociation, since they increase the electronegativity difference between the peroxide oxygens and the aromatic ring.

Electron displacement by electron-donating X group

The greater negative charge on the oxygens produces a larger electrostatic repulsive force between them and a faster rate of dissociation.

In the induced decomposition, electron-withdrawing substituents increase the rate of the reaction. This is because the polystyryl radical is nucleophilic and attacks substrates at positions of low electron density. In the reaction between the polystyryl radical and a benzoyl peroxide

Table 7-4 Effect of substituents on the transfer constants of symmetrically substituted benzoyl peroxides†

Substituents (Same substituent in both rings)	$C = k_{tr}/k_p$
p-CH$_3$O	0.07
H	0.07
p-F	0.22
p-Cl	0.22
p-I	0.29
m-F	0.25
m-I	0.26
m-Br	0.46
p-CN	0.80

† W. Cooper, *J. Chem. Soc.*, 2408 (1952).

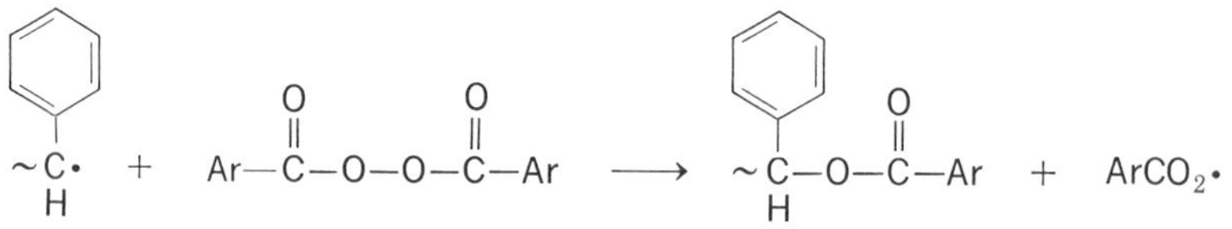

the transition state is stabilized by the ionic resonance form shown below.

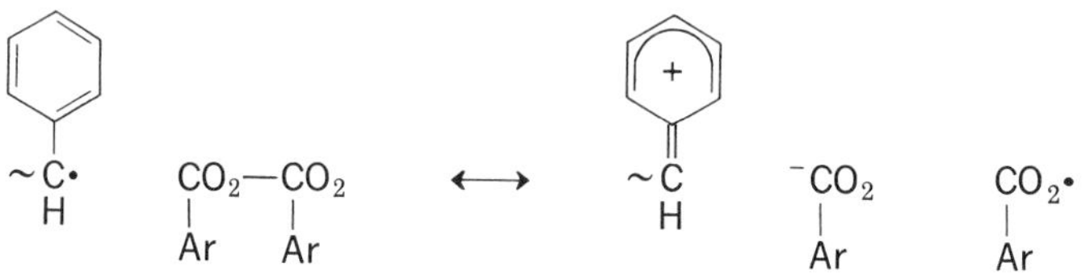

This resonance hybrid leads to the prediction that an electron-withdrawing substituent in the peroxide ring will produce a faster induced decomposition, in agreement with the data in Table 7-4.†

The decomposition of benzoyl peroxide is accelerated by amines. With tertiary amines, radicals are produced at a greatly enhanced rate, and tertiary amines are often used as co-catalysts in polymerization formulas. This is an example of the facilitation of radical formation by substances that might normally be considered ionic catalysts. In the benzoyl peroxide–tertiary amine system, the effect is very striking: A 0.01 M solution of benzoyl peroxide has a half-life of 60,000 hours at 20°C. The addition of 0.01 M dimethylaniline reduces the half-life to 13 min. The products from the reaction of benzoyl peroxide and dimethylaniline (after aqueous hydrolysis) are benzoic acid, methylaniline, formaldehyde, and smaller amounts of p-benzoyloxydimethylaniline. The mechanism of the reaction is complex and not known with certainty. A possible mechanism is shown in reactions (7-22) to (7-24):‡

---

† Alternatively, the mechanism of the attack by the polystyryl radical might be addition to the aromatic ring of the peroxide, with concurrent scission of the peroxide bond, as has been suggested by C. Walling and E. S. Savas, *J. Am. Chem. Soc.*, **82**, 1738 (1960). In this case, similar reasoning would suggest that electron-withdrawing groups in the peroxide ring should increase the rate of attack.

‡ L. Horner, *J. Polymer Sci.*, **18**, 438 (1955); C. Walling and N. Indicator, *J. Am. Chem. Soc.*, **80**, 5814 (1958); C. Walling, "Free Radicals in Solution," John Wiley & Sons, Inc., New York, 1957, pp. 590–595.

$$\phi-N(CH_3)_2 \ + \ \phi-\overset{\overset{O}{\|}}{C}-O-O-\overset{\overset{O}{\|}}{C}-\phi \ \longrightarrow$$

$$\phi-\overset{\overset{CH_3}{|}}{\underset{\underset{CH_3}{|}}{N^+}}-O-\overset{\overset{O}{\|}}{C}\phi \ + \ \phi CO_2^- \qquad (7\text{-}22)$$

(I)

$$[\phi-\overset{\bullet}{N}(CH_3)_2]^+ \ + \ \phi CO_2 \bullet \qquad (7\text{-}23)$$

(II)

$$\phi-\overset{\overset{CH_3}{|}}{\underset{\underset{CH_3}{|}}{N^+}}-O-\overset{\overset{O}{\|}}{C}\phi$$

(I)

$$\phi-\overset{\overset{CH_3}{|}}{N^+}=CH_2 \ + \ \phi CO_2H \qquad (7\text{-}24)$$

(III)

The formulation of reaction (7-22) as an ionic displacement is supported by the fact that electron-donating groups in the aniline ring and electron-withdrawing substituents in benzoyl peroxide accelerate the reaction rate. The initial product (I) is shown to react by two competing paths, one that produces radicals and one that does not. This is indicated by the fact that the efficiency of radical production is low (25% or less) and that the efficiency varies with the nature of the solvent used. The ionic product (III) would lead to the formation of formaldehyde and methylaniline after aqueous hydrolysis, as is observed. Apparently, only the benzoate radical in reaction (7-23) is able to escape and initiate polymerization, since nitrogen is not found in polymers formed by this initiation system. The radical (II) apparently reacts further and is destroyed before it becomes free.

OTHER ACYL PEROXIDES

In the decomposition of alkyl peroxides, ROOR, the nature of the R group has very little effect on the rate of dissociation. The peroxides decompose at similar rates, whether R is ethyl, propyl, isopropyl, or t-butyl. However, in acyl peroxides, RCO—O—O—COR, the nature of the R group has a very pronounced effect on the rate of dissociation. Table 7-5 gives relative rates for the decomposition of a number of acyl peroxides. The data show that the stability of the R group as a free radical

Table 7-5   Relative rates of decomposition of acyl peroxides

R in $R-\overset{O}{\overset{\|}{C}}-O-O-\overset{O}{\overset{\|}{C}}-R$	Relative rate constant		Reference
	60°C	70°C	
Methyl	1	ca. 5	a,d
Ethyl	1	. . .	a
Propyl	1	. . .	a
Isopropyl	100	. . .	a
Phenyl	. . .	1	b,e
Benzyl	. . .	Very fast	c
Cyclopropyl	. . .	0.4	b
Cyclopentyl	. . .	32	b
Cyclohexyl	. . .	60	b

[a] J. Smid and M. Szwarc, *J. Chem. Phys.*, **29**, 432 (1958).
[b] H. Hart and D. P. Wyman, *J. Am. Chem. Soc.*, **81**, 4891 (1959).
[c] P. D. Bartlett and J. E. Leffler, *ibid.*, **72**, 3030 (1950).
[d] M. Levy, M. Steinberg, and M. Szwarc, *ibid.*, **76**, 5978 (1954).
[e] K. Nozaki and P. D. Bartlett, *ibid.*, **68**, 1686 (1946).

influences the rate of decomposition of the acyl peroxide. This implies that there is some C—CO bond stretching in the transition state as well as O—O bond stretching:

$$R-\overset{O}{\overset{\|}{C}}-O-O-\overset{O}{\overset{\|}{C}}-R \longrightarrow R\cdots\overset{O}{\overset{\|}{C}}-O\cdots O-\overset{O}{\overset{\|}{C}}\cdots R$$

Transition state

Thus the ease with which the R group bears an odd electron influences the rate of the O—O bond scission. We shall return to this problem when we discuss peresters.

PROBLEMS

7-1   *t*-Butyl peroxide is allowed to decompose in toluene, ethylbenzene, and isopropylbenzene solutions. How would you expect the *t*-butyl alcohol/acetone ratio to vary in these three solvents?

7-2   Table 7-3 shows that an induced decomposition will be first order if there is present an inhibitor that traps R• radicals and if the radicals effecting the induced decomposition are derived from the solvent. Prove this is true, using the following mechanism:

$$P \xrightarrow{k_d} 2R\bullet$$

$$R\bullet + I \xrightarrow{k_1} \text{Products}$$

$$R\bullet + S \xrightarrow{k_2} \text{Products} + S\bullet$$

$$S\bullet + P \xrightarrow{k_3} R\bullet + \text{Products}$$

Hint: Write the steady-state assumptions for R• and S• and combine them to obtain a relation that involves S• as the only radical species.

7-3 In benzoyl peroxide, induced decomposition could occur by one of two processes. In one, addition to the carbonyl oxygen could precede scission:

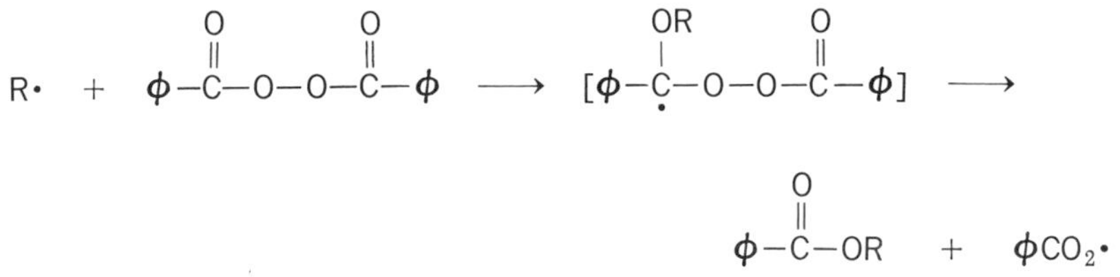

In the other, a direct attack on a peroxidic oxygen could occur:

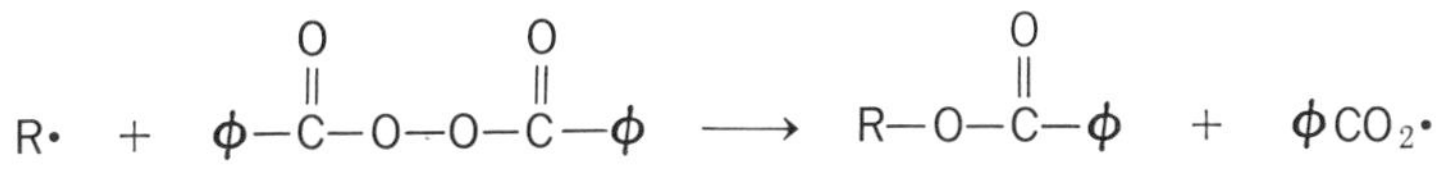

Devise a method for distinguishing these two possibilities. Hint: How do the roles of the two types of oxygens vary in the two mechanisms? Could tracers be used? (See the discussion and references given in W. A. Pryor, "Mechanisms of Sulfur Reactions," McGraw-Hill Book Company, New York, 1962, pp. 48–50.)

7-4 The activation energy for the induced decomposition of ROOR by the polystyryl radical is 22 to 24 kcal/mole, where R is ethyl, propyl, isopropyl, butyl, sec-butyl, or t-butyl. From these facts, would you predict that the induced decomposition occurs by hydrogen abstraction or by attack on the O—O bond? [W. A. Pryor, D. M. Huston, T. R. Fiske, T. L. Pickering, and E. Ciuffarin, *J. Am. Chem. Soc.*, **86**, 4237 (1964).]

7-5 Acetyl peroxide decomposes to form, among other products, methyl acetate and carbon dioxide. Devise an experiment that distinguishes methyl acetate formed by caged radicals from that formed from free acetate radicals. Suggest an experiment to distinguish caged radicals from a molecular, nonradical path forming methyl acetate. [H. J. Shine, J. A. Waters, and D. M. Hoffman, *J. Am. Chem. Soc.*, **85**, 3613 (1963).] Discuss the differences between a nonradical mechanism and a radical process occurring exclusively in a cage. [See, for example, D. F. DeTar and C. Weis, *J. Am. Chem. Soc.*, **79**, 3045 (1957), and R. C. Lamb and J. G. Pacifici, *ibid.*, **86**, 914 (1964).]

7-6 Discuss the average time required for the following processes: (*a*) a bond vibration; (*b*) diffusion from a cage; (*c*) the half-life for a radical combination with a zero activation energy and a typical *A* value. (S. W. Benson, "Foundations of Chemical Kinetics," McGraw-Hill Book Company, New York, 1960, pp. 496, 543–547.)

7-7 In toluene at 80°C, 6-heptenoyl peroxide $(CH_2\!=\!CH\!-\!(CH_2)_4\!-\!CO_2\!-\!)_2$ decomposes to give 1-hexene, 1,5-hexadiene, 1,11-dodecadiene, cyclohexane, methylcyclopentane, and bibenzyl. The first three of these products are formed in about the same yields, whether or not galvinoxyl, a scavenger of oxygenated radicals, is present. However, bibenzyl is entirely eliminated and the yields of the two cyclic compounds are greatly reduced in the presence of this scavenger. Give a mechanism for the decomposition of this peroxide that explains these facts. [R. C. Lamb, P. W. Ayers, and M. K. Toney, *J. Am. Chem. Soc.*, **85**, 3483 (1963).]

SUGGESTIONS FOR FURTHER READING

Davies, A. G.: "Organic Peroxides," Butterworth Scientific Publications, London, 1961.

Edwards, J. O. (ed.): "Peroxide Reaction Mechanisms," Interscience Publishers, Inc., New York, 1962.

Hawkins, E. G. E.: "Organic Peroxides," D. Van Nostrand Company, Inc., Princeton, N.J., 1961.

Tobolsky, A. V., and R. B. Mesrobian: "Organic Peroxides," Interscience Publishers, Inc., New York, 1954.

chapter eight

Thermal Homolysis: Peresters and Peracids

Peresters and peracids are related in the same way as are ordinary esters and acids.

$$\underset{\text{Peracid}}{\underset{\displaystyle \text{R}-\overset{\displaystyle \text{O}}{\overset{\|}{\text{C}}}-\text{O}-\text{OH}}{}} \qquad\qquad \underset{\text{Perester}}{\underset{\displaystyle \text{R}-\overset{\displaystyle \text{O}}{\overset{\|}{\text{C}}}-\text{O}-\text{O}-\text{R}'}{}}$$

Peracids are formed by the reaction of acids, acid chlorides, or anhydrides with hydrogen peroxide. For example, peracetic acid can be prepared by allowing equimolar amounts of acetic acid and 98% hydrogen peroxide to react in the presence of 1% sulfuric acid. At 15°C, equilibrium is reached in 15 hours, giving a 50% solution of peracetic acid:

$$\text{CH}_3-\text{CO}_2\text{H} \;+\; \text{H}_2\text{O}_2 \;\longrightarrow\; \text{CH}_3-\overset{\displaystyle \text{O}}{\overset{\|}{\text{C}}}-\text{O}-\text{OH} \;+\; \text{H}_2\text{O}$$

Peracids are produced as intermediates when aldehydes are oxidized; this can frequently be used as a synthetic route. Peracetic acid is prepared industrially by the oxidation of acetaldehyde:

$$\text{CH}_3-\text{CHO} \xrightarrow{\text{R}\cdot} \text{CH}_3-\overset{\displaystyle \text{O}}{\overset{\|}{\text{C}}}\cdot \xrightarrow{\text{O}_2} \text{CH}_3-\overset{\displaystyle \text{O}}{\overset{\|}{\text{C}}}-\text{O}-\dot{\text{O}}$$

$$\text{CH}_3-\text{CHO} \;+\; \text{CH}_3-\overset{\displaystyle \text{O}}{\overset{\|}{\text{C}}}-\text{O}-\text{O}\cdot \;\longrightarrow\; \text{CH}_3-\overset{\displaystyle \text{O}}{\overset{\|}{\text{C}}}\cdot \;+\; \text{CH}_3-\overset{\displaystyle \text{O}}{\overset{\|}{\text{C}}}-\text{O}-\text{OH}$$

Peresters are formed from acid chlorides and hydroperoxides:

$$\text{R}-\overset{\displaystyle \text{O}}{\overset{\|}{\text{C}}}-\text{Cl} \;+\; \text{R}'-\text{OOH} \;\longrightarrow\; \text{R}-\overset{\displaystyle \text{O}}{\overset{\|}{\text{C}}}-\text{O}-\text{O}-\text{R}' \;+\; \text{HCl}$$

The preparation is especially convenient using t-butyl hydroperoxide, which is available commercially. A number of peresters have been prepared in this way. Table 8-1 gives some examples.

Table 8-1 Peresters and the half-lives of their decomposition reactions†

$t\text{-BuO}-O-\overset{\displaystyle O}{\overset{\|}{C}}-R$	

R	Half-life at 60°, min
CH_3-	5×10^5
$\phi-$	3×10^5
$\phi-CH_2-$	1.7×10^3
ϕ_2CH-	26
$\phi-\overset{\displaystyle CH_3}{\underset{\displaystyle CH_3}{\overset{\|}{\underset{\|}{C}}}}-$	12
$\phi_2\overset{\displaystyle CH_3}{\overset{\|}{C}}-$	6
Cl_3C-	970
$p\text{-}NO_2-C_6H_4-CH_2-$	4,700
$p\text{-}CH_3O-C_6H_4-CH_2-$	880

† P. D. Bartlett and R. R. Hiatt, *J. Am. Chem. Soc.*, **80**, 1398 (1958).

Several different modes of decomposition of peresters have been identified:

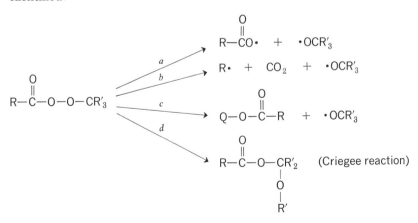

Path (*a*) is simple scission of the O—O bond analogous to that occurring in peroxides. Path (b) is a simultaneous scission of both the O—O bond and the C—C bond to split out carbon dioxide in a manner analogous to the way nitrogen is split from an azo compound. Path (c) is an induced decomposition by the radical Q•. In addition to these three radical decomposition mechanisms, the ionic decomposition shown in (d) has been identified for some peresters. It is the sole decomposition mode for 9-decalyl perbenzoate.†

The reaction rate depends strongly on the ionizing power of the solvent and therefore must involve charged species as intermediates. t-Butyl pertosylate is another example of a perester that reacts entirely by the Criegee mechanism; in methanol as solvent the products are toluene-sulfonic acid and acetone dimethyl ketal.‡

† R. Criegee and R. Kaspar, *Ann. Chem.*, **560**, 127 (1948).
‡ P. D. Bartlett and T. G. Traylor, *J. Am. Chem. Soc.*, **83**, 856 (1961).

t-Butyl trifluoroperacetate and *t*-butyl chloroperformate react either by path (*a*) and (*b*) or by (*d*), depending on the ionizing power of the solvent.†

The half-lives given in Table 8-1 reveal an interesting feature about the decompositions of these peresters: They decompose at a faster rate as the R group is varied so as to form a more stable radical. For example, as R is varied from CH_3 to ϕCH_2 to $\phi_2 CH$, the rate of dissociation increases smoothly. This suggests that the stability of the R group as a free radical affects the rate of the O—O bond scission. The mechanism suggested to explain these facts is the following: Peresters that do not have specially stabilized R groups undergo normal O—O bond scission. However, peresters with R groups that would form relatively stable radicals undergo a synchronous scission of two bonds to split out a molecule of CO_2. In this way, some of the odd electron density is localized on the R group at the transition state. For example, the data in Table 8-1 show that *t*-butyl peracetate and perbenzoate decompose at almost the same rate and that these compounds are the most stable peresters listed. In these compounds, R is methyl and phenyl, respectively, and neither of these groups forms a particularly stable radical. These two peresters, therefore, decompose with simple O—O bond scission:

$$t\text{-Bu}—O—O—CO—CH_3 \longrightarrow t\text{-BuO}\cdot + CH_3—CO—O\cdot$$
$$t\text{-Bu}—O—O—CO—\phi \longrightarrow t\text{-BuO}\cdot + \phi—CO—O\cdot$$

However, *t*-butyl phenylperacetate decomposes 10^2 times faster than the peracetate or perbenzoate. In this case, the decomposition is postulated to occur by scission of two bonds to produce a benzyl free radical.

$$t\text{-Bu}—O—O—CO—CH_2\phi \longrightarrow [t\text{-BuO}\cdots CO_2 \cdots CH_2\phi]$$
$$\text{Transition state}$$
$$\longrightarrow t\text{-BuO}\cdot + CO_2 + \phi CH_2\cdot$$

The localization of some of the odd electron density on the benzyl carbon at the transition state leads to a pronounced rate enhancement. This decomposition may seem unusual at first sight, since ordinary peroxides undergo simple O—O bond scission. However, it is no more unusual than the formation of nitrogen during the dissociation of azo compounds. Compare, for example, this azo compound‡ and perester:§

---

† P. D. Bartlett, in J. O. Edwards (ed.), "Peroxide Reaction Mechanisms," Interscience Publishers, Inc., New York, 1962, p. 1.

‡ S. G. Cohen and C. H. Wang, *J. Am. Chem. Soc.*, **77**, 3628 (1955).

§ P. D. Bartlett and R. R. Hiatt, *J. Am. Chem. Soc.*, **80**, 1398 (1958).

$$\phi\text{—}N{=}N\text{—}CH\phi_2 \longrightarrow \phi\cdot \quad + N_2 + \cdot CH\phi_2$$
$$t\text{-}BuO\text{—}O\text{—}O\text{—}CO\text{—}CH\phi_2 \longrightarrow t\text{-}BuO\cdot + CO_2 + \cdot CH\phi_2$$

At 60°C, the azo compound has a half-life of about 60 min and the perester has a half-life of 26 min.

Table 8-2 gives the activation enthalpy and entropy for the dissociation of three of the compounds from Table 8-1. Notice that the rate constant increases and that both $\Delta H^{\ddagger}$ and $\Delta S^{\ddagger}$ get smaller in going down the table. Since a less positive $\Delta S^{\ddagger}$ acts to produce a slower reaction, the effect of the change in going down Table 8-2 is to cancel part of the rate increase due to the decrease in $\Delta H^{\ddagger}$. The reason for the decrease in enthalpy of activation was discussed above; it occurs because the lower compounds form more stable R radicals and require less energy for bond breaking. The reason for the decrease in entropy in going down the table can be seen from the geometry of the transition state in a reaction in which two bonds are undergoing simultaneous homolysis. For example, in order for the phenyl group in phenylperacetate to delocalize the odd electron, it must be coplanar with the CO_2 in the transition state:

$$t\text{-}BuO\text{—}O\text{—}CO\text{—}CH_2\text{—}\phi \longrightarrow t\text{-}BuO\cdots O\cdots \overset{\overset{\displaystyle O}{\|}}{C}\cdots CH_2{\cdots}\langle\bigcirc\rangle$$

Transition state

This restriction lessens the possible motions in the transition state and lowers its probability and entropy.

Table 8-2 Activation parameters for perester dissociations†

Perester	$\Delta H^{\ddagger}$, kcal/mole	$\Delta S^{\ddagger}$, cal/deg	k, sec^{-1}, at 60°
$t\text{-}BuO\text{—}O\overset{\overset{\displaystyle O}{\|}}{\text{—}C}\text{—}CH_3$	38	17	2×10^{-8}
$t\text{-}BuO\text{—}O\overset{\overset{\displaystyle O}{\|}}{\text{—}C}\text{—}CH_2\phi$	29	3.9	6.8×10^{-6}
$t\text{-}BuO\text{—}O\overset{\overset{\displaystyle O}{\|}}{\text{—}C}\text{—}CH\phi_2$	24	−1.0	4.4×10^{-4}

† P. D. Bartlett and R. R. Hiatt, *J. Am. Chem. Soc.*, **80**, 1398 (1958).

Table 8-3 **Peresters and possible cage decompositions†**

Perester	Relative rate constant, 100°C	Cage reaction, %
$t\text{-BuO}\!-\!\text{O}\!-\!\overset{\displaystyle O}{\overset{\|}{C}}\!-\!\overset{\displaystyle O}{\overset{\|}{C}}\!-\!\text{O}\!-\!\text{OBu-}t$	10^7	0
$t\text{-BuO}\!-\!\text{O}\!-\!\overset{\displaystyle O}{\overset{\|}{C}}\!-\!\text{OBu-}t$	10^2	0
$t\text{-BuO}\!-\!\text{OBu-}t$	1	

† P. D. Bartlett and H. Sakurai, *J. Am. Chem. Soc.*, **84**, 3269 (1962).

The compounds listed in Table 8-3 provide information about the occurrence of cage reactions in peresters. Each compound would give the compound just below it in the table if it were to decompose by loss of CO_2 followed by a cage recombination of the resulting fragments. For example, the first compound, *t*-butyl peroxalate, would yield the second, *t*-butyl monopercarbonate:

$$RO\!-\!O\!-\!\overset{\displaystyle O}{\overset{\|}{C}}\!-\!\overset{\displaystyle O}{\overset{\|}{C}}\!-\!O\!-\!OR \longrightarrow RO\!-\!\overset{\displaystyle O}{\overset{\|}{C}}\!-\!O\!-\!OR + CO_2$$

$$(R = t\text{-Bu})$$

Similarly, loss of CO_2 and cage recombination of the second compound would form the third:

$$R\!-\!O\!-\!\overset{\displaystyle O}{\overset{\|}{C}}\!-\!O\!-\!O\!-\!R \longrightarrow R\!-\!O\!-\!O\!-\!R + CO_2$$

Furthermore, in each case the compound produced would decompose more slowly than the starting perester. Therefore, if these cage products were formed, they could be isolated. In fact, no *t*-butyl peroxide is found in the decomposition of the percarbonate, and neither of the other two compounds is formed in the decomposition of the peroxalate. Therefore, no cage reaction (or, certainly, less than 1%) occurs in the decomposition of the percarbonate or the peroxalate. Results were discussed on page 90 which indicate that cage recombination of acetate radicals does not occur in acetyl peroxide. Thus, there is no evidence for any cage recombination in any of these perester or peroxide reactions. This seems particularly unexpected since C—O, C—N, and N—N couplings do occur. For example,[†] t-butyl monoperoxalate decomposes to give t-butyl carbonate,

the result of a combination between an alkoxy radical and an ROC· radical:

$$R-O-O-\overset{\overset{O}{\|}}{C}-\overset{\overset{O}{\|}}{C}-O-R \quad \xrightarrow[\text{Benzene}]{25°C} \quad CO_2 \quad + \quad R-O-\overset{\overset{O}{\|}}{C}-O-R$$

$$\text{1.5 moles} \qquad\qquad \text{0.5 mole}$$

Galvinoxyl ↓ 25°C, benzene

$$CO_2 \quad + \quad R-O-\overset{\overset{O}{\|}}{C}-O-R$$

$$\text{1.0 mole} \qquad \text{0.4 mole}$$

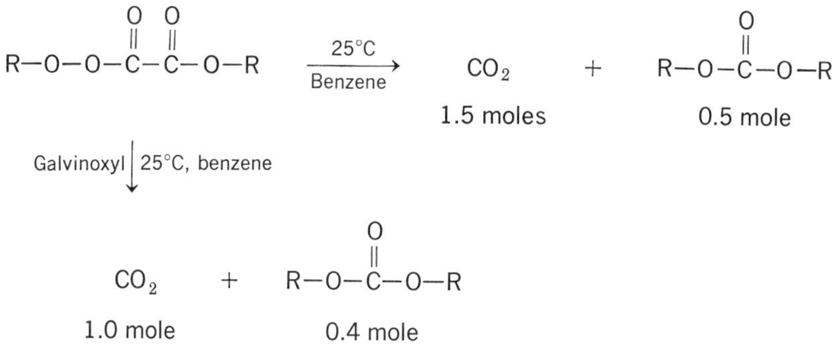

$$(R = t\text{-butyl})$$

The carbonate ester is largely formed in a cage reaction since, as shown above, its yield is not appreciably decreased in the presence of galvinoxyl, which is a very efficient radical scavenger for oxygen radicals.[‡]

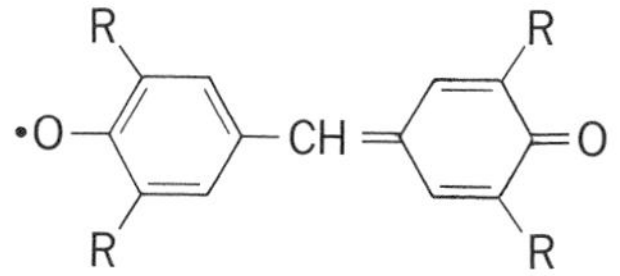

$$(R = t\text{-butyl})$$

Galvinoxyl

PROBLEMS

8-1 Write the products that would be formed from the decomposition of t-butyl trifluoroperacetate by paths (a), (b), and (d) given on page 105.

† P. D. Bartlett, B. A. Gontarev, and H. Sakurai, *J. Am. Chem. Soc.*, **84**, 3101 (1962).

‡ P. D. Bartlett and T. Funahashi, *J. Am. Chem. Soc.*, **84**, 2596 (1962).

8-2 p-Nitro-p'-methoxybenzoyl peroxide decomposes by a radical mechanism in nonpolar solvents and by an ionic mechanism in polar solvents.

a. Predict the products from the radical decomposition in the presence of a hydrogen donor.

b. Write the mechanism for the ionic decomposition. The products after hydrolysis are nitrobenzoic acid, methoxyphenol, and carbonic acid. Discuss this ionic decomposition as a limiting case illustrating charge-separated resonance forms for the transition states of radical reactions. [J. E. Leffler, *J. Am. Chem. Soc.*, **72**, 67 (1956).]

8-3 Decomposition of t-butyl peroxide in toluene containing iodine as a radical scavenger shows that radicals are formed at exactly the rate predicted from gas-phase measurements. Discuss these facts in light of the data in Table 8-3. [P. D. Bartlett and C. Rüchardt, *J. Am. Chem. Soc.*, **82**, 1756 (1960).]

8-4 Explain the activation parameters for the three peresters below:

R in t-BuO—O—CO—R	$\Delta S^{\ddagger}$, cal/deg	$\Delta H^{\ddagger}$, kcal/mole
CH_3	17	38
ϕCH_2	4	29
ϕ—CH=CH—CH_2	−6	23

Consider the number of bonds that break at the transition state. [P. D. Bartlett and R. R. Hiatt, *J. Am. Chem. Soc.*, **80**, 1398 (1958).]

SUGGESTIONS FOR FURTHER READING

Bartlett, P. D.: in J. O. Edwards (ed.), "Peroxide Reaction Mechanisms," Interscience Publishers, Inc., New York, 1962, p. 1.
Swern, D.: *Chem. Rev.*, **45**, 1 (1945).

chapter nine # Thermal Homolysis: Hydrogen Peroxide, Hydroperoxides, and Molecule-induced Homolysis

Hydrogen peroxide is available in aqueous solutions of varying concentrations. This inorganic peroxide is the starting point for the synthesis of all organic peroxidic materials except those which can be prepared by direct oxidation with oxygen. The explosive hazards in handling hydrogen peroxide illustrate the cautions that must be observed in dealing with any peroxidic material. Solutions of hydrogen peroxide of 95 to 100% detonate in the liquid state, but the more dilute solutions sold commercially are safe as long as they are kept pure. However, if organic materials are allowed to contaminate hydrogen peroxide samples, extremely hazardous mixtures result.

The susceptibility of a compound to detonation is related to the amount of oxygen it contains. A rule of thumb is that molecules containing 5% active oxygen and a reactive bond are potentially dangerous. Some examples are given in Table 9-1. As the table shows, the oxygen content of most peroxides puts them in the dangerous class. They are not commercially useful explosives, however, because they are not sufficiently stable to allow safe shipping and their explosions are unpredictable.

Table 9-1   Peroxides and their explosive hazards

Compound	% oxygen	Hazard
Hydrogen peroxide	94	Explosive only when contaminated or at concentrations greater than 90%.
Acetyl peroxide	13	Solid is very hazardous. Only dilute (ca. 30%) solutions are normally handled.
Benzoyl peroxide	7	Explosions of solid have been reported; solutions are safe.
Lauroyl peroxide	4	Not explosive.
Peracetic acid	21	Pure material can be detonated at 110°C. Solutions more concentrated than 69% are exploded on impact. Less dangerous than acetyl peroxide or performic acid.
Performic acid	26	Solutions more concentrated than 47% can be detonated by organic impurities.
t-Butyl peroxide	25	Safe.
Ethyl peroxide	35	Solid is detonated by scratching; detonates at high temperatures (ca. 200°C) in gas phase (especially in presence of oxygen); solutions at moderate temperatures are relatively safe.

Hydrogen peroxide yields hydroxyl radicals either upon heating or upon irradiation:

$$H_2O_2 \xrightarrow[\text{heat}]{\text{Light or}} 2HO\cdot$$

The decomposition of hydrogen peroxide can be catalyzed by iron. A mixture of ferrous ion, hydrogen peroxide, and acid is called Fenton's reagent and is widely used as an oxidant and a source of hydroxyl radicals.

$$H_2O_2 + Fe^{++} + H^+ \longrightarrow HO\cdot + H_2O + Fe^{3+}$$

These reactions will be discussed further in Chap. 11.

Organic hydroperoxides decompose analogously to hydrogen peroxide to yield hydroxyl radicals; their decompositions also can be catalyzed by ferrous ion.

$$ROOH \xrightarrow[\text{heat}]{\text{Light or}} RO\cdot + HO\cdot$$
$$ROOH + Fe^{++} \longrightarrow RO\cdot + OH^- + Fe^{3+}$$

t-BUTYL HYDROPEROXIDE

Tertiary hydroperoxides are readily prepared by alkylation of hydrogen peroxide:

$$ROH \text{ (or } RCl) + H_2O_2 \longrightarrow ROOH + H_2O \qquad (R = \text{tertiary})$$

For this reason, and also because they are more stable and safer to handle than are primary or secondary hydroperoxides, a number of tertiary hydroperoxides are available commercially. Of these, t-butyl hydroperoxide is the most commonly used. The decomposition of t-butyl hydroperoxide, either pure or in inert solvents such as chlorobenzene, gives oxygen and t-butyl alcohol.† The mechanism is

Initiation

$$t\text{-BuOOH} \longrightarrow t\text{-BuO}\cdot + HO\cdot$$

---

† E. R. Bell, J. H. Raley, F. F. Rust, F. H. Seubold, and W. E. Vaughan, *Discussions Faraday Soc.*, **10**, 242 (1951).

Chain

t-BuO• + t-BuOOH $\longrightarrow$ t-BuOH + t-BuOO•

2t-BuOO• $\longrightarrow$ [t-BuOO—OOBu-t] $\longrightarrow$ 2t-BuO• + O_2

As might be expected from this mechanism, solvents that readily form radicals lead to an enhanced rate of decomposition. For example, t-butyl hydroperoxide decomposes at an enhanced rate in alcohols, ethers, and amines.† These solvents all form radicals easily, and the increased rate of decomposition of the hydroperoxide can be attributed to radicals from the solvent taking part in the induced decomposition. The induced decomposition then has the mechanism (SH is a solvent molecule with a labile hydrogen)

Chain

t-BuO• + SH $\longrightarrow$ t-BuOH + S•

S• + t-BuOOH $\longrightarrow$ t-BuOO• + SH

2t-BuOO• $\longrightarrow$ 2t-BuO• + O_2

Radicals from t-butyl hydroperoxide are capable of initiating the polymerization of monomers such as styrene.

$$ROOH \longrightarrow RO• + •OH \tag{9-1}$$

$$RO• + M \longrightarrow RO—M• \xrightarrow{n\text{M}} RO—M_n• $$
$$\text{(Styrene)}$$

However, the growing polystyryl radical is able to attack the hydroperoxide; this adds an induced decomposition pathway to the rate of disappearance of the hydroperoxide.

$$RO—M_n• + ROOH \longrightarrow RO—M_n—H + ROO• \tag{9-2}$$

Since initiation by the hydroperoxide [reaction (9-1)] involves a first-order decomposition of the peroxide and the induced path (9-2) a second-order decomposition, the two pathways can be separated by kinetic analysis. By subtracting the amount of the peroxide that decomposes by the higher-order path, the rate of unimolecular decomposition of the hydroperoxide in styrene solution can be calculated and compared with that in ordinary solvents.‡ This procedure leads to a surprising result: After correction

---

† V. Stannett and R. B. Mesrobian, *J. Am. Chem. Soc.*, **72**, 4125 (1950).

‡ D. H. Johnson and A. V. Tobolsky, *J. Am. Chem. Soc.*, **74**, 938 (1952).

for the amount of bimolecular, induced decomposition, the rate of initiation by the hydroperoxide is faster than that calculated from the rate of the unimolecular decomposition of the hydroperoxide in inert solvents. It is apparent that styrene causes the decomposition of *t*-butyl hydroperoxide to occur at an unexpectedly rapid rate. This phenomenon is called molecule-induced homolysis and is discussed later in this chapter.

CUMYL HYDROPEROXIDE

Cumyl hydroperoxide is another tertiary hydroperoxide that has been studied in detail. The reactions of this hydroperoxide include a β-scission in which acetophenone and methane are produced. In decane at 140°C, the products are those shown below.†

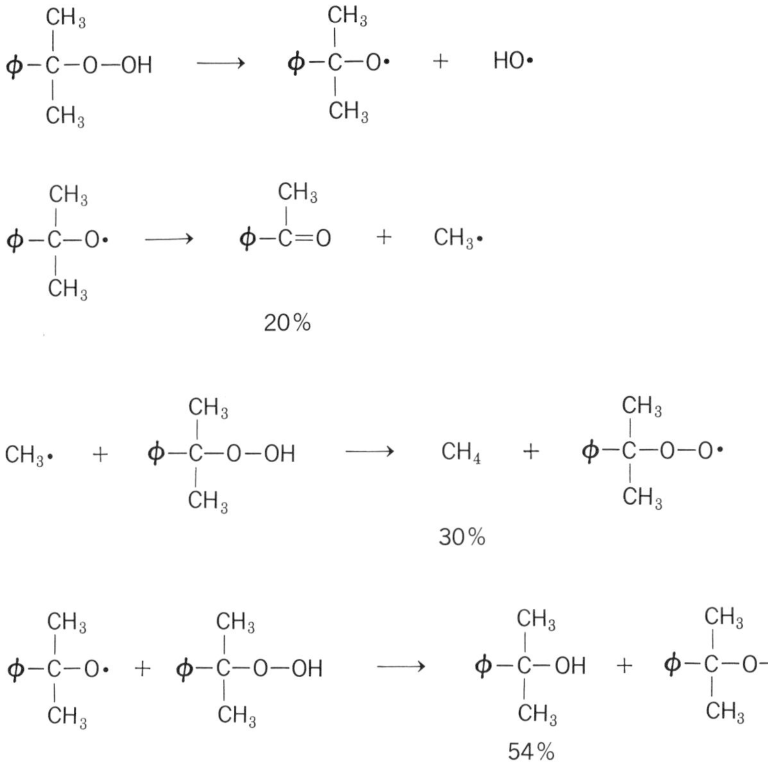

$$\phi-\underset{\underset{CH_3}{|}}{\overset{\overset{CH_3}{|}}{C}}-O-OH \longrightarrow \phi-\underset{\underset{CH_3}{|}}{\overset{\overset{CH_3}{|}}{C}}-O\bullet \ + \ HO\bullet$$

$$\phi-\underset{\underset{CH_3}{|}}{\overset{\overset{CH_3}{|}}{C}}-O\bullet \longrightarrow \phi-\overset{\overset{CH_3}{|}}{C}=O \ + \ CH_3\bullet$$

20%

$$CH_3\bullet \ + \ \phi-\underset{\underset{CH_3}{|}}{\overset{\overset{CH_3}{|}}{C}}-O-OH \longrightarrow CH_4 \ + \ \phi-\underset{\underset{CH_3}{|}}{\overset{\overset{CH_3}{|}}{C}}-O-O\bullet$$

30%

$$\phi-\underset{\underset{CH_3}{|}}{\overset{\overset{CH_3}{|}}{C}}-O\bullet \ + \ \phi-\underset{\underset{CH_3}{|}}{\overset{\overset{CH_3}{|}}{C}}-O-OH \longrightarrow \phi-\underset{\underset{CH_3}{|}}{\overset{\overset{CH_3}{|}}{C}}-OH \ + \ \phi-\underset{\underset{CH_3}{|}}{\overset{\overset{CH_3}{|}}{C}}-O-O\bullet$$

54%　　　　　　　　　　(9-3)

In cumene as solvent, up to 90% of cumyl alcohol is formed, perhaps via the mechanism

†M. S. Kharasch, A. Fono, and W. Nudenberg, *J. Org. Chem.*, **16**, 113 (1951).

$$\phi-\underset{\underset{CH_3}{|}}{\overset{\overset{CH_3}{|}}{C}}-O\cdot \;+\; \phi-\underset{\underset{CH_3}{|}}{\overset{\overset{CH_3}{|}}{C}}-H \;\longrightarrow\; \phi-\underset{\underset{CH_3}{|}}{\overset{\overset{CH_3}{|}}{C}}-OH \;+\; \phi-\underset{\underset{CH_3}{|}}{\overset{\overset{CH_3}{|}}{C}}\cdot$$

$$\phi-\underset{\underset{CH_3}{|}}{\overset{\overset{CH_3}{|}}{C}}\cdot \;+\; \phi-\underset{\underset{CH_3}{|}}{\overset{\overset{CH_3}{|}}{C}}-O-O\cdot \;\longrightarrow\; \left[\phi-\underset{\underset{CH_3}{|}}{\overset{\overset{CH_3}{|}}{C}}-O-O-\underset{\underset{CH_3}{|}}{\overset{\overset{CH_3}{|}}{C}}-\phi\right] \;\longrightarrow\; 2\phi-\underset{\underset{CH_3}{|}}{\overset{\overset{CH_3}{|}}{C}}-O\cdot$$

followed by reaction (9-3). Cumyl hydroperoxide also undergoes an acid-catalyzed decomposition that yields acetone and phenol. The decomposition of cumyl hydroperoxide under homolytic conditions normally gives very little phenol as by-product; for example, in decalin, less than 1% of phenol is formed. However, if acids are added, phenol and acetone are the major products. This acid-catalyzed reaction is used as an industrial synthesis of phenol and acetone, using cumene from petroleum as a raw material.

$$\phi-\underset{\underset{CH_3}{|}}{\overset{\overset{CH_3}{|}}{C}}-O-OH \;+\; H^+ \;\longrightarrow\; \phi-\underset{\underset{CH_3}{|}}{\overset{\overset{CH_3}{|}}{C}}-O^+ \;+\; H_2O$$

$$\Big\downarrow \text{Ionic rearrangement}$$

$$CH_3-\overset{\overset{O}{\|}}{C}-CH_3 \;+\; \phi OH \;\xleftarrow{\;H_2O\;}\; {}^+\underset{\underset{CH_3}{|}}{\overset{\overset{CH_3}{|}}{C}}-O-\phi$$

The initiation of styrene or methyl methacrylate polymerization by cumyl hydroperoxide shows evidence of a molecule-induced decomposition. Polymerization of styrene occurs at 60°C at about 100 times the rate predicted from the known rate of dissociation of cumyl hydroperoxide in benzene. Interestingly, the hydroperoxide reacts to produce radicals at an even faster rate in mixtures of styrene containing pyridine or benzyl alcohol than in pure styrene or styrene-benzene mixtures.†

Molecule-induced homolysis, as we have seen, occurs when t-butyl or cumyl hydroperoxide decomposes in certain olefinic solvents. In the

† A. V. Tobolsky and L. R. Matlack, *J. Polymer Sci.*, **55**, 49 (1961).

following section we shall consider this interesting phenomenon in a general way and discuss a number of systems in which it is believed to occur.

MOLECULE-INDUCED HOMOLYSIS

Molecule-induced homolysis is postulated to occur when radicals are formed at an anomalously rapid rate from the interaction of nonradical species. Most examples of molecule-induced homolysis involve the interaction of olefin solvents with initiators, but other types are also known. As we shall see, molecule-induced homolysis is frequently accompanied by a competing *ionic* decomposition of the initiator, which sometimes makes it difficult to determine whether or not the initiator actually is undergoing homolytic decomposition at an enhanced rate.

In the styrene–t-butyl hydroperoxide system discussed above, a rapid ionic reaction is responsible for the decomposition of a large fraction of the initiator; however, an induced homolysis also must occur since radicals are formed at an anomalously rapid rate.† This was one of the first examples of molecule-induced homolysis that was recognized. However, detailed study of this system is difficult since the initiator decomposes by at least four different paths: unimolecular homolysis; a molecule-induced homolysis which is first order in both hydroperoxide and in styrene; attack on the hydroperoxide by the polystyryl radical;‡ and a polar reaction which leads to styrene oxide and t-butyl alcohol.

Molecule-induced homolysis can be isolated for more detailed study in the m,m'-dibromobenzoyl peroxide–p,p'-dimethoxystilbene system.§ In benzene solution at 45°C, this peroxide and olefin react in two different ways. The first reaction is an easily measured, nonradical process that forms the one-to-one adduct.

$$\underset{\substack{\| \\ Ar-C-O-O-C-Ar}}{\overset{O \qquad\quad O}{}} + \quad RHC{=}CHR \quad\longrightarrow\quad \underset{\substack{| \qquad\quad | \\ RHC{-\!-}CHR}}{\overset{O \qquad\qquad O}{Ar-C-O \quad O-C-Ar}}$$

† C. Walling and Y. W. Chang, *J. Am. Chem. Soc.*, **76**, 4878 (1954); C. Walling and L. Heaton, *ibid.*, **87**, 38 (1965). Also see W. F. Brill and N. Indictor, *J. Org. Chem.*, **29**, 710 (1964).

‡ *Molecule-induced* and *radical-induced* decompositions of initiators must be distinguished. In the former, nonradicals interact to produce radicals. The latter are displacement (S_H2) reactions. (See p. 9.) The radical-induced decomposition of an initiator is sometimes called simply an induced decomposition. (See pp. 82, 93 for examples.)

§ F. D. Greene, W. Adam, and J. E. Cantrill, *J. Am. Chem. Soc.*, **83**, 3461 (1961).

However, a second process is known to occur simultaneously since the radical scavenger galvinoxyl disappears faster if *both* the initiator *and* the olefin are present than if either olefin or peroxide alone is present. The radical process converts about 10% of the peroxide to radicals which then produce a chain reaction of short chain length. This homolysis must be induced by the olefin, since, in the absence of the olefin, the peroxide produces radicals at a slower rate than in its presence.

A molecule-induced homolysis occurs in the reaction of iodine with styrene.† Molecular iodine and styrene interact at 25°C to produce radicals at a rate 10^6 greater than can be explained either by homolysis of iodine or by thermal initiation by the styrene. This interaction mechanism is second-order in styrene and first-order in iodine and could involve the reaction shown below.

$$2\phi CH{=}CH_2 + I_2 \longrightarrow 2\phi\overset{\bullet}{C}H{-}CH_2I$$

The system is complicated by the fact that an ionic reaction occurs simultaneously which also yields styrene diiodide.

Perhaps the most dramatic molecule-induced homolysis yet discovered involves the interaction of *t*-butyl hypochlorite or hypobromite with acetylenic and olefinic solvents.‡ Radical production from mixtures of 2-butyne and *t*-butyl hypochlorite is actually so exothermic that sealed tubes detonate when warmed from liquid nitrogen temperatures. The reactions of styrene have been studied in the most detail. Styrene reacts spontaneously and exothermically with *t*-butyl hypochlorite or hypobromite in the dark at 0°C. The radical nature of the reaction with *t*-butyl hypochlorite is indicated by its inhibition by oxygen or *t*-butyl catechol (a phenolic inhibitor), by the formation of the non-Markovnikov addition product $\phi CHCl{-}CH_2OBu$-*t*, and by the fact that added cyclohexane becomes chlorinated although *t*-butyl hypochlorite and cyclohexane themselves do not react together at 0°C in the dark. The reactivity of cyclohexane relative to styrene is 1:1.1 in the spontaneous dark reaction and 1:1.7 in the more usual light-initiated process. The products of the reaction are very similar for both the light- and the dark-reaction as shown in Table 9-2.

Unimolecular homolysis of the species X—Y can be represented as

$$X{-}Y \longrightarrow X\bullet + Y\bullet$$

† G. Fraenkel and P. D. Bartlett, *J. Am. Chem. Soc.*, **81**, 5582 (1959).
‡ C. Walling, L. Heaton, and D. D. Tanner, *J. Am. Chem. Soc.*, **87**, 1715 (1965).

Table 9-2   Products from the reaction of *t*-butyl hypochlorite and styrene at 40°C both in the dark and with illumination†

	% Yield	
Product	Light	Dark
Acetone	6	4
t-Butyl alcohol	14	11
ϕCHClCH$_2$OBu-*t*	69	63
ϕCHClCH$_2$Cl	2	1

† C. Walling, L. Heaton, and D. D. Tanner, *J. Am. Chem. Soc.*, **87**, 1715 (1965).

The activation energy necessary for this process is equal to the dissociation energy of the X—Y bond.   If the solvent S in which this homolysis occurs is able to interact with the radicals to stabilize them, then the overall energy required for homolysis will be reduced.   This can be shown as below where $(X \cdots S)\cdot$ is a complex between the solvent and the radical X·.

$$X—Y + nS \longrightarrow [(S \cdots X)\cdot \, \cdot(Y \cdots S)] \longrightarrow (S \cdots X)\cdot + (S \cdots Y)\cdot$$
$$\text{Transition state}$$

The effect of this complexation on the energy necessary for homolysis is shown in Fig. 9-1.

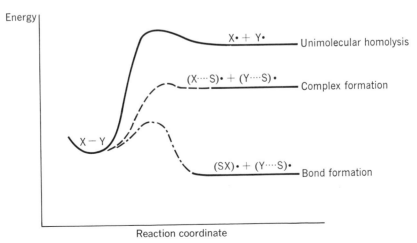

Figure 9-1   Bond formation during homolysis of the initiator X—Y.

In the limiting case, the radical X• may actually bond to a solvent molecule.

$$X—Y + nS \longrightarrow [(X\cdots S)• •(Y\cdots S)] \longrightarrow XS• + •(Y\cdots S)$$
Transition state

In this case, the enthalpy change in the reaction would be reduced by the bond energy of the S—X bond (see the discussion in Chap. 4). If $D(S—X)$ is greater than $D(X—Y)$, the overall reaction will be exothermic. This situation also is illustrated in Fig. 9-1.

Molecule-induced homolysis is most often observed in systems in which the solvent has polarizable electrons and the radicals are relatively electronegative. In these cases, electron donation from the solvent to the nascent radical becomes energetically favorable; examples are the interactions of olefins with halogen molecules and dimethoxystilbene with dibromobenzoyl peroxide.

The pronounced effect of dimethylaniline on the decomposition of benzoyl peroxide was discussed in Chap. 7. The reaction was postulated to involve electron donation by the basic nucleophile to the peroxide O—O bond. Electron-donating solvents can behave as weak nucleophiles, and their ability to induce homolysis can be regarded as part of a continuum with strong nucleophiles such as dimethylaniline at one end and very weak nucleophiles like styrene at the other.† This can be seen by writing the charge-separated resonance structure for the transition state for molecule-induced homolysis by the solvent S:

$$X—Y + nS \longrightarrow [SX• \quad •YS \longleftrightarrow SX\colon^- \quad {}^+YS]$$
Transition state

If the charge-separated structure is the more stable, ions rather than radicals result, and the reaction is an S_N2 displacement by S at the X—Y bond. It is not surprising that ionic processes so often accompany and compete with molecule-induced homolyses.

It is interesting to calculate the thermochemical benefit to be derived from molecule-induced homolysis; consider, for example, the styrene–t-butyl hypochlorite case. The bond energy $D(t\text{-BuO—Cl})$ is approximately 40 kcal/mole, and the exothermicity of the addition of a chlorine

---

† It is interesting that even lithium chloride and bromide appear to produce molecule-induced homolysis of benzoyl peroxide. J. K. Kochi, B. M. Graybill, and M. Kurz, *J. Am. Chem. Soc.*, **86**, 5257 (1964).

atom to styrene is approximately 49 kcal/mole. Therefore, the heats of reaction are:

$$\Delta H,$$
$$\text{kcal/mole}$$

$$t\text{-BuO}\text{---}\text{Cl} \longrightarrow t\text{-BuO}\bullet + \text{Cl}\bullet \qquad\qquad 40$$
$$t\text{-BuO}\text{---}\text{Cl} + \phi\text{CH}\text{==}\text{CH}_2 \longrightarrow t\text{-BuO}\bullet + \text{ClCH}_2\text{---}\overset{\bullet}{\text{C}}\text{H}\phi \qquad -9$$

It is clear that the molecule-induced homolysis, which is actually exothermic, will have a much lower activation energy than simple unimolecular homolysis.

In some systems, olefins themselves can react to generate radicals. For example, 1,1-dichloro-2,2-difluoroethylene reacts with butadiene at 80°C in the dark and in the presence of a polymerization inhibitor to yield a cyclobutane.†

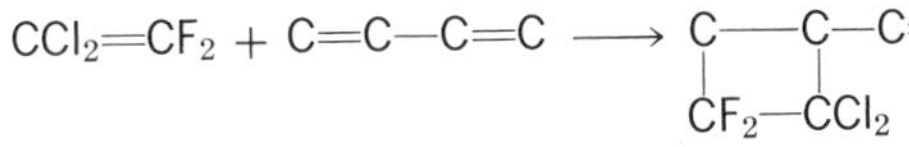

$$\text{CCl}_2\text{==}\text{CF}_2 + \text{C}\text{==}\text{C}\text{---}\text{C}\text{==}\text{C} \longrightarrow \underset{\underset{\text{CF}_2\text{---}\text{CCl}_2}{|\qquad|}}{\text{C}\text{---}\text{C}\text{---}\text{C}\text{==}\text{C}}$$

The evidence suggests that initiation of this process is by bond formation to form the stabilized diradical shown below.

$$\overset{\bullet}{\text{C}}\text{Cl}_2\text{---}\text{CF}_2\text{---}\text{C}\text{---}\overset{\bullet}{\text{C}}\text{---}\text{C}\text{==}\text{C}$$

The thermal polymerization of styrene is another example of molecule-induced homolysis between olefin molecules. Styrene interacts with itself in the dark to form radicals which initiate its own polymerization, and the rate of the process is substantial even at 60°C. The reaction is third order in styrene.‡ In the presence of polymerization inhibitors, 1-phenylnaphthalene and 1-phenyltetralin can be isolated.§ These facts suggest the mechanism shown below, in which the first step is a reversible Diels-Alder condensation. The rate effects of substituting deuterium at the α, β, or ring positions have been shown to be consistent with this mechanism.¶

† P. D. Bartlett, L. K. Montgomery, and B. Seidel, *J. Am. Chem. Soc.*, **86**, 616 (1964).
‡ K. E. Russell and A. V. Tobolsky, *J. Am. Chem. Soc.*, **75**, 5052 (1953); F. R. Mayo, *ibid.*, **75**, 6133 (1953); R. R. Hiatt and P. D. Bartlett, *ibid.*, **81**, 1149 (1959).
§ F. R. Mayo, *Preprints Div. Polymer Chem.*, Am. Chem. Soc., Chicago Meeting, September, 1961, vol. 2, no. 2, p. 55.
¶ W. A. Pryor, R. Henderson, N. V. Carroll, and E. Ciuffarin, American Chemical Society meeting, Abstracts of papers, Atlantic City, September, 1965.

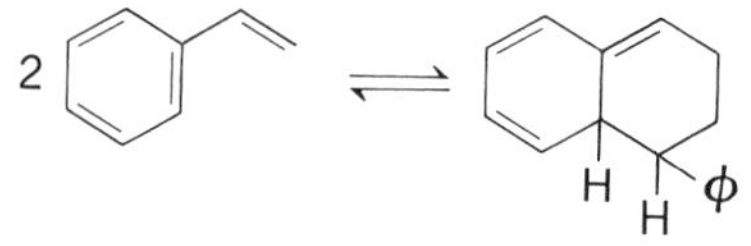

(I)

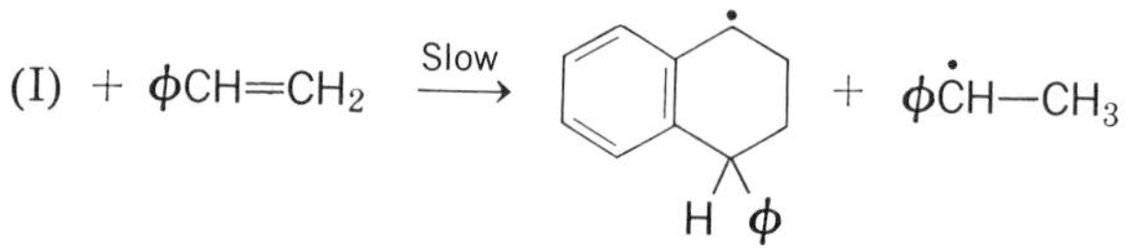

$(I) + \phi CH=CH_2 \xrightarrow{Slow}$ $+ \phi\dot{C}H-CH_3$

It seems clear that the polarizability of the solvent plays a role in determining its effectiveness in inducing homolysis. In all the examples discussed above, the solvents have been unsaturated. However, the saturated but polarizable solvent methyl iodide leads to a 300-fold increase in the rate of decomposition of o-nitrobenzoyl peroxide relative to chloroform as a solvent.[†] An apparently related phenomenon is the increased rate of homolysis of the O—O bond in the perester shown below.[‡]

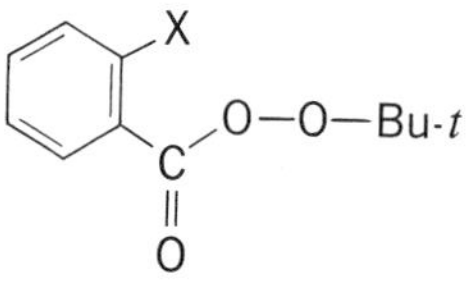

The relative rates of decomposition of this perester at 60°C are

X	k
H	1
t-Bu	4
I	54
MeS	1×10^4
ϕS	2×10^4

Apparently, very polarizable neighboring atoms enhance the O—O bond scission, a phenomenon which might be regarded as intramolecular molecule-induced homolysis.

[†] J. E. Leffler, R. D. Faulkner, and C. C. Petropoulous, *J. Am. Chem. Soc.*, **80**, 5435 (1958).

[‡] W. G. Bentrude and J. C. Martin, *J. Am. Chem. Soc.*, **84**, 1561 (1962).

PROBLEMS

9-1 Pinane can be oxidized by air to pinane hydroperoxide. At 110°C, this hydroperoxide decomposes to form a cyclobutane derivative which gives an iodoform test indicating that it is a methyl ketone. Write a mechanism for the formation of this product. (Hint: The key step is a β-scission.) [G. A. Schmidt and G. S. Fisher, *J. Am. Chem. Soc.*, **76**, 5426 (1954).]

Pinane hydroperoxide

9-2 Write a reasonable structure for the transition state of the decomposition of the perester shown on page 124 for the cases where (*a*) X = I and (*b*) X = φS. Would it be reasonable to ascribe the rate enhancements observed to a steric effect?

9-3 Benzoyl peroxide undergoes decomposition in the solvent methyl iodide at a normal rate, but *o*-nitrobenzoyl peroxide decomposes anomalously rapidly in this solvent. Explain this.

9-4 If acetyl peroxide is allowed to decompose in cyclohexene as solvent, both cyclohexenyl acetate (I) and cyclohexyl acetate (II) are formed.

(I) (II)

It has been postulated that (I) is formed by an S_H2 reaction of cyclohexenyl radicals on the peroxide O—O bond. The combination of cyclohexenyl radicals and acetate radicals to form (I) is held to be improbable since acetate radicals would be expected to decompose before they would collide with another radical.

$$CH_3—CO_2• \xrightarrow[\text{fast}]{\text{Very}} CH_3• + CO_2$$

In view of this, explain the mechanism for formation of (II). Your mechanism should account for the fact that, when acetyl peroxide labeled with O^{18} in the carbonyl group is used, the (II) that is formed has the O^{18} *partially but not entirely* randomized between the two oxygen atoms of (II). [J. C. Martin and E. H. Drew, *J. Am. Chem. Soc.*, **83**, 1232 (1961); H. J. Shine and J. R. Slagle, *ibid.*, **81**, 6309 (1959); H. J. Shine, J. A. Waters, and D. M. Hoffman, *ibid.*, **85**, 3613 (1963).]

9-5 Define and give illustrative examples of: induced decomposition of an initiator, S_H2 reaction of an initiator and a noninitiator, and molecule-induced homolysis of an initiator and of a noninitiator. Discuss the differences in these processes.

9-6 Discuss these facts relating to the formation of styrene diiodide in carbon tetrachloride solution at 25°C: The rate of dissociation of 0.01 M iodine in an inert solvent at 25°C is calculated to be 2×10^{-15} mole l^{-1} sec^{-1} from gas phase data; the rate of radical production from thermal initiation by 0.2 M styrene in an inert solvent is 2×10^{-15} mole l^{-1} sec^{-1}; a mixture of 0.2 M styrene and 0.01 M iodine in carbon tetrachloride destroys DPPH at a rate of 1×10^{-8} mole l^{-1} sec^{-1}; iodine in this solution containing DPPH disappears 15 times faster than the DPPH; the kinetics of the uninhibited formation of styrene diiodide indicates a first-order dependence on iodide and a 3/2-order dependence on styrene. Use an energy versus reaction coordinate diagram to illustrate the thermochemical consequences of molecule-induced homolysis. Illustrate at least one possibility for a transition state which includes one iodine and two styrene molecules. [G. Fraenkel and P. D. Bartlett, *J. Am. Chem. Soc.*, **81**, 5582 (1959).]

SUGGESTIONS FOR FURTHER READING

Wallace, J. G.: Hydrogen Peroxide in Organic Chemistry, E. I. du Pont de Nemours & Company, Electrochemicals Dept., 1962.

Zavgorodnii, S. V.: *Russ. Chem. Rev.* (*English Transl.*), **30**, 133 (1961).

chapter
ten # Thermal Homolysis:
Azo Compounds

Azo compounds constitute a very useful group of initiators. These compounds dramatically exemplify the effect of the stability of the radical being produced on the rate of decomposition of a substance. Azomethane, $CH_3-N=N-CH_3$, decomposes with an activation energy of 51 kcal/mole and undergoes thermal homolysis at useful rates only at temperatures near 400°C.† Table 10-1 gives the activation energy for other azo compounds. Those producing stabilized radicals decompose at enhanced rates; for example, phenylazotriphenylmethane, $\phi_3C-N=N-\phi$, decomposes with an activation energy of 27 kcal/mole and is useful at temperatures near 45 to 80°C.

The C—N and N=N bonds are of normal strengths (70 and 100 kcal/mole, respectively) and do not suggest that azo compounds would be useful initiators. However, the formation of a molecule of nitrogen on dissociation of azo compounds provides a strong driving force for dissociation. (The heat of formation of N_2 is 225 kcal/mole.) In order for the stability of the nitrogen molecule to influence the rate of decomposition of an azo compound, the nitrogen molecule must be partly formed at the transition state:

$$R-N=N-R \longrightarrow [R\cdots N\cong N\cdots R] \longrightarrow 2R\bullet + N_2$$
$$\text{Transition state}$$

This transition state also places some of the odd electron density on the R groups and makes clear why their ability to bear an odd electron influences the rate of decomposition.

The most common azo initiator is azoisobutyronitrile (AIBN), the last compound listed in Table 10-1. This useful initiator was first prepared in 1949 and has been widely used since. It has a half-life of 17 hours at 60°C and 1.3 hours at 80°C. This azo compound decomposes at almost the same rate in benzene, toluene, xylene, acetic acid, aniline, nitrobenzene, dodecyl mercaptan, and isobutyl alcohol. This contrasts very markedly with benzoyl peroxide, for example, which has a rate of decomposition that is very solvent dependent. Furthermore, the rate of decomposition of AIBN in solvents such as toluene is essentially unaffected by inhibitors such as chloranil, iodine, or diphenylpicrylhydrazyl (DPPH) (see page 26 for structure). This implies that radicals do not attack the azo compound to produce an induced decomposition; if they did, the rate of disappear-

---

† Azomethane, like other azo compounds, can be decomposed by photolysis at room temperature.

Table 10-1 Azo compounds

R—N=N—R' R	R'	E_a, kcal/mole	Solvent	Ref.
CH_3	CH_3	51	Gas phase	a
t-Bu	t-Bu	43	Gas phase	b
ϕ_2CH	ϕ_2CH	27	Toluene	c
ϕ	ϕ_3C	27	Benzene	d
$CH_3-\overset{\displaystyle CN}{\underset{\displaystyle CH_3}{C}}$	$CH_3-\overset{\displaystyle CN}{\underset{\displaystyle CH_3}{C}}$	31	Benzene	e

a C. Steel and A. F. Trotman-Dickenson, *J. Chem. Soc.*, 975 (1959).
b A. U. Blackham and N. L. Eatough, *J. Am. Chem. Soc.*, **84**, 2922 (1962).
c S. G. Cohen and C. H. Wang, *ibid.*, **77**, 2457 (1955).
d M. G. Alder and J. E. Leffler, *ibid.*, **76**, 1425 (1954).
e C. E. H. Bawn and S. F. Mellish, *Trans. Faraday Soc.*, **47**, 1216 (1951);
J. P. Van Hook and A. V. Tobolsky, *J. Am. Chem. Soc.*, **80**, 779 (1958).

ance of the azo compound would be lower in the presence of substances that would inhibit the radical chain decomposition. Induced decomposition is negligible for most azo compounds in solution; this sometimes makes them the preferred initiator for studies of radical reactions.

Careful studies of the decomposition reactions of azo compounds have shown the existence of an appreciable cage effect, details of which have been most thoroughly worked out in the case of AIBN. (See page 88 for a discussion of the cage effect.) This initiator is less than 100% efficient in the production of radicals;† that is, instead of producing two radicals per mole, as would be predicted from the simple decomposition (10-1), measurably fewer are formed. This is because an appreciable fraction of the radicals

$$R—N=N—R \longrightarrow 2R\cdot + N_2 \qquad (10\text{-}1)$$

recombine in the solvent cage before they can diffuse apart. The decomposition of AIBN is complicated by the fact that the cyanopropyl radicals combine to form two termination products: tetramethylsuccinonitrile (R—R) and a ketenimine (R—R'):

† J. C. Bevington, *J. Chem. Soc.*, 3707 (1954); *Trans. Faraday Soc.*, **51**, 1392 (1955).

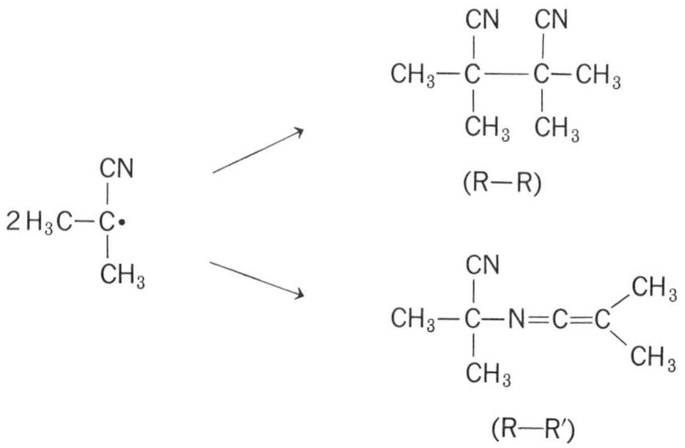

$$2\,H_3C-\underset{\underset{CH_3}{|}}{\overset{\overset{CN}{|}}{C}}\cdot$$

$$CH_3-\underset{\underset{CH_3}{|}}{\overset{\overset{CN}{|}}{C}}-\underset{\underset{CH_3}{|}}{\overset{\overset{CN}{|}}{C}}-CH_3$$

(R—R)

$$CH_3-\underset{\underset{CH_3}{|}}{\overset{\overset{CN}{|}}{C}}-N=C=C\underset{CH_3}{\overset{CH_3}{<}}$$

(R—R′)

Furthermore, they combine to form these two products both in the cage and in solution. Therefore, the decomposition of AIBN involves the reactions shown below.

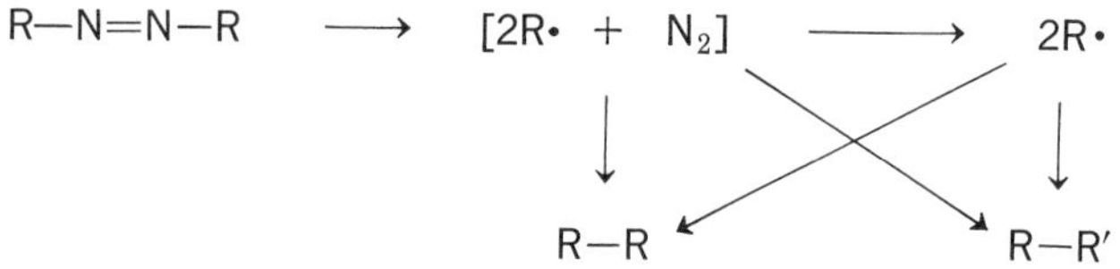

$$R-N=N-R \longrightarrow [2R\cdot + N_2] \longrightarrow 2R\cdot$$

R—R   R—R′

In this scheme, R• is the cyanopropyl radical, brackets represent caged radicals, R—R is the succinonitrile, and R—R′ is the ketenimine. Note that both the caged and the free cyanopropyl radicals are postulated to give both products. One additional complication exists: Although the succinonitrile R—R is a stable product, the ketenimine R—R′ is not. In fact, the ketenimine is an initiator and decomposes with a rate constant like that of AIBN. Therefore, the complete scheme for the decomposition of AIBN is as shown below.†

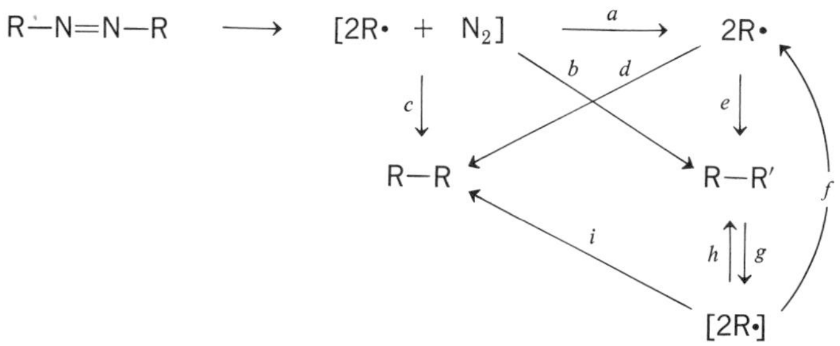

$$R-N=N-R \longrightarrow [2R\cdot + N_2] \overset{a}{\longrightarrow} 2R\cdot$$

(with labeled steps b, c, d, e, f, g, h, i)

R—R   R—R′   (10-2)

[2R•]

† G. S. Hammond, C. S. Wu, O. D. Trapp, J. Warkentin, and R. T. Keys, *J. Am. Chem. Soc.*, **82**, 5394 (1960).

The complex scheme in (10-2) can be described as follows: AIBN decomposes to give cage radicals. These cage radicals can then either (a) escape from the cage to become free radicals, (b) combine to form the ketenimine, or (c) combine to form the succinonitrile. The free radicals also can combine to form either (d) the succinonitrile or (e) the ketenimine. It is of interest that the two termination products R—R and R—R′ are formed in about the same ratio from either cage or free radicals. This is evidence that the combination occurring in the cage is a normal radical combination, rather than some special nonradical process. The ketenimine formed in paths (b) or (e) also dissociates to form cage radicals [path (g)]. These cage radicals have the same three paths open to them as were available to the original cage radicals. They can (f) become free radicals, (i) combine to form succinonitrile, or (h) combine to form the ketenimine.

The scheme given in (10-2) shows two pathways for the formation of tetramethylsuccinonitrile R—R, one from cage radicals and one from free radicals. This leads to the prediction that scavengers that trap all *free* radicals should reduce the yield of R—R to a limiting value representing the amount of R—R formed directly in the cage. This is shown below.

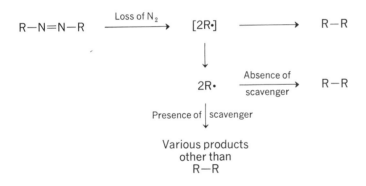

This effect has been demonstrated with a wide range of scavengers. Thiols are very effective hydrogen donors and rapidly react with radicals. Figure 10-1 shows the effect of butanethiol on the yield of tetramethylsuccinonitrile, R—R. As more thiol is added, the yield of succinonitrile rapidly decreases until it levels off at about 20%. This implies that AIBN undergoes about 20% cage recombination; i.e., it is 80% efficient at producing free radicals in this system. Figure 10-2 shows a similar experiment with styrene as the radical scavenger. At low styrene concentrations, very few radicals add to styrene to initiate polymerization, and efficiencies are low. At higher styrene concentrations, more of the radicals find a

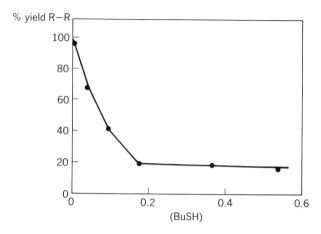

Figure 10-1 Percent yield tetramethylsuccinonitrile (R—R) versus molarity of butanethiol in CCl$_4$ solution. AIBN is initially 0.2 *M*. [*G. S. Hammond, J. N. Sen, C. E. Boozer, J. Am. Chem. Soc.,* **77**, 3244 (1955).]

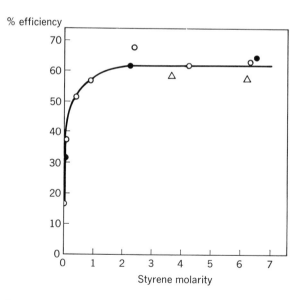

Figure 10-2 Efficiency of AIBN as an initiator of the polymerization of styrene versus the molarity of the styrene (in benzene solution at 60°C). AIBN molarity: ● 6.0 × 10^{-3}; ○ 3.0 × 10^{-3}; △ 1.2 × 10^{-3}. [*J. C. Bevington, Trans. Faraday Soc.,* **51**, 1392 (1955).]

styrene molecule and efficiencies are much higher. However, even in pure styrene all the radicals from AIBN do not initiate, and AIBN is only about 65% efficient.

The only system reactive enough to trap even caged radicals is liquid bromine as solvent. When AIBN is allowed to decompose in liquid bromine, the yield of succinonitrile is zero.†

A number of other azo compounds have been investigated, and their decomposition reactions can be explained by mechanisms similar to the one postulated for AIBN.

The N-nitrosoanilides are also used as initiators. They rearrange *in situ* to diazoacetates, which then dissociate to radicals.

$$\underset{\substack{\text{N}=\text{O} \quad \text{O} \\ | \qquad \parallel \\ \text{Ar}-\text{N}-\!\!-\!\!-\text{C}-\text{R}'}}{} \xrightarrow[\text{step}]{\text{Slow}} \underset{\substack{\text{O} \\ \parallel \\ \text{Ar}-\text{N}=\text{N}-\text{O}-\text{C}-\text{R}'}}{} \xrightarrow{\text{Fast}} \text{Ar}\cdot \; + \; \text{N}_2 \; + \; \text{R}'\text{CO}_2\cdot$$

PROBLEMS

10-1   The rate constant for the liberation of nitrogen from AIBN in benzene solutions is found to be greater than the rate constant for the initiation of the polymerization of styrene by AIBN. Explain this in terms of the scheme given in (10-2).

10-2   When a mixture of $CH_3\!-\!N\!=\!N\!-\!CH_3$ and $CD_3\!-\!N\!=\!N\!-\!CD_3$ is allowed to decompose in isooctane, only C_2H_6 and C_2D_6 are formed. In the gas phase, however, the yields of products are given by the expression

$$\frac{(CH_3\!-\!CD_3)}{[(C_2H_6)(C_2D_6)]^{1/2}} = 2$$

Explain these results.   [R. K. Lyon and D. H. Levy, *J. Am. Chem. Soc.*, **83**, 4290 (1961).]

<hr>

† O. D. Trapp and G. S. Hammond, *J. Am. Chem. Soc.*, **81**, 4876 (1959).

chapter eleven

Radical-forming Redox Reactions

The technique of producing radicals by one-electron oxidation-reduction reactions finds frequent use, since the presence of an unstable initiator is not required and the reactions can be used as a source of radicals at low temperatures. Radicals can be produced by either oxidation or reduction. In the Kolbe electrolysis, salts of organic acids are electrolyzed, and the carboxylate anions undergo oxidation to a radical that loses carbon dioxide. The resulting radicals couple.

$$R-CO_2^- \xrightarrow[-e^-]{Anode} R-CO_2\bullet \longrightarrow R\bullet + CO_2$$
$$2R\bullet \longrightarrow R-R$$

This reaction has some utility in organic syntheses.

The most important radical-forming redox reactions are those involving a metal ion that can undergo a one-electron transfer. Of these, the reaction of hydrogen peroxide with ferrous ion is one of the oldest and best known. Fenton discovered this reaction in 1894, and in 1932 Haber and Weiss proposed a mechanism which, with only slight modification, is accepted today.[†] The reactions occurring when hydrogen peroxide reacts with ferrous ions are as follows:

$$Fe^{++} + H_2O_2 \longrightarrow Fe^{3+} + HO^- + HO\bullet \qquad (11\text{-}1a)$$
$$Fe^{3+} + H_2O_2 \longrightarrow Fe^{++} + HO_2\bullet + H^+ \qquad (11\text{-}1b)$$
$$Fe^{++} + HO\bullet \longrightarrow Fe^3 + OH^- \qquad (11\text{-}1c)$$
$$Fe^{3+} + HO_2^- \longrightarrow Fe^{++} + H^+ + O_2^{\bar{\bullet}} \qquad (11\text{-}1d)$$
$$Fe^{++} + HO_2\bullet \longrightarrow Fe^{3+} + HO_2^- \qquad (11\text{-}1e)$$
$$HO\bullet + H_2O_2 \longrightarrow H_2O + HO_2\bullet \qquad (11\text{-}1f)$$
$$O_2^{\bar{\bullet}} + H_2O_2 \longrightarrow O_2 + OH^- + HO\bullet \qquad (11\text{-}1g)$$

These reactions explain the catalysis of the decomposition of hydrogen peroxide by ferrous ions.

$$2H_2O_2 \xrightarrow{Iron\ salts} 2H_2O + O_2 \qquad (11\text{-}2)$$

Fenton's reagent can be used to oxidize organic materials. Sometimes the oxidized products are dimers, and sometimes they are the result of substitution reactions by hydroxyl radicals. For example, benzene is converted to a mixture of biphenyl and phenol, with higher ratios of phenol to biphenyl if the concentration of ferric ion is kept high. The two prod-

† N. Uri, *Chem. Rev.*, **50**, 375 (1952).

ucts, and the influence of ferric ions on the product distribution, are explained by the mechanism below.†

$$Fe^{++} + H_2O_2 \longrightarrow Fe^{3+} + OH^- + HO\bullet$$

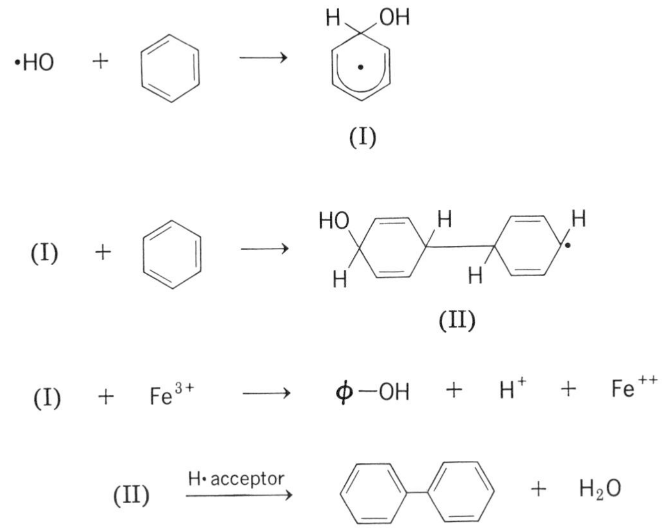

$$\bullet HO + \text{(benzene)} \longrightarrow \text{(I)}$$

(I)

$$(I) + \text{(benzene)} \longrightarrow \text{(II)}$$

(II)

$$(I) + Fe^{3+} \longrightarrow \phi-OH + H^+ + Fe^{++}$$

$$(II) \xrightarrow{H\bullet\,acceptor} \text{(biphenyl)} + H_2O$$

Products can also be formed from the dimerization and disproportionation of (I):

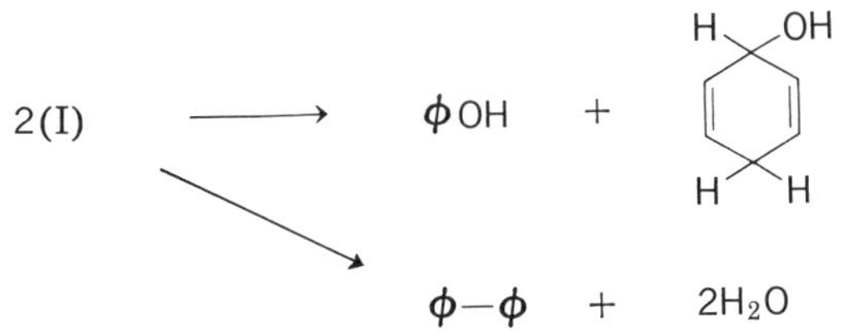

$$2(I) \longrightarrow \phi OH + \text{(cyclohexadiene structure)}$$

$$\phi-\phi + 2H_2O$$

Reaction (11-1a) occurs with ions of other metals and with hydroperoxides, peroxides, and peresters, as well as with hydrogen peroxide. The reaction can be formulated generally as

$$M^I + ROOR \longrightarrow M^{II} + RO\bullet + RO^-$$

where M^I is a transition metal in one valence state, and M^{II} is the next

† J. R. L. Smith and R. O. C. Norman, *J. Chem. Soc.*, 2897 (1963).

higher oxidation valence state. Examples of reactions that fit this formulation are

$$H_2O_2 \xrightarrow{\text{Fe}^{++}, \text{Cr}^{++}, \text{V}^{++}, \text{ or Ti}^{3+}} \text{HO•} + \text{HO}^-$$

$$ROOH \xrightarrow{\text{Fe}^{++}, \text{Co}^{++}, \text{ or Cu}^+} \text{RO•} + \text{HO}^-$$

$$RO-O-\overset{\overset{\displaystyle O}{\|}}{C}-R' \xrightarrow{\text{Cu}^+} \text{RO•} + \text{R'CO}_2^-$$

$$^-O_3S-O-O-SO_3^- \xrightarrow{\text{Fe}^{++}} SO_4^= + SO_4^-\text{•}$$

The most important commercial application of these redox reactions is the use of cumyl hydroperoxide and ferrous ion as a catalyst for the low-temperature emulsion polymerization of styrene-butadiene mixtures to make rubber. The organic monomers are polymerized in oil-like droplets in an aqueous emulsion which is maintained by the addition of soaps and bases. A typical commercial recipe is given in Table 11-1. The mixture is complex, and the purpose of each ingredient is not known in detail. Of interest here are the hydroperoxide, ferrous ion, pyrophosphate (which solubilizes the iron in the reaction solution), and thiol (added to act as a chain transfer agent to reduce molecular weights and produce a more easily handled polymer).

Redox initiators are of importance because they can be used at much lower temperatures than peroxides. Their rates of radical formation can be controlled by varying the concentrations of both the oxidant (the peroxide) and the metal-ion catalyst, as well as by changing the temperature. Furthermore, redox systems are known which can be used as sources of radicals in aqueous solutions.

Another example of a redox reaction that has been developed into a useful synthetic tool is the reaction of peroxidic materials with substrates

Table 11-1   A typical recipe for the emulsion polymerization of styrene-butadiene mixtures

Reagent	Parts by weight	Reagent	Parts by weight
Butadiene	75	Cumyl hydroperoxide	0.17
Styrene	25	Ferrous sulfate	0.017
Water	180	$Na_4P_2O_7 \cdot 10H_2O$	1.5
Thiol	0.5	Fructose	0.5
Sodium hydroxide	0.061		

containing active hydrogens. In the absence of metal ions, a mixture of products usually results. However, metal ions, and particularly copper ions, catalyze a reaction in which the active hydrogen is replaced by an —O—CO—R group. The reaction was discovered by Kharasch and his students and has received extensive study. An example† is the reaction of t-butyl peracetate with cyclohexene catalyzed by cuprous bromide:

$$
\bigcirc + \quad CH_3-\overset{O}{\overset{\|}{C}}-O-O-Bu\text{-}t \quad \xrightarrow{CuBr} \quad \overset{\overset{O}{\overset{\|}{O-C-CH_3}}}{\bigcirc} \tag{11-3}
$$

90%

This is the best synthesis of cyclohexenyl acetate.

The mechanism of this reaction‡ is believed to involve the formation of a t-butoxy radical from the perester by a Haber-Weiss-type decomposition:

$$
CH_3-\overset{O}{\overset{\|}{C}}-O-O-Bu\text{-}t \quad + \quad CuBr \quad \longrightarrow \quad [CH_3-CO_2\bullet\,CuBr] \quad + \quad t\text{-}BuO\bullet \tag{11-4}
$$

The t-butoxy radical then abstracts an allylic hydrogen from cyclohexene:

$$
t\text{-}BuO\bullet \quad + \quad \bigcirc \quad \longrightarrow \quad t\text{-}BuOH \quad + \quad \overset{\bullet}{\bigcirc} \tag{11-5}
$$

Products could result from either a radical process or an ionic one. In the radical process, the cyclohexenyl radical can be visualized as reacting with the complex formed in reaction (11-4):

$$
\overset{\bullet}{\bigcirc} \quad + \quad (CH_3CO_2\bullet\,CuBr) \quad \longrightarrow \quad \overset{\overset{O}{\overset{\|}{O-C-CH_3}}}{\bigcirc} \quad + \quad CuBr \tag{11-6}
$$

Reaction (11-6) is called ligand transfer.

† M. S. Kharasch, G. Sosnovsky, and N. C. Yang, *J. Am. Chem. Soc.*, **81**, 5819 (1959).

‡ C. Walling and A. A. Zavitsas, *J. Am. Chem. Soc.*, **85**, 2084 (1963); J. K. Kochi, *Tetrahedron*, **18**, 483 (1962); *J. Am. Chem. Soc.*, **85**, 1958 (1963).

To visualize the ionic process, the complex in (11-4) can be written as Cu^{II} and a carboxylate anion:

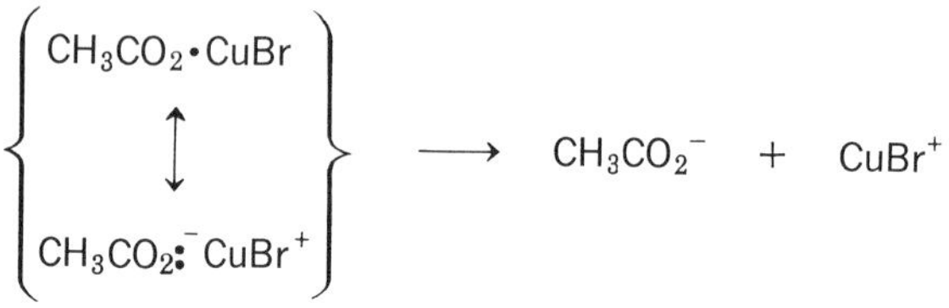

$$\left\{ \begin{array}{c} CH_3CO_2 \cdot CuBr \\ \\ \updownarrow \\ \\ CH_3CO_2^{-} \; CuBr^{+} \end{array} \right\} \quad \longrightarrow \quad CH_3CO_2^{-} \;+\; CuBr^{+} \tag{11-7}$$

Carbonium ions can then be envisioned as being produced by the oxidation of the cyclohexenyl radical by cupric ions

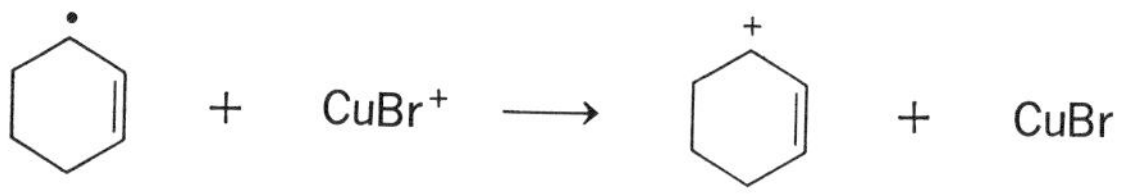

$$\quad + \quad CuBr^{+} \quad \longrightarrow \quad \quad + \quad CuBr \tag{11-8}$$

and products could be formed by the ionic reaction shown below.

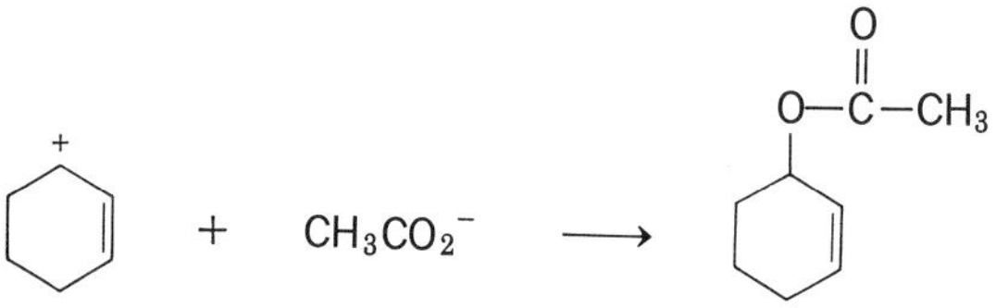

$$\quad + \quad CH_3CO_2^{-} \quad \longrightarrow \quad \tag{11-9}$$

Reaction (11-8), the key step in this ionic sequence, is termed electron transfer.

Some evidence that carbonium ions actually are intermediates in these reactions is obtained from the fact that typical carbonium ion rearrangements occur. For example, 1,2-hydrogen and alkyl migrations sometimes accompany these copper-catalyzed reactions; this type of rearrangement is not thought to occur in radical intermediates.† Also, the products from the reaction of 1-alkenes are similar to those which would result from an allylic carbonium ion rather than an allylic radical. Thus, 1-octene reacts with t-butyl peracetate to give mainly the 3-ester, as shown on the next page.

† P. R. Story, *Tetrahedron Letters*, 414 (1962); C. Walling and A. A. Zavitsas, *J. Am. Chem. Soc.*, **85**, 2084 (1963).

$$C_5H_{11}-CH_2-CH=CH_2$$

$$\downarrow t\text{-BuO}\cdot$$

$$[C_5H_{11}-\overset{\bullet}{C}H-CH=CH_2 \longleftrightarrow C_5H_{11}-CH=CH-\overset{\bullet}{C}H_2]$$

$$\downarrow Cu^{++}$$

$$[C_5H_{11}-\overset{+}{C}H-CH=CH_2 \longleftrightarrow C_5H_{11}-CH=CH-\overset{+}{C}H_2]$$

$$\downarrow CH_3-CO_2^{-}$$

$$C_5H_{11}-\underset{\underset{\displaystyle CO-CH_3}{\displaystyle |}}{\overset{\displaystyle |}{\underset{\displaystyle O}{CH}}}-CH=CH_2 \quad + \quad C_5H_{11}-CH=CH-\underset{\underset{\displaystyle CO-CH_3}{\displaystyle |}}{\overset{\displaystyle |}{\underset{\displaystyle O}{CH_2}}}$$

86:                            14

(Total yield 89%)

Known radical reactions on 1-alkenes give mainly 1-substitution products. For example, the radical chlorination of 1-pentene by t-butyl hypochlorite gives largely the 1-chloride.†

$$C_2H_5-CH_2-CH=CH_2$$

$$40°C \downarrow t\text{-}C_4H_9OCl$$

$$C_2H_5-\underset{\underset{\displaystyle Cl}{\displaystyle |}}{CH}-CH=CH_2 \quad + \quad C_2H_5-CH=CH-\underset{\underset{\displaystyle Cl}{\displaystyle |}}{CH_2}$$

40%   60%

Although the product-forming process may involve carbonium ion reactions, the hydrogen abstraction step (11-5) is a radical process. This is indicated by the fact that the relative reactivities of different substances are those which would be predicted for a reaction in which a t-butoxy

† C. Walling and W. Thaler, *J. Am. Chem. Soc.*, **83**, 3877 (1961).

radical abstracted a hydrogen atom. For example, the relative reactivities of ethylbenzene: cumene: 2-hexene are 1.0:0.4:1.4, both in this copper-catalyzed reaction and in the reaction of these substrates with t-butoxy radicals generated from t-butyl hypochlorite.[†]

The mechanism for these reactions can be summarized in generalized form as below, where RH is any compound having a labile hydrogen. (The symbols Cu[I] and Cu[II] are used so that the anions associated with each of the oxidation states of copper need not be specified.)

Initiation

$$CH_3\text{-}\overset{\displaystyle O}{\overset{\displaystyle \|}{C}}\text{-}O\text{-}O\text{-}Bu\text{-}t \quad + \quad Cu^I \quad \longrightarrow \quad (CH_3CO_2^-Cu^{II}) \quad + \quad t\text{-BuO}\cdot$$

$$t\text{-BuO}\cdot \quad + \quad RH \quad \longrightarrow \quad t\text{-BuOH} \quad + \quad R\cdot$$

Product-forming steps

$$R\cdot \quad + \quad (CH_3CO_2^-Cu^{II}) \quad \longrightarrow \quad R\text{-}O\text{-}\overset{\displaystyle O}{\overset{\displaystyle \|}{C}}\text{-}CH_3 \quad + \quad Cu^I$$

(Ligand transfer)

or, more likely,

$$R\cdot \quad + \quad Cu^{II} \quad \longrightarrow \quad R^+ \quad + \quad Cu^I$$

(Electron transfer)

$$R^+ \quad + \quad CH_3CO_2^- \quad \longrightarrow \quad R\text{-}O\text{-}\overset{\displaystyle O}{\overset{\displaystyle \|}{C}}\text{-}CH_3$$

These copper-ion-catalyzed reactions have been developed into a reaction with broad synthetic utility, and a number of examples are given in Table 11-2.

[†] C. Walling and A. A. Zavitsas, *J. Am. Chem. Soc.*, **85**, 2084 (1963).

Table 11-2 Reactions of active hydrogen donors with peresters catalyzed by copper ions

Active hydrogen compound	Peroxidic compound	Product	% Yield	Ref.
C_5H_{11}—CH_2—CH=CH_2	t-BuO—O—$\overset{\text{O}}{\overset{\|}{C}}$CH₃	C_5H_{11}—CH=CH—CH_2—O—CO—CH₃	12	a
		C_5H_{11}—CH=CH—CH_2—O—CO—CH₃	77	
ϕCH_2—O—$\overset{\text{O}}{\overset{\|}{C}}$—CH₃	t-BuO—O—$\overset{\text{O}}{\overset{\|}{C}}\phi$	ϕ—CH—O—$\overset{\text{O}}{\overset{\|}{C}}$—CH₃, O—CO—$\phi$	35	b
ϕCH_2—O—$\overset{\text{O}}{\overset{\|}{C}}$—$\phi$	t-BuO—O—$\overset{\text{O}}{\overset{\|}{C}}$CH₃	Same product as above	18	b
ϕO—CH_2—CH=CH_2	t-BuO—O—$\overset{\text{O}}{\overset{\|}{C}}$—$\phi$	ϕO—CH—CH=CH_2, O—CO—ϕ	50	b
ϕ—CHO	t-BuO—O—$\overset{\text{O}}{\overset{\|}{C}}$—$\phi$	ϕ—$\overset{\text{O}}{\overset{\|}{C}}$—O—$\overset{\text{O}}{\overset{\|}{C}}$—$\phi$, O—CO—$\phi$	70	b
(1,2,3,4-tetrahydronaphthalene)	t-BuO—O—$\overset{\text{O}}{\overset{\|}{C}}$—$\phi$	(tetralin)—O—CO—ϕ	15	b
C_3H_7—S—C_3H_7	t-BuO—O—$\overset{\text{O}}{\overset{\|}{C}}$—$\phi$	C_3H_7S—CH—C_2H_5, O—CO—ϕ	69	c

[a] C. Walling and A. A. Zavitsas, *J. Am. Chem. Soc.,* **85,** 2084 (1963).
[b] G. Sosnovsky and N. C. Yang, *J. Org. Chem.,* **25,** 899 (1960).
[c] G. Sosnovsky, *Tetrahedron,* **18,** 15 (1962).

PROBLEMS

11-1 Give mechanisms to account for the following products from reactions catalyzed by copper salts:

a. *t*-Butyl hydroperoxide in isopropylbenzene at 100°C gives a 90% yield of
ϕ—C(CH$_3$)$_2$OOBu-*t*.

b. *t*-Butyl hydroperoxide in dioxane at 70°C gives a 50% yield of

c. *t*-Butyl hydroperoxide in dimethylaniline at 25°C gives a 90% yield of
ϕ—N(CH$_3$)CH$_2$—OO—Bu-*t*.

d. *t*-Butyl peroxide reacts with benzaldehyde to give an 83% yield of *t*-butyl benzoate.

e. Benzoyl peroxide in isopropylbenzene in the absence of copper salts gives
ϕ—C(CH$_3$)$_2$—C(CH$_3$)$_2\phi$. In the presence of copper salts at 85°, a 30%

yield of ϕ—C(CH$_3$)$_2$O—$\overset{\displaystyle O}{\overset{\displaystyle \|}{C}}\phi$ is obtained. [M. S. Kharasch and A. Fono, *J. Org. Chem.*, **23**, 324 (1958); **24**, 72 (1959).]

11-2 *a.* Hydrogen peroxide reacts with cyclohexanone to give an adduct which can be represented as shown below.

HO OOH

This material is decomposed by ferrous salts to give 1,12-dodecanedioic acid. Write a mechanism for the reaction.

b. Predict the product of the ferrous ion catalyzed decomposition of 1-phenylcyclohexyl hydroperoxide.

c. The ferrous ion catalyzed decomposition of 1-methylcyclopentyl hydroperoxide in the presence of butadiene gives a 30% yield of 8,12-eicosadien-2,19-dione. Write a mechanism. [S. O. Lawesson and G. Sosnovsky, *Svensk Kem. Tidskr.*, **75**, 343 (1963).]

SUGGESTIONS FOR FURTHER READING

The Kolbe electrolytic reaction

Weedon, B. C. L.: "Advances in Organic Chemistry," vol. I, Interscience Publishers, Inc., New York, 1960, p. 1.

Redox reactions of metal ions

Lawesson, S. O., and G. Sosnovsky: *Svensk Kem. Tidskr.*, **75**, 343 (1963); **75**, 568 (1963). (These review articles are the most complete available and are in English.)

Walling, C.: "Free Radicals in Solution," John Wiley & Sons, Inc., New York, 1957, pp. 564–579.

part three REACTIONS OF RADICALS

Hydrogen Abstraction Reactions

GENERAL FEATURES OF HYDROGEN ABSTRACTIONS

In Chap. 1, radical reactions were divided into three main types: radical-forming reactions, propagation reactions, and terminations. In Part Two we examined ways in which radicals can be produced; we now turn our attention to the propagation reactions of radicals.

Hydrogen abstraction is the most common reaction that radicals undergo. It can be generalized as shown below, where SH is any hydrogen donor.

$$R\cdot + SH \longrightarrow RH + S\cdot$$

Hydrogen transfer occurs either as a principal reaction or as an unavoidable side reaction in almost every radical system.

Ordinarily, the energy required to break a C—H bond is so large that the reaction cannot occur unassisted, and some bond making occurs in the transition state.

$$R\cdot + SH \longrightarrow [R\cdot H \colon S \longleftrightarrow R \colon H \cdot S] \longrightarrow R-H + S\cdot$$
$$\text{Transition state}$$

In this bimolecular process, a radical abstracts a hydrogen atom from another molecule, and the energy necessary for bond breaking is partially supplied by making the new bond. There are a few reactions, however, in which atomic hydrogen is eliminated; examples are the high-temperature pyrolysis and the mercury-sensitized photolysis of ethylene. In the latter most of the reaction is an elimination of molecular hydrogen, but about 4% of the total decomposition involves elimination of a hydrogen atom.[†]

$$Hg \xrightarrow{\quad h\nu \quad} Hg^*$$

$$Hg^* + CH_2{=}CH_2 \longrightarrow Hg + (CH_2{=}CH_2)^*$$

$$(CH_2{=}CH_2)^* \xrightarrow{\text{Mainly}} HC{\equiv}CH + H_2$$
$$\xrightarrow{\text{Some}} CH_2{=}\dot{C}H + H\cdot$$

Attempts have been made to predict the rate of hydrogen abstrac-

[†] P. Kebarle, *J. Phys. Chem.*, **67**, 716 (1963).

tion reactions using transition state theory. The problem is difficult, and most effort has been expended on the simplest hydrogen abstraction reaction, namely, the reaction of hydrogen atoms with hydrogen molecules:†

$$H\cdot + H—H \longrightarrow H—H + H\cdot$$

The rate of this process can be measured experimentally, using isotopic labeling; e.g.,

$$H\cdot + D—D \longrightarrow H—D + D\cdot$$

The rate can also be measured by studying the conversion of *ortho* to *para* hydrogen.‡ The calculations indicate that the transition state for this reaction probably involves three atoms in a straight line:

$$H\cdot + H_2 \longrightarrow [H\cdots H\cdots H]$$
Transition state

If this is correct, then this bimolecular homolytic displacement (S_H2) reaction is analogous in mechanism to an ionic S_N2 reaction involving back-side attack and Walden inversion. It is not known whether all S_H2 reactions involve a back-side-attack mechanism. (See page 9.) Even in the very simple reaction of hydrogen atoms with the hydrogen molecule, the computations are so difficult that the conclusion that the transition state is linear could be in error. The most direct way of answering this question would be to determine whether retention or inversion occurs when a radical displaces a group from an optically active molecule. However, an unambiguous example of a reaction in which a radical attacks an

† The difficulties are discussed in Appendix I in N. N. Semenov, "Some Problems of Chemical Kinetics and Reactivity," vol. 1, Pergamon Press, New York, 1958, p. 285. Also see S. Glasstone, K. J. Laidler, and H. Eyring, "Theory of Rate Processes," McGraw-Hill Book Company, New York, 1941, pp. 88, 91, 110, 222.

‡ Hydrogen exists in two forms: *ortho*, in which the two nuclei have parallel spins, and *para*, in which the spins are antiparallel. Near absolute zero the molecules are mainly in the *para* state, the lowest-level state. At room temperature the gas is about 75% *ortho*. (The two forms are distinguishable by various physical properties.) Since the nuclear spins cancel in *para* hydrogen, this form does not contribute to the magnetic properties of the gas. Paramagnetic substances (for example, O_2, rare-earth elements, and radicals) accelerate the conversion. The mechanism for the conversion as catalyzed by hydrogen atoms is

$$H\cdot + para\text{-}H_2 \longrightarrow ortho\text{-}H_2 + H\cdot$$

asymmetric carbon atom has not yet been reported; hydrogen or halogen abstraction always occurs in preference to attack on carbon. For example, optically active *sec*-butyl iodide reacts with radioactive iodine atoms to give a racemized product containing radioactive iodide. The mechanism of this process involves an attack on iodide by iodine atoms:

$$I\cdot^* \quad + \quad H-\underset{\underset{C_2H_5}{|}}{\overset{\overset{CH_3}{|}}{C}}-I \quad \xrightarrow{\text{Mainly}} \quad H-\underset{\underset{C_2H_5}{|}}{\overset{\overset{CH_3}{|}}{C}}\cdot \quad + \quad I-I^*$$

Optically active   Rapidly racemizes

$$CH_3-\overset{\bullet}{C}H-C_2H_5 \quad + \quad I_2^* \quad \longrightarrow \quad CH_3-\underset{}{\overset{\overset{I^*}{|}}{C}H}-C_2H_5 \quad + \quad I\cdot^*$$

Racemized product
containing radioiodide

The *direct* S_H2 displacement on the carbon nucleus, which would also produce racemization and exchange, occurs very little if at all.†

$$I\cdot^* \quad + \quad H-\underset{\underset{C_2H_5}{|}}{\overset{\overset{CH_3}{|}}{C}}-I \quad \xrightarrow[\text{or none}]{\text{Little}} \quad I^*-\underset{\underset{C_2H_5}{|}}{\overset{\overset{CH_3}{|}}{C}}-H \quad + \quad I\cdot$$

Inverted

Direct proof that radical displacement reactions involve back-side attack will become possible only when a radical displacement at an asymmetrical atom is discovered. However, indirect evidence favoring a back-side-attack mechanism has been obtained through the use of a rate criterion. The ionic S_N2 reaction has a very characteristic rate profile as the R group is varied. The rate is extremely sensitive to the size of the R group, since the attacking Y^- must push past the R group in order to approach the C—X bond from the back side.

$$Y^- \quad + \quad RCH_2-X \quad \longrightarrow \quad \left[Y\cdots\cdots\underset{\underset{H\ H}{\diagdown}}{\overset{\overset{R}{|}}{C}}\cdots\cdots X \right]^- \quad \longrightarrow \quad RCH_2Y \quad + \quad X^-$$

Transition state

† J. E. Bujake, M. W. T. Pratt, and R. M. Noyes, *J. Am. Chem. Soc.*, **83**, 1547 (1961); S. W. Benson, *J. Chem. Phys.*, **38**, 1945 (1963).

The analogous ionic reaction of disulfides is believed to involve the same back-side-attack mechanism, since it follows the same characteristic S_N2 rate profile.

$$Y^- \; + \; RSSR \; \longrightarrow \; [Y\cdots\overset{\displaystyle R}{\overset{|}{S}}\cdots SR]^- \; \longrightarrow \; YSR \; + \; RS^-$$
$$\text{Transition state}$$

The S_H2 displacement reaction by free radicals on disulfides also has been studied:

$$Y\cdot \; + \; RSSR \; \longrightarrow \; [Y\cdots\overset{\displaystyle R}{\overset{|}{S}}\cdots SR] \; \longrightarrow \; YSR \; + \; RS\cdot$$
$$\text{Transition state}$$

It has been found that these two similar ionic and radical displacement reactions on sulfur atoms have related rate profiles.† This is evidence that the S_N2 and the S_H2 reactions involve similar back-side-attack mechanisms when a divalent sulfur is the atom undergoing attack.

We now consider the factors that influence the rates of hydrogen abstraction reactions. Radical transfer processes are influenced by several complex effects which can act in opposing directions. However, if a series of closely related reactions is selected, the effect of one or two factors can frequently be isolated and examined.

One of the most useful generalizations about the rates of hydrogen abstractions concerns the effect of the thermodynamic strengths of the bonds being formed and broken. Reactions of the type

$$R\cdot + SH \longrightarrow [R\cdots H\cdots S] \longrightarrow RH + S\cdot$$
$$\text{Transition}$$
$$\text{state}$$

involve a transition state in which the RH bond is partly formed and the SH bond is partly ruptured, and the strengths of these partial bonds is influenced to some extent by the strengths of the RH and SH bonds themselves. Since the formation of the RH bond provides part of the driving force to break the SH bond, R• radicals that form strong RH bonds and compounds with weak SH bonds should undergo particularly facile hydrogen transfer reactions.‡

---

† W. A. Pryor and T. L. Pickering, *J. Am. Chem. Soc.*, **84**, 2705 (1962); W. A. Pryor and H. Guard, *ibid.*, **86**, 1150 (1964).

‡ J. M. Tedder, *Quart. Rev.* (*London*), **14**, 344 (1960); M. Szwarc, The Transition State, *Chem. Soc.* (*London*), *Spec. Publ.* 16, 1962, p. 95.

In every radical process studied to date, the rates of hydrogen abstractions from aliphatic hydrocarbons increase in the order primary < secondary < tertiary. This order is independent of the nature of the attacking radical and is most easily explained as due to the strengths of the C—H bonds being broken. Thus, tertiary C—H bonds are the weakest, and tertiary hydrogens are abstracted at the fastest rates. Table 12-1 gives data for four radicals which illustrate this point. The data indicate that other factors must also be involved, however, since the selectivity of the radicals varies. For example, the ratio of the rates for abstraction of primary and tertiary hydrogens is 1:50 for methyl radicals and only 1:4 for chlorine atoms. We shall consider this variation in selectivity in further detail below.

The effect on rates of the strength of the bond being formed is illustrated by the data in Table 12-2. In a closely related series of radicals, stronger bonds lead to faster rates. For example, Table 12-2 shows that the halogen atoms abstract hydrogen in the order $F > Cl > Br$ and that this is also the order of the H—X bond strengths. Thus, fluorine abstracts hydrogen at the fastest rate (i.e., with the lowest activation energy) and forms the strongest bond to hydrogen. However, chlorine, trifluoromethyl, hydrogen, and methyl radicals all abstract hydrogen atoms with different activation energies, although they all form bonds to hydrogen of nearly the same strength. One explanation of this is that atoms react faster than

Table 12-1 Relative reactivity of aliphatic hydrogens toward various radicals

	X• + RH $\longrightarrow$ XH + R•			
Type of hydrogen[a]	CH_3• 182°C	ϕ• 60°C	t-BuO• 40°C	Cl• 25°C
Primary	1	1	1	1
Secondary	7	9.3	8	3.6
Tertiary	50	44	44	4.2
Cyclohexane	...	8.3	15	2.5
Reference	b	c	d	e

[a] All data are per hydrogen atom. The reactivities for the methyl radical are for the gas phase; all the others are in solution.

[b] A. F. Trotman-Dickenson, "Gas Kinetics," Butterworth Scientific Publications, London, 1955, p. 225.

[c] R. F. Bridger and G. A. Russell, *J. Am. Chem. Soc.*, **85**, 3754 (1963).

[d] C. Walling and W. Thaler, *ibid.*, **83**, 3877 (1961).

[e] G. A. Russell, *ibid.*, **80**, 4987, 4997 (1958).

Table 12-2   The influence of the strength of the bond being formed on the energy of activation for hydrogen abstraction†

$$X\cdot + \begin{cases} CH_4 \\ C_2H_6 \end{cases} \longrightarrow XH + \begin{cases} CH_3\cdot \\ C_2H_5\cdot \end{cases}$$

$X\cdot$	$D(H-X)$, kcal/mole	CH_4 E_a, kcal/mole	C_2H_6 E_a, kcal/mole
F	136	0.2	0.2
Cl	103	3.9	1.0
CF_3	103	10.3	7.5
H	103	. . .	9.
CH_3	102	14.0	11.2
Br	87	18.3	13.9

† M. Szwarc, *Chem. Soc. (London), Spec. Publ.* 16, 1962, p. 94; J. M. Tedder, *Quart. Rev. (London)* **14**, 338 (1960); A. F. Trotman-Dickenson, "Gas Kinetics," Butterworth Scientific Publications, London, 1954, pp. 179, 191.

multiatomic radicals. In the reaction of multiatomic radicals, some bond reorganization probably occurs at the transition state. That is, a nearly planar radical such as methyl might be forced into a more pyramidal geometry at the transition state, and this change in geometry would require energy.

Radical (Very shallow pyramid)   Transition state (Deeper pyramid)   Methane (Tetrahedral)

We have seen that the selectivities of the radicals listed in Table 12-1 vary greatly. The *selectivity* and the *reactivity* of a radical can frequently be related. For the two reactions

$$CH_3\cdot + RH \longrightarrow CH_4 + R\cdot$$
$$Cl\cdot + RH \longrightarrow HCl + R\cdot$$

the data in Tables 12-1 and 12-2 show that methyl radicals are *more selective* and *less reactive* than are chlorine atoms; that is, methyl radicals are

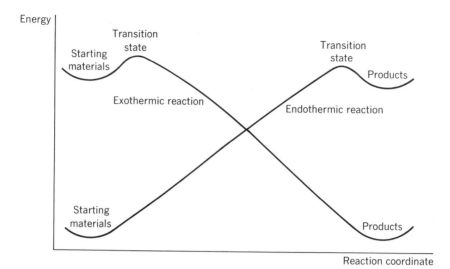

Figure 12-1 Selectivity and exothermicity of reactions.

more selective in their reactions with the three types of hydrogen atoms, but they are less reactive and require a larger activation energy to abstract a given type of hydrogen atom. This inverse relationship between the selectivity and the reactivity of a radical can be explained most easily in terms of the extrathermodynamic relationship between the activation energy and the heat of reaction.† Figure 12-1 shows an energy diagram for a generalized exothermic and an endothermic reaction. In the exothermic reaction, the reactants are of high energy relative to the products, and the transition state lies near the starting materials along the reaction coordinate. Therefore, the structure of the transition state must be very similar to that of the starting materials. This implies that bond breaking cannot have proceeded very far at the transition state and that the reaction rate is not very sensitive to the exact nature and strength of the bond being broken.

For the endothermic reaction, the situation is quite different. The reactants are of low energy, and the transition state resembles products more than starting materials. In these reactions, a considerable amount of bond reorganization can have occurred at the transition state, and the

† G. S. Hammond, *J. Am. Chem. Soc.*, **77**, 334 (1955); K. B. Wiberg and L. H. Slaugh, *ibid.*, **80**, 3033 (1958); J. E. Leffler and E. Grunwald, "Rates and Equilibria of Organic Reactions," John Wiley & Sons, Inc., New York, 1963, pp. 162–168.

rate of such reactions is frequently very sensitive to the nature and strength of the bonds being broken.

It should be stressed that this relationship between the heat of reaction and the rate of reaction is not a thermodynamic one. Although there need not be any direct relationship, in practice it is usually found that very reactive species produce exothermic reactions. Since the extent of bond breaking at the transition state is small, these reactions are usually relatively insensitive to the exact nature of the bond being broken.

Two other factors frequently influence the rates of hydrogen abstraction reactions. One is the polar effect, which was discussed briefly in Chap. 1 and will be considered in detail later in this chapter. The second is the solvent effect. As was pointed out on page 14, this effect usually is so much smaller in radical reactions than in ionic reactions that it is used as a diagnostic tool for identifying radical processes. However, in some radical reactions the effects of changing solvents are very significant. One notable example is the chlorination of 2,3-dimethylbutane. The data in Table 12-3 show that the product distribution is completely altered by a change in solvent.† The mechanism of this reaction is shown below.

$$Cl\cdot + RH \longrightarrow R\cdot + HCl$$
$$R\cdot + Cl_2 \longrightarrow RCl + Cl\cdot$$

Thus, the location of the chlorine in the product depends on which hydrogen atom is abstracted by the chlorine atom. Tertiary C—H bonds are

† G. A. Russell, *J. Am. Chem. Soc.*, **80**, 4987 (1958). Note that the product distribution depends not on the dielectric constant, as it might in ionic reactions, but on the ability of the solvents to complex with a chlorine atom.

Table 12-3 The product distribution in the chlorination of 2,3-dimethylbutane†

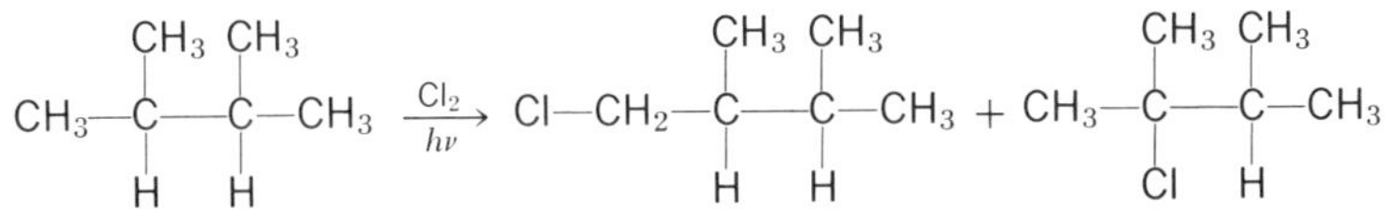

Solvent	I, %	II, %
Carbon tetrachloride	60	40
Benzene	10	90
Carbon disulfide	5	95

† G. A. Russell, *J. Am. Chem. Soc.*, **80**, 4987 (1958).

weaker than primary and therefore should be broken more easily. However, there are 12 primary and only 2 tertiary hydrogens in 2,3-dimethylbutane. In carbon tetrachloride as solvent, the chlorine atom is very reactive and shows little selectivity, and the larger number of primary hydrogens leads to the formation of a larger amount of primary alkyl chloride. However, benzene and carbon disulfide complex with the chlorine atom to stabilize it and make it more selective in its reactions.

$$Cl\cdot + CS_2 \rightleftharpoons (CS_2\cdot Cl)$$
$$(CS_2\cdot Cl) + RH \longrightarrow HCl + R\cdot + CS_2$$

It should be noted that, even in carbon tetrachloride, tertiary hydrogens are more reactive than are primary. Table 12-3 shows that a 60% yield of the primary halide is obtained; however, there are six times as many primary hydrogens as tertiary. The relative selectivity *per hydrogen* for tertiary as compared with primary hydrogens therefore is 40/1 to 60/6, or 4:1. Thus, tertiary hydrogens are four times more reactive than primary even in carbon tetrachloride.

Bimolecular abstraction reactions always have a rate proportional to the concentration of a molecular species and the concentration of radicals. For example, the rate of the reaction

$$R\cdot + SH \longrightarrow RH + S\cdot$$

is

$$\text{Rate} = k(R\cdot)(SH)$$

The concentration of radicals in kinetic systems usually is not measurable by direct methods.† Consequently, the rate constants for radical reactions generally are obtained as ratios in such a manner that the radical concentrations are not required. This is best made clear by an example: The rate

----

† Electron paramagnetic resonance (EPR) measures the concentrations of radicals directly, as was discussed in Chap. 2. However, present EPR instruments cannot detect radicals below about 10^{-8} M and usually are not sensitive enough to detect the very low steady-state concentrations of radicals present in radical reactions. The instruments are constantly being improved, and direct measurement of the absolute values of rate constants may eventually become more practical.

In unusual cases in which radicals are stable enough to exist at ordinary concentrations, reactions can be followed by the usual techniques. An example of this is discussed on page 328.

of the abstraction of hydrogen by methyl radicals can be obtained relative to the rate of their dimerization without measuring the concentration of the methyl radicals. For the reactions

$$CH_3\bullet + RH \xrightarrow{k_1} CH_4 + R\bullet \qquad (12\text{-}1)$$

$$2CH_3\bullet \xrightarrow{k_2} C_2H_6 \qquad (12\text{-}2)$$

the rates are

$$\frac{d(CH_4)}{dt} = k_1(CH_3\bullet)(RH) \qquad (12\text{-}3)$$

$$\frac{d(C_2H_6)}{dt} = k_2(CH_3\bullet)^2$$

and, therefore,

$$\frac{k_1(RH)}{k_2^{1/2}} = \frac{d(CH_4)/dt}{[d(C_2H_6)/dt]^{1/2}}$$

On rearrangement, this gives

$$\frac{k_1}{(k_2)^{1/2}} = \frac{1}{(RH)} \frac{[\text{Rate of formation of methane}]}{[\text{Rate of formation of ethane}]^{1/2}} \qquad (12\text{-}4)$$

Thus, the rate constant for reaction (12-1) can be obtained relative to the rate constant for the dimerization of methyl radicals [reaction (12-2)]. In this procedure, the absolute concentration of methyl radicals is never required.

In one case, however, a rate constant has been obtained by direct measurement. This is the gas-phase exchange of hydrogen atoms with hydrogen molecules:

$$H\bullet + H_2 \xrightarrow{k_5} H_2 + H\bullet \qquad (12\text{-}5)$$

In this reaction, the concentration of hydrogen atoms in the gas phase can be measured by techniques based on measuring rates of diffusion or by mass spectrometry, and the rate constant is found to be given by[†]

$$k_5 = 4 \times 10^{10}\, e^{-7,500/RT} \qquad \text{liter mole}^{-1}\ \text{sec}^{-1}$$

[†] A. F. Trotman-Dickenson, "Free Radicals," Methuen & Co., Ltd., London, 1959, p. 63. Other techniques for measuring the rate of this exchange were discussed on page 151.

ABSTRACTION OF HYDROGEN BY METHYL RADICALS

Methyl radicals can be generated from a number of sources, the most common of which are azomethane, t-butyl peroxide, acetyl peroxide, dimethylmercury, and acetone:

$$CH_3-N{=}N-CH_3 \longrightarrow 2CH_3\cdot + N_2$$

$$\underset{\substack{\| \\ O}}{CH_3-\overset{O}{\overset{\|}{C}}-O-O-\overset{O}{\overset{\|}{C}}-CH_3} \longrightarrow 2CH_3\cdot + 2CO_2$$

$$\underset{\substack{| \\ CH_3}}{CH_3-\overset{CH_3}{\overset{|}{C}}-O-O-\overset{CH_3}{\overset{|}{C}}-CH_3} \longrightarrow 2\,CH_3-\overset{CH_3}{\underset{CH_3}{\overset{|}{\underset{|}{C}}}}-O\cdot \longrightarrow \begin{array}{l} 2\,CH_3-\overset{O}{\overset{\|}{C}}-CH_3 \\ + \\ 2CH_3\cdot \end{array}$$

$$CH_3-\overset{O}{\overset{\|}{C}}-CH_3 \xrightarrow{\text{Light}} CH_3\cdot + CH_3CO\cdot$$

$$CH_3-Hg-CH_3 \longrightarrow 2CH_3\cdot + Hg$$

Methyl radicals abstract hydrogen from any hydrogen donor present in the system; this abstraction reaction competes with the normal termination reaction.

$$CH_3\cdot + RH \xrightarrow{k_1} CH_4 + R\cdot \tag{12-1}$$

$$2CH_3\cdot \xrightarrow{k_2} C_2H_6 \tag{12-2}$$

As discussed above, the ratio of the rate of formation of methane to the square root of the rate of formation of ethane gives the ratio of rate constants (corrected for concentration):

$$\frac{k_1}{(k_2)^{1/2}} = \frac{1}{(RH)} \frac{[\text{Rate of formation of methane}]}{[\text{Rate of formation of ethane}]^{1/2}} \tag{12-4}$$

The absolute value of the rate constant k_2 has been measured by the technique of rotating sectors.† In this manner, k_2 is obtained as

† R. Gomer and G. B. Kistiakowsky, *J. Chem. Phys.*, **19**, 85 (1951); A. Shepp, *ibid.*, **24**, 939 (1956). This method involves measuring the rate of formation of ethane relative to methane both under conditions of steady illumination and during periods of alternating light and dark. The reasoning is complex, and a discussion of the method is postponed until we discuss vinyl polymerization in Chap. 15.

$$k_2 = 2 \times 10^{10} \text{ liter mole}^{-1} \text{ sec}^{-1} \qquad (12\text{-}6)$$

From Eqs. (12-4) and (12-6), the rate of abstraction of hydrogen atoms from RH by methyl radicals is

$$k_1 = \frac{1}{(RH)} \frac{[\text{Rate of formation of methane}]}{[\text{Rate of formation of ethane}]^{1/2}}$$

$$\times (2 \times 10^{10})^{1/2} \text{ liter mole}^{-1} \text{ sec}^{-1} \qquad (12\text{-}7)$$

Trotman-Dickenson has tabulated a large number of rate constants obtained by this method; Table 12-4 gives typical data. The table shows that the rate constants are not entirely independent of the radical source, but differences are probably within experimental error. Note that the rate of hydrogen abstraction increases in the alkane series as the substrate is made more branched; this reflects the fact that primary hydrogens are abstracted at the slowest rate. Methanol and methyl ether have similar reactivity. This implies that hydrogen abstraction is from the methyl

Table 12-4   Rate constants for the abstraction of hydrogen atoms by methyl radicals†

		$CH_3\bullet + RH \xrightarrow{k} CH_4 + R\bullet$	
RH	Source of methyl radicals	$k \times 10^{-2}$ liter mole^{-1} sec^{-1} at 182°C	$E_a,$ kcal/mole
Acetone	Acetone	120	9.7
Acetone	t-Butyl peroxide	100	9.5
Hexane	Acetone	170	8.1
2-Methylpropane	Acetone	220	7.6
2-Methylpropane	Azomethane	100	6.6
2-Methylpropane	$Hg(CH_3)_2$	160	7.4
2,3-Dimethylbutane	Acetone	350	6.9
2,3-Dimethylbutane	$Hg(CH_3)_2$	250	6.8
Methanol	Acetone	60	8.2
Dimethyl ether	Acetone	90	9.5
Acetaldehyde	t-Butyl peroxide	2,200	7.5
t-Butyl peroxide	t-Butyl peroxide	60	11.7
Azomethane	Azomethane	200	7.6
HCl	Acetone	3×10^5	2.3

† A. F. Trotman-Dickenson, "Gas Kinetics," Butterworth Scientific Publications, London, 1955. The units have been converted from cc mole^{-1} sec^{-1} to those given here.

groups in both of these compounds. Acetaldehyde is more reactive than is methanol or methyl ether; in aldehydes the hydrogen attached to the carbonyl group is very labile.

$$CH_3\cdot + CH_3{-}CHO \longrightarrow CH_4 + CH_3{-}CO\cdot$$

The data indicate that both t-butyl peroxide and azomethane are themselves attacked by radicals. Generally, t-butyl peroxide is not regarded as especially reactive toward radicals, and azo compounds are thought to be extremely unreactive toward induced decompositions. However, as the rate constants show, attack on these compounds by methyl radicals occurs at appreciable rates in the gas phase.

The effect of the substitution of deuterium for hydrogen on the rate of hydrogen abstraction reactions has been investigated in several compounds. The complete theory of isotope effects is complex, and review articles on this subject may be consulted for details.[†] However, the relevant principle may be briefly stated as follows: Substitution of deuterium for hydrogen produces a change in rate if the substituted C—H bond is partially broken in the transition state. In reactions of the type

$$R\cdot + SH \longrightarrow [R\cdots H\cdots S] \longrightarrow RH + S\cdot$$
$$\text{Transition state}$$

$$R\cdot + SD \longrightarrow [R\cdots D\cdots S] \longrightarrow RD + S\cdot$$
$$\text{Transition state}$$

deuterium is transferred more slowly than hydrogen. This effect is called the *primary kinetic isotope effect* and is usually expressed as the ratio of the rate constants for the hydrogen and the deuterium compound, k_H/k_D. Values of k_H/k_D for hydrogen abstractions vary from slightly over 1 to about 8. In particular, substantial values of k_H/k_D are observed in methyl radical reactions:[‡]

$$CH_3\cdot + RH(D) \longrightarrow CH_3{-}H(D) + R\cdot$$

This indicates that the R—H bond is appreciably stretched in the transition state.

† K. B. Wiberg, *Chem. Rev.*, **55**, 713 (1955); F. H. Westheimer, *ibid.*, **61**, 265 (1961); K. B. Wiberg and E. L. Motell, *Tetrahedron*, **19**, 2009 (1963).
‡ M. Szwarc, *Chem. Soc. (London)*, *Spec. Publ.* **16**, 1962, p. 94; W. M. Jackson, J. R. McNesby, and B. deB. Darwent, *J. Chem. Phys.*, **37**, 1610 (1962).

A correlation is frequently observed between the magnitude of the isotope effect and the activation energy. It is not surprising that reactions having a large activation energy frequently show a high selectivity between isotopic substituents. (See the discussion on page 156 on selectivity and reactivity.) An example of this is the reaction of N-bromosuccinimide with toluene, ethylbenzene, and cumene (isopropylbenzene). In this series of compounds the activation energy decreases, and the values of k_H/k_D (at 77°C) are 4.8, 2.7, and 1.8, respectively.[†]

Most of the data discussed above have applied to the gas-phase reactions of methyl radicals. However, the available data suggest that the relative rates of reaction of methyl radicals with a series of hydrogen donors are the same in solution as in the gas phase. Relative rates of reaction in solution can be obtained by the following procedure: Methyl radicals are generated in mixtures of various hydrogen donors with carbon tetrachloride. The two reactions shown below then occur in competition.

$$CH_3\cdot + RH \xrightarrow{k_8} CH_4 + R\cdot \qquad (12\text{-}8)$$

$$CH_3\cdot + CCl_4 \xrightarrow{k_9} CH_3Cl + CCl_3\cdot \qquad (12\text{-}9)$$

The rates of these two processes are

$$\frac{d(CH_4)}{dt} = k_8(CH_3\cdot)(RH)$$

$$\frac{d(CH_3Cl)}{dt} = k_9(CH_3\cdot)(CCl_4)$$

Dividing one rate by the other gives

$$\frac{d(CH_4)}{d(CH_3Cl)} = \frac{k_8}{k_9}\frac{(RH)}{(CCl_4)} \qquad (12\text{-}10)$$

This will be recognized as an example of the technique of solving for a ratio of rate constants such that all radical concentrations cancel out. If small amounts of methyl radicals are used, the concentrations of RH and CCl_4 remain substantially unchanged during reaction and can be set equal to their initial concentrations. Also, $\Delta(CH_4)$ and $\Delta(CH_3Cl)$ can be taken as

[†] K. B. Wiberg and E. L. Motell, *Tetrahedron*, **19**, 2009 (1963). A more sophisticated rationale for the proportionality between the kinetic isotope effect and activation energy is given in this reference.

Table 12-5   Rates of hydrogen abstraction by methyl radicals relative to abstraction of chlorine from carbon tetrachloride at 100°C†

Substrate	k_8/k_9	Substrate	k_8/k_9
Benzene	0.039	1-Octene	3.2
Methyl benzoate	0.062	Cyclohexane	4.8
Acetone	0.40	Chloroform	11.1
Toluene	0.75	Methyl acetate	21
Carbon tetrachloride	(1.00)		

† F. G. Edwards and F. R. Mayo, *J. Am. Chem. Soc.*, **72**, 1265 (1950).

approximations for the differential quantities. Since both (CH_4) and (CH_3Cl) are initially zero, $\Delta(CH_4)/\Delta(CH_3Cl)$ is equal to the ratio of methane to chloromethane in the products. Therefore, Eq. (12-10) becomes

$$\frac{k_8}{k_9} = \frac{(CCl_4)}{(RH)} \frac{[\text{Yield of methane}]}{[\text{Yield of chloromethane}]} \tag{12-11}$$

That is, relative values of k_8 can be obtained from the ratio of methane to chloromethane that is formed, corrected for the initial concentration ratio of the reactants. Table 12-5 gives data obtained by this technique, with acetyl peroxide as the source of methyl radicals. The data show that

Table 12-6   Relative rates of hydrogen abstraction by methyl radicals in the gas phase and in solution†

$$CH_3\bullet + RH \xrightarrow{k_8} CH_4 + R\bullet$$
$$CH_3\bullet + CCl_4 \xrightarrow{k_9} CH_3Cl + \bullet CCl_3$$

Substrate	k_8/k_9 (Solution) 100°C	k_8 (Gas phase) 100°C	$\left[\dfrac{k_8 \text{ in the gas phase}}{\text{Relative } k_8 \text{ in solution}}\right]$
Benzene	0.04	0.091	2.3
Acetone	0.40	1.0	2.5
Toluene	0.75	1.9	2.5
1-Octene	3.2	7.7	2.4
Cyclohexane	4.8	3.0	0.6

† F. G. Edwards and F. R. Mayo, *J. Am. Chem. Soc.*, **72**, 1265 (1950). Gas-phase data are absolute values of the rate constants ($\times 10^{-3}$) extrapolated to 100°C, using the data similar to that given in Table 12-4. See A. F. Trotman-Dickenson, "Free Radicals," Methuen & Co., Ltd., London, 1959, p. 70.

benzene is relatively inert to hydrogen abstraction. Acetone and toluene react more slowly than does carbon tetrachloride. Cyclohexane is an unusually reactive hydrocarbon. Octene, which has allylic hydrogens, reacts more rapidly than a saturated alkane.

Table 12-6 compares the relative rate constants obtained in solution with the gas-phase data compiled by Trotman-Dickenson. The table shows that the relative rates of hydrogen abstraction by methyl radicals are the same in the gas phase and in solution. We conclude that relative rates of hydrogen abstraction by reactive, relatively nonpolar radicals such as methyl are not greatly affected by solvents.

ABSTRACTION OF HYDROGEN BY ALKOXY RADICALS

Alkoxy radicals may be produced in a variety of ways, including the decomposition of alkyl nitrites, alkyl peroxides, and hypohalites. Simple alkoxy radicals react largely by hydrogen abstraction. For example, t-butyl methyl peroxide and methyl nitrite both yield methoxy radicals which abstract hydrogen from various hydrogen donors:

$$t\text{-BuO-OCH}_3 \xrightarrow{200°C} CH_3O\bullet + t\text{-BuO}\bullet$$

$$CH_3O\text{-NO} \xrightarrow{120°C} CH_3O\bullet + NO$$

$$CH_3O\bullet + RH \longrightarrow CH_3OH + R\bullet$$

When RH is an active donor such as cyclohexane, almost quantitative yields of methanol are formed.

More complex alkoxy radicals usually react in more than one way. The t-butoxy radical, for example, can either abstract a hydrogen atom from a hydrogen donor RH or undergo β-scission to form acetone. These two processes are shown below.

$$t\text{-BuO}\bullet + RH \xrightarrow{k_{12}} t\text{-BuOH} + R\bullet \tag{12-12}$$

$$t\text{-BuO}\bullet \xrightarrow{k_{13}} CH_3\bullet + CH_3\text{-CO-CH}_3 \tag{12-13}$$

By reasoning similar to that used to derive Eq. (12-11), the following equation can be derived.

$$\frac{k_{12}}{k_{13}} = \frac{[\text{Yield of } t\text{-BuOH}]}{[\text{Yield of acetone}]} \frac{1}{(RH)} \tag{12-14}$$

This equation has been used to obtain the relative reactivities of a series of hydrogen donors with t-butyl peroxide as the source of t-butoxy radicals. The reaction mixtures are analyzed for the ratio of t-butyl alcohol to acetone, and these are converted to relative values of k_{12}, using Eq. (12-14). Table 12-7 gives data obtained in this manner from decompositions of t-butyl peroxide at 135°C.

Table 12-7 also gives data obtained with t-butyl hypohalite as the source of the t-butoxy radicals. In the presence of two hydrogen donors, RH and SH, the following reactions occur:

$$\text{RH} + t\text{-BuO}\bullet \xrightarrow{k_{15}} \text{R}\bullet + t\text{-BuOH} \tag{12-15}$$

$$\text{R}\bullet + t\text{-BuOCl} \longrightarrow \text{RCl} + t\text{-BuO}\bullet$$

$$\text{SH} + t\text{-BuO}\bullet \xrightarrow{k_{16}} \text{S}\bullet + t\text{-BuOH} \tag{12-16}$$

$$\text{S}\bullet + t\text{-BuOCl} \longrightarrow \text{SCl} + t\text{-BuO}\bullet$$

The following equation can be derived by a process similar to that used to obtain Eq. (12-11).

$$\frac{d(\text{RH})}{d(\text{SH})} = \frac{k_{15}}{k_{16}} \frac{(\text{RH})}{(\text{SH})} \tag{12-17}$$

This can be rearranged and integrated to give

$$\frac{k_{15}}{k_{16}} = \frac{d(\text{RH})/(\text{RH})}{d(\text{SH})/(\text{SH})} = \frac{\log\,[(\text{RH})/(\text{RH})_0]}{\log\,[(\text{SH})/(\text{SH})_0]} \tag{12-18}$$

where (RH) and (SH) are the concentrations of the two hydrogen donors at time t, and $(\text{RH})_0$ and $(\text{SH})_0$ are their initial concentrations. With gas-phase chromatography, it is quite easy to obtain the molar ratios of the two hydrogen donors RH and SH. With this powerful and convenient analytical tool and Eq. (12-18), a series of rate constants for hydrogen abstraction from various hydrogen donors can be obtained relative to the rate constant for some standard hydrogen donor SH. Table 12-7 gives data obtained in this manner at 40°C, with cyclohexane as the standard hydrogen donor and t-butyl hypohalite as the radical source.

Table 12-7 also gives relative rate constants obtained using t-butyl peroxide as the radical source, and good agreement is obtained in the data for the two different sources of t-butoxy radicals. Note that the usual order of hydrogen atom reactivity, namely, primary < secondary < tertiary, is followed in the series toluene/ethylbenzene/isopropylbenzene and in the series toluene/diphenylmethane/triphenylmethane.

Table 12-7   Relative rates of hydrogen abstraction by *t*-butoxy radicals from *t*-butyl peroxide or *t*-butyl hypohalite

$$RH + t\text{-BuO}\bullet \xrightarrow{k_{12}} R\bullet + t\text{-BuOH}$$

| RH | Relative k_{12} values (per hydrogen)[a] using | |
	t-Butyl peroxide at 135°C[b]	*t*-Butyl hypohalite at 40°C[c]
Toluene	1.0	1.0
Ethylbenzene	3.2	3.2
Isopropylbenzene	5.1, 6.4[d]	6.8
m-Xylene	1.2	1.2
p-Xylene	1.5	1.5
t-Butylbenzene	0.1	0.3
Cyclohexane	2.0	1.5
Tetralin	7.6	. . .
Diphenylmethane	4.2[d]	4.7
Triphenylmethane	. . .	9.6

[a] In the aromatic substrates only benzylic hydrogens are considered to be reactive.
[b] A. L. Williams, E. A. Oberright, and J. B. Brooks, *J. Am. Chem. Soc.*, **78**, 1190 (1956).
[c] C. Walling and B. B. Jacknow, *J. Am. Chem. Soc.*, **82**, 6108 (1960).
[d] J. H. T. Brooks, *Trans. Faraday Soc.*, **53**, 327 (1957).

ABSTRACTION OF HYDROGEN BY PHENYL RADICALS

The relative reactivities of a series of hydrogen donors toward phenyl radicals have been obtained with phenylazotriphenylmethane as the radical source. This azo compound undergoes rapid thermal homolysis at 60°C. When it is allowed to decompose in mixtures of the hydrogen donor RH and carbon tetrachloride, the following reactions occur:

$$\phi\text{—N}{=}\text{N—C}\phi_3 \longrightarrow \phi\bullet + N_2 + \phi_3C\bullet$$
$$\phi\bullet + RH \xrightarrow{k_{19}} \phi H + R\bullet$$ (12-19)
$$\phi\bullet + CCl_4 \xrightarrow{k_{20}} \phi Cl + \bullet CCl_3$$ (12-20)

By a method identical to that used to derive Eq. (12-11), we obtain

$$\frac{k_{19}}{k_{20}} = \frac{(CCl_4)}{(RH)} \frac{[\text{Yield of benzene}]}{[\text{Yield of chlorobenzene}]}$$ (12-21)

The ratio of benzene to chlorobenzene can easily be obtained by using gas-phase chromatography. From this ratio and Eq. (12-21), relative values of k_{19} can be calculated. Table 12-8 gives examples of data of this type. With the data for toluene, ethylbenzene, isopropylbenzene, and t-butylbenzene, the reactivities of a primary to a secondary to a tertiary benzylic hydrogen can be calculated to be $1:4.6:9.7$.† With the data for methyl disulfide, ethyl disulfide, isopropyl disulfide, and t-butyl disulfide, hydrogens alpha to an S—S bond can be obtained as $1:3.2:9.1$. Thus, hydrogens adjacent to a sulfur atom have a reactivity very similar to benzylic hydrogens. The data of Table 12-1 show the selectivity of phenyl radicals toward primary, secondary, and tertiary aliphatic hydrogens to be $1:9.3:44$. These data can be combined with the data of Table 12-8 to give the series of relative values of k_{19} (per hydrogen atom) shown below. (The symbols $1°$, $2°$, and $3°$ imply primary, secondary, and tertiary atoms.)

Aliphatic			Benzylic		
$1°$	$2°$	$3°$	$1°$	$2°$	$3°$
0.12	1.0	4.8	1.0	4.6	9.7

† Table 12-8 gives the reactivities of these four hydrogens shown below. As

Compound	k_{19}/k_{20}	Number and type of hydrogens	
		α to phenyl	β to phenyl
Toluene	0.27	3 primary	None
Ethylbenzene	0.84	2 secondary	3 primary
Isopropylbenzene	0.93	1 tertiary	6 primary
t-Butylbenzene	0.11	None	9 primary

shown, these four substrates contain four types of hydrogens, and the reactivity of each type can be obtained from simultaneous equations. The reactivity of a single primary α hydrogen is $0.27/3 = 0.09$, from the data for toluene. Similarly, a primary β hydrogen has the activity $0.11/9 = 0.01$, from the data on t-butylbenzene. The reactivity of a secondary α hydrogen can then be calculated from the data for ethylbenzene by subtracting the activity due to the β hydrogens:

Secondary α hydrogen $= \frac{1}{2}[0.84 - 3(.01)] = 0.41$

Similarly, isopropylbenzene gives

Tertiary α hydrogen $= 0.93 - 6(.01) = 0.87$

Then the reactivity series of $1°:2°:3°$ benzylic hydrogens is $0.09:0.40:0.86$ or $1:4.6:9.7$.

Table 12-8 Relative reactivities of hydrogen donors toward phenyl radicals†

Hydrogen donor	k_{19}/k_{20}	Hydrogen donor	k_{19}/k_{20}
Hexane	0.96	Triphenylmethane	3.5
2,3-Dimethylbutane	1.19	Chloroform	3.2
Cyclohexane	1.08	Chloromethane	0.07
Cyclohexene	4.4	Methyl ether	0.28
Toluene	0.27	Acetone	0.17
p-Phenoxytoluene	0.26	Acetic acid	0.09
p-Nitrotoluene	0.22	Methyl acetate	0.09
p-Methyltoluene	0.79	Methyl disulfide‡	0.57
Ethylbenzene	0.84	Ethyl disulfide‡	1.5
Isopropylbenzene	0.93	Isopropyl disulfide‡	1.9
t-Butylbenzene	0.11	t-Butyl disulfide‡	0.25
Diphenylmethane	1.4		

† R. F. Bridger and G. A. Russell, *J. Am. Chem. Soc.*, **85**, 3754 (1963).
‡ W. A. Pryor and H. Guard, *ibid.*, **86**, 1150 (1964).

Thus a primary benzylic hydrogen (as in toluene) has the same reactivity toward a phenyl radical as does a secondary aliphatic hydrogen. Primary aliphatic hydrogens are much less reactive.

The magnitude of the kinetic isotope effect has been measured for the reaction of phenyl radicals with toluene and with acetone.† For the reaction with ϕ—CH_3 versus ϕ—CD_3, k_H/k_D was found to be 4.5; for the reaction with CH_3—CO—CH_3 versus CD_3—CO—CD_3, k_H/k_D was found to be 4.2. Both these values indicate that a considerable amount of bond breaking has occurred at the transition state. (See the discussion on page 162.)

The influence of polar factors on the reactions of phenyl radicals can be judged from the rate differences between toluene and the ring-substituted toluenes listed in Table 12-8.

$$\phi\cdot \;+\; CH_3{-}\!\!\left\langle\!\!\bigcirc\!\!\right\rangle\!\!{-}X \;\xrightarrow{k_X}\; \phi H \;+\; \cdot CH_2{-}\!\!\left\langle\!\!\bigcirc\!\!\right\rangle\!\!{-}X$$

Electron-withdrawing X groups give slightly smaller values of k_X, and electron donors give slightly larger values. These data obey the Hammett equation with the low ρ value of -0.1, indicating that the phenyl radical is rather insensitive to polar effects.

† R. F. Bridger and G. A. Russell, *J. Am. Chem. Soc.*, **85**, 3754 (1963).

Table 12-9 Relative reactivities (per hydrogen) of hydrogen donors toward several radicals

Hydrogen donor	Radical				
	Methyl 65°C	Phenyl 60°C	t-Butoxy 40°	Chlorine atoms 40°	Bromine atoms 40°
Cyclohexane	. . .	1.0	1.5	2.0	0.004
Toluene[a]	(1)	(1)	(1)	(1)	(1)
Ethylbenzene[a]	4.1	4.6	3.2	2.5	17.2
Isopropylbenzene[a]	12.9	9.7	6.9	5.5	37.0
Reference	b	c	d	c, e	c, f

[a] Only benzylic hydrogens are considered labile.
[b] J. A. Meyer, V. Stannett, and M. Szwarc, *J. Am. Chem. Soc.*, **83**, 25 (1961).
[c] R. F. Bridger and G. A. Russell, *ibid.*, **85**, 3754 (1963).
[d] C. Walling and W. Thaler, *ibid.*, **83**, 3877 (1961).
[e] G. A. Russell, *ibid.*, **80**, 4987, 4997 (1958).
[f] G. A. Russell and C. DeBoer, *ibid.*, **85**, 3136 (1963).

RELATIVE RATES OF HYDROGEN ABSTRACTION BY VARIOUS RADICALS

Table 12-9 compares the relative reactivities for a series of radicals toward several common hydrogen donors. These data were all obtained by techniques similar to those described in the preceding sections. Note that methyl, phenyl, and t-butoxy radicals all have similar reactivities; the more reactive chlorine atom is somewhat less selective, and the less reactive bromine atom is considerably more selective.

POLAR EFFECTS IN HYDROGEN ABSTRACTIONS

Hydrogen abstraction reactions illustrate the polar effects that frequently influence radical reactions. The data in Table 12-10 compare the reactivity of methyl radicals and chlorine atoms toward the hydrogens in propionic acid. Methyl radicals attack an α hydrogen 7.8-fold *faster* than a β hydrogen, whereas chlorine atoms attack an α hydrogen only $\frac{1}{30}$ as fast as a β hydrogen. These facts are most easily explained in terms of a polar effect due to the electron-removing carboxylic acid group. The relatively electronegative chlorine atom prefers to attack those hydrogens furthest removed from the electronegative carboxy group. The reverse is true for the relatively electropositive methyl radical. In analogy with the terminology used in ionic reactions, the chlorine atom can be thought of as a relatively electrophilic radical, whereas methyl radicals are relatively nucleophilic.

Another example of a polar effect can be seen in Table 12-9. Note that chlorine and t-butoxy radicals abstract a hydrogen from cyclohexane faster than from toluene, whereas the reverse is true for bromine atoms. Two factors must be considered to explain these facts: the inductive electron-withdrawing effect of a phenyl group and the resonance stability of a benzylic radical.† In terms of these two factors, the hydrogen abstraction rates in Table 12-9 can be explained as follows: Chlorine and t-butoxy are electrophilic radicals. Therefore, the electron-removing inductive effect of a phenyl substituent acts to retard their attack on adjacent hydrogen atoms. Furthermore, they are so reactive that there is relatively little C—H bond breaking at the transition state, and the weaker benzylic C—H bond is not broken significantly faster than an aliphatic C—H bond. However, for the less electronegative and more selective bromine atom, the situation is reversed. Bromine is a less electronegative atom than is chlorine and is less repelled by the inductive effect of the phenyl substituent. Furthermore, there is extensive C—H bond breaking at the transition state in the reactions of bromine atoms. This leads to an increased odd electron density at the benzylic position at the transition state and considerable resonance stabilization due to the phenyl group. In summary, the transition state for reaction of the electronegative and unselective chlorine atom with toluene can be represented as shown below. (t-Butoxy would be similar.)

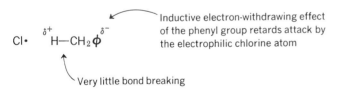

Cl• $\overset{\delta^+}{}$ H—CH$_2$ $\overset{\delta^-}{}\phi$

Inductive electron-withdrawing effect of the phenyl group retards attack by the electrophilic chlorine atom

Very little bond breaking

† G. A. Russell and H. C. Brown, *J. Am. Chem. Soc.*, **77**, 4578 (1955).

Table 12-10   Relative selectivity of Cl• and CH$_3$• toward the hydrogens in propionic acid†

Relative selectivity	CH$_3$—CH$_2$—CO$_2$H	
CH$_3$•	1	7.8
Cl•	30	1

† J. M. Tedder, *Quart. Rev.* (*London*), **14**, 340 (1960).

The transition state for the reaction of bromine atoms has much more bond breaking and can be represented by the two resonance structures shown below.

As discussed on page 95, the correlation of the rates of radical reactions by the Hammett equation demonstrates the occurrence of polar effects in homolytic reactions. The reactions of both bromine and chlorine atoms with ring-substituted toluenes have been studied from this viewpoint, and both reactions are correlated by the Hammett equation. However, in both cases the rates are correlated by σ^+ values better than by the usual values of σ. The σ^+ constants were developed to apply to ionic reactions in which a positive charge capable of resonance interaction with the benzene ring is generated at the transition state.† Although these σ^+ constants might have been expected to correlate only the rates of reactions in which there is considerable ionic character, it has been found that actually many homolytic reactions involving electrophilic radicals are correlated better by σ^+ than by σ. Examples‡ are hydrogen abstraction reactions from $ArCH_3$ by t-BuO•, Cl•, and Br•. This is a particularly striking demonstration of the polar effects that can arise in homolytic reactions.

The reaction of chlorine atoms with substituted toluenes is shown in reaction (12-22).§

† H. C. Brown and Y. Okamoto, *J. Am. Chem. Soc.*, **80**, 4979 (1958).

‡ At present it appears that the reactions of some radicals are correlated better by σ and some better by σ^+. In fact, although bromine reactions are correlated much better by σ^+ than by σ, the reactions of chlorine atoms are correlated almost as well by σ as by σ^+. This area is the subject of current research, and the criteria that distinguish between reactions correlated by σ and by σ^+ are not known at present. However, for our purposes, this distinction is not critical. The two points made here are that the reactions of both chlorine and bromine atoms involve substantial polar effects and that a larger amount of C—H bond breaking occurs at the transition state in the bromine atom reactions. For discussion of the correlation of radical reactions by the Hammett equation and the differences between σ and σ^+, see G. A. Russell, *J. Org. Chem.*, **23**, 1407 (1958), and J. A. Howard and K. U. Ingold, *Can. J. Chem.*, **41**, 1744 (1963).

§ C. Walling and B. Miller, *J. Am. Chem. Soc.*, **79**, 4181 (1957); G. A. Russell and R. C. Williamson, *ibid.*, **86**, 2357 (1964).

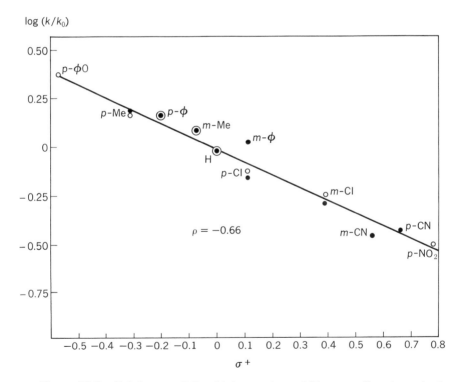

$$\text{Cl}\bullet \ + \ \ \overset{\text{CH}_3}{\underset{\text{X}}{\bigcirc}} \ \longrightarrow \ \text{HCl} \ + \ \overset{\dot{\text{C}}\text{H}_2}{\underset{\text{X}}{\bigcirc}} \qquad\qquad (12\text{-}22)$$

Figure 12-2 shows the data for reaction (12-22) plotted in the form of the Hammett equation

$$\log \frac{k}{k_0} = \sigma^+\rho$$

where k_0 is the rate of reaction with toluene, k is the rate of reaction with X—C_6H_4—CH_3, and σ^+ is a constant for each X group. The points define a straight line with slope $\rho = -0.66$. This negative value of ρ indicates

Figure 12-2 Relative reactivity of toluenes toward Cl• versus the σ^+ constant. [Open circles are data of G. A. Russell and R. C. Williamson, *J. Am. Chem. Soc.*, **86**, 2357 (1964), at 40°C; closed circles are data of C. Walling and B. Miller, *ibid.*, **79**, 4181 (1957), at 70°C.]

that electron-donating substituents increase the rate of reaction (12-22), in agreement with previous data indicating that the chlorine atom is an electrophilic radical. The transition state for this hydrogen abstraction can be represented by the two resonance forms shown below.

$$\text{Cl} \cdot \quad \text{H} : \text{CH}_2 - \underset{}{\bigcirc} - X \quad \longleftrightarrow \quad \overset{-}{\text{Cl}} : \quad \overset{\cdot}{\text{H}} \overset{+}{\text{CH}}_2 - \underset{}{\bigcirc} - X$$

These resonance forms predict that electron-donating X groups should stabilize the transition state and speed the reaction.

A parallel study has been made of the reaction of bromine atoms with substituted toluenes:

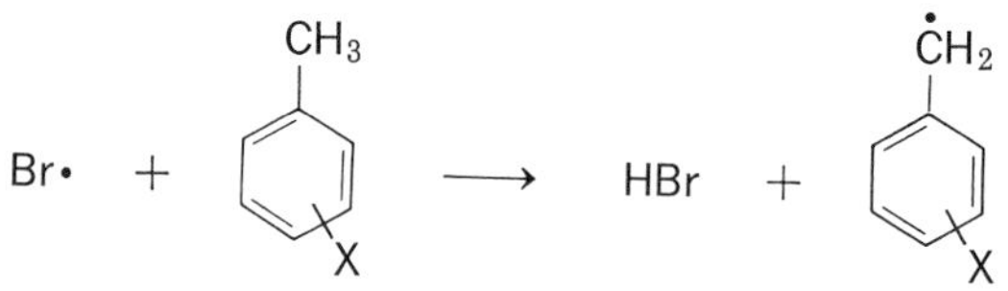

$$\text{Br} \cdot \quad + \quad \underset{X}{\overset{CH_3}{\bigcirc}} \quad \longrightarrow \quad \text{HBr} \quad + \quad \underset{X}{\overset{\dot{C}H_2}{\bigcirc}} \qquad (12\text{-}23)$$

As we have seen, bromine atom reactions involve a larger amount of bond breaking at the transition state than do the reactions of chlorine atoms. Therefore, in hydrogen abstractions from ring-substituted toluenes, the substituents will be *more* effective in influencing the relative stabilities of the transition states (and, hence, the rates) of bromine atom reactions. Figure 12-3 shows data for reaction (12-23), and the Hammett equation is obeyed. As predicted, ρ for bromine atom reactions is -1.36 at $80°C$, considerably larger than the $\rho = -0.66$ for chlorine reactions. Therefore, the resonance hybrid for bromine atom reactions is analogous to that for chlorine but with a significantly larger amount of charge separation and positive charge on the benzyl carbon. That is, the resonance forms shown on the right below are more important than are the comparable forms in chlorine atom reactions.

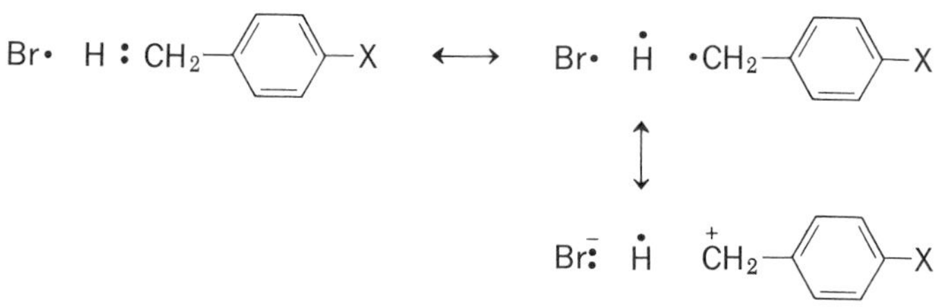

$$\text{Br} \cdot \quad \text{H} : \text{CH}_2 - \underset{}{\bigcirc} - X \quad \longleftrightarrow \quad \text{Br} \cdot \quad \overset{\cdot}{\text{H}} \quad \cdot \text{CH}_2 - \underset{}{\bigcirc} - X$$

$$\updownarrow$$

$$\overset{-}{\text{Br}} : \quad \overset{\cdot}{\text{H}} \quad \overset{+}{\text{CH}}_2 - \underset{}{\bigcirc} - X$$

Figure 12-4 shows the activation energy and heat of reaction for the reaction of chlorine and bromine atoms with toluene. These diagrams

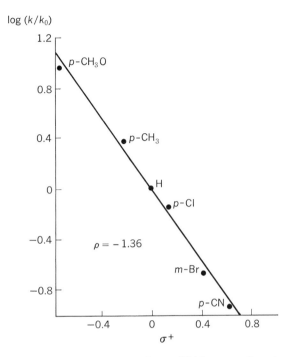

Figure 12-3 Relative reactivity of toluenes toward Br• at 80°C versus the σ^+ constant. [*R. E. Pearson and J. C. Martin, J. Am. Chem. Soc.*, **85**, 3142 (1963).]

show the much larger exothermicity and lower activation energy for the reaction of chlorine compared with bromine atoms. In terms of the principle discussed on page 156, less bond reorganization of the substrate occurs at the transition state in the reaction of chlorine atoms. Chlorination, therefore, would be expected to be less selective than bromination. The lower value of ρ observed in the chlorination of toluenes is in accord with this prediction.

All the above facts point to a larger activation energy and a larger selectivity in the reactions of bromine atoms with toluenes than those of chlorine atoms. This suggests that the kinetic isotope effect might be larger in bromine atom reactions when deuterium is substituted for hydrogen. (Refer to the discussion on page 162.) In agreement with this, k_H/k_D is 4.6 for the reaction of ϕCH_2D with bromine atoms and 1.3 with chlorine atoms (both in carbon tetrachloride at 77°C).†

† G. A. Russell and H. C. Brown, *J. Am. Chem. Soc.*, **74**, 3995 (1952); K. B. Wiberg and L. H. Slaugh, *ibid.*, **80**, 3033 (1958); C. Walling and B. Miller, *ibid.*, **79**, 4181 (1957).

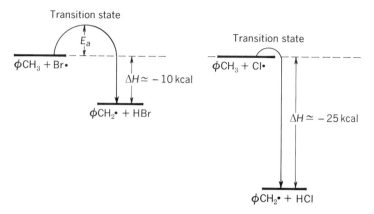

Figure 12-4 A comparison of the activation energy and exothermicity in the reactions of Br• and Cl• with toluene.

PROBLEMS

12-1 Derive Eq. (12-17). Explain how gas-phase chromatography and equations similar to (12-17) would allow three or more hydrogen donors to be compared *in one single experiment.*

12-2 Derive Eq. (12-21).

12-3 Using the data in Table 12-8, show that the reactivity of hydrogen atoms alpha to a disulfide bond is $1:3.2:9.1$ for $1°:2°:3°$. Calculate the relative reactivity for $1°$ hydrogen atoms alpha to the disulfide bond compared with $1°$ hydrogens beta to the disulfide link.

12-4 Using the data of Table 12-8, compare the reactivity (per hydrogen atom) of hydrogens alpha to an ether link, a disulfide link, a ketone carbonyl bond, and an ester carbonyl bond.

12-5 Using Fig. 12-4, discuss the structure of the transition state relative to the starting materials for chlorination and bromination of toluene. In which reaction is there more bond breaking at the transition state? Which would have the larger ρ in a Hammett equation correlation?

12-6 Predict the sign and approximate magnitude of ρ in a Hammett equation correlation of the reaction of benzoyloxy radicals (from benzoyl peroxide) with benzyl ethers at $90°C$.

$$X-\!\!\left\langle\!\!\!\bigcirc\!\!\!\right\rangle\!\!-CH_2-O-CH_2\phi$$

[R. L. Huang, H. H. Lee, and S. H. Ong, *J. Chem. Soc.*, 3336 (1962).]

12-7 The reaction of $\phi CH_2 D$ with methyl radicals from acetyl peroxide at $125\,^\circ C$ gives bibenzyl, methane, and CO_2. The value of k_H/k_D can be calculated from either the deuterium incorporated in the methane or the deuterium remaining in the bibenzyl. It is found that the former method gives $k_H/k_D = 9$ and the latter gives 7. Give a mechanism that explains this discrepancy if methyl radicals abstract ring hydrogens as well as benzylic hydrogens. If this is the correct explanation, which value is the true k_H/k_D? [S. H. Wilen and E. L. Eliel, *J. Am. Chem. Soc.*, **80**, 3309 (1958).]

12-8 In the discussion of molecule-induced homolysis in Chap. 9, it was claimed that complexing of halogen atoms can lead to a *faster* rate of dissociation of the halogen. In this chapter it has been stated that complexing of chlorine atoms increases their selectivity and, presumably, *decreases* their reactivity. Are these statements contradictory? Prove your point using energy-reaction coordinate diagrams.

SUGGESTIONS FOR FURTHER READING

Lewis, E. S., and M. C. R. Symons: *Quart. Rev. (London)*, **12**, 230 (1958).

Mayo, F. R., and C. Walling: *Chem. Rev.*, **46**, 191 (1950).

Szwarc, M.: The Transition State, *Chem. Soc. (London)*, *Spec. Publ.* 16, 1962, pp. 91–117.

Tedder, J. M.: *Quart. Rev. (London)*, **14**, 336 (1960).

Trotman-Dickenson, A. F.: "Free Radicals," Methuen & Co., Ltd., London, 1959, pp. 61–91.

chapter
thirteen Halogenation

We have already seen several examples of the radical chain processes by which the halogens oxidize organic materials:

$$X\bullet + RH \longrightarrow R\bullet + HX$$
$$R\bullet + X_2 \longrightarrow RX + X\bullet$$

In this chapter the details will be considered more fully. In addition to halogenation by the halogens themselves, certain halogen-carrying substances can be used. The most common are N-bromosuccinimide and the hypohalites. Use of these compounds sometimes leads to increased selectivity in halogenation reactions.

HALOGENATION BY FLUORINE

Fluorine reacts with organic molecules with considerable violence, and organic fluorides, therefore, usually are produced by indirect methods. However, fluorination can be studied in the gas phase by diluting the fluorine with nitrogen or other inert gases. The reactions are very fast and exothermic, and the usual products include all possible polyfluoro compounds as well as CF_4. Both steps in the chain sequence are extremely exothermic. For example, for methane, the heats of reaction are

	ΔH, kcal/mole
$F\bullet + CH_4 \longrightarrow HF + CH_3\bullet$	-32
$CH_3\bullet + F_2 \longrightarrow CH_3F + F\bullet$	-70

Fluorination occurs in the dark even at $-80°C$. The simple initiation step shown below seems unlikely because of its large, endothermic heat of reaction.

$$F_2 \longrightarrow 2F\bullet \qquad \Delta H = 37 \text{ kcal}$$

Therefore, bimolecular processes have been suggested for the initiation step. For example, the redox reaction between fluorine and methane

$$F_2 + CH_4 \longrightarrow HF + F\bullet + CH_3\bullet$$

should have a heat of reaction of 5 kcal/mole:

$$\Delta H = D(F\text{—}F) + D(CH_3\text{—}H) - D(H\text{—}F) = 37 + 102 - 134 = 5$$

180

The reaction of fluorine with olefins is predicted to be slightly exothermic. For example, the reaction with ethene can be calculated to have a heat of reaction of about -2 kcal/mole:

$$CH_2{=}CH_2 + F_2 \longrightarrow FCH_2{-}CH_2 + F\bullet \qquad \Delta H = -2 \text{ kcal/mole}$$

Radical-producing reactions such as these between fluorine and olefins or alkanes are examples of molecule-induced homolysis. (See pages 119 to 124.) Apparently fluorine is particularly susceptible to interactions that produce radicals, as indicated by facts such as these:

1. Small amounts of fluorine can act as initiators in the chlorination or the oxidation of olefins in the dark at temperatures as low as $0°C$.
2. The $Cl_2C{=}CCl_2$-fluorine system produces fluorine atoms even at $-78°C$, although unassisted homolysis is negligibly slow at this temperature.†

HALOGENATION BY CHLORINE

Radical chlorination is of enormous utility and has been the subject of literally hundreds of investigations. When mixtures of hydrocarbons and chlorine are heated to $200°C$ or are irradiated with light of wavelength less than 4875 A, a chain reaction occurs:

	ΔH, kcal/mole
$Cl_2 \longrightarrow 2Cl\bullet$	58
$Cl\bullet + CH_4 \longrightarrow HCl + CH_3\bullet$	-1
$CH_3\bullet + Cl_2 \longrightarrow CH_3Cl + Cl\bullet$	-23

From the bond strengths, $D(CH_3{-}Cl) = 81$, $D(CH_3{-}H) = 102$, $D(H{-}Cl) = 103$, and $D(Cl{-}Cl) = 58$, the heats of the reactions can be calculated as shown above. The chlorine atom is much less reactive than the fluorine, and only one of the steps in the chain is significantly exothermic. However, neither reaction has an appreciable activation energy, and chain lengths as large as 10^6 are observed.

The rates of the gas-phase chlorination reactions of simple alkanes have been extensively investigated.‡   If hydrogen and chlorine are

† W. T. Miller, S. D. Koch, and F. W. McLafferty, *J. Am. Chem. Soc.*, **78**, 4992 (1956).

‡ A. F. Trotman-Dickenson, "Gas Kinetics," Butterworth Scientific Publications, London, 1955, pp. 181–188; H. O. Pritchard, J. B. Pyke, and A. F. Trotman-Dickenson, *J. Am. Chem. Soc.*, **77**, 2629 (1955).

allowed to react, hydrogen chloride is produced by the radical chain shown below.

$$Cl\bullet + H_2 \xrightarrow{k_1} HCl + H\bullet \qquad\qquad (13\text{-}1)$$

$$H\bullet + Cl_2 \longrightarrow HCl + Cl\bullet$$

From a detailed analysis of this system, the rate constant for the reaction of chlorine atoms with hydrogen can be obtained, and k_1 is found to be $8 \times 10^{10} \, e^{-5,500/RT}$ liter mole^{-1} sec^{-1}. Then, by allowing chlorine to react with mixtures of hydrogen and methane, the relative rate constants for the reaction of chlorine atoms with these two substrates can be obtained.

$$Cl\bullet + H_2 \longrightarrow HCl + H\bullet$$

$$Cl\bullet + CH_4 \longrightarrow HCl + CH_3\bullet$$

Then, mixtures of methane and another organic compound can be investigated, and the relative rate constant for the next higher reaction can be calculated. In this way, the rate constant for the reaction of chlorine atoms with any compound can be related to that for the reaction with hydrogen. For example, if chlorine atoms are allowed to react with a mixture of two hydrocarbons, RH and SH, the ratio of the rate constants k_{RH}/k_{SH} is given as

$$Cl\bullet + RH \xrightarrow{k_{RH}} HCl + R\bullet$$

$$Cl\bullet + SH \xrightarrow{k_{SH}} HCl + S\bullet$$

$$-\frac{d(RH)}{dt} = k_{RH}(RH)(Cl\bullet)$$

$$-\frac{d(SH)}{dt} = k_{SH}(SH)(Cl\bullet)$$

$$\frac{k_{RH}}{k_{SH}} = \frac{d(RH)/(RH)}{d(SH)/(SH)} = \frac{\log\,[(RH)_0/(RH)]}{\log\,[(SH)_0/(SH)]}$$

In this manner, the relative rate constants for the two compounds can be obtained and eventually related back to the reaction of chlorine with hydrogen. Table 13-1 gives data so obtained. The comparison between hydrogen and methane is interesting; the reaction with methane requires almost 2 kcal/mole less activation energy but the pre-exponential A term favors the reaction with hydrogen. If the pre-exponential term A is asso-

Table 13-1 **Arrhenius parameters for the gas-phase chlorination of compounds†**

$$Cl\bullet + RH \xrightarrow{\ k\ } HCl + R\bullet$$
$$k = Ae^{-E_a/RT}$$

RH	Second substance used in competition experiment	log A	E_a, cal/mole
H_2	. . .	10.9	5500
CH_4	H_2	10.4	3900
C_2H_6	CH_4	11.1	1000
CH_3—CH_2—CH_3	C_2H_6	10.3	700
CH_3—$\underset{\underset{\textstyle CH_3}{\vert}}{\overset{\overset{\textstyle CH_3}{\vert}}{C}}$—H	C_2H_6	11.4	700
$(CH_3)_4C$	C_2H_6	11.3	900
CH_3Cl	CH_4	10.7	3400
C_2H_5Cl	C_2H_6	10.7	1500

† A. F. Trotman-Dickenson, "Gas Kinetics," Butterworth Scientific Publications, London, 1955, p. 188; "Free Radicals," Methuen & Co., Ltd., London, 1959, p. 65. Rates are in reciprocal seconds and concentrations in moles per liter.

ciated with the probability of the reaction, then the smaller A value for methane might be taken to mean that some change in geometry of the carbon atom occurs in the transition state and this decreases the probability of the reaction. Table 13-1 also shows the familiar phenomenon of tertiary hydrogens reacting faster than secondary, and primary hydrogens reacting most slowly of all.

A considerable amount is known about the nature of the products formed from chlorination of organic substances. In 1936, Hass, McBee, and Weber formulated the following rules:†

1. Carbon skeleton rearrangements do not occur during chlorination.
2. Every possible monochloride is formed.
3. Hydrogen atoms are substituted at rates in the order $3° > 2° > 1°$.
4. At increasing temperatures these relative rates approach $1:1:1$.
5. Liquid-phase chlorination gives higher rates than vapor phase at any given temperature.
6. Moisture, surfaces, and light have no effect on reactivity ratios.

† For a discussion see C. Walling, "Free Radicals in Solution," John Wiley & Sons, Inc., New York, 1957, p. 357.

Table 13-2   Selectivity of chlorinations in the gas phase†,‡

$$C—C—C—C$$
1   3.6   3.6   1

$$C—C—C—\overset{\overset{\displaystyle O}{\|}}{C}—Cl$$
1   3   0.2

$$C—C—C—CH_2Cl$$
1   3.7   2.1   0.8

$$C—C—C—CO_2CH_3$$
1   3   0

$$C—C—C—CH_2F$$
1   3.7   1.7   0.9

† These selectivities are per hydrogen atom and are normalized so that the terminal atoms in each molecule are given unit activity.

‡ J. M. Tedder, *Quart. Rev.* (*London*), **14**, 342 (1960); H. Singh and J. M. Tedder, *J. Chem. Soc.*, 4737 (1964); C. Walling, "Free Radicals in Solution," John Wiley & Sons, Inc., New York, 1957, p. 364.

Table 13-2 gives some relative reactivities† obtained from the analysis of the products of chlorination of various substrates in the gas phase. The data show that electronegative substituents slow the chlorination of nearby carbon atoms. For example, compare the first two lines in the table: a chlorine substituent does not alter the relative reactivity of the 3- and 4-carbons. However, the chlorine substituent greatly decreases the relative reactivity at the 1- and 2-carbons. This is the manifestation of a polar effect much like that discussed in the preceding chapter. There we saw that electron-withdrawing substituents in toluene slowed the rate of chlorination. In these aliphatic cases also, the electron-withdrawing chlorine substituent slows further chlorination.‡

Thus far we have considered gas-phase chlorinations; we now turn to the equally useful liquid-phase reactions. The interaction of chlorine with some olefinic solvents causes molecule-induced homolysis of the Cl—Cl bond. (See the discussion on pages 119 and 122.) For example, in cyclohexene at 25°C, chlorine rapidly reacts *in the absence of light and oxygen* to give products (I), (II), and (III).

† The relative reactivity is defined as the relative rate of reaction at any position in a molecule, corrected to a per-hydrogen basis. For example, chlorination of butanoyl chloride produces 30% of the 4-chloro, 65% of the 3-chloro, and 5% of the 2-chloro derivative. The selectivity at the 4-position to that at the 3-, to that at the 2-position, is 30/3:65/2:5/2, or 10:32:2.5. If the activity at the 4-position is taken as unity, this becomes 1:3.2:0.25, as shown at the top of the second column of Table 13-2.

‡ H. Singh and J. M. Tedder, *J. Chem. Soc.*, 4737 (1964).

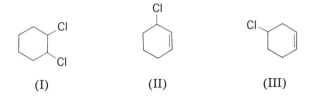

(I)   (II)   (III)

These three products are formed in the molar ratio of $2:1:0.6$ in pure cyclohexene as solvent. If the cyclohexene is diluted with a non-olefin solvent or if oxygen is present, the amount of product (III) drops to zero. The most likely explanation of these facts is that (I), (II), and (III) are produced by radical chlorination of cyclohexene, and (I) and (II) are produced in a concurrent, ionic process. The ionic reactions are shown below.

(I)   (II)

No ionic pathway to product (III) is known; this product must arise from a radical mechanism. Therefore, it appears that the interaction of cyclohexene and chlorine produces radicals *at a rapid rate at 25°C in the dark.* The presence of chlorine atoms is conclusively demonstrated by the fact that cyclohexane also becomes chlorinated if it is present; that is, mixtures of cyclohexene and cyclohexane lead to the formation of product (IV) in addition to (I), (II), and (III).

(IV)

Since cyclohexane would be expected to be inert to ionic chlorination processes, this is powerful evidence that chlorine atoms must be produced in an interaction between chlorine and cyclohexene, and these relatively unselective chlorine atoms then abstract hydrogen from both cyclohexane and cyclohexene. Several of the molecule-induced homolysis reactions discussed on page 120 involved kinetic orders in olefin that were larger than unity. It is, therefore, of interest that the radical-producing reaction in this system also has an order in cyclohexene which is larger than 1. This is indicated by the fact that dilution of cyclohexene with a non-olefin solvent gradually reduces the yields of the radical products and favors the formation of the ionic products (I) and (II). Therefore, the radical process involves a higher kinetic order in olefin than does the ionic process. Since ionic chlorination of cyclohexene is at least first order in olefin, the radical process must be more than first order. These reactions are outlined below.

An investigation of the effect of the structure of the olefin on the molecule-induced homolysis of chlorine has shown that different olefins vary in their effectiveness. In particular, isobutylene does not induce radical formation although the other butene isomers do.†

† M. L. Poutsma, *J. Am. Chem. Soc.*, **87**, 2161, 2172 (1965).

Table 13-3   Relative rate constants† for the liquid-phase chlorination of butylbenzene at 40°C‡

$$\overset{\alpha}{\phi - CH_2} - \overset{\beta}{CH_2} - \overset{\gamma}{CH_2} - \overset{\delta}{CH_3}$$

Butylbenzene, M	Solvent	k_α	k_β	k_γ	k_δ
6.3	None	13.9	7.3	9.2	1.0
1.0	Benzene	20	10	13	1.0
3.0	CCl$_4$	8.5	4.7	6.0	1.0
1.0	CCl$_4$	6.6	3.8	5.0	1.0
0¶	CCl$_4$	5.9	2.7	4.0	1.0

† Per hydrogen atom.
‡ G. A. Russell, A. Ito, and D. G. Hendry, *J. Am. Chem. Soc.*, **85**, 2976 (1963).
¶ Extrapolated to zero concentration of the substrate butylbenzene.

As was discussed in the previous chapter (page 157), liquid-phase chlorinations show a pronounced solvent effect, and the isomer distribution obtained in the chlorination of any substrate depends on the solvent used. When aralkyl hydrocarbons are chlorinated, the substrate itself can complex with the chlorine atom; therefore the *concentration of the substrate* as well as the nature of any solvent used can be expected to influence isomer distribution. Table 13-3 illustrates this in the chlorination of butylbenzene. Note that, as butylbenzene is diluted with carbon tetrachloride (a solvent that does not complex with chlorine atoms), the selectivity of the chlorination decreases. As expected, benzene as solvent leads to very high selectivities. By extrapolating the data obtained with carbon tetrachloride as solvent to infinite dilution, the reactivities shown in the last line of Table 13-3 are obtained. Note that the benzylic hydrogens are the most labile and that the β hydrogens have a *decreased* activity. This decrease in activity at the β position can be explained as due to the electron-withdrawing inductive effect of the phenyl group.

Table 13-4 combines liquid-phase data extrapolated to infinite dilution with gas-phase data. Relative rate constants per hydrogen atom are given for many hydrocarbons. (The liquid- and gas-phase results were combined by making the reasonable assumption that the rate of reaction of cyclopentane is the same in both phases.†) The data show that substitution of either a phenyl or an alkyl group activates hydrogens to similar extents. Thus, the series CH$_4$, ϕ—CH$_3$, ϕ_2CH$_2$, ϕ_3CH has the relative

† G. A. Russell, A. Ito, and D. G. Hendry, *J. Am. Chem. Soc.*, **85**, 2976 (1963).

Table 13-4 Reactivities of carbon-hydrogen bonds toward chlorine atoms at 40°C (liquid-phase reactivities have been extrapolated to infinite dilution)[†]

RH[‡]	Solvent	Relative reactivity (per hydrogen atom)
Methane	Vapor[¶]	0.0044
Ethane	Vapor	1.05
Propane (1°)	Vapor	1.25
(2°)	Vapor	4.42
Butane (1°)	Vapor	1.47
(2°)	Vapor	5.15
i-Butane (1°)	Vapor	1.29
(3°)	Vapor	6.25
2,3-Dimethylbutane (1°)	Reactants	1.0
(3°)	Reactants	3.9
Cyclohexane	Cyclohexane	2.7
Toluene	Cyclohexane	1.4
Ethylbenzene (α)	Cyclohexane	3.5
(β)	Cyclohexane	1.8
Isopropylbenzene (α)	Cyclohexane	7.8
(β)	Cyclohexane	2.2
t-Butylbenzene	CCl_4	0.63
Diphenylmethane	Cyclohexane	2.7
Triphenylmethane	Nitrobenzene	10
CH_3Cl	Vapor	0.066
CH_2Cl_2	Reactants	0.011
$CHCl_3$	Reactants	0.0051

[†] G. A. Russell, A. Ito, and D. G. Hendry, *J. Am. Chem. Soc.*, **85**, 2976 (1963).
[‡] 1°, 2°, and 3° refer to primary, secondary, and tertiary hydrogen atoms.
[¶] Vapor-phase data are those of H. O. Pritchard, J. B. Pyke, and A. F. Trotman-Dickenson, *J. Am. Chem. Soc.*, **77**, 2629 (1955), and J. H. Knox and R. L. Nelson, *Trans. Faraday Soc.*, **55**, 937 (1959).

reactivities 1:320:615:2,300, and the series CH_4, CH_3—CH_3, $(CH_3)_2CH_2$, $(CH_3)_3CH$ has the relative reactivities 1:240:1,000:1,400. This result agrees with the conclusion reached in the previous chapter that very little C—H bond breaking occurs at the transition state of chlorine-atom reactions and that the reaction is relatively insensitive to resonance stabilization by α phenyl groups.

HALOGENATION BY BROMINE

The bromine atom is considerably more stable than the chlorine atom, and the second step in the chain sequence for bromination is endothermic.

$$\begin{array}{lc} & \Delta H, \\ & \text{kcal/mole} \\ CH_3\cdot + Br_2 \longrightarrow CH_3-Br + Br\cdot & -21 \\ Br\cdot + CH_4 \longrightarrow CH_3\cdot + HBr & 15 \end{array}$$

Brominations, therefore, require elevated temperatures for any but the most activated C—H bonds.

Solvent effects are less important in bromine atom reactions than in those of chlorine atoms, and liquid-phase and vapor-phase results can be combined to give the data in Table 13-5. As has been noted before, bromine atoms are more selective than chlorine atoms. The total range of relative rates from methane to triphenylmethane is over 10^9 for bromination and only 10^3 for chlorination (see Table 13-4).

The data in Table 13-6 compare fluorine, chlorine, and bromine atoms in their selectivity toward the four types of hydrogens in 1-fluorobutane. Fluorine is very unselective, chlorine is intermediate, and bromine is quite selective.

Table 13-5 Relative reactivities of carbon-hydrogen bonds toward bromine atoms at 40°C†

RH	Phase	Relative rate (per hydrogen atom)
Methane	Vapor‡	0.0007
Ethane	Vapor	1.0
Propane (2°)	Vapor	220
i-Butane (3°)	Vapor	19×10^3
Toluene (α)	CCl$_4$	64×10^3
Ethylbenzene (α)	CCl$_4$	1×10^6
Isopropylbenzene (α)	CCl$_4$	2.3×10^6
Diphenylmethane (α)	CCl$_4$	0.6×10^6
Triphenylmethane (α)	CCl$_4$	1.1×10^6

† G. A. Russell and C. DeBoer, *J. Am. Chem. Soc.*, **85**, 3136 (1963).
‡ G. C. Fettis, J. H. Knox, and A. F. Trotman-Dickenson, *J. Chem. Soc.*, 4177 (1960).

Table 13-6   Relative selectivities of the halogens in reaction with 1-fluorobutane†

| | Relative selectivity | | | |
	CH_2F——CH_2——CH_2——CH_3			
F_2 at 20°C	<0.3	0.8	1.0	1
Cl_2 at 78°C	0.9	1.7	3.7	1
Br_2 at 146°C	10	9	88	1

† J. M. Tedder, *Quart. Rev.* (*London*), **14**, 343 (1960).

HALOGENATION BY IODINE

The iodine atom is very stable, and long chain lengths cannot be achieved in iodination. The heats of reaction for the two steps in the iodination of methane are

$$\Delta H,\ \text{kcal/mole}$$

$$I_2 + CH_3\bullet \longrightarrow CH_3I + I\bullet \qquad -18$$
$$I\bullet + CH_4 \longrightarrow HI + CH_3\bullet \qquad +33$$

Hydrogen abstraction by iodine atoms is appreciably endothermic, and iodine atoms do not react with alkanes at moderate temperatures. However, iodine atoms react with alkyl iodides to abstract iodide. The reaction involving optically active *sec*-butyl iodide was discussed on page 152. Table 13-7 gives the relative rates of abstraction of iodine atoms from a series of alkyl iodides by iodine atoms and by methyl radicals. The rate profiles are very similar. These data are most easily explained if the iodine atom attacks alkyl iodides on iodide. If the attack is on iodide,

$$I\bullet + RI \longrightarrow R\bullet + I_2$$

then isopropyl iodide would be expected to react *faster* than methyl iodide, since a secondary carbon-iodine bond is weaker than a primary. However, if the attack were on carbon in an S_H2 process

Table 13-7   Relative rates for reaction of I·
and CH_3· with alkyl iodides[†]

$$CH_3· + RI \longrightarrow CH_3I + R·$$
$$I· + RI \longrightarrow I—I + R·$$

R in	Relative rates	
RI	CH_3·	I·
CH_3	1	1
C_2H_5	4	1.7
i-C_3H_7	19	29
t-C_4H_9	37	
neo-C_5H_{11}	. . .	2.4

[†] J. E. Bujake, M. W. T. Pratt, and R. M. Noyes, *J. Am. Chem. Soc.*, **83**, 1547 (1961); F. W. Evans, R. J. Fox, and M. Szwarc, *ibid.*, **82**, 6414 (1960).

then isopropyl iodide should react *more slowly* than methyl iodide, since approach to its more hindered carbon atom would be slower.[†]   This conclusion agrees with the results discussed on page 152.

At high temperatures in the gas phase, iodine abstracts hydrogen atoms from hydrocarbons to produce dehydrogenated products.   For example, at 685°C ethane reacts with iodine to produce a 72% yield of ethylene and 10% of acetylene.   Propane, butane, and pentane give similar results.[‡]

Hexane gives small amounts of hexene and major amounts of benzene.[§]   In all these cases, the iodine is converted to hydrogen iodide:

$$R—CH_2—CH_3 + I_2 \longrightarrow R—CH=CH_2 + 2HI$$

These reactions are thought to be radical processes since they occur in the gas phase at high temperatures and because of their similarity to other radical halogenation processes.[¶]

[†] For further discussion, see S. W. Benson, *J. Chem. Phys.*, **38**, 1945 (1963); W. A. Pryor and T. L. Pickering, *J. Am. Chem. Soc.*, **84**, 2705 (1962).

[‡] J. H. Raley, R. D. Mullineaux, and C. W. Bittner, *J. Am. Chem. Soc.*, **85**, 3174 (1963).

[§] R. D. Mullineaux and J. H. Raley, *J. Am. Chem. Soc.*, **85**, 3178 (1963).

[¶] For a discussion of the mechanism, see S. W. Benson, *J. Chem. Phys.*, **38**, 1945 (1963).

HALOGENATION BY HYPOHALITES

Hypohalites frequently are used as halogenation agents. t-Butyl hypochlorite is an easily synthesized† liquid which reacts with hydrocarbons to yield alkyl chlorides. The chain mechanism for this reaction is

$$t\text{-BuO}\cdot + RH \longrightarrow t\text{-BuOH} + R\cdot$$
$$R\cdot + t\text{-BuOCl} \longrightarrow RCl + t\text{-BuO}\cdot$$

Relative reactivities of various hydrocarbons toward t-butyl hypochlorite have been measured; they parallel the reactivity of these compounds toward t-butyl peroxide, indicating that the species abstracting a hydrogen is the t-butoxy radical in both cases. (See the discussion of alkoxy radicals on pages 165 to 167.) In some compounds, t-butyl hypochlorite leads to different products than does molecular chlorine. For example, cyclopropane yields chlorocyclopropane with t-butyl hypochlorite:

However, chlorine leads to major amounts of 1,3-dichloropropane:‡

The lower of these two reactions is interesting in that it could be an example of an S_H2 reaction on a carbon atom.

---

† Care must be exercised. C. P. C. Bradshaw and A. Nechvatal, *Proc. Chem. Soc.*, 213 (1963), found that hypohalite preparations may explode if the temperature is allowed to exceed 20°C.

‡ C. Walling and P. S. Fredericks, *J. Am. Chem. Soc.*, **84**, 3326 (1962).

Hypohalite compounds provide a convenient route to alkoxy radicals and permit detailed study of their reactions. For example, alkoxy radicals can be generated as below:

$$ROH \xrightarrow{HOCl} ROCl \xrightarrow{Light} RO\bullet + Cl\bullet$$

Hypohalites from tertiary alcohols have been studied most thoroughly; they react by β-scission and by hydrogen abstraction.

In unsymmetrical alkoxy radicals, more than one alkyl group can be eliminated. Normally, the products formed in largest yield are those resulting from elimination of the most stable radical. (See page 12 for some typical data.) It has been found that alkyl groups are eliminated as the free radical from alkoxy radicals in the order t-butyl > isopropyl > benzyl $\simeq$ ethyl > chloromethyl > methyl.† One unexpected anomaly is observed in studies of this type: Olefins as solvents lead to a very pronounced increase in k_d relative to k_a. Thus, in the absence of olefins, the hypohalite below reacts both by abstracting a hydrogen atom from cyclohexane and by eliminating the benzyl radical.

---

† C. Walling and A. Padwa, *J. Am. Chem. Soc.*, **85**, 1593 (1963).

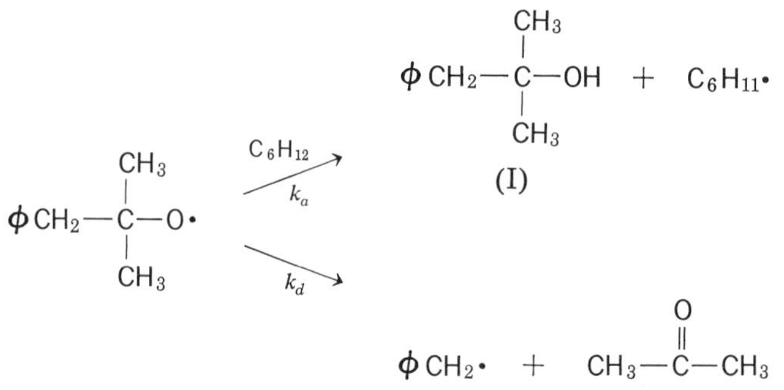

$$\phi CH_2-\underset{\underset{CH_3}{|}}{\overset{\overset{CH_3}{|}}{C}}-O\cdot \quad \overset{C_6H_{12}}{\underset{k_a}{\nearrow}} \quad \phi CH_2-\underset{\underset{CH_3}{|}}{\overset{\overset{CH_3}{|}}{C}}-OH \;+\; C_6H_{11}\cdot \qquad (I)$$

$$\underset{k_d}{\searrow} \quad \phi CH_2\cdot \;+\; CH_3-\overset{\overset{O}{\|}}{C}-CH_3$$

In one case, cyclohexyl chloride is the product, and, in the other, benzyl chloride is produced:

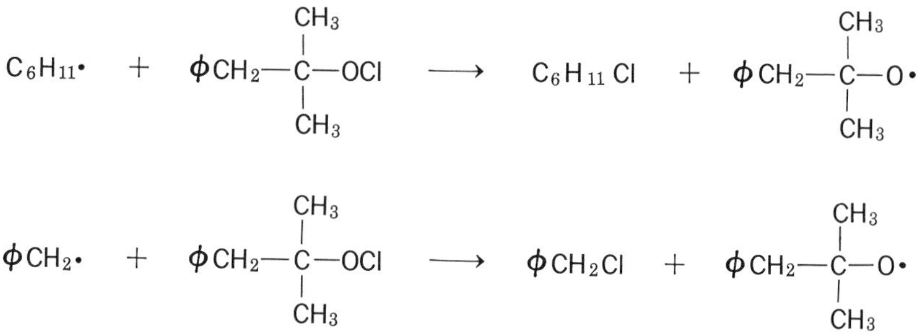

$$C_6H_{11}\cdot \;+\; \phi CH_2-\underset{\underset{CH_3}{|}}{\overset{\overset{CH_3}{|}}{C}}-OCl \;\longrightarrow\; C_6H_{11}\,Cl \;+\; \phi CH_2-\underset{\underset{CH_3}{|}}{\overset{\overset{CH_3}{|}}{C}}-O\cdot$$

$$\phi CH_2\cdot \;+\; \phi CH_2-\underset{\underset{CH_3}{|}}{\overset{\overset{CH_3}{|}}{C}}-OCl \;\longrightarrow\; \phi CH_2 Cl \;+\; \phi CH_2-\underset{\underset{CH_3}{|}}{\overset{\overset{CH_3}{|}}{C}}-O\cdot$$

In pure cyclohexane as solvent, $k_d/k_a = 2$, indicating that the alkoxy radical shown above cleaves twice as fast as it abstracts hydrogen from cyclohexane. In cyclohexene, on the other hand, the only reaction that can be observed is decomposition, *and benzyl chloride and acetone are the only products.* No alcohol (I) is found. This seems surprising since cyclohexene, with allylic hydrogens, might have been expected to be a better hydrogen donor than cyclohexane. Even more unexpected is the finding that the addition of as little as 4% of cyclohexene to cyclohexane leads to a complete change in the reaction with cyclohexane; then only decomposition products are obtained, and both the cyclohexane and the cyclohexene are recovered unchanged. This is another example of the great effect of olefinic substances on the rate of some radical reactions.† (See, for example, pages 119 to 124.)

---

† The solvent dependence of alkoxy radical reactions is discussed by C. Walling and P. J. Wagner, *J. Am. Chem. Soc.*, **86**, 3368 (1964).

HALOGENATION BY *N*-BROMOSUCCINIMIDE

N-bromosuccinimide (NBS) brominates organic compounds in a reaction that can be initiated by benzoyl peroxide or other typical radical sources and by light. The reaction was recognized to be a radical chain process in 1944 and has been studied extensively as a useful synthetic tool.† The special feature of NBS that makes it particularly useful is its extreme selectivity; allylic and benzylic bromination can be effected in excellent yield. The examples below illustrate this.

50–80%

$$CH_2{=}CH{-}CH_3 \longrightarrow CH_2{=}CH{-}CH_2Br$$

29%

$$\phi CH{=}CH{-}CH_3 \longrightarrow \phi CH{=}CH{-}CH_2Br$$

75%

$$\phi CH_3 \longrightarrow \phi CH_2Br$$

At first it was thought that these reactions involved the succinimidyl radical as a halogen carrier, much as the *t*-butoxy radical is involved in the reactions of *t*-butyl hypochlorite. However, recent studies have shown this to be incorrect. These studies have mainly involved benzylic brominations of substituted toluenes, but the evidence indicates that probably all brominations by NBS involve the mechanism shown below.

$$Br\cdot \; + \; RH \longrightarrow HBr \; + \; R\cdot$$

$$R\cdot \; + \; Br_2 \longrightarrow R{-}Br \; + \; Br\cdot$$

† For reviews, see C. Djerassi, *Chem. Rev.*, **43**, 271 (1948); C. Walling, "Free Radicals in Solution," John Wiley & Sons, Inc., New York, 1957, pp. 381–386.

In this mechanism, low concentrations of bromine function as the active bromination agent; NBS merely acts as a bromine reservoir. This mechanism was first proposed in 1953 by Goldfinger to explain chlorinations by *N*-chlorosuccinimide, and its applicability to brominations by NBS now has been amply confirmed.† In terms of this scheme, allylic bromination by molecular bromine occurs in preference to addition to the double bond. This competition is illustrated below for the case of cyclohexene.

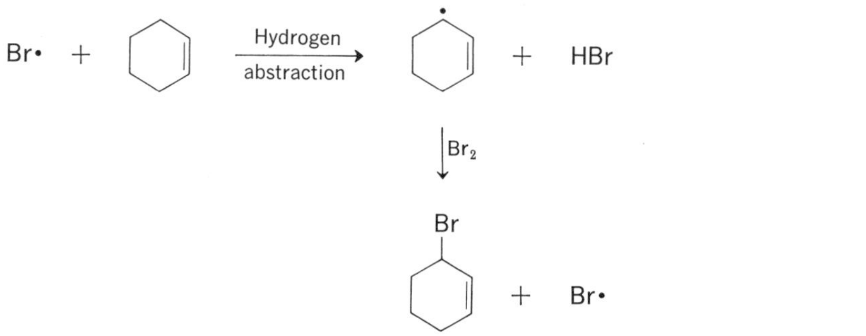

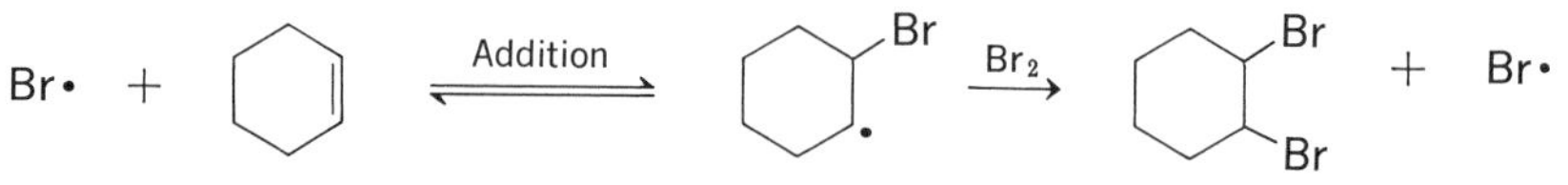

Since the addition of bromine atoms to the double bond is reversible, a low bromine concentration favors the hydrogen abstraction step. This explanation is supported by the fact that bromination by slow photolysis of molecular bromine also favors allylic bromination.‡ Actually, the hydrogen abstraction step shown in the above scheme is also reversible:

Br• + RH ⇌ R• + HBr

However, NBS reacts with hydrogen bromide and keeps its concentration low and minimizes reversal of the above reaction. Thus NBS is a convenient reagent for maintaining a low concentration of bromine at the expense of hydrogen bromide.

† B. P. McGrath and J. M. Tedder, *Proc. Chem. Soc.*, 1511 (1961); R. E. Pearson and J. C. Martin, *J. Am. Chem. Soc.*, **85**, 354, 3142 (1963); G. A. Russell, C. DeBoer, and K. M. Desmond, *ibid.*, **85**, 365 (1963); C. Walling, A. L. Rieger, and D. D. Tanner, *ibid.*, **85**, 3129 (1963); G. A. Russell and K. M. Desmond, *ibid.*, **85**, 3139 (1963).
‡ B. P. McGrath and J. M. Tedder, *Proc. Chem. Soc.*, 1511 (1961).

Table 13-8 Relative reactivities of hydrocarbons toward three halogenating reagents†

Hydrocarbon	Chlorine (40°)	t-Butyl hypochlorite (40°)	NBS (80°)
Cyclohexene	. . .	36	129
Toluene	(1)	(1)	(1)
Ethylbenzene	. . .	3.2	24
Isopropylbenzene	4.0	6.8	50
Cyclohexane	2.3	1.5	0.003
2,3-Dimethylbutane	3.4	4.2	0.1

† C. Walling, A. L. Rieger, and D. D. Tanner, *J. Am. Chem. Soc.*, **85**, 3129 (1963).

In the competitive bromination of substituted toluenes, it is found that molecular bromine and NBS show identical relative reactivities.† Both molecular bromine and NBS react with substituted toluenes at rates that obey the Hammett equation, using σ^+ rather than the usual σ values (see pages 95, 172), and the ρ for both reactions is -1.39.‡ This coincidence makes it very probable that the active species is molecular bromine in both reactions.

Table 13-8 illustrates the greater selectivity of NBS as compared with chlorine or *t*-butyl hypochlorite as a halogenation agent. The ratio of rates of cyclohexene and cyclohexane is 4×10^4 for NBS and only 24 for *t*-butyl hypochlorite. These data indicate that NBS is the preferred reagent for selective halogenation of complex molecules.

PROBLEMS

13-1 Using the dissociation energies given on page 180, calculate the heat of reaction for

$$F \cdot + CH_4 \longrightarrow HF + CH_3 \cdot$$

† In fact, *N*-bromotetrafluorosuccinimide, *N*-bromotetramethylsuccinimide, NBS, and bromine all have identical reactivities [R. E. Pearson and J. C. Martin, *J. Am. Chem. Soc.*, **85**, 354, 3142 (1963)]; and *N*-bromoacetamide and various *N*-bromohydantoins have very similar reactivities [C. Walling and A. L. Rieger, *J. Am. Chem. Soc.*, **85**, 3134 (1963)].

‡ R. E. Pearson and J. C. Martin, *J. Am. Chem. Soc.*, **85**, 354, 3142 (1963).

13-2 Derive an expression for the ratio of the rate constants for the reaction of chlorine atoms with hydrogen molecules and with methane. Your equation should involve only the concentrations of nonradical species.

13-3 Give an explanation for the fact that the activation energy for the reaction of chlorine atoms with RH decreases in the order $CH_4 > CH_3Cl > C_2H_5Cl > C_2H_6$.

13-4 Explain why the ratio of rate constants for the halogenation of triphenyl-methane to methane is 10^9 for bromination and only 10^3 for chlorination. What would this ratio be for fluorination?

13-5 Predict the relative amounts of ketones that would be found from the decomposition of the following hypohalites. [See page 12 for an example; F. D. Greene et al., *J. Org. Chem.*, **28**, 55 (1963).]

a.
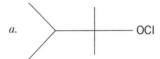

b.
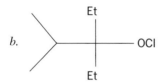

13-6 As discussed on page 194, the decomposition of $\phi CH_2C(CH_3)_2OCl$ in cyclohexane gives both benzyl chloride and cyclohexyl chloride. However, in cyclo-hexene, benzyl chloride is the only halide produced. What is the mechanism for the reaction in cyclohexane? Is cyclohexene normally a better hydrogen donor than cyclohexane? Cite data to illustrate your statement. Explain the results in cyclo-hexene.

13-7 The top line in Table 13-3 gives the relative rate constants for the chlorination of the four aliphatic carbon atoms of butylbenzene in the absence of a solvent; the bottom line gives these rate constants extrapolated to zero concentration of butyl-benzene in carbon tetrachloride. Explain the differences in these data.

13-8 Electron-withdrawing groups do not have the same effect on chlorination and bromination. Although chlorination is retarded more strongly at the α than at the β position, bromination may show the reverse reactivity pattern. For example, consider these data on gas-phase chlorinations and brominations [H. Singh and J. M. Tedder, *J. Chem. Soc.*, 4737 (1964)]:

Chlorination, 75°C			
C——C——C——C			
1	3.6	3.6	1
C——C——C——CH$_2$F			
1	3.7	1.7	0.9
C——C——C——CH$_2$Cl			
1	3.7	2.1	0.8
C——C——C——C——CF$_3$			
1	4.3	1.2	0.04
C——C——C——C——COCl			
1	3.9	2.1	0.2
C——C——C——C——CO$_2$Me			
1	3.6	2.4	0.4

Bromination, 160°C			
C——C——C——C			
1	80	80	1
C——C——C——CH$_2$F			
1	90	7	9
C——C——C——CH$_2$Cl			
1	80	32	34
C——C——C——C——CF$_3$			
1	90	7	1
C——C——C——C——COCl			
1	77	32	29
C——C——C——C——CO$_2$Me			
1	77	35	41

[The numbers are relative reactivities per hydrogen atom.]   Give an explanation for the trends observed.

13-9   For each of the three reactions below, calculate the heat of reaction when the halogen X_2 is fluorine, chlorine, bromine, or iodine.

$$\text{>C=C<} + X_2 \longrightarrow X-\overset{|}{C}-\overset{\bullet}{\underset{|}{C}}- + X\bullet$$

$$2\ \text{>C=C<} + X_2 \longrightarrow 2X-\overset{|}{C}-\overset{\bullet}{\underset{|}{C}}-$$

$$RH + X_2 \longrightarrow R\bullet + HX + X\bullet$$

In the light of your calculated values, comment on the reasonableness of each of the reactions as a possible source of radicals at 0°C for each of the four halogens.   Comment also on the kinetic consequences of your calculations and any differences between the halogens.   [W. T. Miller and A. L. Dittman, *J. Am. Chem. Soc.*, **78**, 2793 (1956); M. L. Poutsma, *ibid.*, **87**, 2161 (1965).]

SUGGESTIONS FOR FURTHER READING

Bratolyubov, A. S.: *Russ. Chem. Rev.* (*English Transl.*), **30**, 602 (1961).   (Chlorination of alkanes.)

Chiltz, G., P. Goldfinger, G. Huybrechts, G. Martens, and G. Verbeke: *Chem. Rev.*, **63**, 355 (1963).   (Kinetics of chlorination in the gas phase.)

Tedder, J. M.: *Quart. Rev.* (*London*), **14**, 336 (1960).   (Transfer reactions in general.)

Walling, C.: "Free Radicals in Solution," John Wiley & Sons, Inc., New York, 1957, chap. 8.

chapter
fourteen Addition
Reactions

Many types of species add to the carbon-carbon double bond in radical chain processes:

$$AB \quad + \quad {>}C{=}C{<} \quad \xrightarrow[\text{photolysis}]{\text{Initiators or}} \quad -\overset{|}{\underset{A}{C}}-\overset{|}{\underset{B}{C}}-$$

The mechanisms of these processes involve the reactions shown below.

$$B\cdot \quad + \quad {>}C{=}C{<} \quad \longrightarrow \quad B-\overset{|}{\underset{|}{C}}-\overset{|}{\underset{|}{C}}\cdot \qquad (14\text{-}1)$$

$$B-\overset{|}{\underset{|}{C}}-\overset{|}{\underset{|}{C}}\cdot \quad + \quad AB \quad \longrightarrow \quad B-\overset{|}{\underset{|}{C}}-\overset{|}{\underset{|}{C}}-A \quad + \quad B\cdot \qquad (14\text{-}2)$$

$$B-\overset{|}{\underset{|}{C}}-\overset{|}{\underset{|}{C}}\cdot \quad + \quad {>}C{=}C{<} \quad \longrightarrow \quad B-\overset{|}{\underset{|}{C}}-\overset{|}{\underset{|}{C}}-\overset{|}{\underset{|}{C}}-\overset{|}{\underset{|}{C}}\cdot \qquad (14\text{-}3)$$

$$B-(\overset{|}{\underset{|}{C}}-\overset{|}{\underset{|}{C}})_n\cdot \quad + \quad {>}C{=}C{<} \quad \longrightarrow \quad B-(\overset{|}{\underset{|}{C}}-\overset{|}{\underset{|}{C}})_n-\overset{|}{\underset{|}{C}}-\overset{|}{\underset{|}{C}}\cdot \qquad (14\text{-}4)$$

$$B-(\overset{|}{\underset{|}{C}}-\overset{|}{\underset{|}{C}})_n-\overset{|}{\underset{|}{C}}-\overset{|}{\underset{|}{C}}\cdot \quad + \quad AB \quad \longrightarrow \quad B-(\overset{|}{\underset{|}{C}}-\overset{|}{\underset{|}{C}})_n-\overset{|}{\underset{|}{C}}-\overset{|}{\underset{|}{C}}-A \quad + \quad B\cdot$$

$$(14\text{-}5)$$

Radicals are generated in any of the usual ways, and the radical B· can then add to an olefin in reaction (14-1). A number of possibilities then exist for further reaction.

1. The simplest possibility is for (14-1) to be very rapidly reversed. If this reversal is rapid, no addition product is formed, but the addition and elimination of B can produce chemical transformations. For example, *cis* olefins can be isomerized to *trans:* The addition of B

$$B\cdot \quad + \quad \underset{H}{\overset{R}{>}}C{=}C\underset{H}{\overset{R}{<}} \quad \longrightarrow \quad B-\overset{R}{\underset{H}{C}}-\overset{\cdot}{\underset{H}{C}}\overset{R}{<}$$

produces an intermediate radical which rapidly undergoes rotation about its carbon-carbon single bond.

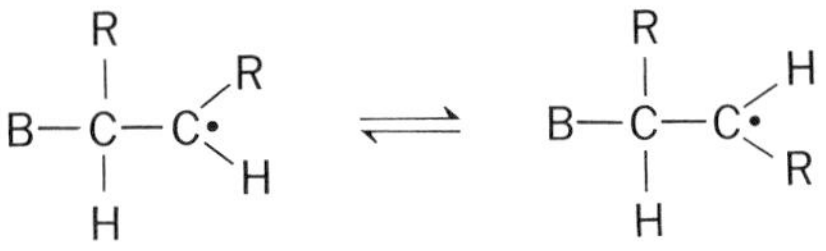

Both conformations of the radical then eliminate B, one producing *cis* and one *trans* olefin.

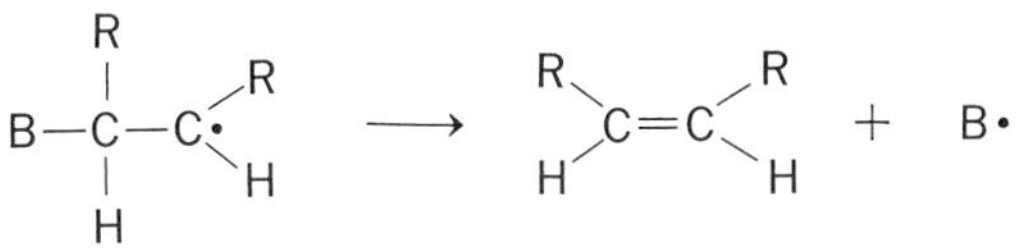

Cis

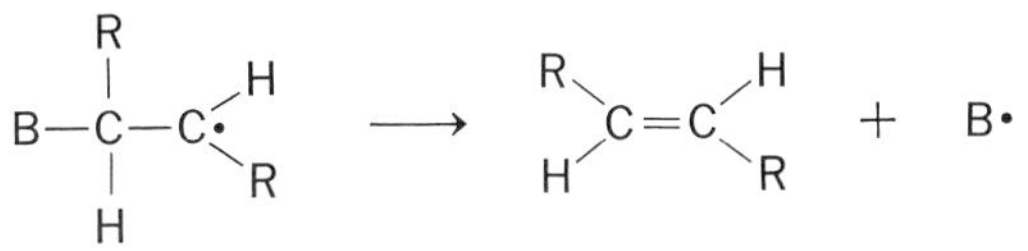

Trans

One example of this process is the isomerization of *cis* to *trans* stilbene by bromine and light.†

2. If AB is a good transfer agent, the transfer reaction (14-2) will have a large rate constant. In this case, excellent yields of the one-to-one adduct can be formed.

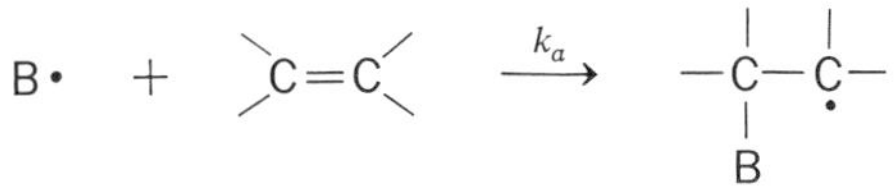

(14-1)

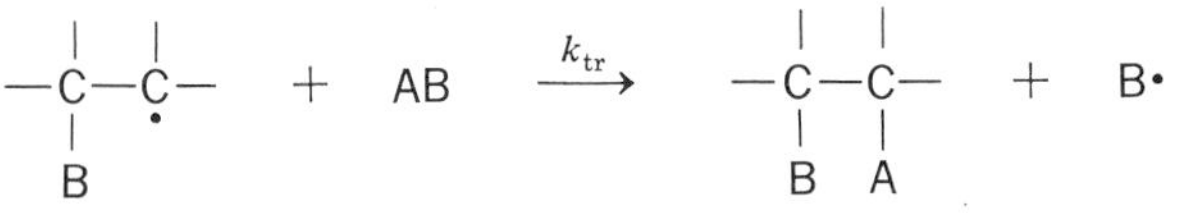

(14-2)

As shown above, this is a chain process. If AB is a good transfer agent, the chain length may be very large; i.e., thousands of moles of adduct may be

† For further examples, see C. Walling, "Free Radicals in Solution," John Wiley & Sons, Inc., New York, 1957, pp. 302–308.

produced for each mole of B• generated in the initiation step. High yields of adduct require that a sufficient concentration of AB be present so that reaction (14-2) will occur rapidly. However, if AB is a good transfer agent, k_{tr} and k_a will both be large, and even moderate AB/olefin ratios will assure good yields. An example of this process is the peroxide or light-initiated addition of hydrogen bromide to 1-butene to produce 1-bromo-butane in 95 to 100% yield.

3. If AB is only a moderately active transfer agent and if the olefin undergoes radical polymerization, then reactions (14-3) and (14-4) will have larger rate constants than (14-2). In this case, polymerization to form a low-molecular-weight polymer occurs, as is shown below:

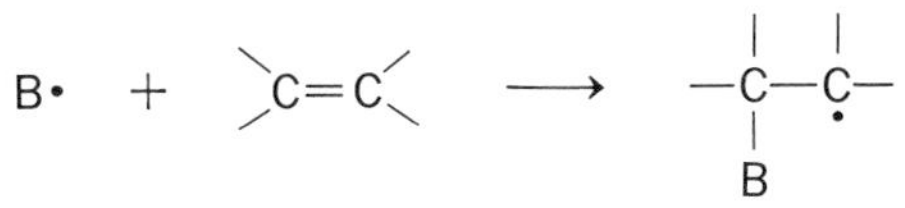

$$B\cdot \ + \ \underset{\diagdown}{\overset{\diagup}{C}}=\underset{\diagup}{\overset{\diagdown}{C}} \quad \longrightarrow \quad -\underset{\underset{B}{|}}{\overset{|}{C}}-\overset{|}{\underset{\cdot}{C}}- \tag{14-1}$$

$$-\underset{\underset{B}{|}}{\overset{|}{C}}-\overset{|}{\underset{\cdot}{C}}- \ + \ n\underset{\diagdown}{\overset{\diagup}{C}}=\underset{\diagup}{\overset{\diagdown}{C}} \quad \longrightarrow \quad -\underset{\underset{B}{|}}{\overset{|}{C}}-\overset{|}{C}-(\overset{|}{C}-\overset{|}{C}-)_n\cdot \tag{14-4}$$

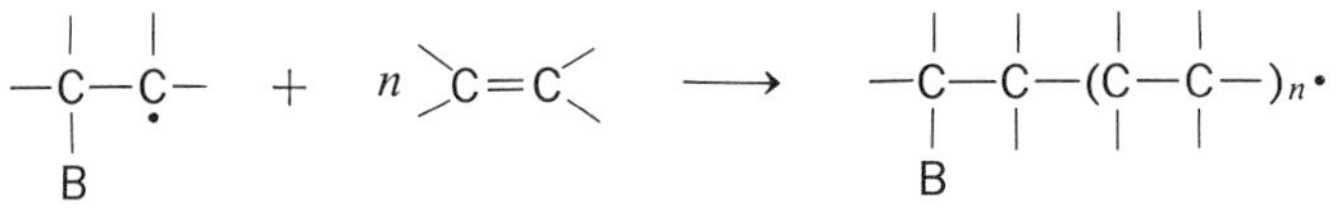

$$(\text{I})$$

$$(\text{I}) \ + \ \text{AB} \quad \longrightarrow \quad -\underset{\underset{B}{|}}{\overset{|}{C}}-\overset{|}{C}-(\overset{|}{C}-\overset{|}{C})_n-\text{A} \ + \ \text{B}\cdot$$

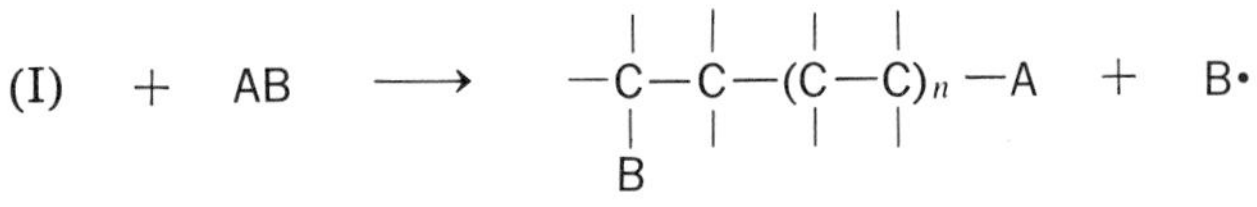

$$(\text{II})$$

$$\tag{14-5}$$

Low-molecular-weight polymers such as (II) are called telomers. Note that (II) has part of the telomerization agent AB on each end. These telomers frequently are undesirable by-products, but in some cases they are useful synthetic products. For example, ethylene reacts with carbon tetrachloride as shown below.†

$$CH_2{=}CH_2 + CCl_4 \xrightarrow[90°C]{\text{AIBN}} Cl_3C{-}(CH_2{-}CH_2)_n{-}Cl$$

† A. N. Nesmeyanov, R. Kh. Freidlina, and L. I. Zakharkin, *Quart. Rev.* (*London*), **10**, 360 (1956).

When a 20 to 1 mole ratio of ethylene to CCl_4 is used, products are formed which can be separated into the fractions shown below.

9%; $n = 2$ 44%; $n_{av} = 19$

12%; $n = 3$ 11%; $n_{av} = 40$

24%; $n = 4 - 7$

Some of these fractions have commercial use; for example, hydrolysis of a middle fraction gives carboxylic acids useful in soap manufacture.

4. If AB is a poor transfer agent and if excess olefin is used, reactions (14-1) to (14-5) occur in a process that can be abbreviated as shown below. (M is a polymerizable olefin, i.e., a monomer.)

$$B\bullet + M \xrightarrow{k_a} B\text{—}M\bullet \qquad (14\text{-}1)$$

$$B\text{—}M_n\bullet + M \xrightarrow{k_p} B\text{—}M^\bullet_{n+1} \qquad (14\text{-}4)$$

$$B\text{—}M_n\bullet + AB \xrightarrow{k_{tr}} B\text{—}M_n\text{—}A + B\bullet \qquad (14\text{-}5)$$

In this case, the rate constant for the addition reaction (14-4) is equal to k_p, the propagation rate constant for the polymerization of the monomer. The transfer constant C is defined as

$$C = \frac{k_{tr}}{k_p}$$

If C is about 0.1 or smaller and if AB is not present in great excess, polymerization of M occurs and AB acts merely as a solvent. The value of n in A—M_n—B is called the degree of polymerization, and n may be 10^3 or larger. In these cases, one molecule of AB is incorporated into each large polymeric molecule. An example of this process is the polymerization of styrene in carbon tetrachloride as a solvent.† The transfer constant for carbon tetrachloride toward styrene is 0.01. Polymerization of styrene in an equimolar mixture with carbon tetrachloride produces a polymer with an average degree of polymerization of 70 (as determined from the chlorine content of the polymer).

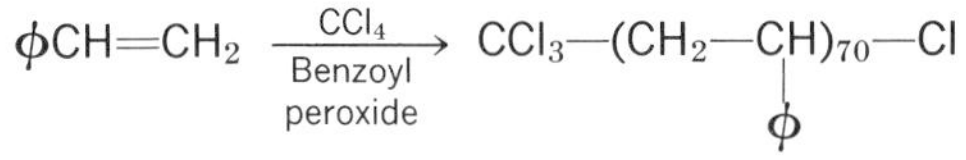

$$\phi CH\text{=}CH_2 \xrightarrow[\text{Benzoyl peroxide}]{CCl_4} CCl_3\text{—}(CH_2\text{—}\underset{\phi}{\overset{|}{CH}})_{70}\text{—}Cl$$

If higher styrene/carbon tetrachloride ratios are used, the degree of polymerization approaches 10,000.

† F. R. Mayo, *J. Am. Chem. Soc.*, **70**, 3689 (1948).

In summary, we have seen that good transfer agents (e.g., hydrogen bromide, bromine, and hydrogen sulfide) can be added to olefins to produce excellent yields of the one-to-one adduct. Poorer transfer agents (e.g., carbon tetrachloride) can be added to produce telomers. The use of poor transfer agents or of an excess of a polymerizable olefin leads to the formation of a polymeric molecule incorporating a molecule of the transfer agent.

In this chapter, we shall discuss additions to produce one-to-one adducts and telomers. We shall take up the transfer reactions of polymeric radicals in Chap. 15.

ADDITION OF THE HYDROGEN HALIDES AND THE HALOGENS

Hydrogen bromide is an extremely reactive hydrogen donor which adds to olefins to give excellent yields of the one-to-one adduct. The addition of hydrogen bromide to olefins has historical interest since it is one of the first reactions shown to occur by either an ionic or a radical mechanism.[†]

During the 1920s, various workers studied the addition of hydrogen bromide to allyl bromide; some reported that the product was predominantly 1,2-dibromopropane, and some reported 1,3-dibromopropane. Since the 1,2-dibromo compound would be predicted by Markovnikov's rule, occurrence of the 1,3-compound was regarded as anomalous. This reaction was studied with great thoroughness by Kharasch and his students, and in 1937 Kharasch in America and Hey and Waters in England independently proposed a radical chain mechanism for the non-Markovnikov addition of hydrogen bromide to olefins.[‡] Careful study by the Kharasch group showed that the facts were these: In the dark and in the absence of all radical-producing materials, hydrogen bromide slowly adds to allyl bromide by an ionic mechanism to form the expected Markovnikov product, the 1,2-dibromide. In the presence of air, light, or any peroxidic materials, a much faster radical addition occurs to produce the 1,3-dibromide.

† A fascinating account of the experimental work that led to the understanding of the radical addition of hydrogen bromide is given by Frank R. Mayo in W. A. Waters (ed.), "Vistas in Free Radical Chemistry," Pergamon Press, New York, 1959, pp. 139–142. Much of the history of the early research on radical reactions is described in this book.

‡ M. S. Kharasch, H. Engelmann, and F. R. Mayo, *J. Org. Chem.*, **2**, 288 (1937); F. R. Mayo and C. Walling, *Chem. Rev.*, **27**, 351 (1940); D. H. Hey and W. A. Waters, *ibid.*, **21**, 169 (1937).

$$CH_3-\underset{\underset{Br}{|}}{CH}-CH_2Br$$

Ionic product

Dark
Slow

$$CH_2=CH-CH_2Br$$

Light or air or peroxides
Fast

$$CH_2-CH_2-CH_2Br$$
$$\underset{Br}{|}$$

Radical product

Kharasch and his coworkers subsequently showed that terminal olefins usually give non-Markovnikov products from radical addition reactions.

These radical addition processes were originally called "abnormal" addition or the peroxide effect or sometimes Kharasch additions. It is more appropriate, however, simply to refer to one addition process as radical and one as ionic.

The stabilities of radicals and carbonium ions increase in the same order, namely, $1° < 2° < 3°$. It is clear from the schematic equations below that this fact is responsible for the formation of different products in the two mechanisms. In the ionic case, the proton adds first and forms the more stable secondary carbonium ion; in the radical case, a bromine atom adds first to produce the more stable secondary radical.

Ionic addition

$$RCH=CH_2 + H^+ \longrightarrow R\overset{+}{C}H-CH_3 \xrightarrow{Br^-} R-\underset{\underset{Br}{|}}{CH}-CH_3$$

Radical addition

$$RCH=CH_2 + Br\bullet \longrightarrow R\overset{\bullet}{C}H-CH_2Br \xrightarrow{HBr} R-CH_2-CH_2Br + Br\bullet$$

The stereochemistry of the radical addition of hydrogen bromide has been investigated, and a preference for *trans* addition is usually found. For example, deuterium bromide adds to the two isomeric 2-butenes at -60 to $-78°C$ with complete stereospecificity; *cis*-2-butene gives *threo*-3-deutero-2-bromobutane, and the *trans* olefin gives the *erythro* product:[†]

† P. S. Skell and R. G. Allen, *J. Am. Chem. Soc.*, **81**, 5383 (1959).

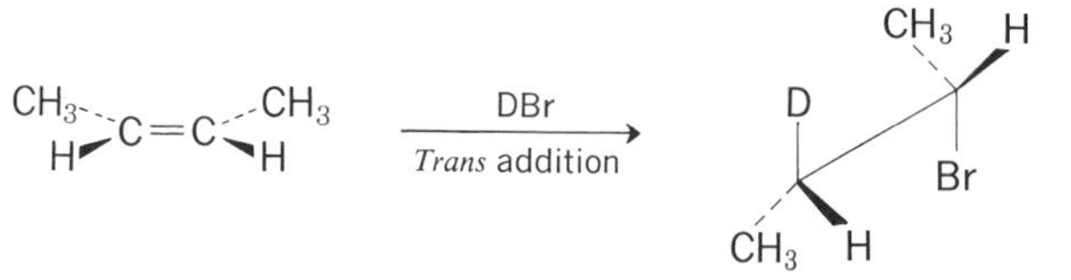

Cis   Threo

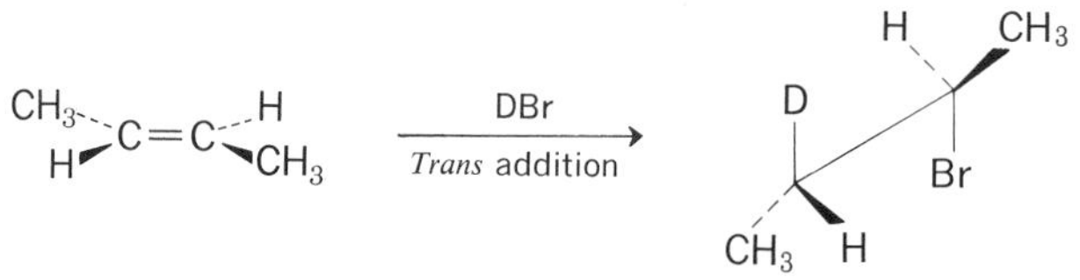

Trans   Erythro

In the 2-bromo-2-butene system, hydrogen bromide additions can occur to give either stereospecific or nonstereospecific products.† Under the conditions shown below, with low temperatures and a large excess of hydrogen bromide, stereospecific products are formed.

Cis   Meso

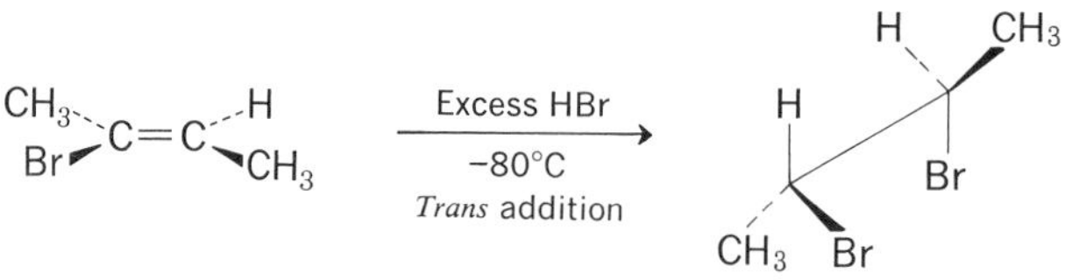

Trans   dl

At higher temperatures and at lower ratios of hydrogen bromide to olefin, the stereochemical preference for *trans* addition decreases, until at 25°C the same mixture of products is obtained from either olefin. This suggests that the mechanism involves two different conformations of the inter-

† H. L. Goering and D. W. Larsen, *J. Am. Chem. Soc.*, **81**, 5937 (1959).

mediate radical, which equilibrate *before* transfer occurs if the concentration of hydrogen bromide is sufficiently low.

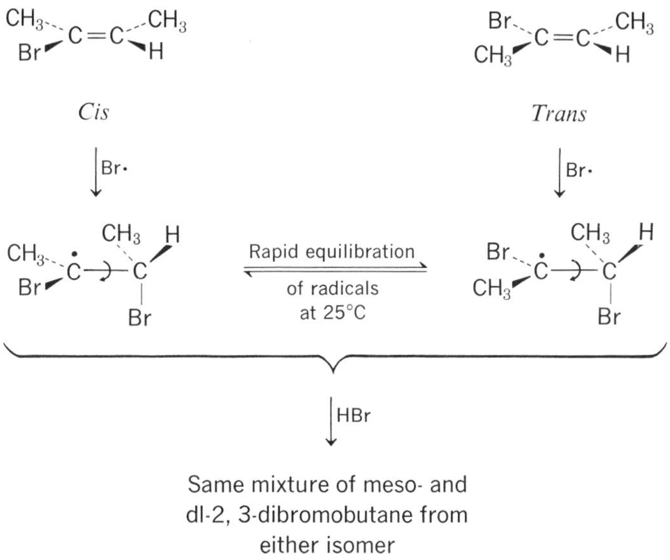

$$CH_3 \diagdown C = C \diagup CH_3 \atop Br \diagup \qquad \diagdown H$$

Cis

$$Br \diagdown C = C \diagup CH_3 \atop CH_3 \diagup \qquad \diagdown H$$

Trans

↓ Br·

↓ Br·

CH₃ H
$CH_3 \diagdown \overset{\bullet}{C} \to C \diagup$
Br⁄ $\quad$ ⟍
$\qquad$ Br

Rapid equilibration
of radicals
at 25°C

CH₃ H
$Br \diagdown \overset{\bullet}{C} \to C \diagup$
CH₃⁄ $\quad$ ⟍
$\qquad$ Br

↓ HBr

Same mixture of meso- and
dl-2, 3-dibromobutane from
either isomer

At higher hydrogen bromide concentrations, the two intermediate radicals are trapped, and different final products are obtained from the two olefins.

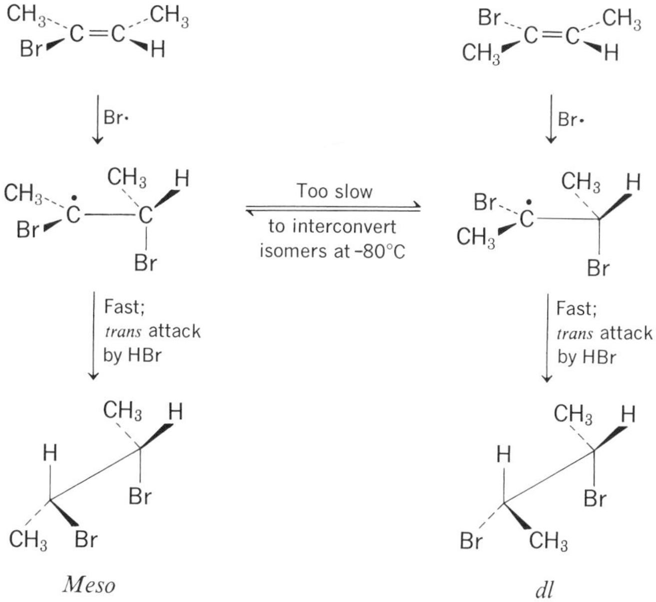

$$CH_3 \diagdown C = C \diagup CH_3 \atop Br \diagup \qquad \diagdown H$$

$$Br \diagdown C = C \diagup CH_3 \atop CH_3 \diagup \qquad \diagdown H$$

↓ Br·

↓ Br·

CH₃ H
$CH_3 \diagdown \overset{\bullet}{C} - C$
Br⁄
$\qquad$ Br

Too slow
to interconvert
isomers at –80°C

CH₃ H
$Br \diagdown \overset{\bullet}{C}$
CH₃⁄
$\qquad$ Br

Fast;
trans attack
by HBr

Fast;
trans attack
by HBr

CH₃ H
H
$\qquad$ Br
CH₃ Br

Meso

CH₃ H
H
$\qquad$ Br
Br CH₃

dl

Notice that *trans* addition is explained by assuming that the intermediate radicals abstract hydrogen from HBr from the side opposite to the bromine substituent.

An alternative explanation of these same facts can be given, using bridged radicals. In this hypothesis, bromine atoms add to an olefin via a bridged structure.

$$
\begin{array}{cc}
\underset{Br}{\overset{CH_3}{\diagdown}}C=C\underset{H}{\overset{CH_3}{\diagup}} & \underset{CH_3}{\overset{Br}{\diagdown}}C=C\underset{H}{\overset{CH_3}{\diagup}} \\
Cis & Trans
\end{array}
$$

$$ \downarrow Br\cdot \qquad\qquad \downarrow Br\cdot $$

$$
\begin{array}{cc}
\text{CH}_3 \;\; \text{C} \cdots \text{C} \;\; \text{CH}_3 \\
\text{Br} \qquad \text{Br} \qquad \text{H} \\
(\text{I})
\end{array}
\qquad
\begin{array}{cc}
\text{Br} \;\; \text{C} \cdots \text{C} \;\; \text{CH}_3 \\
\text{CH}_3 \qquad \text{Br} \qquad \text{H} \\
(\text{II})
\end{array}
$$

If it is postulated that these bridged radicals are attacked by the transfer agent *trans* to the bromine bridge, then stereospecific *trans* addition can be explained. For example, radical (I) from the *cis* olefin would give *meso* product:

$$
\text{CH}_3 \;\; \text{C} \cdots \text{C} \;\; \text{CH}_3 \quad \xrightarrow[\text{attack}]{Trans} \quad Meso
$$

At higher temperatures and lower hydrogen bromide concentrations, the two bridged radicals (I) and (II) could be postulated to interconvert by a mechanism involving open-chain radicals.†

† For further discussion of the stereochemistry of radical addition processes and the occurrence of bridged radicals, see H. L. Goering, P. I. Abell, and B. F. Aycock, *J. Am. Chem. Soc.*, **74**, 3588 (1952); P. S. Skell, R. C. Woodworth, and J. H. McNamara, *ibid.*, **79**, 1253 (1957); P. S. Skell, D. L. Tuleen, and P. D. Readio, *ibid.*, **85**, 2849 (1963); P. I. Abell and L. H. Piette, *ibid.*, **84**, 916 (1962); N. P. Neureiter and F. G. Bordwell, *ibid.*, **82**, 5354 (1960); B. A. Bohm and P. I. Abell, *Chem. Rev.*, **62**, 599 (1962).

Steric factors can lead to a predominance of *cis* addition of hydrogen bromide to olefins. Addition to the bicyclic olefin below occurs primarily from the less hindered *exo* side.†

The product is primarily the *trans* dibromide, indicating that both the initial attack by bromine atoms and the hydrogen transfer by HBr occur preferentially from the *exo* side.

As we have seen, radical addition of hydrogen bromide to most olefins occurs very rapidly. In contrast, radical addition of hydrogen chloride can be achieved only under special circumstances, and hydrogen iodide does not add to olefins in radical processes. Table 14-1 gives the energetics for the addition of these three hydrogen halides to ethylene. Only in the case of hydrogen bromide are both steps exothermic. Although hydrogen iodide is an excellent transfer agent and donates a hydrogen to a radical in a very exothermic step, the iodine atom is stable and does not add to

† N. A. LeBel, *J. Am. Chem. Soc.*, **82**, 623 (1960).

Table 14-1   **Energetics of the addition of the hydrogen halides to ethylene†**

$$X\bullet + CH_2{=}CH_2 \longrightarrow X{-}CH_2{-}CH_2\bullet \qquad (14\text{-}1)$$
$$X{-}CH_2{-}CH_2\bullet + HX \longrightarrow X{-}CH_2{-}CH_3 + X\bullet \qquad (14\text{-}2)$$

	ΔH, kcal/mole	
HX	Reaction (14-1) (Addition)	Reaction (14-2) (Transfer)
HBr	-5	-11
HCl	-26	5
HI	7	-27

† C. Walling, "Free Radicals in Solution," John Wiley & Sons, Inc., New York, 1957, p. 241.

olefins with release of energy. Therefore, for hydrogen iodide, reaction (14-1) is a bottleneck and does not occur rapidly. In the case of hydrogen chloride, the situation is reversed: The chlorine atom is very reactive and adds to olefins in a very exothermic reaction, but hydrogen chloride does not transfer a hydrogen in an exothermic step. Thus, only hydrogen bromide is predicted to add to olefins in reactions with long chain length.

Radical additions of hydrogen chloride can be forced to occur under favorable circumstances. However, the reversibility of the reactions can lead to radical rearrangements, and radical addition of hydrogen chloride can actually produce Markovnikov products. For example,† the radical addition of hydrogen chloride to propene may involve the following steps:

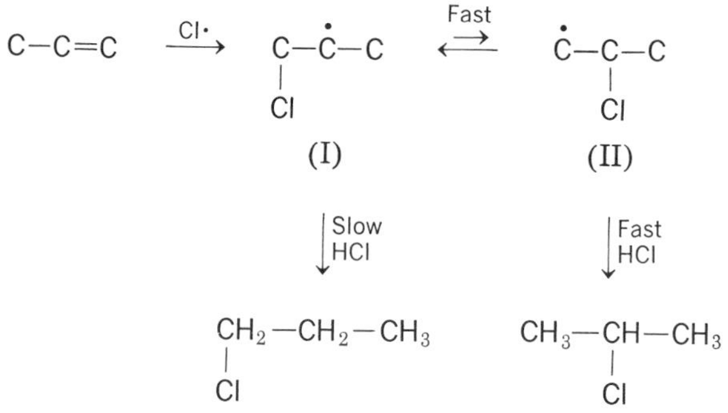

As the scheme above shows, although the equilibrium between (I) and (II) favors (I), transfer to the less hindered radical (II) is faster than transfer

† F. R. Mayo, *J. Am. Chem. Soc.*, **84**, 3964 (1962).

to (I), and secondary chloride is formed. Direct evidence for the isomerization of (I) to (II) is the fact that propyl chloride is converted to isopropyl chloride on irradiation with gamma rays in the presence of hydrogen chloride.

This 1,2-migration of a halogen atom is known to occur also in the bromo analogue of (I). However, in the presence of hydrogen bromide the transfer reaction is so fast that the first-formed radical is trapped and little or no rearrangement occurs. Therefore, hydrogen bromide adds to propene under radical conditions to give only the non-Markovnikov product.

The addition of the halogens to olefins can now be considered briefly. Table 14-2 gives the energetics for the two reactions involved in the chain. Both chlorine and bromine would be predicted to add to olefins in reactions with long chain lengths. Iodine adds only in special situations and prefers to react with alkyl halides at the halogen atom, as discussed on page 191.

Table 14-2   Energetics of the addition of the halogens to ethylene†

$$X\cdot + CH_2{=}CH_2 \longrightarrow X{-}CH_2{-}CH_2\cdot \qquad (14\text{-}1)$$
$$X{-}CH_2{-}CH_2\cdot + X_2 \longrightarrow X{-}CH_2{-}CH_2{-}X + X\cdot \qquad (14\text{-}2)$$

	ΔH, kcal/mole	
	Reaction (14-1)	Reaction (14-2)
X_2	(Addition)	(Transfer)
Br_2	−5	−17
Cl_2	−26	−19
I_2	7	−13

† C. Walling, "Free Radicals in Solution," John Wiley & Sons, Inc., New York, 1957, p. 241.

ADDITION OF THE HALOMETHANES

The addition reactions of halomethanes to olefins illustrate the factors that control the relative yields of one-to-one adduct and telomer. In mixtures of CX_4 and monomers, radicals can react either with CX_4 or with the monomeric olefin M.

$$X_3C—M_n^\bullet + M \xrightarrow{k_p} X_3C—M_{n+1}^\bullet \tag{14-4}$$

$$X_3C—M_n^\bullet + CX_4 \xrightarrow{k_{tr}} X_3C—M_n—X + {}^\bullet CX_3 \tag{14-5}$$

In the case of the radical where n in (14-4) and (14-5) is 1, the competition between CX_4 and M for reaction with $X_3C—M^\bullet$ determines whether one-to-one product or telomer is formed:

$$X_3C—M^\bullet + CX_4 \xrightarrow{k_{tr}} X_3C—M—X + {}^\bullet CX_3 \tag{14-2}$$

$$X_3C—M^\bullet + M \xrightarrow{k_p} X_3C—M_2^\bullet \xrightarrow[\text{leads to telomer}]{\text{Further reaction}} \tag{14-3}$$

Clearly, the ratio of one-to-one product to telomer depends on the activity of CX_4 as a transfer agent and on the polymerizability of the monomer M.

First, we shall consider the transfer reactivity of CX_4. It is reasonable to expect that the monomeric radical $X_3C—M^\bullet$ and the polymeric radical $X_3C—M_n^\bullet$ will react similarly. The relative rates of reaction of $X_3C—M_n^\bullet$ with halomethanes are known; they are given by values of the transfer constant $C = k_{tr}/k_p$. Values of C decrease in the order $CBr_4 > CBrCl_3 > CCl_4 > CH_2Cl_2 > CH_3Cl$; that is, polymeric radicals react fastest with CBr_4 and slowest with CH_3Cl. It is reasonable to expect the ratios of rate constants for reactions (14-2) and (14-3) to decrease in the same order, and this implies that CBr_4 should give the highest yields of one-to-one product and CH_3Cl the lowest.

Now consider the reactivity of the monomer: clearly, as it becomes more reactive toward self-polymerization, reaction (14-3) increases in rate relative to (14-2), and the yield of one-to-one product decreases.

Table 14-3 gives examples of these principles. In additions to 1-octene, the yields of the one-to-one product decrease as the transfer agent becomes poorer. However, 1-octene is quite unreactive toward self-polymerization, and good yields of the one-to-one product are obtained even with a transfer agent as poor as carbon tetrachloride. Styrene follows a similar pattern, but since it is much more reactive to-

Table 14-3   Additions of halomethanes to 1-octene and to styrene†

Halomethane	Initiator‡	Product	% Yield
		Additions to 1-octene	
CBr_4	L,A	$Br_3C—CH_2—\overset{\overset{\displaystyle Br}{\vert}}{CH}—C_6H_{13}$	96
$CBrCl_3$	L,A	$Cl_3C—CH_2—\overset{\overset{\displaystyle Br}{\vert}}{CH}—C_6H_{13}$	88
CCl_4	A	$Cl_3C—CH_2—\overset{\overset{\displaystyle Cl}{\vert}}{CH}—C_6H_{13}$	85
$CHCl_3$	B	$Cl_3C—CH_2—CH_2—C_6H_{13}$	22
		Additions to styrene	
CBr_4	L	$Br_3C—CH_2—\overset{\overset{\displaystyle Br}{\vert}}{CH}—\phi$	96
$CBrCl_3$	A	$\begin{cases} Cl_3C—CH_2—\overset{\overset{\displaystyle Br}{\vert}}{CH}—\phi \\ \text{Telomer} \end{cases}$	78 10
CCl_4	A	Telomer	90

† C. Walling, "Free Radicals in Solution," John Wiley & Sons, Inc., New York, 1957, p. 252; M. S. Kharasch, E. V. Jensen, and W. H. Urry, *J. Am. Chem. Soc.*, **69**, 1100 (1947); M. S. Kharasch, O. Reinmuth, and W. H. Urry, *ibid.*, **69**, 1105 (1947).

‡ L = light, A = acetyl peroxide, B = benzoyl peroxide.

ward self-polymerization than is 1-octene, it gives appreciable amounts of telomer even with a transfer agent as reactive as $CBrCl_3$.

Table 14-4 gives a number of examples of the types of products that can be formed from these addition reactions of halogen derivatives to olefins.

Table 14-4   Examples of radical addition reactions†

AB	Olefin	Product	% Yield
CCl_3CN	1-Octene	$NC—CCl_2—CH_2—CHCl—C_6H_{13}$	66
CCl_3COCl	1-Octene	$Cl—CO—CCl_2—CH_2—CHCl—C_6H_{13}$	81
$CF_2{=}CFI$	Ethene	$CF_2{=}CF—CH_2—CH_2I$	67
CF_3I	Ethene	$CF_3—CH_2—CH_2I$	82 (plus telomer)

† C. Walling, "Free Radicals in Solution," John Wiley & Sons, Inc., New York, 1957, p. 252.

ADDITION OF THIOLS AND HYDROGEN SULFIDE

Thiols and hydrogen sulfide can add to olefins either by an ionic or by a radical mechanism, Markovnikov adducts being produced in one case and non-Markovnikov in the other. The ability to obtain either product gives these reactions the same synthetic utility as hydrogen bromide additions.[†]

Hydrogen sulfide normally adds via an ionic mechanism; however, intense light sources such as mercury arcs induce the radical addition. With thiols, the radical path is the usual one, and purified materials and complete absence of light and oxygen are necessary to achieve the ionic addition. Elemental sulfur is an excellent radical scavenger, and in its presence thiols or hydrogen sulfide add to olefins by an ionic mechanism to give Markovnikov products.

$$RSH + C_6H_{13}-CH=CH_2 \quad \xrightarrow[\text{180°C}]{\text{Sulfur}} \quad C_6H_{13}-\underset{\underset{SR}{|}}{CH}-CH_3$$

$$\xrightarrow[\text{180°C}]{\text{Peroxide}} \quad C_6H_{13}-CH_2-CH_2-SR$$

Investigations of the stereochemistry of the addition of hydrogen sulfide to cyclic olefins has shown that stereoselectivity can sometimes be obtained if high concentrations of hydrogen sulfide are present. In the presence of high concentrations of hydrogen sulfide, the transfer rate is fast; low concentrations allow time for the two intermediate radicals to interconvert. For example, with 1-chlorocyclohexene, more *cis* product is obtained when higher concentrations of hydrogen sulfide are used.[‡] As shown in the equations at the top of page 217, the *cis* adduct results from an overall *trans* addition of H_2S to the olefin. In this process either *both* the addition and the transfer steps must occur from the axial direction, or both must be equatorial; both are shown as axial in the equations given here. The important feature for our present discussion is that high concentrations of hydrogen sulfide are able to scavenge the intermediate radical, whatever its conformation, before it has time to invert.

[†] W. A. Pryor, "Mechanisms of Sulfur Reactions," McGraw-Hill Book Company, New York, 1962, pp. 75–93, 162–164.

[‡] H. L. Goering, D. I. Relyea, and D. W. Larsen, *J. Am. Chem. Soc.*, **78**, 348 (1956).

Table 14-5 gives the relative rates of addition of the thiyl radical from dodecanethiol to various olefins. The data show a polar effect and imply that the thiyl radical is electrophilic. Olefins with electron-donating substituents react faster than those with electron-withdrawing groups. A transition state in which the thiyl radical has a partial negative charge explains these data. For example, in the addition to vinyl butyl ether, the transition state can be pictured as

$$RS\overset{\cdot\cdot}{\underset{-}{}}\ \overset{\cdot}{C}H_2\!-\!\overset{+}{C}H\!-\!OBu \longleftrightarrow RS\overset{\cdot\cdot}{\underset{-}{}}\ \overset{\cdot}{C}H_2\!-\!CH\!=\!\overset{+}{O}Bu$$

A few further features of the radical additions of sulfur compounds should be mentioned. A great variety of sulfur species can be added to olefins; these include the bisulfite ion, sulfur dioxide, sulfenyl halides, sulfonyl halides, sulfuryl halides, sulfur chloride pentafluoride, and thiol-acids. Some of these reagents have utility in synthetic work. For example, addition of thiolacetic acid is sometimes used to produce the equivalent

Table 14-5   Radical addition of dodecanethiol to olefins at 60°C†

$$C_{12}H_{25}S\cdot + RCH{=}CH_2 \xrightarrow{k_a} C_{12}H_{25}S{-}CH_2{-}\overset{\bullet}{C}HR$$

Olefin	Relative k_a
$\phi CH{=}CH_2$	17
$C_4H_9O{-}CH{=}CH_2$	4
$C_6H_{13}{-}CH{=}CH_2$	(1.00)
$CH_3{-}\overset{O}{\overset{\|}{C}}{-}O{-}CH{=}CH_2$	0.8
$ClCH_2{-}CH{=}CH_2$	0.7
Cyclohexane	0.2

† C. Walling and W. Helmreich, *J. Am. Chem Soc.*, **81**, 1144 (1959).

of the non-Markovnikov addition of hydrogen sulfide without the inconvenience of working with hydrogen sulfide gas.

$$RCH{=}CH_2 \xrightarrow[\text{Peroxide}]{CH_3{-}\overset{O}{\overset{\|}{C}}{-}SH} R{-}CH_2{-}CH_2{-}S{-}\overset{O}{\overset{\|}{C}}{-}CH_3$$

$$\downarrow \text{Hydrolysis}$$

$$R{-}CH_2{-}CH_2{-}SH$$

Many of these sulfur species add to acetylenic compounds as well as to olefins, but these reactions have been studied much less.

ADDITION OF VARIOUS SPECIES TO OLEFINS TO PRODUCE NEW CARBON-CARBON BONDS

Addition reactions that produce new carbon-carbon bonds have special interest in synthetic work. Most study has been devoted to the addition of various halomethane derivatives, and this work has already been discussed. In this section, various other molecules that have been added to olefins to produce new carbon-carbon bonds will be briefly mentioned.†

Aldehydes are excellent hydrogen donors, and they readily add to

† C. Walling and E. S. Huyser, in A. C. Cope (ed.), "Organic Reactions," vol. 13, John Wiley & Sons, Inc., New York, 1963, pp. 91–149.

olefins to produce ketones. Virtually any aldehyde can be added to any olefin, and good yields of the one-to-one adduct usually are produced if an excess of aldehyde is used. Only ethylene gives appreciable amounts of telomer. For example, butyraldehyde adds to 1-octene:

$$C_3H_7-CHO \;+\; C_6H_{13}-CH{=}CH_2 \;\xrightarrow{\text{Peroxide}}\; C_3H_7-\overset{\displaystyle O}{\overset{\|}{C}}-(CH_2)_7-CH_3$$

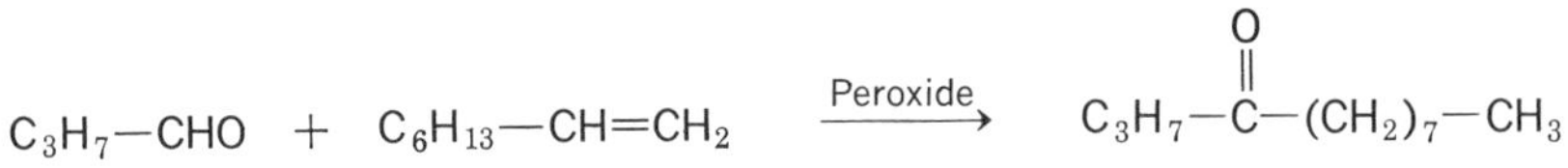

57%

Heptaldehyde adds to 1-octene to give a 75% yield of hexyl octyl ketone. The chain in these additions is

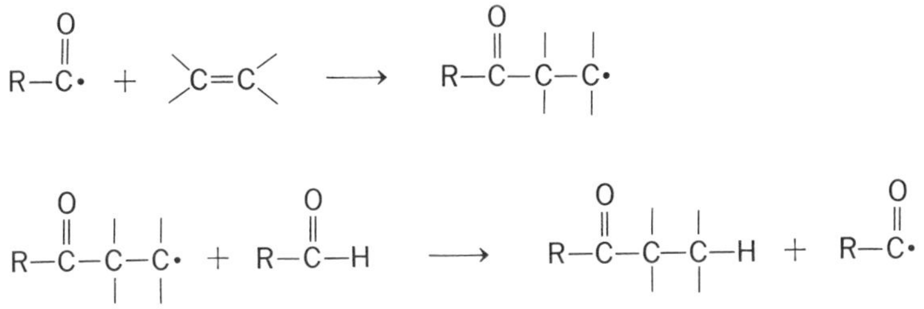

$$R-\overset{\displaystyle O}{\overset{\|}{C}}{\cdot} \;+\; {>}C{=}C{<} \;\longrightarrow\; R-\overset{\displaystyle O}{\overset{\|}{C}}-\overset{|}{\underset{|}{C}}-\overset{|}{\underset{|}{C}}{\cdot}$$

$$R-\overset{\displaystyle O}{\overset{\|}{C}}-\overset{|}{\underset{|}{C}}-\overset{|}{\underset{|}{C}}{\cdot} \;+\; R-\overset{\displaystyle O}{\overset{\|}{C}}-H \;\longrightarrow\; R-\overset{\displaystyle O}{\overset{\|}{C}}-\overset{|}{\underset{|}{C}}-\overset{|}{\underset{|}{C}}-H \;+\; R-\overset{\displaystyle O}{\overset{\|}{C}}{\cdot}$$

Primary and secondary alcohols add to olefins in a chain reaction that includes the steps shown below.

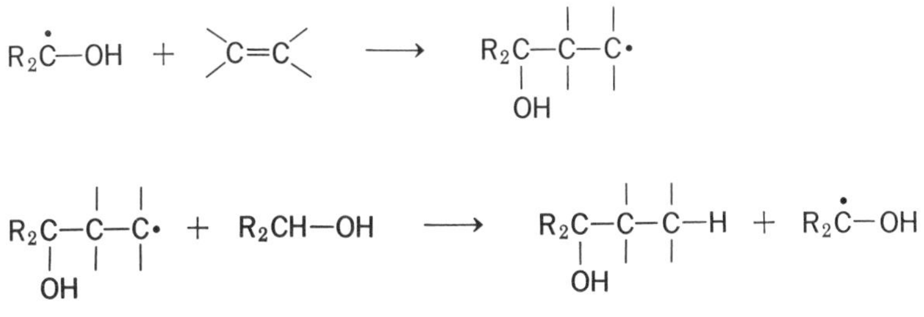

$$R_2\overset{\displaystyle \cdot}{C}-OH \;+\; {>}C{=}C{<} \;\longrightarrow\; R_2C-\overset{|}{\underset{\underset{OH}{|}}{C}}-\overset{|}{\underset{|}{C}}{\cdot}$$

$$R_2C-\overset{|}{\underset{\underset{OH}{|}}{C}}-\overset{|}{\underset{|}{C}}{\cdot} \;+\; R_2CH-OH \;\longrightarrow\; R_2C-\overset{|}{\underset{\underset{OH}{|}}{C}}-\overset{|}{\underset{|}{C}}-H \;+\; R_2\overset{\displaystyle \cdot}{C}-OH$$

Tertiary alcohols have no α hydrogen atom and do not react. The transfer constants of alcohols are small, and a large excess of the alcohol must be used; light, peroxides, or azo compounds can serve as initiators. For example,† isopropyl alcohol adds to 1-octene (24:1 mole ratio) to give 46% of the one-to-one product plus some telomer:

† W. H. Urry, F. W. Stacey, E. S. Huyser, and O. O. Juveland, *J. Am. Chem. Soc.*, **76**, 450 (1954).

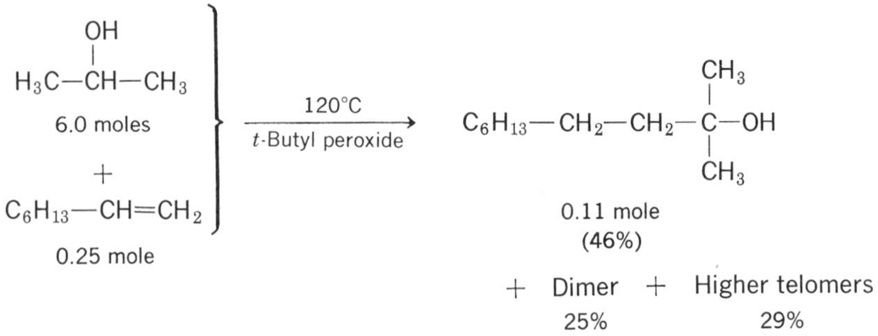

$$\left.\begin{array}{c} \overset{\displaystyle OH}{\underset{\displaystyle |}{H_3C-CH-CH_3}} \\ \text{6.0 moles} \\ + \\ C_6H_{13}-CH=CH_2 \\ \text{0.25 mole} \end{array}\right\} \xrightarrow[\textit{t-Butyl peroxide}]{120°C} \quad C_6H_{13}-CH_2-CH_2-\overset{\displaystyle CH_3}{\underset{\displaystyle CH_3}{\overset{\displaystyle |}{\underset{\displaystyle |}{C}}}}-OH$$

0.11 mole
(46%)

+   Dimer   +   Higher telomers
25%   29%

Telomer formation with a given olefin decreases in the order methanol > primary alcohol > secondary alcohol. Also, less telomer is obtained at elevated temperatures. By using high alcohol/olefin ratios and sufficiently high reaction temperatures, most secondary alcohols can be added to olefins to obtain good yields of the one-to-one product.

The α carbon-hydrogen bond of an amine can also be added to olefins. Light or t-butyl peroxide can be used as initiator, but benzoyl peroxide is ineffective because the decomposition of the peroxide is catalyzed by the amine. Amines have small transfer constants (about 0.1), and some telomer is generally produced. However, acceptable yields of the one-to-one product can be obtained by the use of large excesses of amine. Examples are shown below.†

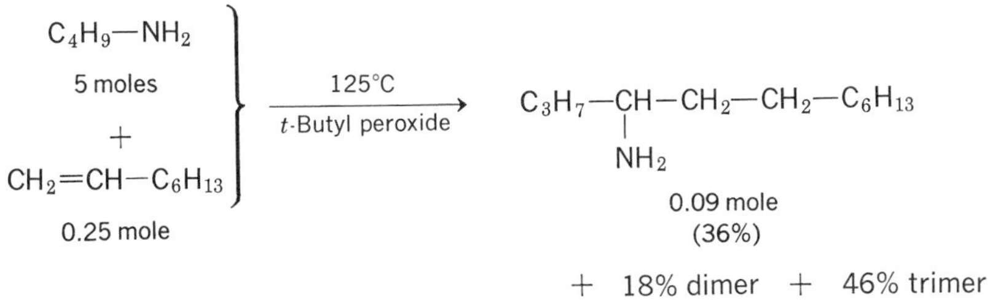

$$\left.\begin{array}{c} C_4H_9-NH_2 \\ \text{5 moles} \\ + \\ CH_2=CH-C_6H_{13} \\ \text{0.25 mole} \end{array}\right\} \xrightarrow[\textit{t-Butyl peroxide}]{125°C} \quad C_3H_7-\overset{\displaystyle }{\underset{\displaystyle NH_2}{\overset{\displaystyle |}{CH}}}-CH_2-CH_2-C_6H_{13}$$

0.09 mole
(36%)

+   18% dimer   +   46% trimer

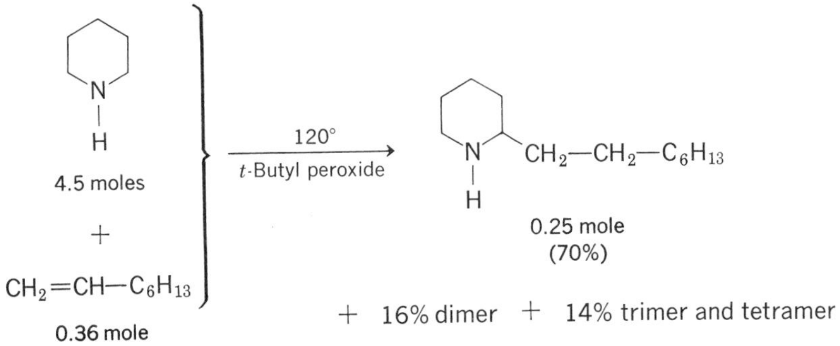

$$\left.\begin{array}{c} \text{(piperidine N-H)} \\ \text{4.5 moles} \\ + \\ CH_2=CH-C_6H_{13} \\ \text{0.36 mole} \end{array}\right\} \xrightarrow[\textit{t-Butyl peroxide}]{120°} \quad \text{(piperidine)} N-CH_2-CH_2-C_6H_{13}$$

0.25 mole
(70%)

+   16% dimer   +   14% trimer and tetramer

† W. H. Urry and O. O. Juveland, *J. Am. Chem. Soc.*, **80**, 3322 (1958).

Table 14-6   Typical radical-induced additions to 1-octene[a]

Reagent (Equivalents)[b]	Initiator (Equivalents)[c]	°C	Product, % yield
CH_3CO_2H (300)	TBP (0.15)	105	$n\text{-}C_8H_{17}\text{—}CH_2CO_2H$, 69%
$CH_3\text{—}CO\text{—}CH_3$ (22)	IPK (0.24)	56	$n\text{-}C_8H_{17}\text{—}CH_2\text{—}CO\text{—}CH_3$, 32%
$CH_2Cl\text{—}CO_2Et$ (11)	TBP (0.10)	155	$n\text{-}C_8H_{17}\text{—}CHCl\text{—}CO_2Et$, 73%
$CH_3CO\text{—}SCH_2CH_3$ (22)	TBP (0.10)	155	$n\text{-}C_8H_{17}\text{—}CH(CH_3)\text{—}S\text{—}COCH_3$, 8%;
			$n\text{-}C_8H_{17}\text{—}CH_2\text{—}CH_2\text{—}S\text{—}COCH_3$, 1%;
			$n\text{-}C_8H_{17}\text{—}CH_2CO\text{—}S\text{—}CH_2CH_3$, 1%
$CH_3CO_2CH_3$ (100)	IPK (0.24)	57	$n\text{-}C_8H_{17}\text{—}CH_2\text{—}CO\text{—}OCH_3$, 8%;
			$n\text{-}C_8H_{17}\text{—}CH_2O\text{—}COCH_3$, 1%
Cyclohexane (60)	BP (0.50)	82	Octylcyclohexane, 42%

[a] J. C. Allen, J. I. G. Cadogan, and D. H. Hey, *J. Chem. Soc.*, 1918 (1965); J. I. G. Cadogan, D. H. Hey, and S. H. Ong, *ibid.*, 1939 (1965).
[b] Per one equivalent of 1-octene.
[c] TBP is *t*-butyl peroxide, IPK is diisopropyl peroxydicarbonate, and BP is benzoyl peroxide.

Some esters are attacked by radicals at the α carbon-hydrogen bond, and the resultant radical can add to olefins. For example, diethyl malonate adds to 1-octene under radical conditions to produce diethyl octyl-malonate. Similarly, some ethers, acetals, ketones, amides, and even certain hydrocarbons add to terminal olefins. The data in Table 14-6 illustrate some of these useful processes using 1-octene as a typical terminal olefin.[†]

RELATIVE RATES OF ADDITION REACTIONS

We now turn to the factors that influence the rates of these addition processes. The rate of the addition of radical X• to an olefin is influenced by the stabilities of the X• radical, the olefin, and the radical formed by the addition; steric hindrance to the addition step; and polar factors. Table 14-7 gives the rate constants for addition and transfer in the reactions of thiols with olefins. The butanethiyl radical adds to styrene faster than to pentene, since addition to styrene produces a benzyl radical that is stabilized by resonance.

$$RS\bullet + CH_2{=}CHR' \longrightarrow RS\text{—}CH_2\text{—}\overset{\bullet}{C}HR'$$
$$RS\bullet + CH_2{=}CH\phi \longrightarrow RS\text{—}CH_2\text{—}\overset{\bullet}{C}H\phi$$

[†] J. C. Allen, J. I. G. Cadogan, and D. H. Hey, *J. Chem. Soc.*, 1918 (1965); C. Walling and E. S. Huyser, in A. C. Cope (ed.), "Organic Reactions," vol. 13, John Wiley & Sons, Inc., New York, 1963, pp. 118–149.

Table 14-7 Rate constants for addition and transfer processes in the reactions of thiols with olefins†

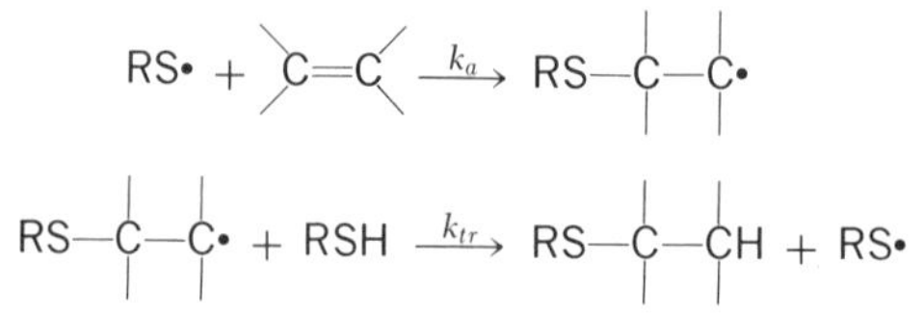

$$RS\bullet + {>}C{=}C{<} \xrightarrow{k_a} RS{-}\overset{|}{\underset{|}{C}}{-}\overset{|}{\underset{|}{C}}\bullet$$

$$RS{-}\overset{|}{\underset{|}{C}}{-}\overset{|}{\underset{|}{C}}\bullet + RSH \xrightarrow{k_{tr}} RS{-}\overset{|}{\underset{|}{C}}{-}\overset{|}{C}H + RS\bullet$$

Olefin	Thiol	k_a	k_{tr}
		(liter mole^{-1} sec^{-1} at 25°C)	
Styrene	Butanethiol	8×10^8	1.2×10^3
1-Pentene	Butanethiol	7×10^6	1.4×10^6

† M. Onyszchuk and C. Sivertz, *Can. J. Chem.*, **33**, 1034 (1955); C. Sivertz, *J. Phys. Chem.*, **63**, 34 (1959).

On the other hand, since the radical from styrene is resonance stabilized, it abstracts hydrogen from the thiol more slowly.

The importance of steric factors in these radical addition reactions is indicated by the fact that terminal olefins usually react faster and give better yields of products than do internal olefins. Also, the direction of addition of radicals to terminal olefins is probably a result of a steric effect, as well as of the slightly higher stability of secondary radicals compared with primary. The effects of polar factors on radical addition reactions can be seen in data such as those given in Table 14-5.

Extensive data have been published on the addition of methyl radicals to various olefins, acetylenes, and aromatic compounds.† These data are obtained in the following manner: A methyl radical source is allowed to decompose in a mixed solvent consisting of isooctane and the unsaturated compound being investigated. Acetyl peroxide is most often used as the methyl source, but azomethane and *t*-butyl peroxide also can be used. The methyl radicals abstract hydrogen from the isooctane (SH) to produce methane:

$$CH_3\bullet + SH \xrightarrow{k_6} CH_4 + S\bullet \tag{14-6}$$

However, in the presence of the unsaturated compound A, some of the methyl radicals undergo an addition reaction:

† M. Szwarc and J. H. Binks, "Theoretical Organic Chemistry," Kekule Symposium, 1958, Butterworth Scientific Publications, London, 1958.

$$CH_3\cdot + A \xrightarrow{k_7} CH_3A\cdot \qquad (14\text{-}7)$$

The ratio of k_7/k_6 can be calculated from the decrease in the amount of methane produced when the unsaturated compound A is present, compared with when it is absent. Table 14-8 gives data obtained in this way.

The data in Table 14-8 illustrate the various factors that influence the rates of addition processes. Addition occurs fastest to terminal olefins. Very highly substituted olefins react slowly, owing to steric hindrance, even if they would give stable radicals upon addition. For example, tetraphenylethene reacts more slowly than does di- or triphenylethene. Styrene, however, reacts much faster than does propene. In this case, the

Table 14-8 Rate constants at 65°C for the addition of methyl radicals to double bonds relative to abstraction of hydrogen from isooctane†

Compound	k_7/k_6
Ethylene	26
Ethoxyethylene	6
Propene	22
Methylpropene	36
2-Methyl-2-butene	6
cis-2-Butene	3
trans-2-Butene	7
Styrene	796
1,1-Diphenylethene	1,500
cis-1,2-Diphenylethene	29
trans-1,2-Diphenylethene	104
1,1,2-Triphenylethene	48
Tetraphenylethene	8
Ethyl maleate	333
Ethyl fumarate	2,000
Butadiene	2,015
2,3-Dimethylbutadiene	2,200
2,4-Hexadiene	180
2,5-Dimethyl-2,4-hexadiene	20
1,4-Diphenylbutadiene	380
1,1,4,4-Tetraphenylbutadiene	60

† M. Szwarc and J. H. Binks, "Theoretical Organic Chemistry," Kekule Symposium, 1958, Butterworth Scientific Publications, London, 1958, pp. 271, 272, 278.

phenyl substituent stabilizes the radical being formed without hindering the addition step.

$$CH_3\bullet + CH_2{=}CH\phi \longrightarrow CH_3{-}CH_2{-}\overset{\bullet}{C}H\phi$$

$$CH_3\bullet + CH_2{=}CH{-}CH_3 \longrightarrow CH_3{-}CH_2{-}\overset{\bullet}{C}H{-}CH_3$$

The same type of data can be collected for addition of methyl radicals to aromatic hydrocarbons. For example, benzene reacts as shown below.

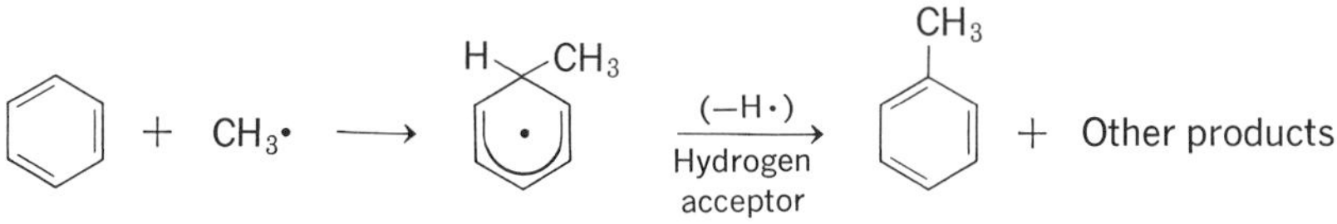

Table 14-9 gives data of this type. The relative rates of methylation of an aromatic compound can be correlated with the *localization energy* of the compound, a quantity that can be calculated using molecular orbital techniques.† The localization energy is defined as the π-bonding energy necessary to isolate one electron from the resonating system and localize it on a given atom. Such localization produces a new resonating system consisting of one less atom and one less electron. The localized system has the same π-bond structure as the transition state for methylation. For benzene, for example, localization leaves a pentadienyl radical. (See the above equation.) The π-bonding energy, which can readily be obtained by the molecular orbital method, is then calculated for both the starting material and the localized system which is taken as an approximation for the transition state. Thus, for example, the π-bonding energy of benzene and of the pentadienyl radical are calculated. The difference should be proportional to the energy required to methylate benzene, and therefore to the activation energy (of the logarithm of the rate constant) for reaction (14-7). Figure 14-1 shows the localization energies plotted versus the logarithm of the relative rates of methyl addition. The localization energies calculated in this simple manner predict the rate of the additions very well.

If the rate patterns for methyl additions reflect general principles that govern radical additions, then other radicals should show qualitatively similar patterns. Figure 14-2 is a log-log graph of the rates of methyl additions versus the relative rates of addition of ethyl, propyl, phenyl, and trichloromethyl radicals to the same aromatic systems, and the correlation

† A. Streitwieser, "Molecular Orbital Theory for Organic Chemists," John Wiley & Sons, Inc., New York, 1960, pp. 335, 400.

Table 14-9   Relative rates of addition of methyl radicals to aromatic compounds†

Substrate	Relative rate	Substrate	Relative rate
(Ethene)	(85)	Benzanthracene	515
Benzene	1	Anthracene	820
Naphthalene	22	Naphthacene	9,250
Phenanthrene	27	Pyridine	3

† M. Szwarc and J. H. Binks, "Theoretical Organic Chemistry," Kekule Sy...posium, 1958, Butterworth Scientific Publications, London, 1958, pp. 263, 276, 278.

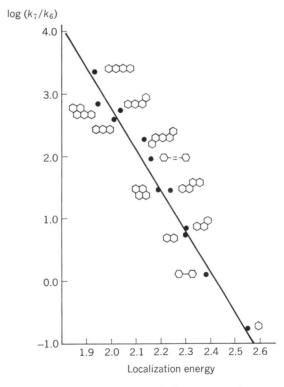

Figure 14-1   Relative rates of addition of methyl radicals to aromatic compounds versus the localization energy for the compounds. (*M. Szwarc and J. H. Binks, "Theoretical Organic Chemistry," Kekule Symposium, 1958, Butterworth Scientific Publications, London, 1958, p. 266.*)

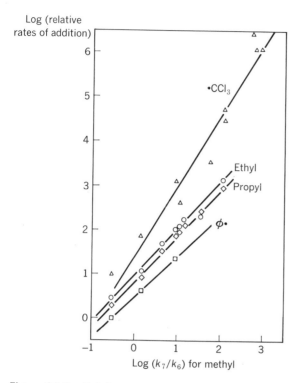

Figure 14-2 Relative rates of addition of phenyl, ethyl, propyl, and trichloromethyl radicals to aromatic compounds versus the relative rates of addition of methyl radicals to the same compounds. (*A. F. Trotman-Dickinson*, "*Free Radicals*," *Methuen & Co., London*, 1959, p. 109.)

is excellent. The slopes of these lines indicate the relative selectivity of the radicals involved:

Ethyl	1.0
Propyl	1.0
Phenyl	1.0
Trichloromethyl	2.0

Thus, the alkyl radicals and phenyl radicals all select among aromatic positions similarly. The trichloromethyl radical is about twice as selective as methyl radicals on this scale. The same treatment of the data for the polystyryl radical shows that it is also about twice as selective as methyl radicals.

PROBLEMS

14-1 Write the mechanism for the isomerization of *cis-* to *trans*-stilbene (ϕCH=CHϕ) initiated by light and bromine.

14-2 Write the mechanism for the light-initiated addition of hydrogen bromide to 1-butene to produce 1-bromobutane. Why is the one-to-one adduct produced in this case and not in that of Prob. 14-1?

14-3 Write the complete mechanism for the production of trimeric product from the AIBN-initiated addition of carbon tetrachloride to ethylene.

14-4 Demonstrate that the ratio of the yield of one-to-one adduct to the total yield of telomers (dimers and higher) is given by the expression

$$\frac{1:1 \text{ Addend}}{\text{Telomers}} = \frac{k_2(\text{AB})}{k_a(\text{M})}$$

The equations are

$$\text{B}\bullet + \text{M} \xrightarrow{k} \text{BM}\bullet$$

$$\text{BM}\bullet + \text{AB} \xrightarrow{k_2} \text{BMA} + \text{B}\bullet$$

$$\text{BM}\bullet + \text{M} \xrightarrow{k_a} \text{BM}_2\bullet$$

$$\text{BM}_n\bullet + \text{M} \xrightarrow{k_p} \text{BM}_{n+1}\bullet$$

$$\text{BM}_n\bullet + \text{AB} \xrightarrow{k_{tr}} \text{BM}_n\text{A} + \text{B}\bullet$$

where M is the monomeric olefin. If reactivity is independent of chain length, certain of these rate constants become equal. Using this simplification, rewrite the above expression for the yields of the adducts.

14-5 On page 205, the adduct from the telomerization of styrene with carbon tetrachloride is given as Cl_3C—$(CH_2$—$CH\phi)_n$—Cl. Why is this a more likely structure than Cl_3C—$(CH\phi$—$CH_2)_n$—Cl? Why is more high-molecular-weight telomer produced at high styrene/carbon tetrachloride ratios?

14-6 Why is the "peroxide effect" a poor name for the non-Markovnikov addition of hydrogen bromide to a terminal olefin?

14-7 Use the data in Table 14-1 to explain why hydrogen iodide and hydrogen chloride do not add to olefins in chain processes.

14-8 Write the probable structure for the dimeric product resulting from the addition of isopropyl alcohol to 1-octene.

14-9 In the addition of carbon tetrachloride to ethylene, the ratio of the rate constants for abstraction of chlorine from carbon tetrachloride relative to the rate of addition to ethylene has been measured for radicals of differing molecular weights. The transfer constant for the n-mer is defined as

$$C_n = \frac{k_{tr,n}}{k_{p,n}}$$

where the rate constants are for the processes shown below.

$$BM_n \cdot + AB \xrightarrow{k_{tr,n}} BM_nA + B\cdot$$

$$BM_n \cdot + M \xrightarrow{k_{p,n}} BM_{n+1}\cdot$$

At $27°C$, $C_1 = 0.07$, $C_2 = 3.0$, $C_3 = 9.7$, $C_4 = 18$, and for very large n, $C_n = 31$. Using an argument based on polar contributions to the transition states, explain this trend of rising values of the transfer constant. [C. David and P. A. Gosselain, *Tetrahedron*, **18**, 639 (1962).]

14-10 In the addition of chloroform to ethylene at $28°C$, $C_1 = 0.2$, $C_2 = 1.3$, $C_3 = 1.5$. (See Prob. 14-9 for definitions.) Explain this trend. [F. W. Mellows and M. Burton, *J. Phys. Chem.*, **66**, 2164 (1962).]

14-11 In the addition of carbon tetrachloride to styrene at $60°C$, $C_1 = 6 \times 10^{-4}$, $C_2 = 25 \times 10^{-4}$, $C_3 = 69 \times 10^{-4}$, and C_4 and all higher transfer constants equal 115×10^{-4}. (See Prob. 14-9 for definitions.) Explain this trend. Comment on why the transfer constant for carbon tetrachloride is so much larger toward ethylene than toward styrene. (See Prob. 14-9.) [F. R. Mayo, *J. Am. Chem. Soc.*, **70**, 3689 (1948).]

14-12 Rationalize the trend of the transfer constants (toward styrene at $60°C$) for the following transfer agents:

CBr_4	2.2
CCl_4	1.1×10^{-2}
$CHCl_3$	5×10^{-5}

[G. Henrici-Olivé and S. Olivé, *Fortschr. Hochpolymer.-Forsch.*, **2**, 496 (1961).]

14-13 In Table 14-8, explain the trend of the values of k_7/k_6 for ethylene, butadiene, 2,3-dimethylbutadiene, and 1,4-diphenylbutadiene.

14-14 The t-butyl peroxide–initiated reaction of either *cis* or *trans* 4-t-butylcyclohexanol with 1-octene at $150°C$ gives 1-octyl-4-t-butyl-1-cyclohexanol in about 40% yield.

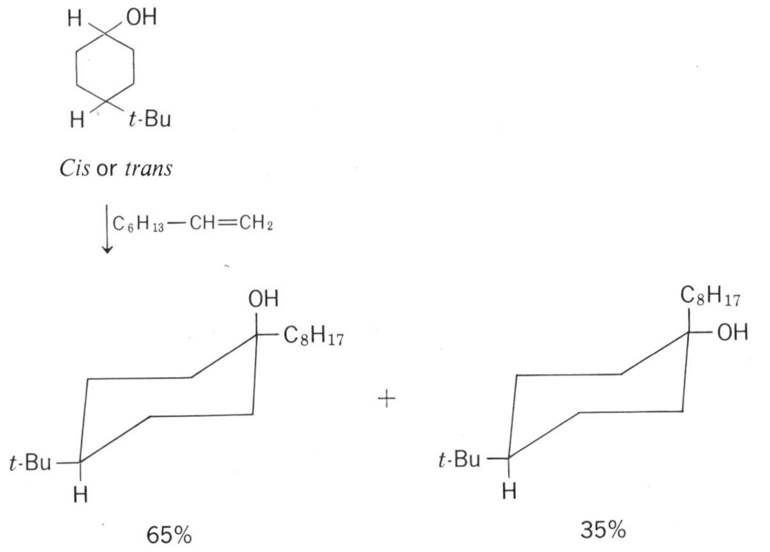

Cis or *trans*

$$C_6H_{13}-CH=CH_2$$

65%

+

35%

Both *cis* and *trans* give the same isomer distribution of products, namely, about 65% axial hydroxyl and 35% equatorial. Discuss the mechanism for the addition of alcohols to olefins. Explain the stereochemistry of the above addition, assuming that the cyclohexyl radical is planar. Then explain the stereochemistry, assuming that the rates of inversion of pyramidal cyclohexyl radicals exceed their rates of addition to 1-octene. [R. J. Gritter and R. J. Albers, *J. Org. Chem.*, **29**, 728 (1964).]

14-15 Optically active 1-chloro-2-methylbutane gives optically active 1-chloro-2-bromo-2-methylbutane on bromination.

a. Explain this, assuming that bridged radicals are more stable than open-chain radicals in this series.

b. Then explain it assuming either that bridged radicals are not formed at all or that they are less stable than open-chain radicals and are formed only from open-chain radicals. Which explanation do you prefer? (See pages 35 to 39 and 210.)

14-16 A mixture of 5 mmoles of ethyl 2-cyano-6-heptenoate and 2.5 mmoles of benzoyl peroxide was refluxed for 24 hours in 126 g of cyclohexane. A product was obtained (62% yield) which could be hydrolyzed to give 1,1-cyclohexanedicarboxylic acid. Write a mechanism for the reaction and identify the product. [J. I. G. Cadogan, D. H. Hey, and S. H. Ong, *J. Chem. Soc.*, 1932 (1965).]

14-17 The reactivities of various olefins toward addition of hydrogen bromide have been measured relative to ethylene as standard. Typical values at 40°C are:

Ethylene	(1)
Propylene	15
1-Butene	20
2-Butene	69
Isobutylene	286
Vinyl chloride	0.3

Rationalize the trends in these values, and compare the reactions of bromine atoms and methyl radicals. [P. I. Abell, *Trans. Faraday Soc.*, **60**, 2214 (1964).]

SUGGESTIONS FOR FURTHER READING

Bohm, B. A., and P. I. Abell: *Chem. Rev.*, **62**, 599 (1962). (On the stereochemistry of radical additions.)

Cadogan, J. I. G., and D. H. Hey: *Quart. Rev. (London)*, **8**, 308 (1954).

Stacey, F. W., and J. F. Harris: in A. C. Cope (ed.), "Organic Reactions," vol. 13, John Wiley & Sons, Inc., New York, 1963, pp. 150–376.

Walling, C., and E. S. Huyser: in A. C. Cope (ed.), "Organic Reactions," vol. 13, John Wiley & Sons, Inc., New York, 1963, pp. 91–149.

Radical
Polymerizations

A polymer is a large molecule which either occurs in nature or is man-made; we shall limit our discussion to man-made polymers. A polymer can be considered to be formed from a simple unit, called the mer, which is repeated many times to form the polymer chain. Polymers formed in radical processes usually have 10^3 to 10^5 repeat units per molecule and have molecular weights of 10^5 to 10^7.

The progress in polymer chemistry since the 1930s is one of the most significant accomplishments of chemical research in recent years. A glance around an average room reveals man-made fabrics, structural materials, table tops, dishes, and many other items that only a few years ago would have been made of wood or metal or other natural products.

Synthetic polymers can be made by either ionic or radical processes. Some of the commercial plastics are produced by both processes, but most are made by one process or the other. The subject of ionic polymerization is beyond the bounds of this text, and a detailed discussion of radical polymerizations is more suited to an advanced textbook.† However, certain types of information about free radicals can best be obtained by studies of polymeric radicals, and it is important that these be discussed here. Before this is done, however, it will be interesting to examine the range of useful plastics that can be produced by radical polymerization processes.

EXAMPLES OF USEFUL POLYMERS

Polymerization reactions are divided into two types. All free radical polymerizations are *addition polymerizations*, in which the repeating unit in the chain is identical with the monomer. An example of an addition polymerization is the formation of polyethylene:‡

$$nCH_2{=}CH_2 \longrightarrow (-CH_2{-}CH_2{-})_n$$

Some ionic polymerizations also occur by addition, but most involve a process called *condensation polymerization*.§ In this type of reaction,

† A list of advanced texts is given at the end of this chapter.

Notice that the nature of the end of the polymeric chain is not specified. Polymer molecules have very high molecular weights and, consequently, a very small number of end groups per gram of polymer. Usually the experimental determination of the nature of these end groups is very difficult, but their nature can be inferred from the mechanism by which the polymer molecules are formed. We shall consider these mechanisms later in this chapter.

§ The division into addition and condensation polymers was originally proposed by Carothers. More recently, Flory has proposed a division of polymers based on

232

a small molecule is split from the monomers when they react. An example is the formation of nylon from adipic acid and hexamethylenediamine:

$$n\,CO_2H-(CH_2)_4-CO_2H \ + \ n\,NH_2-(CH_2)_6-NH_2 \ \xrightarrow[\text{Catalysis}]{\text{Acid}}$$

$$\begin{matrix} O & & O & H & & & H \\ \| & & \| & | & & & | \\ \end{matrix}$$
$$-(C-(CH_2)_4-C-N-(CH_2)_6-N)_n \ + \ 2n\,H_2O$$

The simplest and the most useful polymer is polyethylene. Two processes are used for its production. The older, radical process gives material with a melting point of about 110°C; this is called "high-pressure" polyethylene. The newer ionic process produces material with a melting point of about 140°C; it is called either "low-pressure" or "high-density" polyethylene. Despite the somewhat broader utility of the higher-melting, stiffer material produced by the ionic process, the radical process is still used because it yields more transparent material, which is superior in certain applications. In the radical process, ethylene at about 1,000 atm is heated to 200°C in the presence of a small, controlled amount of air or peroxide, and polymer is removed continuously. The air or peroxide reacts with ethylene to produce radicals [reaction (15-1)]. These primary radicals then add to the monomer to initiate the polymerization [reaction (15-2)]. The resulting radical, which contains one monomer unit, adds another to produce a dimer, which reacts to form a trimer, etc.

Initiation

$$CH_2{=}CH_2 \ \xrightarrow[\text{peroxide}]{\text{Air or}} \ \text{Radicals (R·)} \qquad (15\text{-}1)$$

$$R{·} + CH_2{=}CH_2 \longrightarrow R{-}CH_2{-}CH_2{·} \qquad (15\text{-}2)$$

Propagation

$$R{-}(CH_2{-}CH_2)_n{·} + CH_2{=}CH_2 \longrightarrow R{-}(CH_2{-}CH_2)_n{-}CH_2{-}CH_2{·} \qquad (15\text{-}3)$$

polymerization mechanisms: polymerizations are either chain reactions or step reactions. The former involve formation of an active center which grows in a chain process until termination. In the latter, new bonds are formed by the stepwise reaction of any of the functional groups present. All radical polymerizations are chain processes; most, but not all, ionic polymerizations are step reactions.

Termination

$$2R-CH_2-CH_2 \bullet \quad \begin{cases} \xrightarrow{\text{Combination}} R-CH_2-CH_2-CH_2-CH_2-R \quad (15\text{-}4) \\ \\ \xrightarrow{\text{Disproportionation}} R-CH=CH_2 + R-CH_2-CH_3 \quad (15\text{-}5) \end{cases}$$

Finally, growth is stopped when two chains interact either by combination (15-4) or by disproportionation (15-5). Polyethylene has been commercially produced in the United States since 1943. Today it is used in sheeting and films, in flexible bottles and trays, as a coating and insulation for electrical wires, and in many other useful applications.

Substitution of different groups for one or more of the hydrogens in ethylene produces monomers that form other useful polymers. Table 15-1 gives examples of some of the most commonly used plastics.

KINETICS OF POLYMERIZATIONS

The mechanism for the polymerization of a monomer can be symbolized by the equations shown below.

Initiation   *Rate law*

$I \longrightarrow 2R\bullet$ $R_d = k_d(I)$

$R\bullet + M \longrightarrow M\bullet$ $R_i = k_i(R\bullet)(M)$

Propagation

$M\bullet + M \longrightarrow M_2\bullet$

In general

$M_n\bullet + M \longrightarrow M_{n+1}^{\bullet}$ $R_p = k_p(M\bullet)(M)$

Termination

$M_n\bullet + M_m\bullet \longrightarrow M_{n+m}$ $R_{t,c} = k_{t,c}(M\bullet)^2$

$M_n\bullet + M_m\bullet \longrightarrow M_n + M_m$ $R_{t,d} = k_{t,d}(M\bullet)^2$

In general

$M_n\bullet + M_m\bullet \longrightarrow$ Polymer $R_t = k_t(M\bullet)^2$

Table 15-1 Examples of plastics produced by addition polymerization using radical initiators†

Polymer (and common trade name)	Monomer used	Properties of the plastic	Uses
Polyethylene	$CH_2{=}CH_2$	Flexible, semiopaque, inert to most chemicals.	Containers; film; pipe; electrical insulation.
Polystyrene	$CH_2{=}CH\phi$	Clear, rigid, somewhat brittle; air bubbles can be incorporated to give foamed plastics of varying densities.	Containers; the foamed plastic is used as insulation and packing material.
Poly(vinyl chloride) (Geon, Koroseal, Tygon)	$CH_2{=}CHCl$	Rigid; organic materials such as esters can be mixed into the polymer to "plasticize" it, giving a clear, flexible plastic.	Pipes; insulation; plasticized material is used in shower curtains, leather-ette, and hoses.
Poly(vinylidene chloride)	$CH_2{=}CCl_2$	Translucent and rigid.	Usually polymerized in mixtures with vinyl chloride to give Saran copolymers.
Polychlorotrifluoro-ethylene (Kel-F)	$CF_2{=}CFCl$	Chemically inert.	Low polymers are used as high-temperature greases; high polymers are used as chemically inert gaskets.
Polytetrafluoro-ethylene (Teflon)	$CF_2{=}CF_2$	Unusually high melting point (327°C), chemical inertness, and flexibility.	Gaskets; chemically resistant parts; electrical insulation.
Poly(methyl methacrylate) (Plexiglas, Lucite)	$CH_2{=}\underset{\underset{CO_2CH_3}{\mid}}{\overset{\overset{CH_3}{\mid}}{C}}$	Clear and semiflexible.	Watch lenses; contact lenses; aircraft windows.
Polyacrylonitrile (Orlon, Acrilan)	$CH_2{=}\underset{\underset{C{\equiv}N}{\mid}}{CH}$	Crystalline, strong, high luster.	Fibers.
Styrene-butadiene copolymer	$CH_2{=}CH\phi,$ $CH_2{=}CH{-}CH{=}CH_2$	Rubbery; usually polymerized as an emulsion in water stabilized by soaps and other additives.	Material with ca. 25% styrene and 75% butadiene is major synthetic rubber used in tires; ca. 80% styrene in copolymer gives a more rigid polymer used in helmets, bowling balls, and luggage.

† J. K. Stille, "Introduction to Polymer Chemistry," John Wiley & Sons, Inc., New York, 1962, pp. 149–180.

where I is an initiator, R• is a low-molecular-weight radical, M is a molecule of monomer, and M_n• is a polymeric radical with n monomer units in the chain. Note that there are two termination reactions but that both have the same kinetic law and a generalized equation can be written. The simplifying assumption is made that the rate constant for any reaction is independent of the chain length of the polymeric radical taking part in the reaction. Thus, for example, in the propagation reaction, $M_{200}^\bullet$ is assumed to add another monomer unit at the same rate as does $M_{201}^\bullet$. This assumption is necessary in order to derive simple rate laws. Addition polymerizations frequently involve chain lengths of 1,000 or more, and a kinetic expression containing 1,000 different values for the propagation rate constant would be unworkable. Once this simplifying assumption is made, the polymeric radicals can be abbreviated as M• without giving a subscript denoting their size, as shown in the rate expressions on page 234.

A number of simple expressions can be derived from this scheme. It is reasonable to assume that a steady state in radical concentrations will rapidly be reached at which the rates of formation and destruction of radicals are equal. At the steady state,

Rate of formation of radicals = Rate of destruction of radicals

The rate of formation of radicals is given by $2k_df(I)$, where f is the fraction of the primary radicals that escape cage recombination and are able to initiate polymerization, and the factor of 2 arises because each initiator molecule forms two radicals. The rate of destruction of radicals is given by $2k_t(M•)^2$, where the factor of 2 accounts for the destruction of two radicals in each reaction. Therefore,

$$2k_df(I) = 2k_t(M•)^2$$

$$\text{and} \quad (M•) = \left(\frac{\text{Rate of formation of radicals}}{2k_t}\right)^{1/2}$$

$$= \left[\frac{k_df(I)}{k_t}\right]^{1/2} \tag{15-6}$$

Equation (15-6) is a useful expression for the concentration of radicals present in the reacting system. The rate of formation of polymer is given by

$$\frac{-d(M)}{dt} = R_P = k_i(R•)(M) + k_p(M•)(M)$$

In chain reactions, the monomer molecules consumed in the initiation step can be neglected, and the rate of consumption of monomer can be approximated as

$$R_P = k_p(M\cdot)(M) \tag{15-7}$$

Substitution of (15-6) into (15-7) gives

$$R_P = \frac{k_p}{k_t^{1/2}} (M)[k_d f(I)]^{1/2} \tag{15-8a}$$

or, more generally,

$$R_P = \frac{k_p}{k_t^{1/2}} (M)(\text{Rate of formation of radicals}/2)^{1/2} \tag{15-8b}$$

Equation (15-8a) predicts that the rate of formation of polymer should be proportional to the square root of the initiator concentration; this is borne out for a large number of initiators. The equation also predicts that the rate will be proportional to the concentration of monomer; this is frequently found to be true.

The ratio of rate constants $k_p/k_t^{1/2}$ can be obtained very easily from Eq. (15-8a) by measuring the rate of polymer formation using an initiator with a known rate of decomposition. This ratio of $k_p/k_t^{1/2}$ represents the polymerizability of the monomer; a larger value means that a given amount of initiator will produce more polymer in a given time. Table 15-2 gives values of this ratio for several common monomers. The table also gives the absolute values of propagation and termination rate constants. (We shall see how these are obtained below.) Notice that the polymerizability of a monomer is given not by the magnitude of the propagation constant

Table 15-2   Rate constants for some common monomers at 25°C†

	$k_p/k_t^{1/2}$	k_p	$k_t \times 10^{-7}$
p-Methoxystyrene	0.00284	2.9	0.10
Styrene	.014	40	.79
Methyl methacrylate	.055	275	2.5
Vinyl acetate	.18	1,000	3.0
Methyl acrylate	.20	1,500	5.5

† Rate constants are in liter mole^{-1} sec^{-1}.   G. M. Burnett, "Mechanism of Polymer Reactions," Interscience Publishers, Inc., New York, 1954, pp. 223, 234.

k_p but by the ratio $k_p/k_t^{1/2}$. Thus, vinyl acetate and methyl acrylate have about the same polymerizability, but the latter has a larger propagation constant.

The kinetic chain length ν is the number of monomer molecules consumed by each primary radical. This is given by

$$\nu = \frac{-d(M)/dt}{\text{Rate of formation of radicals}} \qquad (15\text{-}9)$$

For example, if propagation occurs 100 times as fast as initiation, then, on an average, each *polymeric radical* will grow to $M_{100}^{\bullet}$. The actual size of the *polymer molecule* depends on the termination mechanism. The number of monomer units in the average polymer molecule is called the degree of polymerization and is symbolized $\bar{P}$. If termination occurs by disproportionation, the average polymer has a degree of polymerization equal to the kinetic chain length and $\bar{P} = \nu$. If termination is by combination, the average polymer contains a number of monomer units equal to twice the kinetic chain length, $\bar{P} = 2\nu$.

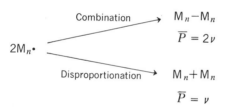

Regardless of the termination mechanism, Eq. (15-9) can be written as

$$\nu = \frac{R_P}{\begin{array}{l}\text{[Rate of}\\\text{destruction}\\\text{of radicals]}\end{array}} = \frac{k_p(M\bullet)(M)}{2k_t(M\bullet)^2} = \frac{k_p(M)}{2k_t(M\bullet)} \qquad (15\text{-}10)$$

and, using (15-7), this becomes

$$\nu = \frac{k_p^2(M)^2}{2k_t R_P} \qquad (15\text{-}11)$$

Notice from (15-9) that the chain length is inversely proportional to the rate of initiation; faster rates of initiation lead to lower-molecular-weight polymers. This has been amply confirmed. Also note in (15-11) that the chain length obtained for a monomer at any given rate of polymerization is a function of the nature of the monomer, not of the initiator. Since $k_p/k_t^{1/2}$ is the polymerizability of a monomer, it is not surprising that the square of this ratio appears in the expression for chain length. This suggests another method for obtaining $k_p/k_t^{1/2}$. If the chain length ν could be measured, Eq. (15-11) could be used to calculate $k_p/k_t^{1/2}$. The degree of polymerization, $\bar{P}$, can be measured by techniques that are suitable for measuring the molecular weights of high-molecular-weight substances.† If the termination mechanism is known, the degree of polymerization, $\bar{P}$, can be related to the kinetic chain length, ν, and (15-11) can be solved for the value of k_p^2/k_t.

Termination mechanisms for polymers can be investigated by several techniques, only one of which will be given here: A radioactive initiator is used, and the number of initiator molecules that are incorporated into each polymer is determined. If termination is by combination, 1 mole of initiator is incorporated into each mole of polymer; disproportionation implies that ½ mole of initiator is incorporated into each mole of polymer. The scheme shown below illustrates this.

$$\text{R—R} \longrightarrow 2\text{R}\cdot$$

$$\text{R}\cdot \longrightarrow n\,\text{M} \longrightarrow \text{R—M}_n\cdot$$

$$2\text{R—M}_n\cdot \quad \underset{\text{Disproportionation}}{\overset{\text{Combination}}{\rightleftarrows}} \quad \begin{array}{l} \text{R—M}_n\text{—M}_n\text{—R} \\ \text{R—M}_n \ + \ \text{R—M}_n \end{array}$$

Experiments such as this have been done for most of the common monomers. The most common termination mechanism is combination, but some disproportionation occurs with certain monomers.

We can summarize this method for determining k_p^2/k_t as follows: The degree of polymerization, $\bar{P}$, can be obtained from the molecular weight of the polymer. Then, if termination is by combination,

$$\bar{P} = 2\nu \tag{15-12}$$

and the value of k_p^2/k_t can be calculated from (15-11).

---

† These techniques include sensitive analyses for the numbers of end groups in a given amount of polymer, osmotic pressure, the ultracentrifuge, or light scattering. An introductory description of these processes is given in W. J. Moore, "Physical Chemistry," Prentice-Hall, Inc., Englewood Cliffs, N.J., 3d ed., 1963, chap. 19.

EVALUATION OF INDIVIDUAL RATE CONSTANTS

So far, the rate constants for propagation and termination have been obtained only as ratios. We met the same situation in dealing with monomeric radicals; because of the difficulty in measuring the concentrations of radicals, rate-constant ratios are more easily obtained than are absolute values of rate constants. The absolute values of the propagation and termination rate constants can be evaluated, but the method is somewhat complex. It is beyond our present purposes to examine these procedures in detail, but qualitatively the idea is as follows. Measurements of the rate of polymerization and the degree of polymerization under steady-state conditions cannot give the absolute values of k_p or k_t. An additional parameter must be obtained, and the one usually used is the lifetime of a radical, τ, which is the average time from the creation of a radical chain to its destruction. The lifetime of a growing chain is equal to the concentration of radicals divided by their rate of destruction:

$$\tau_s = \frac{(M\cdot)_s}{2k_t(M\cdot)_s^2} = \frac{1}{2k_t(M\cdot)_s} \tag{15-13}$$

and, from (15-7),

$$\tau_s = \frac{k_p(M)}{2k_t(R_P)_s} \tag{15-14}$$

where the subscript s refers to concentrations at the steady state. If τ_s could be measured at the steady state, then k_p/k_t could be obtained from (15-14). This ratio, combined with the known value of k_p^2/k_t, would allow calculation of k_p and k_t.

Methods for determining τ_s involve measurements at non-steady-state conditions. One method is to initiate polymerization by photoactivation of an initiator. If steady illumination is used, the steady state is rapidly reached. However, if a flickering light is used, the rate of polymerization varies from one value to another. Rapidly flickering light can be achieved by rotating a solid, light-proof disk with a pie-shaped wedge cut in it between the light and the reaction solution, as shown in Fig. 15-1. The ratio of the light to the dark periods is then simply the ratio of the size of the pie-shaped wedge to the size of the rest of the disk. During the flashing cycles, the concentration of radicals $(M\cdot)$ and, consequently, the rate of polymerization, R_P, oscillate. We shall consider two extreme cases: one where the flickering rate is fast compared with τ_s and one where it is slow.

Light

Spinning disk

Reaction system

Figure 15-1

At slow flickering rates, the rate of polymerization during the light period is the steady-state value, $R_{P,s}$, and the rate during the dark period is zero. The average rate of polymerization is the average between these two values. If the light is on one-fourth of the time, then

$$R_{P,\text{av}} = \frac{R_{P,s}}{4}$$

If the flickering rate is fast compared with τ_s, the radicals produced during the light period do not have time to die out entirely during the dark period, and the rate during the dark period is not zero. The average rate is just that produced by the light that strikes the reaction solution. If the light is on one-fourth of the time, then one-fourth as much light strikes the solution as with steady illumination, and one-fourth as much initiator decomposes. However, since the rate of polymerization varies with the square root of the rate of formation of radicals [see Eq. (15-8b)], the average rate of polymerization is

$$R_{P,\text{av}} = \frac{R_{P,s}}{\sqrt{4}} = \frac{R_{P,s}}{2} \tag{15-15}$$

Thus, as the time of the flickering cycle passes through a value equal to τ_s, the rate of polymerization changes. If this rate is plotted versus the duration of the illumination, the value of τ_s can be obtained.

Table 15-3 gives data obtained by these methods for vinyl acetate under a particular set of experimental conditions. The lifetime of a growing chain is about 4 sec, and in that time it grows to 10^4 monomer units in length. It then terminates in a reaction with a bimolecular rate constant equal to over 10^7 liter mole^{-1} sec^{-1}. The chains grow despite this enormous termination rate constant because the concentration of radicals is extremely low (about $10^{-8}\ M$).

Table 15-3   Absolute rate constants for the polymerization of pure vinyl acetate at 25°C†

R_i	$= 1 \times 10^{-9}$ mole liter^{-1} sec^{-1}
$R_{P,s}$	$= 0.5 \times 10^{-4}$ mole liter^{-1} sec^{-1}
k_p^2/k_t	$= 3 \times 10^{-2}$ liter mole^{-1} sec^{-1}
τ_s	$= 4$ sec
k_p/k_t	$= 3 \times 10^{-5}$
k_p	$= 1,000$ liter mole^{-1} sec^{-1}
k_t	$= 3 \times 10^7$ liter mole^{-1} sec^{-1}
(M•)	$= 0.4 \times 10^{-8}$ mole/liter

† H. Kwart, H. S. Broadbent, and P. D. Bartlett, *J. Am. Chem. Soc.*, **72**, 1060 (1950); W. I. Bengough and H. W. Melville, *Proc. Roy. Soc. (London)*, Ser. A, **230**, 429 (1955).

COPOLYMERIZATIONS

Many useful plastics can be produced by allowing two different monomers to copolymerize, and the subject, therefore, has great practical interest. Furthermore, since the growing polymeric radical can add to either one of the two olefins present, the relative reactivities of the olefins can be calculated from the composition of the copolymer. However, the analysis of the system must allow for the fact that two different radicals are present. When two monomers copolymerize, the following reactions can occur:

	Rate
M₁• + M₁ ⟶ M₁•	$k_{11}(M_1\bullet)(M_1)$
M₁• + M₂ ⟶ M₂•	$k_{12}(M_1\bullet)(M_2)$
M₂• + M₁ ⟶ M₁•	$k_{21}(M_2\bullet)(M_1)$
M₂• + M₂ ⟶ M₂•	$k_{22}(M_2\bullet)(M_2)$

where M_1 is the first monomer, M_2 is the second, and $M_1\bullet$ and $M_2\bullet$ are the polymeric radicals having monomer 1 or monomer 2 on the end of the chain. Assume that the reactivity of the polymeric radical depends only on the end monomer and not on the composition of the rest of the chain. Also assume the steady state in both $M_1\bullet$ and $M_2\bullet$, so that

$$k_{21}(M_2\bullet)(M_1) = k_{12}(M_1\bullet)(M_2) \tag{15-16}$$

The rate of disappearance of the two monomers is given by

$$\frac{-d(M_1)}{dt} = k_{11}(M_1 \cdot)(M_1) + k_{21}(M_2 \cdot)(M_1) \qquad (15\text{-}17)$$

$$\frac{-d(M_2)}{dt} = k_{12}(M_1 \cdot)(M_2) + k_{22}(M_2 \cdot)(M_2) \qquad (15\text{-}18)$$

The following rate ratios are defined:

$$r_1 = \frac{k_{11}}{k_{12}}$$

$$r_2 = \frac{k_{22}}{k_{21}}$$

Division of (15-17) by (15-18) yields

$$\frac{d(M_1)}{d(M_2)} = \frac{(M_1)}{(M_2)} \left[\frac{k_{11}(M_1 \cdot) + k_{21}(M_2 \cdot)}{k_{12}(M_1 \cdot) + k_{22}(M_2 \cdot)} \right]$$

This can be written in the form †

$$\frac{d(M_1)}{d(M_2)} = \frac{(M_1)}{(M_2)} \left[\frac{r_1(M_1) + (M_2)}{(M_1) + r_2(M_2)} \right]$$

This important relation gives the relative rates of incorporation of the two monomers into the polymer as a function of their concentrations and r_1 and r_2.

The rate ratios r_1 and r_2 are called monomer reactivity ratios. For $r_1 > 1$, the polymeric radical ending with monomer 1 prefers to react with its own monomer rather than with monomer 2; for $r_1 < 1$, the polymeric radical ending in monomer 1 prefers to react with monomer 2. In the special situation where $r_1 = r_2 = 1$, the polymeric radical has no preference for either monomer, regardless of which monomer is on the end of the chain. In that case, the two monomers are distributed randomly along the polymer chain in a ratio depending only on the ratio of monomer concentrations in the reaction mixture. If r_1 and r_2 are both very small, the polymer will have alternating units of monomer 1 and 2.

† Multiply through by $(M_2)/k_{21}(M_2 \cdot)$ and substitute (15-16) into the resulting equation.

Table 15-4 Copolymer reactivity ratios at 60°C†

M₁	M₂	r_1	r_2
Styrene	Methyl methacrylate	0.5	0.5
Styrene	p-Nitrostyrene	0.2	1.1
Styrene	p-Chlorostyrene	0.7	1.0
Styrene	p-Methoxystyrene	1.2	0.8
Styrene	Acrylonitrile	0.4	0.04
Styrene	Vinyl acetate	55	0.01
Styrene	Ethyl vinyl ether	90	ca. 0
Styrene	Butadiene	0.78	1.4
Styrene	Vinyl chloride	17	0.02
Vinyl acetate	Vinyl chloride	0.2	1.7
Vinyl acetate	Methyl methacrylate	0.01	20

† L. J. Young, *J. Polymer Sci.*, **54**, 411 (1961).

Table 15–4 gives values of some typical reactivity ratios. For example, in the styrene–methyl methacrylate system, r_1 and r_2 both equal 0.5, meaning that each polymeric radical has about twice as much tendency to react with the opposite monomer unit. This type of preference for the cross-addition reaction is best explained as due to polar influences.

TRANSFER IN POLYMERIZATIONS

In transfer reactions, the growing polymer radical reacts with a substance that terminates one chain and starts another growing. For example, consider reaction with a hydrogen donor RH:

$$M_n\cdot + RH \xrightarrow{k_{tr}} M_n\!-\!H + R\cdot \qquad (15\text{-}19)$$

$$R\cdot + M \xrightarrow{k_a} M\cdot$$

In the simplest case, the rate constant for the addition of R· to the monomer is very large, and no retardation of polymerization results from transfer. In this case, the molecular weight of the polymer produced in the presence of RH is reduced but the rate of formation of polymer is unchanged. †

----

† If the reinitiation step is slow or if termination steps involving the primary radicals become important, then transfer slows the rate of polymer formation as well as producing molecular weight reduction.

Transfer, therefore, is a process in which molecular weight is changed without a change in the rate of polymerization, and the quantitative theory of transfer reactions requires an analysis of the factors that influence molecular weight. One measure of molecular weight is the degree of polymerization, defined as

$$\bar{P} = \frac{\text{Monomer units used}}{\text{Polymer molecules formed}} \qquad (15\text{-}20)$$

We shall restrict our attention to the common situation in which transfer occurs without retardation and where termination is entirely by combination. (Styrene plus an active hydrogen donor exemplifies this situation.) For the simple polymerization scheme below,

$$\text{M}\bullet + \text{M} \xrightarrow{k_p} \text{M}\bullet$$

$$2\text{M}\bullet \xrightarrow{k_t} \text{Polymer}$$

the degree of polymerization can be obtained from Eq. (15-20) as

$$\bar{P} = \frac{k_p(\text{M}\bullet)(\text{M})}{k_t(\text{M}\bullet)^2} = \frac{k_p(\text{M})}{k_t(\text{M}\bullet)}$$

Now, however, we consider the addition of reaction (15-19) as another way in which polymer molecules can be formed. Then, the degree of polymerization becomes

$$\bar{P} = \frac{k_p(\text{M}\bullet)(\text{M})}{k_t(\text{M}\bullet)^2 + k_{tr}(\text{M}\bullet)(\text{RH})}$$

On inversion and elimination of radical concentrations, using (15-7), this becomes

$$\frac{1}{\bar{P}} = \frac{k_t(\text{M}\bullet)}{k_p(\text{M})} + \frac{k_{tr}(\text{RH})}{k_p(\text{M})}$$

$$= \frac{k_t R_P}{k_p^2(\text{M})^2} + C_{\text{RH}} \frac{(\text{RH})}{(\text{M})}$$

where the transfer constant C is the ratio of k_{tr}/k_p for the particular transfer agent RH. Actually, all species present in the reaction system, including the monomer and the polymer, can function as transfer agents. Usually transfer studies are held to low conversions where transfer to the polymer can be neglected; however, transfer to monomer is important. Therefore, the transfer equation can be written as

$$\frac{1}{\bar{P}} = \frac{k_t R_P}{k_p{}^2(M)^2} + \text{Sum of all transfer terms}$$

$$= \frac{k_t R_P}{k_p{}^2(M)^2} + C_M + \Sigma_i C_i \frac{(i)}{(M)} \tag{15-21}$$

where C_M is the transfer constant of the monomer, C_i is that of any additional solvent or transfer agent present, and (i) is the molarity of the transfer agent. If the transfer agent is not an initiator, its presence does not change the rate of polymerization, and the first two terms of (15-21) are a constant. In that case, the transfer equation becomes

$1/\bar{P} \times 10^5$

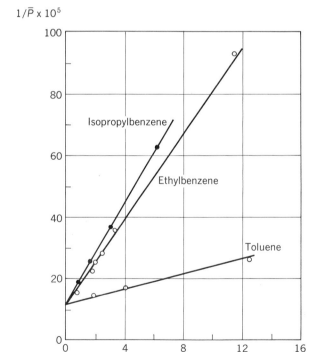

Figure 15-2   Transfer by hydrocarbon solvents to the polystyryl radical at 60°C.   [R. A. Gregg and F. R. Mayo, Discussions Faraday Society, **2,** 328 (1947).]

$$\frac{1}{P} = \text{const} + C_i \frac{(i)}{(M)} \tag{15-22}$$

and a graph of the inverse of the degree of polymerization versus the mole ratio of the transfer agent to monomer should be a straight line with a slope equal to the transfer constant. Figure 15-2 gives such a graph for a number of hydrocarbon solvents in the polymerization of styrene.

The transfer behavior shown in Fig. 15-2 might have been predicted. Isopropylbenzene is a better transfer agent than is ethylbenzene, which is better than toluene. The rate of hydrogen abstraction by the polystyryl radical in the transfer step, therefore, is $3° > 2° > 1°$. Table 15-5 gives additional transfer constants. Most hydrocarbons are poor transfer agents. The table shows that thiols, carbon tetrabromide, and pentaphenylethane are very effective transfer agents.

Table 15-5 Transfer constants at 60°C†

| | Transfer constant toward radical from | |
Transfer agent	Styrene	Vinyl acetate
Benzene	0.6×10^{-5}	
Toluene	1.6×10^{-5}	
Isopropylbenzene	18×10^{-5}	
Cyclohexane	0.4×10^{-5}	70×10^{-5}
Diphenylmethane	28×10^{-5}	
Triphenylmethane	65×10^{-5}	
Isopropyl alcohol	8×10^{-5}	
Propionic acid	0.5×10^{-5}	
Butyraldehyde	57×10^{-5}	$6,500 \times 10^{-5}$
Acetone	5×10^{-5}	120×10^{-5}
Aniline	20×10^{-5}	
Butyl chloride	0.4×10^{-5}	
Butyl iodide	18×10^{-5}	
Methyl disulfide	940×10^{-5}	
Chloroform	5×10^{-5}	1.3×10^{-2}
Carbon tetrabromide	2.2	ca. 40
Carbon tetrachloride	1.1×10^{-2}	
Pentaphenylethane	2.0	
Butanethiol	22	48
Hydrogen sulfide	ca. 5	
Styrene	8×10^{-5}	
Vinyl acetate	. . .	22×10^{-5}

† G. Henrici-Olivé and S. Olivé, *Fortschr. Hochpolymer.-Forsch.*, **2**, 496 (1961).

PROBLEMS

15-1 Using the data of Table 15-4, discuss the structure of (a) the styrene-acrylonitrile copolymer and (b) the styrene–vinyl acetate copolymer.

51-2 Draw a resonance structure for the transition state which rationalizes the alternation of monomers in the styrene–methyl methacrylate copolymer.

15-3 Table 15-5 gives the transfer constants for a number of substances. Write the equation for the chemical process representing the most likely mechanism for transfer by toluene, isopropyl alcohol, butanethiol, carbon tetrabromide, butyl iodide, and methyl disulfide.

15-4 Using radioactive AIBN as an initiator, a sample of styrene is polymerized to an average degree of polymerization of 1.0×10^4. The AIBN has activity equal to 1.0×10^8 counts/min/mole in a liquid scintillation counter. If 1.00 g of the polystyrene has an activity of 100 counts/min, show that the termination mechanism is combination.

15-5 Using the equation on page 243 which describes copolymerization, calculate the composition of the polymer formed in the first 1% of the polymerization if the concentrations of M_1 and M_2 are equal and (a) $r_1 = r_2 = 1$; (b) $r_1 = 0.01$, $r_2 = 10$; (c) $r_1 = r_2 = 0.01$; (d) $r_1 = r_2 = 10$.

15-6 In pure styrene at 60°C, polystyrene formed by thermal self-initiated polymerization (i.e., no added initiators) has a degree of polymerization of 1.0×10^4 and a rate of polymerization of 2×10^{-6} mole liter^{-1} sec^{-1}. Give the rate of polymerization and the degree of polymerization for a 50% solution by volume of styrene in toluene (435 g toluene and 450 g styrene per liter). Assume small conversion to polymer. Repeat the calculation for a 0.1% by volume solution of carbon tetrabromide in styrene. Use the densities of 3.42 g/ml for carbon tetrabromide and 0.90 g/ml for styrene and assume no volume change on mixing.

15-7 The polymerization of styrene can be initiated by *t*-butyl peroxide at 60°C. If a solution of 1.0 *M* peroxide and 7.0 *M* styrene is used, the rate of polymerization is found to be 1.05×10^{-5} mole liter^{-1} sec^{-1} and the degree of polymerization is 3.23×10^3. Calculate the transfer constant for *t*-butyl peroxide. Use the value for C_M given in Table 15-5. [W. A. Pryor, A. Lee, and C. E. Witt, *J. Am. Chem. Soc.*, **86**, 4229 (1964).]

SUGGESTIONS FOR FURTHER READING

Bamford, C. H., W. G. Barb, A. D. Jenkins, and P. F. Onyon: "Kinetics of Vinyl Polymerization by Radical Mechanisms," Butterworth Scientific Publications, London, 1958.

Bevington, J. C.: "Radical Polymerization," Academic Press Inc., New York, 1961.

Billmeyer, F. W., Jr.: "Textbook of Polymer Science," Interscience Publishers, John Wiley & Sons, Inc., New York, 1962.

Burnett, G. M.: "Mechanism of Polymer Reactions," Interscience Publishers, Inc., New York, 1954.

D'Alelio, G. F.: "Fundamental Principles of Polymerization," John Wiley & Sons, Inc., New York, 1952.

Flory, P. J.: "Principles of Polymer Chemistry," Cornell University Press, Ithaca, N.Y., 1953.

Stille, J. K.: "Introduction to Polymer Chemistry," John Wiley & Sons, Inc., New York, 1962.

chapter
sixteen Aromatic
Substitution

Aromatic substitutions by radical mechanisms are of great practical use-fulness since the products are different from those obtained in the analo-gous ionic substitutions. In the latter, the familiar pattern is that electron-donating groups such as alkyl or alkoxy are *ortho*- and *para*-directing and lead to enhanced rates of substitution; electron-withdrawing groups, such as nitro, lead to *meta* substitution products and deactivation of the ring. In the radical process, these rules no longer hold. Homolytic substitution by phenyl radicals from benzoyl peroxide, for example, is *faster* on *either* nitrobenzene or toluene than on benzene itself, and both nitrobenzene and toluene are substituted mainly at the *ortho* position. The differences in the two mechanisms are shown below for substitution on chlorobenzene.

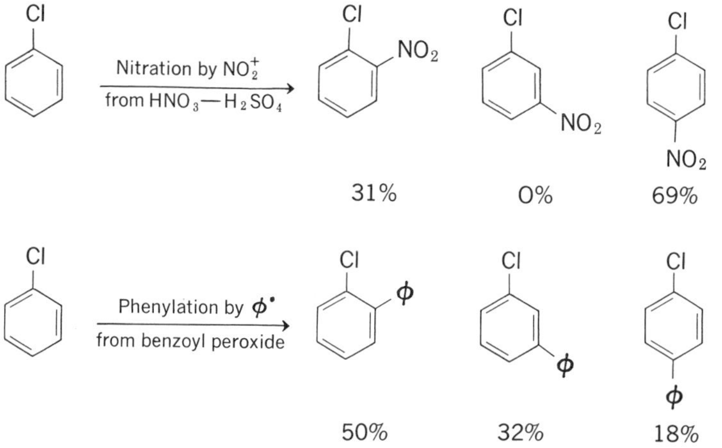

Nitration of chlorobenzene, a typical ionic substitution reaction involving the electrophilic NO_2^+ ion, gives mainly *para* product. Further, since a halogen is a slightly deactivating substituent (although *ortho-para* directing), chlorobenzene is attacked only 0.03 times as fast as benzene itself. In phenylation of chlorobenzene, the product is mainly *ortho*. Further, chlorobenzene reacts about 1.4 times faster than benzene.

The suggestion that there might be two possible mechanisms for aromatic substitution was first made by Hey in 1934, and in 1937 Hey and Waters outlined the ionic and radical mechanisms in detail and sug-gested the utility of the radical path. Despite an enormous amount of work since that time, the mechanism of homolytic aromatic substitution is still not entirely clear. The difficulty is that monosubstitution products are usually obtained together with intractable tars which are the result of further reactions, and only recently have physical techniques allowing

252

accurate analysis of the product mixtures become available. In early work, the products were identified by isolation. Frequently the *para* isomer is the least soluble in the reaction mixture and crystallizes from it most easily. Therefore, older work frequently implied that products were mainly *para*. More modern analyses for the reaction mixtures by spectroscopy or by gas-phase chromatography have indicated that products other than the *para* isomer are formed.

PHENYLATION

The homolytic substitution reaction that has been studied most thoroughly is phenylation. The phenyl radical can be generated in several ways:

$$\phi-\overset{\overset{\displaystyle O}{\|}}{C}-O-O-\overset{\overset{\displaystyle O}{\|}}{C}-\phi \longrightarrow 2\phi CO_2\bullet \longrightarrow 2\phi\bullet + 2CO_2 \qquad (16\text{-}1a)$$

$$\phi-\overset{\overset{\displaystyle N=O}{|}}{N}-CO-CH_3 \longrightarrow \phi\bullet + N_2 + CH_3CO_2\bullet \qquad (16\text{-}1b)$$

$$\phi-N=N-C\phi_3 \longrightarrow \phi\bullet + N_2 + \phi_3C\bullet \qquad (16\text{-}1c)$$

$$\phi N_2^+Cl^- + NaOH \longrightarrow \phi\bullet + N_2 + NaCl + OH\bullet \qquad (16\text{-}1d)$$

$$Ar-H \xrightarrow{\phi\bullet} Ar-\phi \qquad (16\text{-}2)$$

If the substituting species in (16-2) were a free phenyl radical, it would be anticipated that any of these sources of phenyl radicals would lead to the same rate behavior and isomer ratios. This fundamental prediction has not been tested in any detail. However, the data which are available suggest that different sources of radicals give similar, but not necessarily identical, behavior.

Reaction (16-1a) is the familiar decomposition of benzoyl peroxide. When the decomposition occurs in aromatic solvents, nuclear substitution of the solvent occurs. The product is the result of phenyl radicals from the peroxide attacking the solvent; very little, if any, of the other two possible products are formed. For example, if the solvent is Ar—H, the products are as shown below.

$$Ar-H \xrightarrow{\phi\bullet} Ar-\phi + \phi-\phi + Ar-Ar$$
$$\qquad\qquad \text{Mainly} \qquad \text{Much less}$$

Reaction (16-1b) was developed by Hey and his students. *N*-Nitrosoacetanilide (acylphenylnitrosamine), prepared by nitrosation of acylphenylamine with nitrosyl chloride, rearranges *in situ* to the diazoester:

$$\underset{\substack{\text{N}=\text{O} \\ | \\ \phi-\text{N}-\text{CO}-\text{CH}_3 \\ \textit{N}\text{-Nitrosoacetanilide}}}{} \xrightarrow{\text{Rearrangement}} \underset{\substack{\text{O} \\ \| \\ \phi-\text{N}=\text{N}-\text{O}-\text{C}-\text{CH}_3 \\ \text{Phenyldiazo acetate}}}{}$$

This rearrangement is the rate-determining step; the diazoester undergoes rapid homolysis to phenyl radicals.

$$\underset{\substack{\text{O} \\ \|}}{\phi-\text{N}=\text{N}-\text{O}-\text{C}-\text{CH}_3} \longrightarrow \phi\cdot \ + \ \text{N}_2 \ + \ \text{CH}_3-\text{CO}_2\cdot$$

Reaction (16-1c) also was first investigated by Hey. Phenylazotriphenylmethane decomposes rapidly at 60°C and is a convenient phenyl source; the more stable trityl radical does not interfere in the phenylation reaction.

Reaction (16-1d), the so-called Gomberg reaction, utilizes diazonium salts produced by the diazotization of aniline with nitrous acid as a radical source. Strong base converts the diazonium salt (usually the chloride) to the covalent diazohydroxide, and this species decomposes to form phenyl radicals. The system is heterogeneous: The diazonium salt is converted to the hydroxide in the aqueous phase, and the covalent diazohydroxide diffuses into the organic phase, decomposes, and leads to phenylation of the organic substrate. Even though the yields are only 10 to 40% and tars are produced, the reaction is of interest since the starting materials are readily available.

Table 16-1 gives data for the phenylation of a number of substrates, using three sources of phenyl radicals. Note that nitrobenzene, chlorobenzene, bromobenzene, and toluene all react faster than benzene. In the ionic electrophilic substitution reaction, an electrophilic species such as NO_2^+ attacks the aromatic ring; therefore, electron-donating substituents speed the reaction and electron-withdrawing substituents retard the rate. However, in homolytic substitutions where neutral radicals attack, any polar effects would be expected to be much smaller, and both electron-withdrawing and electron-donating groups can stabilize the transition state.

Direct evidence that both electron-donating and electron-withdrawing groups stabilize a system containing an odd electron comes from studies of the dissociation of ring-substituted hexaphenylethanes.

Table 16-1   Relative rates of phenylation of substituted benzenes†

X in X—ϕ	Phenyl source		
	Benzoyl peroxide 70°	NO $\mid$ ϕ—N—COCH$_3$ 20°	ϕ_3Bi photolysis 80°
NO$_2$	4.0	3.1	
H	(1.0)	(1.0)	(1.0)
Cl	1.4	1.5	
Br	1.7	1.8	
CH$_3$	1.7‡	1.8	1.7

† G. H. Williams, "Homolytic Aromatic Substitution," Pergamon Press, New York, 1960, p. 57; R. Huisgen and R. Grashey, *Ann. Chem.*, **607**, 46 (1957).

‡ Hydrogen abstraction from the methyl group occurs to the extent of about 15%.

$$Ar_3C—CAr_3 \xrightleftharpoons{K_{eq}} 2Ar_3C\cdot \qquad (16\text{-}3)$$

For example,† the equilibrium constant K_{eq} for the dissociation of hexaphenylethane is 2×10^{-3} at 25°C in benzene. The constant for the compound having four *p*-methyl substituents is sevenfold larger; that with six *o*-methoxy groups is 600-fold larger; and the compound containing six *p*-nitro groups is 100% dissociated.

Table 16-1 also shows that phenyl radicals from benzoyl peroxide, nitrosoacetanilide, or from photolysis of triphenylbismuth all give approximately the same rate ratio for phenylation of toluene relative to benzene. (The data are complicated by the fact that they are measured at different temperatures, and this rate ratio is undoubtedly temperature dependent. Also, in toluene some hydrogen abstraction from the side chain occurs, and products from this reaction were measured only for the peroxide reaction.)

Table 16-2 gives data on the isomer distribution of the product from phenylation, using benzoyl peroxide. The table shows very different behavior from that obtained in ionic substitutions. Both electron-donating and electron-withdrawing substituents give products in similar ratios.

† G. W. Wheland, "Advanced Organic Chemistry," John Wiley & Sons, Inc., New York, 3d ed., 1960, p. 774.

Table 16-2   Isomer distribution of products from phenylation of C_6H_5—X using benzoyl peroxide at $80°C$†

	Isomer % in [structure of X on ring with φ]		
X in C_6H_5—X	Ortho	Meta	Para
NO_2	62	10	28
Cl	50	32	18
Br	49	33	18
CH_3	67	19	14

† G. H. Williams, "Homolytic Aromatic Substitution," Pergamon
Press, New York, 1960, p. 68.

MECHANISMS OF PHENYLATION USING BENZOYL PEROXIDE

Three reactions between a phenyl radical and an aromatic substrate can
be envisioned:

$$\phi\cdot + ArH \longrightarrow \begin{cases} \phi{-}Ar + H\cdot & (16\text{-}4a) \\ \phi H + Ar\cdot & (16\text{-}4b) \\ (\phi ArH)\cdot & (16\text{-}4c) \end{cases}$$

Reaction (16-4a) is a direct displacement of H• by φ•; (16-4b) is a hydrogen
abstraction; (16-4c) is addition of phenyl to the aromatic ring to form an
addition complex. Of these three possibilities, reaction (16-4b) is usually
an unimportant side reaction. It would be expected to lead to the formation of Ar—Ar, and, as was pointed out above, this is a minor product.

The biaryl product Ar—φ could result either from the direct displacement reaction (16-4a) or from a two-step sequence involving the
addition complex shown in (16-4c). This two-step mechanism is shown
in greater detail below for the case where Ar—H is benzene.

$$\phi\cdot + \phi H \longrightarrow [\text{cyclohexadienyl radical with } \phi \text{ and } H] \qquad (16\text{-}5)$$

$$\phi\text{-}H \text{ radical} + R\bullet \longrightarrow \phi\text{-}\phi + RH \qquad (16\text{-}6)$$

In this scheme, $R\bullet$ is any radical present in the system, including $\phi\bullet$. In the reaction of benzoyl peroxide with benzene it has been established that the chief mode of formation of biphenyl is the two-step sequence shown in (16-5) and (16-6) rather than the direct displacement shown in (16-4a). Calculations based on bond energies show that (16-4a) is endothermic whereas the sum of (16-5) and (16-6) is exothermic. However, the most convincing evidence establishing the two-step mechanism has been obtained from the careful examination of reaction products that is made possible by modern analytical techniques.

The reaction of benzoyl peroxide with benzene (run in dilute solution to minimize products resulting from the induced decomposition) has been found to give the following mixture of products:†

$$\phi\text{-}\overset{O}{\overset{\|}{C}}\text{-}O\text{-}O\text{-}\overset{O}{\overset{\|}{C}}\text{-}\phi \;\xrightarrow[\text{Benzene}]{\text{Reflux}}\; CO_2 \;+\; \phi CO_2H \;+\; [\text{dihydrobiphenyl}] \;+\; \phi\text{-}\phi$$

$$0.01M \qquad\qquad\qquad 1.77 \qquad 0.08 \qquad\qquad 0.18 \qquad\qquad 0.36$$

$$+\; \phi\text{-}\overset{O}{\overset{\|}{C}}\text{-}O\text{-}\phi \;+\; [\text{product}] \;+\; [\text{product}]$$

$$0.03 \qquad\qquad\qquad 0.22 \qquad\qquad\qquad 0.27$$

where the numbers under the products give the moles formed per mole of peroxide. The material balance is excellent: The yield of CO_2 indicates that $(1.77 + 0.08 + 0.03)/2.0$, or 94% of the peroxide decomposed. The products given account for 82% of the phenyl groups from the peroxide as follows:

$$\begin{aligned}
&.08\\
&.18\\
&.36\\
&.03\\
2 \times .22 =\; &.44\\
2 \times .27 =\; &\underline{.54}\\
&1.63 \text{ moles of phenyl groups per mole of peroxide}
\end{aligned}$$

† D. F. DeTar, 17th Organic Symposium, June, 1961.

The nature of these products clearly implicates the addition complex as an intermediate in the reaction sequence. The complex reacts by disproportionation, combination, and loss of hydrogen.

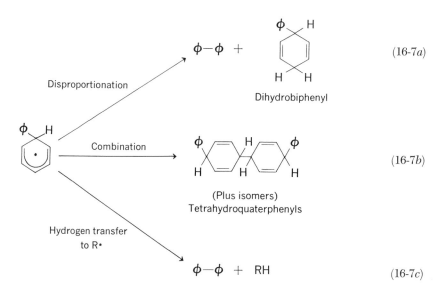

(16-7a)

(16-7b)

(16-7c)

A detailed study of the yields of these reaction products gives still more mechanistic information.† Figure 16-1 shows the variation in the yield (mole/mole of peroxide) of biphenyl, dihydrobiphenyl, benzoic acid, and methyl benzoate as a function of the initial concentration of benzoyl peroxide. Extrapolation to infinite dilution, where no induced decomposition could occur, shows that the yield of benzoic acid would be zero and the yields of biphenyl and dihydrobiphenyl would be equal. This suggests the chief reaction producing biphenyl at low concentrations of peroxide is the disproportionation reaction (16-7a). At infinite dilution the yield of biphenyl is about 0.24 mole/mole of peroxide; most of the remaining radicals are converted to tetrahydroquaterphenyls by reaction (16-7b).

As the initial concentration of the peroxide is increased, induced decomposition becomes a major path for product formation. An induced decomposition which appears particularly reasonable is that involving the addition complex.

† D. H. Hey, M. J. Perkins, and G. H. Williams, *J. Chem. Soc.*, 3412 (1964).

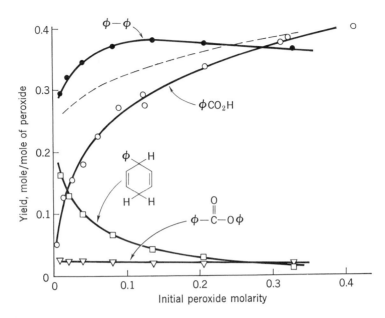

Figure 16-1 Yield of biphenyl, dihydrobiphenyl, benzoic acid, and phenyl benzoate from the reaction of benzoyl peroxide with benzene at 80°C. [*From D. H. Hey, M. J. Perkins, and G. H. Williams, J. Chem. Soc., 3412 (1964).*]

$$\underset{H}{\overset{\phi}{\bigodot}} \cdot \ + \ \phi CO_2 - CO_2\phi \ \longrightarrow \ \overset{\phi}{\bigodot} \ + \ \phi CO_2H \ + \ \phi CO_2 \cdot$$

$$(16\text{-}7d)$$

If the yields of biphenyl formed at higher concentrations are due to the sum of (16-7a) and (16-7d), then the yield of biphenyl should equal the sum of the yields of dihydrobiphenyl plus benzoic acid. Figure 16-1 shows this sum as a dashed line, and it is approximately equal to the biphenyl yield. Reaction (16-7d) is hydrogen donation from a radical species to a peroxide. A similar step has been identified as responsible for the increased rate of decomposition of *t*-butyl peroxide in certain alcohols and amines.† The mechanism for the reaction in 2-butanol, for example, is shown below.

† E. S. Huyser and C. J. Bredeweg, *J. Am. Chem. Soc.*, **86**, 2401 (1964); E. S. Huyser, C. J. Bredeweg, and R. M. VanScoy, *ibid.*, **86**, 4148 (1964).

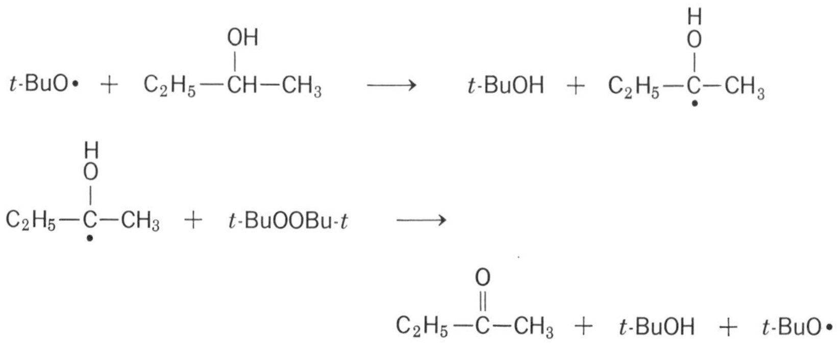

$$t\text{-BuO}\cdot \;+\; \underset{\displaystyle \overset{\displaystyle OH}{|}}{C_2H_5-CH-CH_3} \;\longrightarrow\; t\text{-BuOH} \;+\; \underset{\displaystyle \overset{\displaystyle \overset{H}{O}}{|}}{C_2H_5-\underset{\bullet}{C}-CH_3}$$

$$\underset{\displaystyle \overset{\displaystyle \overset{H}{O}}{|}}{C_2H_5-\underset{\bullet}{C}-CH_3} \;+\; t\text{-BuOOBu-}t \;\longrightarrow$$

$$C_2H_5-\overset{\displaystyle \overset{O}{\|}}{C}-CH_3 \;+\; t\text{-BuOH} \;+\; t\text{-BuO}\cdot$$

The reaction of the addition complex with benzoate radicals might also appear probable at higher peroxide concentrations.

However, kinetic analysis plus other data has indicated that this reaction accounts for 5% or less of the total products from the reactions of benzoyl peroxide with benzene.[†] In phenylation reactions of substituted benzene derivatives, however, abstraction of hydrogen by benzoate radicals can become the main reaction pathway which produces biphenyl.

Figure 16-1 shows that the yield of phenyl benzoate remains constant as the peroxide concentration changes. Ester probably arises from several reactions, but apparently these reactions vary in different ways with peroxide concentration such that their sum remains approximately constant. Three possible ester-forming reactions are shown below.

$$\phi\cdot + \phi CO_2-CO_2\phi \longrightarrow \phi CO_2\phi + \phi CO_2\cdot \qquad (16\text{-}8a)$$

$$\phi CO_2-CO_2\phi \longrightarrow \phi CO_2\phi + CO_2 \qquad (16\text{-}8b)$$

$$\phi CO_2\cdot + \phi H \longrightarrow (\phi CO_2\phi H)\cdot \xrightarrow{R\cdot} \phi CO_2\phi + RH \qquad (16\text{-}8c)$$

Reaction (16-8a) is induced decomposition, (16-8b) is cage decomposition, and (16-8c) is the two-step mechanism by benzoate instead of by phenyl radicals. In concentrated solutions, reaction (16-8a) undoubtedly occurs, and it is probable that some ester is also formed by the cage reaction

[†] D. H. Hey, M. J. Perkins, and G. H. Williams, *J. Chem. Soc.*, 3412 (1964).

(16-8*b*). Under the usual concentration conditions, however, reaction (16-8*c*) apparently is the main path responsible for ester formation. This follows from the fact that *p*-chlorobenzoyl peroxide gives only phenyl *p*-chlorobenzoate and no *p*-chlorophenyl *p*-chlorobenzoate.†

$$\underset{\text{(Ar}=p\text{-chlorophenyl})}{\overset{O\quad\quad O}{\overset{\|\quad\quad\|}{Ar C-O-O-CAr}}} \quad\xrightarrow{\text{Benzene}}\quad \underset{\text{Formed}}{\overset{O}{\overset{\|}{\phi O-CAr}}} \quad+\quad \underset{\text{Not formed}}{\overset{O}{\overset{\|}{Ar O-CAr}}}$$

Notice that one consequence of the two-step mechanism for biaryl formation is that the yield of biphenyl can be lower than the total amount of the addition complex which was formed, since some of the addition complex can be converted to dihydrobiphenyl or to tetrahydroquaterphenyls. This illustrates a critical difficulty in obtaining fundamental information from such reactions. If the phenylation of a substituted benzene is studied, it cannot necessarily be assumed that there is any relation between the relative yield of a *meta*-substituted biphenyl and the relative rate of attack at the *meta* position. It is conceivable that the product from *meta* attack is preferentially diverted to dimerization products and does not appear as a biphenyl-type product. For example, on page 224, the results of methyl radical addition to aromatic compounds were discussed, and it was pointed out that good agreement is obtained between product analysis and theoretically calculated reactivities. Data such as these must be treated with caution since other products are formed, and the ultimate products isolated may not correctly reflect the relative rate at which attack actually occurred at any given position.‡

Table 16-3 gives the relative rates of reaction of a series of substituted phenyl radicals with nitrobenzene, benzene, and toluene. The *p*-nitrophenyl radical attacks these substrates in the order ϕ—CH$_3$ > ϕ—H > ϕ—NO$_2$. Therefore, the *p*-nitrophenyl radical is an electrophilic radical that attacks benzene rings faster if they contain electron-donating groups. The unsubstituted phenyl radical attacks both toluene and nitrobenzene faster than benzene. The *p*-methylphenyl radical attacks nitrobenzene at the fastest relative rate.

† D. F. DeTar, 17th Organic Symposium, June, 1961; B. M. Lynch and R. B. Moore, *Can. J. Chem.*, **40**, 1461 (1962).

‡ A. L. J. Beckwith and W. A. Waters, *J. Chem. Soc.*, 1665 (1957); A. L. J. Beckwith, *ibid.*, 2248 (1962).

Table 16-3   Relative rates for arylation of nitrobenzene and toluene by various aryl radicals at 80°C†

Substrate	Radical			
	NO$_2$	Cl		CH$_3$
Nitrobenzene	0.9	1.5	4.0	5.1
Benzene	(1)	(1)	(1)	(1)
Toluene	2.6	1.3	1.7	1.0

† G. H. Williams, "Homolytic Aromatic Substitution," Pergamon Press, New York, 1960, p. 67. A correction has been made for the fact that benzene has six reactive positions whereas toluene and nitrobenzene have only five.

PROBLEMS

16-1   Phenyl radicals from benzoyl peroxide react with benzene to form a cyclohexadienyl radical. This radical would be expected to disproportionate, dimerize, abstract hydrogen, and donate hydrogen. Exemplify each of these processes with an equation.

16-2   Referring to Fig. 16-1, list the equations which represent the most important pathway at low peroxide concentrations for formation of: biphenyl, dihydrobiphenyl, benzoic acid, and methyl benzoate. Do the same for high peroxide concentrations.

16-3   Rationalize the fact that the p-nitrophenyl radical reacts with toluene faster than with nitrobenzene, whereas the reverse is true for the p-methylphenyl radical.

16-4   A prediction of the mechanism given in Eq. (16-7) has been tested by E. L. Eliel, S. Meyerson, Z. Welvart, and S. H. Wilen, *J. Am. Chem. Soc.*, **82**, 2936 (1960). They studied the decomposition of benzoyl peroxide in C$_6$H$_5$D. Using 0.4 M peroxide, they found the following isomer content for the bibenzyl product: 25% C$_6$H$_5$—C$_6$H$_5$, 74% C$_{12}$H$_9$D, 1% C$_{12}$H$_8$D$_2$. Explain how each of these products could arise.

16-5   Consider the arylation reaction of ϕ—X with benzoyl peroxide. Is it possible for the relative yields of *ortho-*, *meta-*, and *para-*substituted biphenyls *not* to be equal to the relative rate at which phenyl radicals attack the *ortho, meta,* and *para* positions? Draw reactions which indicate at least one way in which phenyl radicals might attack the *para* position faster than the *meta* but a larger yield of *meta* substitution product be isolated.

16-6 When benzene is arylated with *N*-nitrosoacetanilide, it is found that the yield of biphenyl is much larger than the yield of CO_2. This suggests that acetate radicals are not involved in the reaction since they would decompose to form CO_2. Suggest a mechanism involving an induced decomposition which produces biphenyl without generating acetate radicals. [D. B. Denney, N. E. Gershman, and A. Appelbaum, *J. Am. Chem. Soc.*, **86**, 3180 (1964).]

SUGGESTIONS FOR FURTHER READING

Augood, D. R., and G. H. Williams: *Chem. Rev.*, **57**, 123 (1957).

Dermer, O. C., and M. T. Edmison: *Chem. Rev.*, **57**, 77 (1957).

Williams, G. H.: "Homolytic Aromatic Substitution," Pergamon Press, New York, 1960.

chapter
seventeen Rearrangements

Rearrangements of free radicals, although not commonplace, do occur in some systems. Most often a radical rearrangement is only a nuisance and makes the product mixture even more complex than usual. Sometimes, however, radical rearrangements can be utilized in syntheses. The first radical rearrangement was identified by Urry and Kharasch in 1944, and the subject has become clarified only in the last decade.

Rearrangements occur very frequently in carbonium ion systems, occasionally in free radical systems, and very infrequently in carbanion systems. Simple molecular orbital principles give an insight into why this should be true.† In the rearrangement from (I) to (III), the system must pass through the triangular configuration (II):

$$\begin{array}{ccc} \text{(I)} & \text{(II)} & \text{(III)} \end{array}$$

The energy of activation for the rearrangement step can be related to the difference in energy between (I) and the transition state (II). The three orbitals for a three-atom structure such as (II) consist of one bonding orbital and two degenerate antibonding orbitals. Electrons in the antibonding orbitals destabilize the system and raise its energy. In the case of a carbonium ion, only two electrons are present, and they can be paired and put in the lowest bonding orbital (see Fig. 17-1a). For the radical, one more electron is present, and it must go into one of the antibonding orbitals (Fig. 17-1b). In the case of the carbanion, two electrons must go into these orbitals, and this system would be predicted to be the least stable of the three (Fig. 17-1c). (As Fig. 17-1c shows, the carbanion transition state would be predicted to be a triplet.)

1,2-ARYL MIGRATIONS

By far the largest number of radical rearrangements are those where an aryl group moves from one position to the adjacent atom. The radical undergoing rearrangement can be generated in a number of ways. For

† A. Streitwieser, "Molecular Orbital Theory for Organic Chemists," John Wiley & Sons, Inc., New York, 1961, pp. 380–381; J. D. Roberts, "Molecular Orbital Calculations," W. A. Benjamin, Inc., New York, 1962, pp. 118–121; H. E. Zimmerman and A. Zweig, J. Am. Chem. Soc., 83, 1196 (1961).

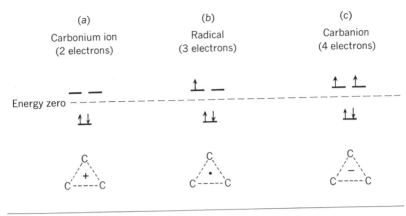

(a)
Carbonium ion
(2 electrons)

(b)
Radical
(3 electrons)

(c)
Carbanion
(4 electrons)

Energy zero

Figure 17-1   Energy levels for a triangular structure of three orbitals.

example, the treatment of phenylisovaleraldehyde with peroxides gives the following results:†

$$\phi-\underset{\underset{C}{|}}{\overset{\overset{C}{|}}{C}}-C-CHO \xrightarrow{R\cdot} \phi-\underset{\underset{C}{|}}{\overset{\overset{C}{|}}{C}}-C-\overset{O}{\overset{\|}{C}\cdot} \xrightarrow{-CO} \phi-\underset{\underset{C}{|}}{\overset{\overset{C}{|}}{C}}-C\cdot$$

(IV)

(IV) $\xrightarrow{\text{Rearrangement}}$ $\cdot\underset{\underset{C}{|}}{\overset{\overset{C}{|}}{C}}-C-\phi$ (17-1)

(IV) $+$ $\phi-\underset{\underset{C}{|}}{\overset{\overset{C}{|}}{C}}-C-CHO \longrightarrow \phi-\underset{\underset{CH_3}{|}}{\overset{\overset{CH_3}{|}}{C}}-CH_3 + \phi-\underset{\underset{C}{|}}{\overset{\overset{C}{|}}{C}}-C-\overset{O}{\overset{\|}{C}\cdot}$ (17-2)

$\cdot\underset{\underset{C}{|}}{\overset{\overset{C}{|}}{C}}-C-\phi + \phi-\underset{\underset{C}{|}}{\overset{\overset{C}{|}}{C}}-C-CHO \longrightarrow H-\underset{\underset{CH_3}{|}}{\overset{\overset{CH_3}{|}}{C}}-CH_2\phi + \phi-\underset{\underset{C}{|}}{\overset{\overset{C}{|}}{C}}-C-\overset{O}{\overset{\|}{C}\cdot}$

This system is a particularly favorable one for rearrangement since a primary radical rearranges to a more stable tertiary one.   In pure aldehyde as

† S. Winstein and F. H. Seubold, *J. Am. Chem. Soc.*, **69**, 2916 (1947); F. H. Seubold, *ibid.*, **75**, 2532 (1953).

solvent, 60% of the hydrocarbon product is of the rearranged structure. Therefore, under these conditions, reaction (17-1) is slightly faster than (17-2). If this mechanism is correct, the amount of rearrangement depends on the concentration of hydrogen donors in the system. In pure aldehyde, the most active hydrogen donor is the aldehyde itself. Therefore, if the aldehyde concentration is decreased, the rate of reaction (17-1) should increase relative to reaction (17-2) and a larger amount of rearrangement should be observed. In agreement with this, the amount of rearrangement increases from 60 to 80% when the aldehyde is diluted to 1 M with chlorobenzene as solvent. The addition of a very active hydrogen donor (such as a thiol) should cause (**IV**) to be converted to unrearranged product even faster, and less rearrangement should be observed. This has been confirmed in related systems.

These considerations rule out a mechanism whereby reactions (17-1) and (17-2) are compressed into a single step in which the phenyl pushes out the CO. The transition state for this hypothetical single-step process is shown below.

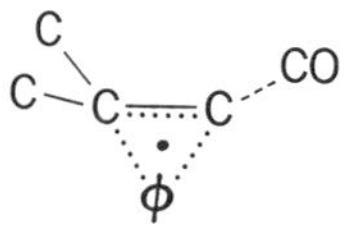

Not observed

Rearrangements of radicals generated from the decarbonylation of aldehydes also occur in the related triphenyl system.[†]

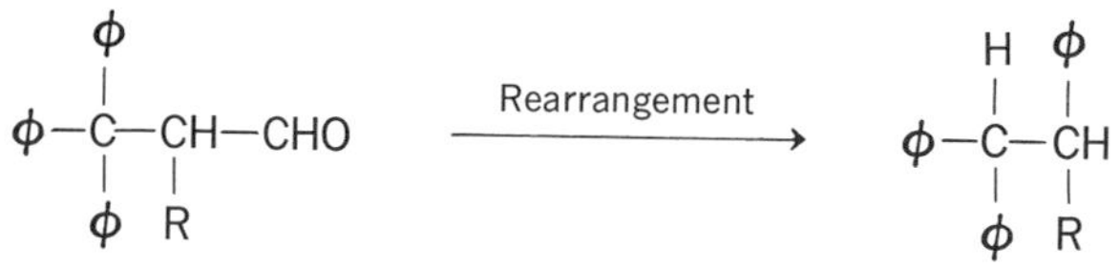

$(R = H, CH_3)$

Cyclic aldehydes may also undergo decarbonylation with rearrangement.[‡]

[†] D. Y. Curtin and J. C. Kauer, *J. Org. Chem.*, **25**, 880 (1960).
[‡] J. W. Wilt and H. Philip, *J. Org. Chem.*, **25**, 891 (1960).

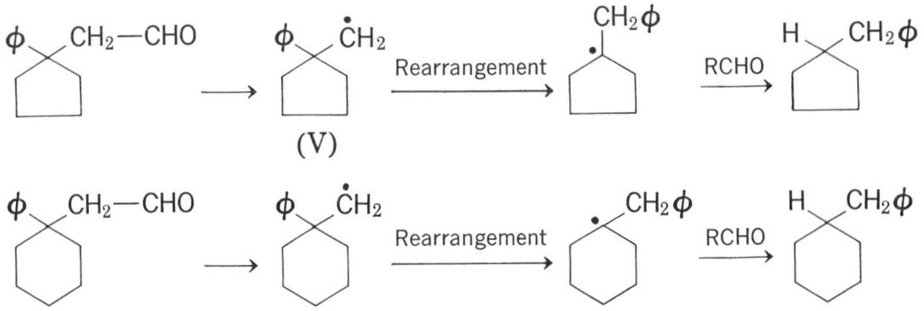

ϕ–CH$_2$—CHO $\rightarrow$ ϕ–$\overset{\bullet}{C}$H$_2$ $\xrightarrow{\text{Rearrangement}}$ (V) $\xrightarrow{\text{RCHO}}$

ϕ–CH$_2$—CHO $\rightarrow$ ϕ–$\overset{\bullet}{C}$H$_2$ $\xrightarrow{\text{Rearrangement}}$ $\xrightarrow{\text{RCHO}}$

In the cyclopentyl compound shown above, the extent of rearrangement increases from 63 to 92% when the aldehyde is diluted to 1 M with chlorobenzene. The rearrangement decreases to less than 2% if benzyl mercaptan is added; this very active hydrogen donor traps the first radical (V) before it rearranges.

In the above cases, a primary or secondary radical rearranges to a more stable tertiary radical. The rearrangement from one primary radical to another primary radical also occurs in some circumstances. For example, 3-phenylpropanal-2-C-14 rearranges to the extent of 4% at 170°C. The addition of thiophenol reduces the amount of rearrangement, indicating that the mechanism most likely involves radicals.†

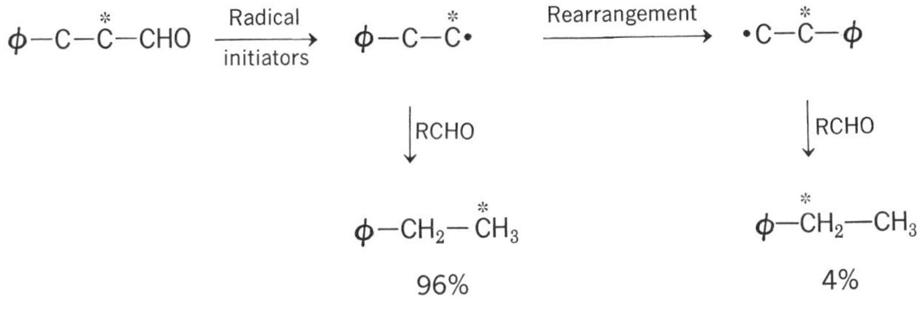

ϕ–C–$\overset{*}{C}$–CHO $\xrightarrow[\text{initiators}]{\text{Radical}}$ ϕ–C–$\overset{*}{C}\cdot$ $\xrightarrow{\text{Rearrangement}}$ $\cdot$C–$\overset{*}{C}$–ϕ

$\downarrow$RCHO $\qquad\qquad\qquad\qquad\qquad$ $\downarrow$RCHO

ϕ–CH$_2$–$\overset{*}{C}$H$_3$ $\qquad\qquad\qquad\qquad$ ϕ–$\overset{*}{C}$H$_2$—CH$_3$

96% $\qquad\qquad\qquad\qquad\qquad\qquad$ 4%

All the cases considered so far involve radicals generated in decarbonylation reactions of aldehydes. However, radicals generated in other ways may also rearrange. For example, when neophyl chloride is treated with a Grignard reagent in the presence of cobaltous bromide, the products include t-butylbenzene, isobutylbenzene, 2-methyl-3-phenyl-1-propene, 2,2-dimethylstyrene, and a mixture of dimers. The radical mechanism shown below has been suggested to explain these products.‡

† L. H. Slaugh, *J. Am. Chem. Soc.*, **81**, 2262 (1959).
‡ W. H. Urry and M. S. Kharasch, *J. Am. Chem. Soc.*, **66**, 1438 (1944).

$$RMgBr \;+\; CoBr_2 \;\longrightarrow\; RCoBr \;+\; MgBr_2$$

$$RCoBr \;\longrightarrow\; R\cdot \;+\; CoBr$$

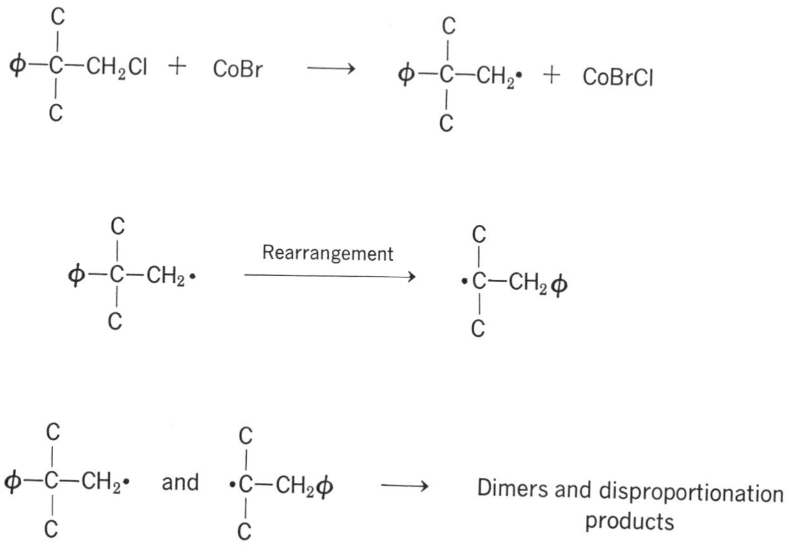

$$\phi-\underset{\underset{C}{|}}{\overset{\overset{C}{|}}{C}}-CH_2Cl \;+\; CoBr \;\longrightarrow\; \phi-\underset{\underset{C}{|}}{\overset{\overset{C}{|}}{C}}-CH_2\cdot \;+\; CoBrCl$$

$$\phi-\underset{\underset{C}{|}}{\overset{\overset{C}{|}}{C}}-CH_2\cdot \quad\xrightarrow{\text{Rearrangement}}\quad \cdot\underset{\underset{C}{|}}{\overset{\overset{C}{|}}{C}}-CH_2\phi$$

$$\phi-\underset{\underset{C}{|}}{\overset{\overset{C}{|}}{C}}-CH_2\cdot \quad\text{and}\quad \cdot\underset{\underset{C}{|}}{\overset{\overset{C}{|}}{C}}-CH_2\phi \;\longrightarrow\; \text{Dimers and disproportionation products}$$

An ionic rearrangement could also be proposed. Carbonium ions could be generated by the redox reaction:

$$R\cdot + CoBr_2 \longrightarrow R^+ + CoBr + Br^-$$

(See the discussion of redox reactions in Chap. 11.) It is possible, therefore, that the rearrangement step shown above involves carbonium ions rather than radicals. However, it is noteworthy that the amount of rearrangement here is similar to that found in the radical rearrangement of the comparable aldehyde. (See page 267.)

Radicals may also be generated from azo compounds, as in the following example:†

† C. G. Overberger and H. Gainer, *J. Am. Chem. Soc.*, **80**, 4561 (1958).

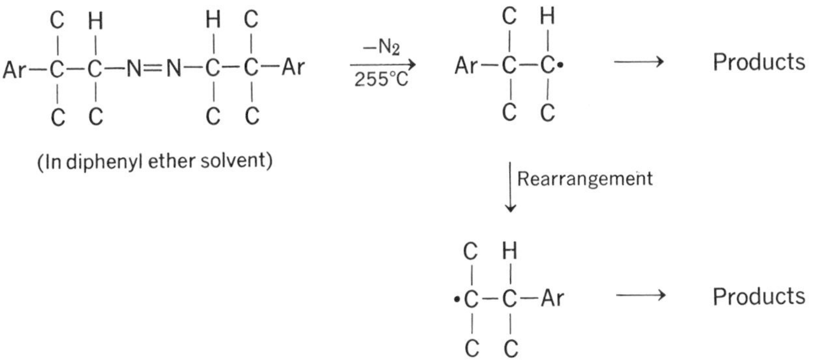

$$
\underset{\substack{\text{(In diphenyl ether solvent)}}}{\overset{\substack{C\;\;H\qquad\qquad H\;\;C \\ |\;\;\;| \qquad\qquad |\;\;\;| \\ Ar-C-C-N{=}N-C-C-Ar \\ |\;\;\;| \qquad\qquad |\;\;\;| \\ C\;\;C \qquad\qquad C\;\;C}}{}}
\xrightarrow[255°C]{-N_2}
\underset{\substack{C\;\;C}}{\overset{\substack{C\;\;H \\ |\;\;\;| \\ Ar-C-C\bullet \\ |\;\;\;|}}{}}
\longrightarrow \quad \text{Products}
$$

$$\Big\downarrow \text{Rearrangement}$$

$$
\underset{\substack{C\;\;C}}{\overset{\substack{C\;\;H \\ |\;\;\;| \\ \bullet C-C-Ar \\ |\;\;\;|}}{}}
\longrightarrow \quad \text{Products}
$$

The rearranged and the unrearranged radicals both form products by disproportionation reactions, and so alkanes and alkenes of both rearranged and unrearranged structure are obtained. In the case where Ar = phenyl, 23% rearrangement occurs.

Hydrocarbons also can serve as the radical source. If alkylbenzenes are heated to 400–525°C in the presence of hydrogen abstractors, rearrangements occur. For example, alkyl bromides effect the rearrangement of isopropylbenzene to propylbenzene:[†]

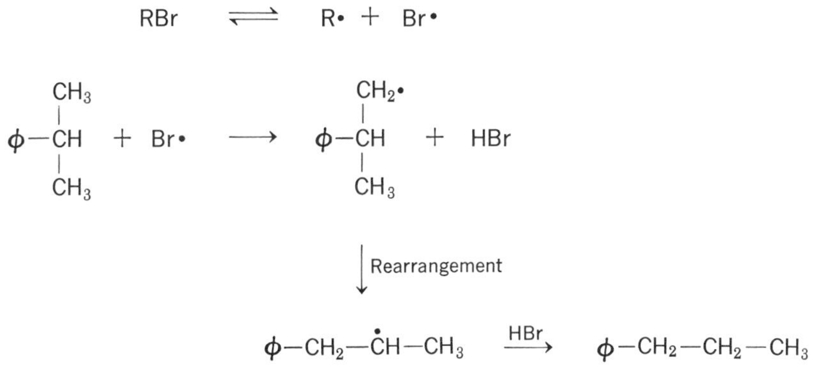

$$RBr \quad \rightleftharpoons \quad R\bullet + Br\bullet$$

$$
\underset{\substack{CH_3}}{\overset{\substack{CH_3 \\ | \\ \phi-CH \\ |}}{}} + Br\bullet \longrightarrow
\underset{\substack{CH_3}}{\overset{\substack{CH_2\bullet \\ | \\ \phi-CH \\ |}}{}} + HBr
$$

$$\Big\downarrow \text{Rearrangement}$$

$$\phi-CH_2-\overset{\bullet}{C}H-CH_3 \xrightarrow{HBr} \phi-CH_2-CH_2-CH_3$$

Abstraction of the tertiary, benzylic hydrogen occurs preferentially but does not lead to a rearrangement.

Relative rates for the migration of substituted phenyl groups can be obtained by an analysis of the rearrangement of the aryl-substituted isovaleraldehydes.[‡] The reactions that occur are shown below.

[†] L. H. Slaugh and J. H. Raley, *J. Am. Chem. Soc.*, **82**, 1259 (1960).
[‡] C. Rüchardt, *Chem. Ber.*, **94**, 2609 (1961); C. Rüchardt and S. Eichler, *ibid.*, **95**, 1921 (1962).

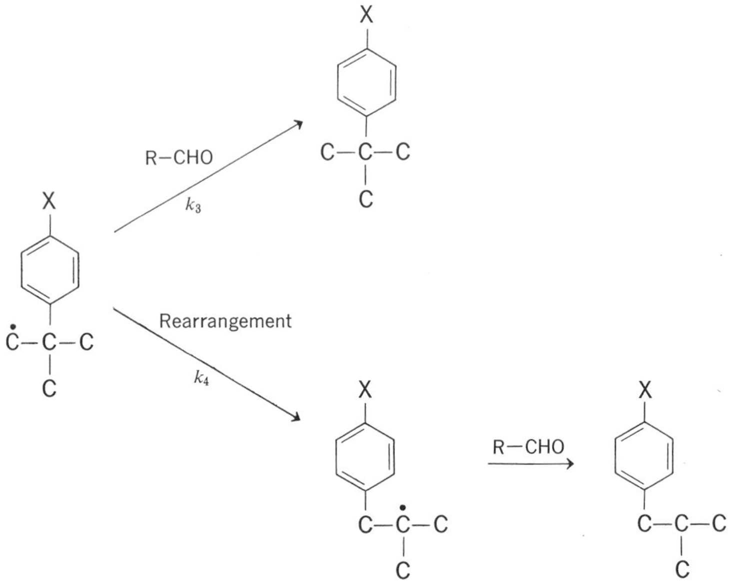

(17-3)

(17-4)

$(R = Ar - C(CH_3)_2 - CH_2)$

The following equation can be easily obtained:

$$\frac{k_4}{k_3} = \frac{\% \text{ yield rearranged product}}{\% \text{ yield unrearranged product}} \text{ (RCHO)} \tag{17-5}$$

If k_3 is assumed to be a constant independent of X, the values of k_4 obtained for different substituents can be compared. The results obtained are

X	Relative k_4
Cl	1.8
H	1.0
CH_3	0.6
CH_3O	0.35

These rate constants are correlated by the Hammett equation with $\rho \cong 1$. The transition state, therefore, can be described by the resonance structures shown below.

Electron-withdrawing X groups would be predicted to stabilize this charge distribution and increase the extent of rearrangement, as is observed.

In the above examples, we have considered radical migrations to carbon atoms. Radicals also can migrate to other atoms. For example, aryl groups can migrate to oxygen in certain alkoxy radicals. The hydroperoxide below rearranges as shown:†

(Ar = p-nitrophenyl)

Note that a p-nitrophenyl group migrates in preference to phenyl. In carbonium ion rearrangements, phenyl migrates more easily than does p-nitrophenyl.

1,2-ALKYL AND HYDROGEN MIGRATIONS

There is no unambiguous evidence that 1,2-hydrogen or alkyl group migrations occur in radical reactions. In the few systems where such migrations have been postulated, other more probable paths could also explain the products. It is not unexpected that 1,2-aryl migrations are more common in radical reactions than are 1,2-alkyl or hydrogen migrations; in carbonium ion rearrangements, groups migrate in the order aryl > alkyl or hydrogen.

† P. D. Bartlett and J. D. Cotman, *J. Am. Chem. Soc.*, **72**, 3095 (1950).

1,2-HALOGEN MIGRATIONS

Halogen atoms migrate; this type of rearrangement was discussed briefly on page 212 in connection with the addition of hydrogen halides to olefins. The addition of hydrogen bromide to halogen-containing olefins frequently leads to rearrangements. An example in which the product is entirely of the rearranged structure is given below.†

$$Br\cdot \ + \ C=C-CCl_3 \ \longrightarrow \ Br-C-\overset{\cdot}{C}-CCl_3$$

$$Br-C-\overset{\cdot}{C}-CCl_3 \ \xrightarrow{\text{Rearrangement}} \ Br-C-\underset{\underset{Cl}{|}}{C}-\overset{\cdot}{C}Cl_2$$

$$Br-C-\underset{\underset{Cl}{|}}{C}-\overset{\cdot}{C}Cl_2 + \ HBr \ \longrightarrow \ BrCH_2-\underset{\underset{Cl}{|}}{CH}-CHCl_2 \ + \ Br\cdot$$

This mechanism leads to the prediction that any radical could effect the rearrangement; in accord with this, the radical addition of thiols or bromine also leads to rearranged products:

$$C=C-CCl_3 \ \xrightarrow{RS\cdot} \ RS-C-\overset{\cdot}{C}-CCl_3 \ \xrightarrow{\text{Rearrangement}}$$

$$RS-C-\underset{\underset{Cl}{|}}{C}-\overset{\cdot}{C}Cl_2 \ \xrightarrow{RSH} \ RS-CH_2-\underset{\underset{Cl}{|}}{CH}-CHCl_2$$

$$C=C-CCl_3 \ \xrightarrow{Br\cdot} \ Br-C-\overset{\cdot}{C}-CCl_3 \ \xrightarrow{\text{Rearrangement}}$$

$$Br-C-\underset{\underset{Cl}{|}}{C}-\overset{\cdot}{C}Cl_2 \ \xrightarrow{Br_2} \ BrCH_2-\underset{\underset{Cl}{|}}{CH}-\underset{\underset{Br}{|}}{C}Cl_2$$

The light-initiated chlorinations of isopropyl bromide and propyl bromide by t-butyl hypohalite both give 1-bromo-2-chloropropane as one of the products.‡

† R. Kh. Freidlina, V. N. Kost, and M. Ya. Khorlina, *Russ. Chem. Rev.* (*English Transl.*), **31**, 7 (1962).

‡ P. S. Skell, R. G. Allen, and N. D. Gilmour, *J. Am. Chem. Soc.*, **83**, 504 (1961).

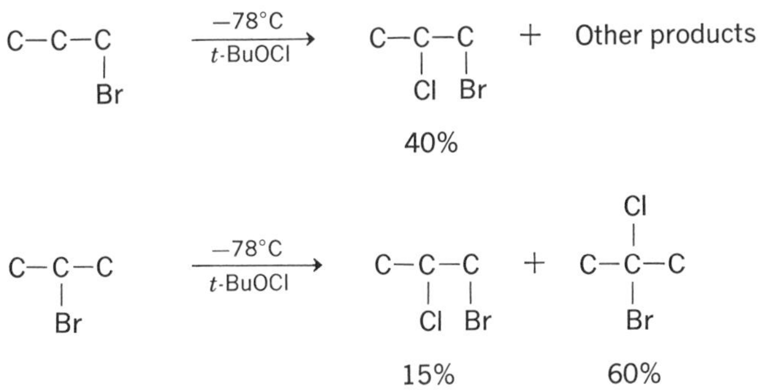

C—C—C $\xrightarrow[t\text{-BuOCl}]{-78°C}$ C—C—C + Other products
   | | |
  Br   Cl Br

                      40%

                                             Cl
                                           |
C—C—C $\xrightarrow[t\text{-BuOCl}]{-78°C}$ C—C—C + C—C—C
   | | | |
  Br   Cl Br   Br

                     15%   60%

The reaction of isopropyl bromide must involve the rearrangement.

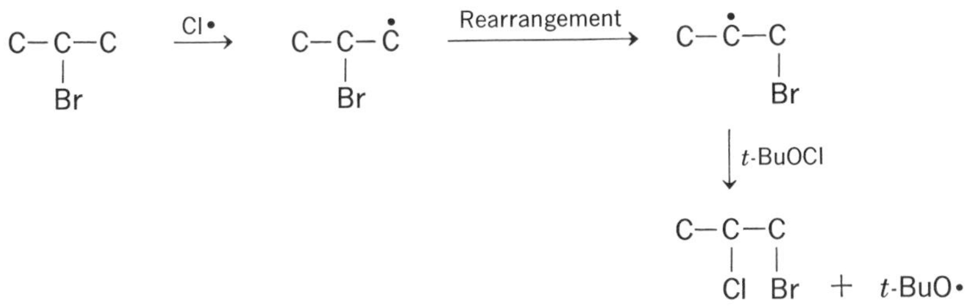

C—C—C $\xrightarrow{\;Cl•\;}$ C—C—Ċ $\xrightarrow{\text{Rearrangement}}$ C—Ċ—C
   | | |
  Br   Br   Br

                                                       ↓ t-BuOCl

                                           C—C—C
                                             | |
                                         Cl Br + t-BuO•

CIS-TRANS REARRANGEMENTS

It was pointed out in the discussion of HX additions to olefins that reversible additions can produce *cis-trans* isomerizations. Iodine, hydrogen bromide, or thiols add to olefins reversibly, and examples are known in which each of these lead to isomerizations. For example, thiols isomerize *cis*-2-butene.

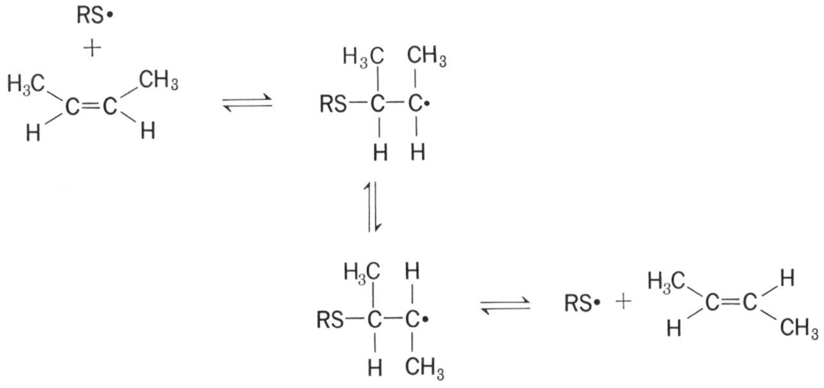

A related and particularly interesting example has been discovered during the addition of deuterated methanethiol to 2-butene.† At $-70°C$, the deuterated thiol adds to either *cis-* or *trans-*2-butene to produce the same mixture of isomers. Under these conditions, the isomerization of the intermediate radical is rapid relative to hydrogen transfer from the thiol.

$$
\begin{array}{cc}
\underset{\textit{Trans}}{\overset{\displaystyle CH_3 \;\; C=C \;\; H}{\quad H \qquad CH_3}} & \underset{\textit{Cis}}{\overset{\displaystyle CH_3 \;\; C=C \;\; CH_3}{\quad H \qquad H}}
\end{array}
$$

$\Big\downarrow CH_3S\cdot$ $\Big\downarrow CH_3S\cdot$

$$
\begin{array}{ccc}
CH_3-\overset{\displaystyle CH_3 \;\; S}{\underset{H}{C}}-\overset{\bullet}{\underset{CH_3}{C}}\cdots H & \underset{\text{of radicals}}{\overset{\text{Rapid equilibration}}{\rightleftharpoons}} & CH_3-\overset{\displaystyle CH_3 \;\; S}{\underset{H}{C}}-\overset{\bullet}{\underset{H}{C}}\cdots CH_3
\end{array}
$$

$\Big\downarrow CH_3SD$

$$
CH_3-\overset{\displaystyle CH_3 \quad \atop \displaystyle S \quad D}{\underset{\displaystyle H \quad CH_3}{C-C}}-H
$$

Equilibrium mixture of
threo and *erythro* isomers

However, when DBr is added, the two isomeric olefins give two different products:

† P. S. Skell and R. G. Allen, *J. Am. Chem. Soc.*, **82**, 1511 (1960).

Thus, when the faster transfer agent DBr is present, the two isomeric intermediate radicals are trapped before they can isomerize. It is interesting that the *addition* of DBr is not observed; DSCH$_3$ is the only species that adds. Thus, the reaction below occurs faster than Br• can add to the olefins.

$$Br• + CH_3SD \longrightarrow CH_3S• + DBr$$

RING-OPENING AND RING-CLOSING REACTIONS

The peroxide-initiated addition of carbon tetrachloride to β-pinene gives rearranged chloride in high yield:

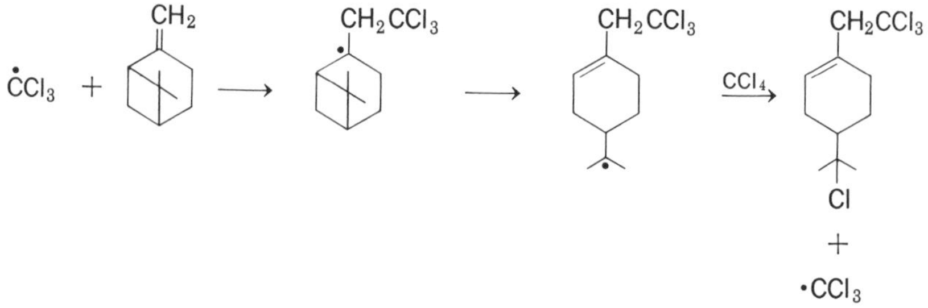

$\dot{C}Cl_3$ + [structure: methylenecyclohexane with CH₂] ⟶ [structure: cyclohexane with CH₂CCl₃ and radical] ⟶ [structure: cyclohexene with CH₂CCl₃ and radical] $\xrightarrow{CCl_4}$ [structure: cyclohexene with CH₂CCl₃ and Cl]

+

·CCl₃

Thiolacetic acid, however, adds to give mainly unrearranged product. This faster transfer agent traps the first-formed radical. The rearrangement reaction is a β-scission, but in a cyclic system this can result in a rearranged product.

An interesting ring opening is observed during the chlorination of spiropentane.†

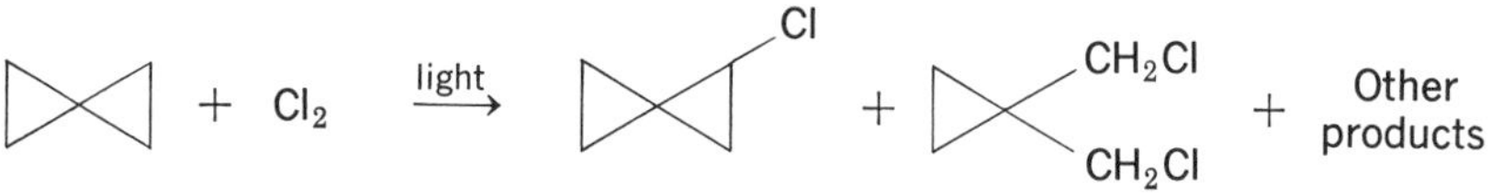

[structure: spiropentane] + Cl₂ $\xrightarrow{light}$ [structure: chlorospiropentane with Cl] + [structure: with CH₂Cl and CH₂Cl] + Other products

The dichloride product could be the result of the reaction

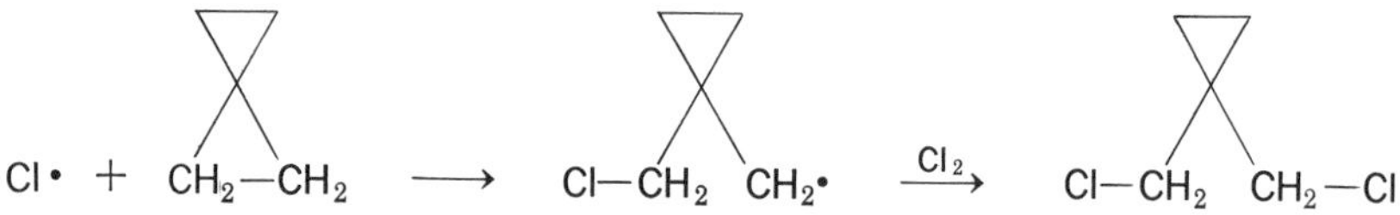

Cl· + [structure: CH₂—CH₂] ⟶ [structure: Cl—CH₂ CH₂·] $\xrightarrow{Cl_2}$ [structure: Cl—CH₂ CH₂—Cl]

(This reaction is similar to that discussed on pages 192 to 193.)

There are other systems that undergo β-scission reactions to form ring-opened products. For example, the substituted pyran below undergoes ring opening at 125°C in a peroxide-initiated reaction.‡

† D. E. Applequist, G. F. Fanta, and B. W. Henrikson, J. Am. Chem. Soc., 82, 2368 (1960).

‡ E. S. Huyser, J. Org. Chem., 25, 1820 (1960).

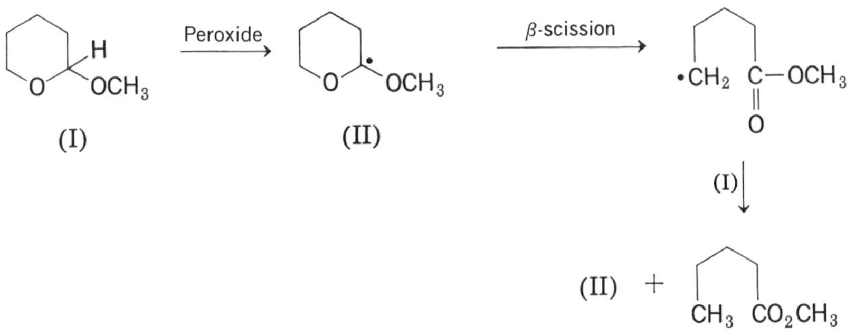

Ring closures are the reverse of these ring-opening β-scission reactions. One example is the formation of a tricyclic compound by the addition of p-thiocresol to norbornadiene:†

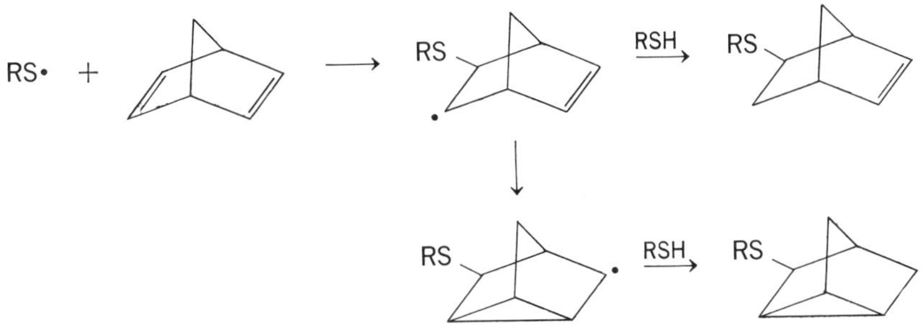

The extent of ring closure was found to decrease as more thiocresol was added, indicating that the first radical could be trapped by a high concentration of transfer agent before ring closure occurred.

An interesting reaction in which both a ring opening and a ring closure occur is the decomposition of azocamphane.‡ Pyrolysis at 300°C gives a mixture of products including some of the rearranged material shown below.

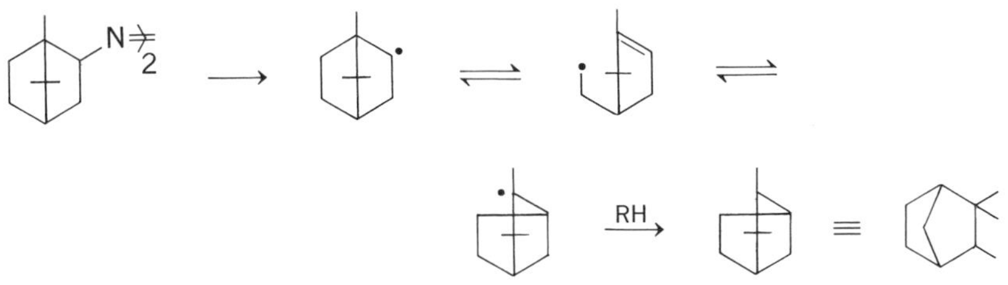

† S. J. Cristol, G. D. Brindell, and J. A. Reeder, *J. Am. Chem. Soc.*, **80**, 635 (1958).
‡ J. A. Berson, C. J. Olson, and J. S. Walia, *J. Am. Chem. Soc.*, **82**, 5000 (1960).

Approximately the same mixture of products is obtained by pyrolysis of the azo compound below, which gives the second radical produced in the sequence shown on page 279.

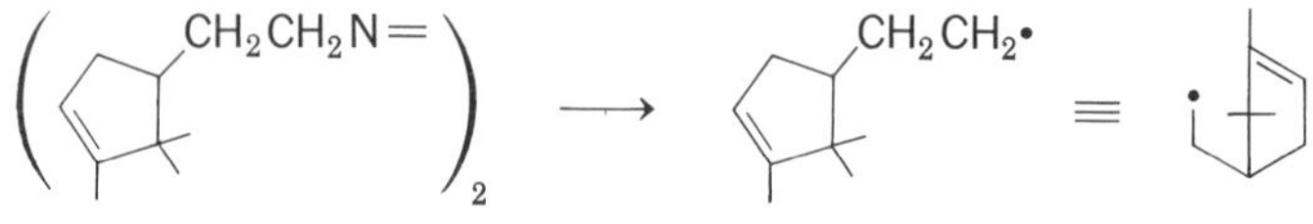

INTRAMOLECULAR HYDROGEN TRANSFER

Terminal radicals can "bite back" on themselves and abstract a hydrogen from the fourth or fifth carbon down the chain:

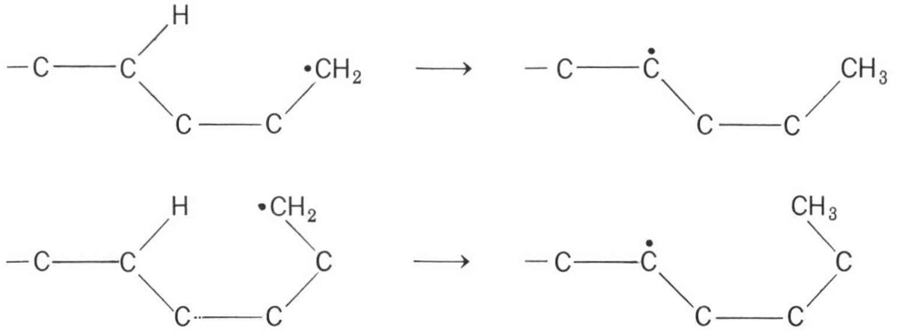

This reaction is favored by the driving force for converting a primary to a secondary radical, and the five- or six-membered quasi-ring transition state provides a low-energy pathway.

As we shall see below, good evidence has been obtained for 1,4- and 1,5-hydrogen transfer reactions. However, even the sterically less favorable 1,3-hydrogen transfer has been postulated in the reaction of butyl radicals produced from pentanal.† The products of photolysis are 1-butene, butane, and octane, as would be expected from butyl radicals.

$$C_4H_9-CHO \xrightarrow{-H} C_4H_9\cdot + CO$$

$$\downarrow$$

Dimerization and disproportionation

† J. A. Kerr and A. F. Trotman-Dickenson, *J. Chem. Soc.*, 1602 (1960); also see, however, A. S. Gordon and J. R. McNesby, *J. Chem. Phys.*, **33**, 1882 (1960) and C. P. Quinn, *Trans. Faraday Soc.*, **59**, 2543 (1963).

However, large amounts of propene are also formed. This could result from the 1,3-rearrangement:

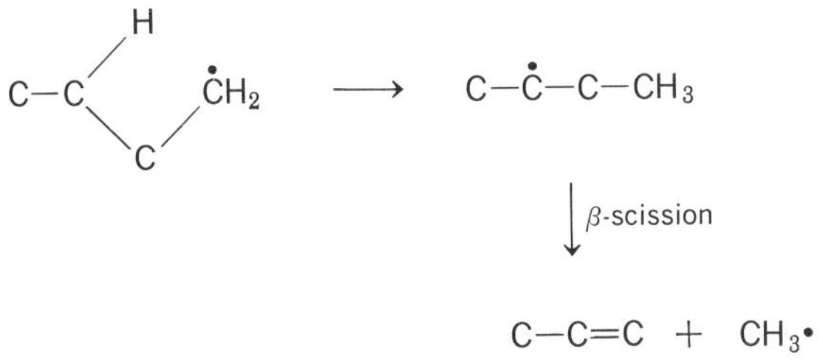

$$C-C=C \ + \ CH_3\bullet$$

The transition state would involve a strained four-membered ring. However, the alternative mechanism involves an even less probable 1,2-hydrogen transfer:

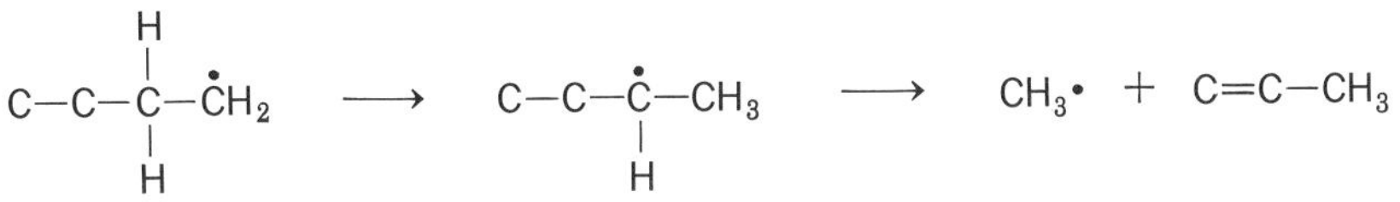

A 1,4-hydrogen transfer may occur in the reaction of methyl radicals with ethylene.† Propene is a major product, and the mechanism shown below has been suggested.

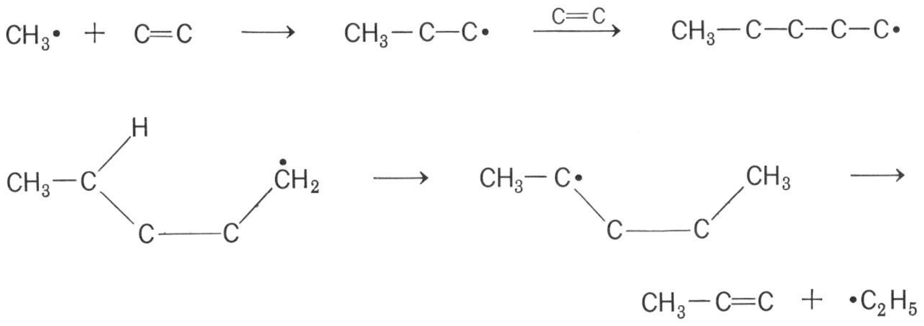

$$CH_3\bullet \ + \ C{=}C \ \longrightarrow \ CH_3{-}C{-}C\bullet \ \xrightarrow{\ C=C\ } \ CH_3{-}C{-}C{-}C{-}C\bullet$$

$$CH_3{-}C{=}C \ + \ \bullet C_2H_5$$

The products also contain 1-butene, which could result from a 1,5-rearrangement of primary heptyl radicals:

† A. S. Gordon and J. R. McNesby, *J. Chem. Phys.*, **31**, 853 (1959); **33**, 1882 (1960).

$$C-C-C-C-C\bullet \quad \xrightarrow{C=C} \quad C-C-C-C-C-C-C\bullet \quad \longrightarrow$$

$$C-C-\overset{\bullet}{C}-C-C-C-C \quad \longrightarrow \quad C-C-C{=}C + \overset{\bullet}{C}-C-C$$

Support for this mechanism was obtained by the use of $D_3C\bullet$ radicals. At 300°C, the propene consisted of 30% C_3H_6, 20% C_3H_5D, 30% $C_3H_4D_2$, and 20% $C_3H_3D_3$. This suggests exchange reactions that separate the deuterium atoms. One possible mechanism involving a series of rapid 1,4- and 1,5-hydrogen transfer reactions is shown below.

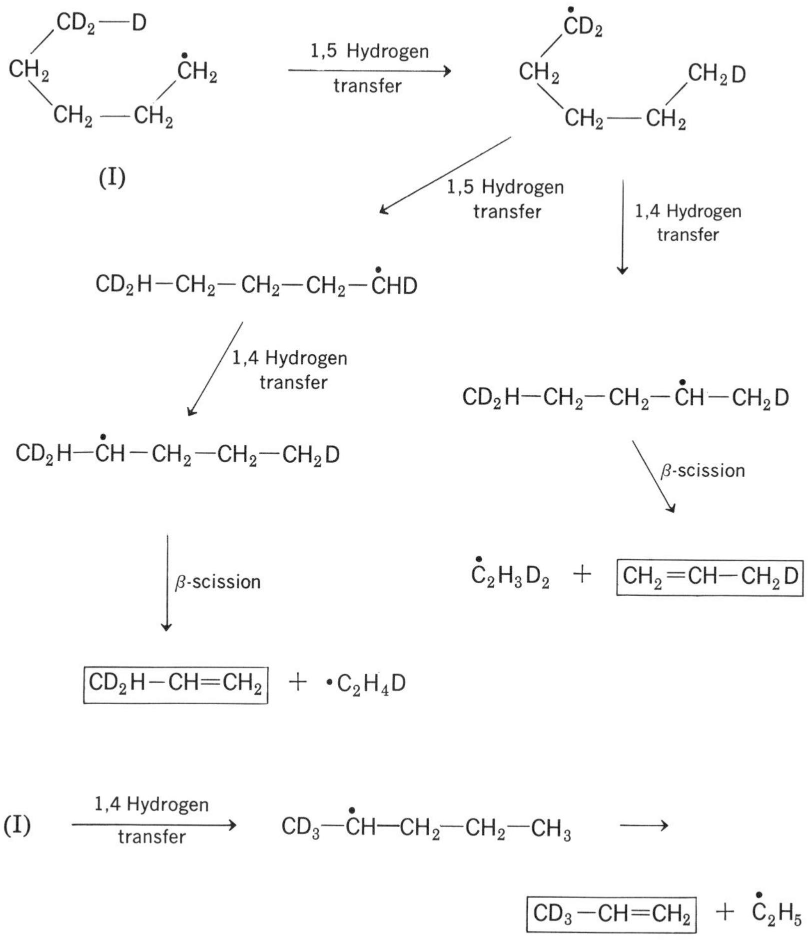

$$CD_2H-CH_2-CH_2-CH_2-\overset{\bullet}{C}HD$$

$$CD_2H-\overset{\bullet}{C}H-CH_2-CH_2-CH_2D$$

$$CD_2H-CH_2-CH_2-\overset{\bullet}{C}H-CH_2D$$

$$\overset{\bullet}{C}_2H_3D_2 \;+\; \boxed{CH_2{=}CH-CH_2D}$$

$$\boxed{CD_2H-CH{=}CH_2} \;+\; \bullet C_2H_4D$$

$$(I) \quad \xrightarrow[\text{transfer}]{\text{1,4 Hydrogen}} \quad CD_3-\overset{\bullet}{C}H-CH_2-CH_2-CH_3 \quad \longrightarrow$$

$$\boxed{CD_3-CH{=}CH_2} \;+\; \overset{\bullet}{C}_2H_5$$

An example of a 1,5-hydrogen transfer with synthetic utility occurs in the Hofmann-Loffler reaction, where an *N*-chloroamine is converted to a pyrrolidine by irradiation in acid solution followed by treatment with base. The mechanism is believed to be †

(I)   (II)   (III)

(III)   (I)   (IV)   (II)

The further reaction of compound (**IV**) with base produces the pyrrolidine:

(**IV**)

Alkoxy radicals also can bite back to abstract hydrogen. An example of a 1,5-transfer occurs in the reactions of the alkoxy radical from the hypohalite shown on the next page.‡

† S. Wawzonek and P. J. Thelen, *J. Am. Chem. Soc.*, **72**, 2118 (1950); E. J. Corey and W. R. Hertler, *ibid.*, **82**, 1657 (1960).

‡ F. D. Greene, M. L. Savitz, F. D. Osterholtz, H. H. Lau, W. N. Smith, and P. M. Zanet, *J. Org. Chem.*, **28**, 55 (1963).

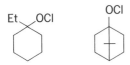

PROBLEMS

17-1 Predict the products from the decompositions of the two hypohalites below in carbon tetrachloride at 80°C. In both cases, rearranged products are obtained. [F. D. Greene et al., *J. Org. Chem.*, **28**, 55 (1963).]

17-2 Draw resonance structures explaining why *p*-nitrophenyl would migrate in preference to phenyl in the rearrangement of $ArC\phi_2$—O•.

17-3 If *t*-butylbenzene is refluxed with *t*-butyl peroxide, isobutylbenzene is formed. Give a complete mechanism for this reaction. What other products might be expected? What effect would added benzyl mercaptan have on the product composition? [H. Pines and C. N. Pillai, *J. Am. Chem. Soc.*, **82**, 2921 (1960).]

17-4 The peroxide $(\phi—CH(CH_3)—CH_2—CO—O—)_2$ was refluxed in benzene for 5 hours and the products were (moles per 100 moles peroxide): CO_2, 158; $\phi—CH(CH_3)—CH_2—CO_2H$, 27; $\phi CH=CH—CH_3$, 4; $\phi CH_2CH_2CH_3$, 8; $\phi CH(CH_3)_2$, 19; and $C_{18}H_{22}$, 23. Write a mechanism explaining the formation of these products. [W. Rickatson and T. S. Stevens, *J. Chem. Soc.*, 3960 (1963).]

17-5 Derive Eq. (17-5).

SUGGESTIONS FOR FURTHER READING

Fish, A.: *Quart. Rev. (London)*, **18**, 243 (1964). Chiefly concerned with gas-phase processes.

Freidlina, R. K., V. N. Kost, and M. Y. Khorlina: *Russ. Chem. Rev. (English Transl.)*, **31**, 1 (1962).

Heusler, K., and J. Kalvoda: *Angew. Chem. (Intern. Ed. Engl.)*, **3**, 525 (1964). Considers intramolecular hydrogen transfers in steroids.

Walling, C.: in P. de Mayo (ed.), "Molecular Rearrangements," vol. I, Interscience Publishers, Inc., New York, 1963.

chapter
eighteen Autoxidation

Autoxidation is the slow oxidation of an organic compound by oxygen, the term "slow" meaning that the oxidation is not accompanied by a flame. These processes are ubiquitous and very important. They include the hardening that occurs in the air-drying of paints and varnishes, the deterioration of rubber and plastic materials in air, the slow combustion of organic fuels, and many industrial oxidation processes in which oxygen is used as the oxidant. Oxygen is a diradical, and it is not surprising that these autoxidation processes have radical mechanisms.

The most common autoxidation is that in which compounds with labile hydrogens react to form hydroperoxides:

$$RH + O_2 \longrightarrow ROOH$$

Examples of this reaction are the oxidation of isopropylbenzene,

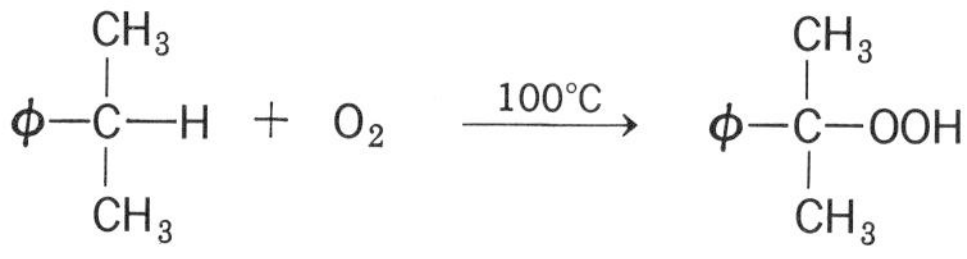

$$\phi-\underset{\underset{CH_3}{|}}{\overset{\overset{CH_3}{|}}{C}}-H \; + \; O_2 \quad \xrightarrow{100°C} \quad \phi-\underset{\underset{CH_3}{|}}{\overset{\overset{CH_3}{|}}{C}}-OOH$$

89% yield

of Tetralin,

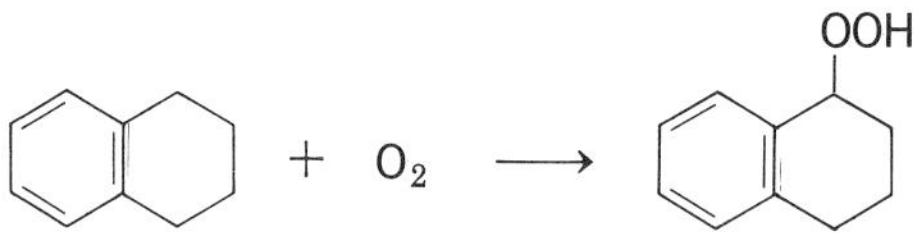

60% yield

and of cyclohexene,

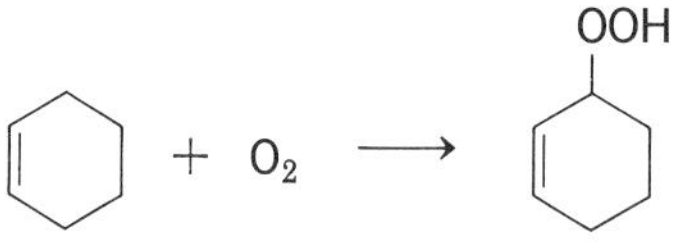

20% yield

These oxidative chain reactions involve the propagation steps shown below.

$$R\cdot + O_2 \longrightarrow ROO\cdot \qquad\qquad (18\text{-}1)$$
$$ROO\cdot + RH \longrightarrow ROOH + R\cdot \qquad\qquad (18\text{-}2)$$

Occasionally, the product of autoxidation is not the hydroperoxide ROOH but instead is a molecule with the general formula ROH or ROOR. For example, the oxidation of benzaldehyde gives benzoic acid:

$$\phi-\overset{\overset{\textstyle O}{\|}}{C}-H \quad \xrightarrow{O_2} \quad \phi-\overset{\overset{\textstyle O}{\|}}{C}-OH$$

In this case, the mechanism involves the prior formation of the peracid, which then reacts with a molecule of benzaldehyde, as shown below.

$$\phi-\overset{\overset{\textstyle O}{\|}}{C}-H \quad + \quad O_2 \quad \longrightarrow \quad \phi-\overset{\overset{\textstyle O}{\|}}{C}-OOH$$

$$\phi-\overset{\overset{\textstyle O}{\|}}{C}-OOH \quad + \quad \phi-\overset{\overset{\textstyle O}{\|}}{C}-H \quad \longrightarrow \quad 2\phi-\overset{\overset{\textstyle O}{\|}}{C}-OH$$

The oxidation of 10-phenylxanthene is an example of a reaction of the type

$$RH \xrightarrow{O_2} ROOR$$

The oxidation involves an initiation step

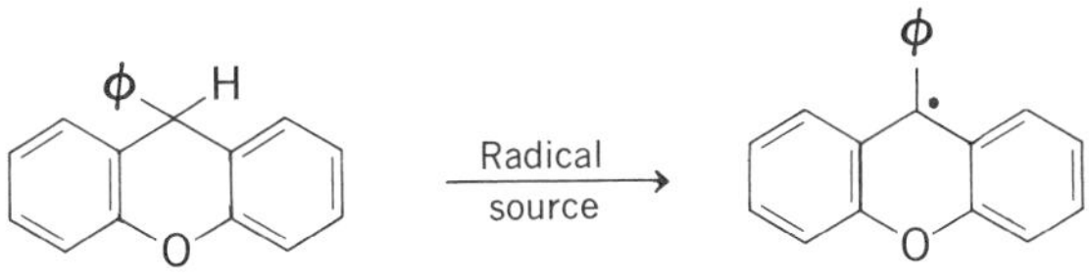

(I)

followed by

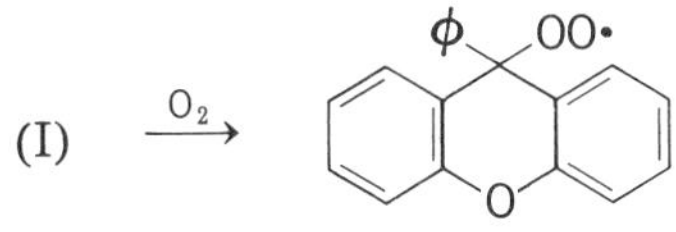

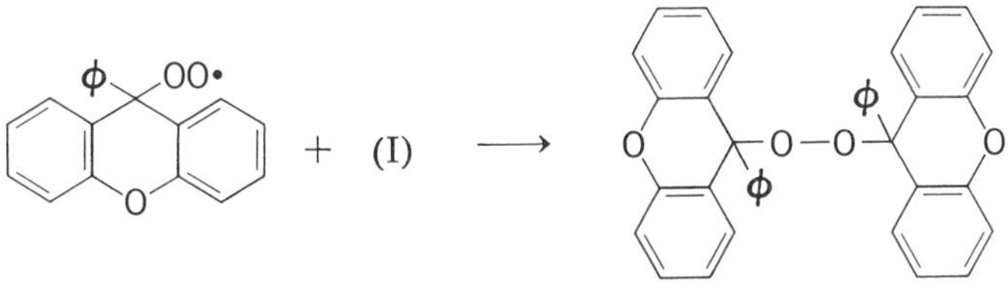

$$(I) \xrightarrow{O_2}$$

(18-3)

INITIATION, PROPAGATION, AND TERMINATION PROCESSES

Autoxidations can be initiated by peroxides, hydroperoxides, azo compounds, or any radical source. Frequently initiation occurs spontaneously. The most likely process responsible for these spontaneous initiations is the molecule-induced homolysis shown below.†

$$RH + O_2 \longrightarrow R\cdot + \cdot O{-}OH$$

The chain given in reactions (18-1) and (18-2) can terminate in three different ways:

$R\cdot + O_2 \longrightarrow ROO\cdot$	(18-1)
$ROO\cdot + RH \longrightarrow ROOH + R\cdot$	(18-2)
$2ROO\cdot \longrightarrow$ Nonradical products	(18-4)
$ROO\cdot + R\cdot \longrightarrow$ Nonradical products	(18-5)
$2R\cdot \longrightarrow$ Nonradical products	(18-6)

Normally, reaction (18-1) is very fast, and the only important termination reaction is that involving two $ROO\cdot$ radicals [reaction (18-4)]. However, reactions (18-5) and (18-6) occur in some systems. For example, reaction (18-3) shown on page 289 is an example of process (18-5). Since the ratio of $R\cdot$ to $ROO\cdot$ depends on the concentration of oxygen in the system, the contribution of the three possible termination reactions varies as the partial pressure of oxygen is changed. Figure 18-1 shows data for the oxidation of ethyl linoleate. At very low oxygen pressures, where reaction (18-1) is slow and the majority of the radicals are of the $R\cdot$ type, termination is mainly by reaction (18-6). At higher oxygen pressures, termination is mainly by the cross-termination mechanism [reaction (18-5)]. However, when the oxygen pressure becomes as high as 100 mm, reaction (18-1) has become so fast that the majority of the radicals are present as peroxy radicals and the main termination mechanism is reaction (18-4).

The possible products of autoxidation schemes are conveniently represented by the flow diagram of Fig. 18-2. The reaction marked (a) is the initiation process. Reaction (b) is peroxidation of the alkyl radical. The $ROO\cdot$ radicals may then react by paths (c), (d), or (e). Path (c) is the reaction forming such products as those discussed on page 288 and is part of the chain sequences (18-1) and (18-2). Path (d) is exemplified by reac-

† C. F. H. Tipper, *Quart. Rev. (London)*, **11**, 318 (1957); M. Seakins and C. Hinshelwood, *Proc. Royal Soc. (London)*, Ser. A, **276**, 324 (1963).

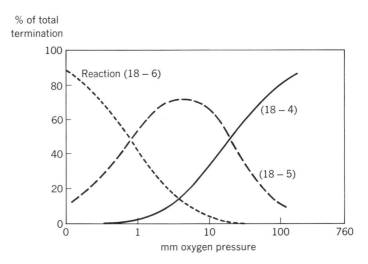

Figure 18-1 Relative contribution of the three termination reactions in the autoxidation of ethyl linoleate at 45°C. [*L. Bateman, Quart. Revs.,* **8,** 147 (1954).]

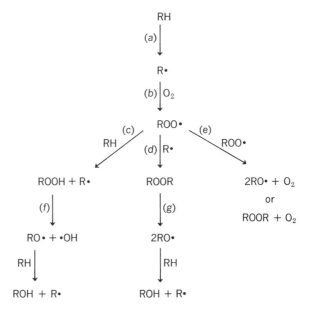

Figure 18-2 An outline of the types of reactions which occur in autoxidation systems.

tion (18-3) and is a termination step. Both (*c*) and (*d*), however, produce peroxidic materials that may undergo homolysis under some reaction conditions. These possibilities are shown as paths (*f*) and (*g*). If these homolyses occur, alkoxy radicals are formed, and alcohols may be reaction products.

Path (*e*) represents a possible reaction type that has been shown to occur when RH is isopropylbenzene. In that case, the oxidation has been studied, using a mixture of labeled oxygen molecules consisting of O^{16}—O^{16} and O^{18}—O^{18}. Path (*e*) leads to the prediction that some O^{16}—O^{18} should be formed during autoxidation. This is shown in the scheme below, where $O°$—$O°$ is the O^{18}—O^{18} molecule.

$$RH \xrightarrow[60°C]{AIBN} R\bullet$$

$$R\bullet + O—O \longrightarrow ROO\bullet$$
$$R\bullet + O^*—O^* \longrightarrow R\overset{**}{O}\overset{*}{O}\bullet$$
$$ROO\bullet + R\overset{**}{O}\overset{*}{O}\bullet \longrightarrow [RO\overset{**}{O}\overset{*}{O}R] \longrightarrow RO\bullet + O—\overset{*}{O} + R\overset{*}{O}\bullet \qquad (18\text{-}7)$$

It was found that O^{16}—O^{18} is produced during autoxidation of isopropyl-benzene. The data indicated that reaction (18-7) occurred from 1.7 to 2.6 times for each termination step in the reaction sequence, larger values being obtained for oxidations with longer chain lengths. These facts imply that the reaction of two ROO• radicals in this system sometimes produces chain termination and sometimes leads to chain continuance.†

The effect of the chemical nature of the R group on the rate of oxidation of RH can be studied by obtaining rates of autoxidation under conditions of high oxygen pressure. In the system below,

$$RH \xrightarrow{Catalyst, R_i} R\bullet$$

$$R\bullet + O_2 \xrightarrow{k_1} ROO\bullet \qquad (18\text{-}1)$$

$$ROO\bullet + RH \xrightarrow{k_2} ROOH + R\bullet \qquad (18\text{-}2)$$

$$2ROO\bullet \xrightarrow{k_t} \text{Nonradical products} \qquad (18\text{-}4)$$

The steady-state condition is that

$$R_i = 2k_t(ROO\bullet)^2$$

---

† P. D. Bartlett and T. G. Traylor, *J. Am. Chem. Soc.*, **85**, 2407 (1963).

Table 18-1   Oxidizability of hydrocarbons†

RH	Relative $k_2/k_t^{1/2}$	RH	Relative $k_2/k_t^{1/2}$
Tetralin	3.0	p-Methyltoluene (p-xylene)	0.052
Benzyl ether	7.0	Ethylbenzene	0.18
Toluene	0.015	Cumene (isopropyl benzene)	1.0
p-Nitrotoluene	0.0063		

† G. A. Russell, *J. Am. Chem. Soc.*, **78**, 1047 (1956).

and, therefore, at the steady state,

$$\frac{-d(\text{RH})}{dt} = k_2(\text{RH})(\text{ROO}\bullet) = \frac{k_2}{(2k_t)^{1/2}}(\text{RH})(R_i)^{1/2} \tag{18-8}$$

where R_i is the rate of initiation, k_t is the termination rate constant, and the oxygen pressure is sufficiently high so that (18-4) is the only important termination process. If the rates of disappearance of different substrates RH are compared at a constant value of the rate of initiation, then relative values for $k_2/k_t^{1/2}$ can be obtained from Eq. (18-8). This ratio represents the oxidizability of the substrate in the same way that the ratio of $k_p/k_t^{1/2}$ represents the polymerizability of a monomer in radical polymerization (see page 237). Table 18-1 gives values for this ratio for various hydro-carbons. Notice that, in the oxidation of toluenes, electron-withdrawing substituents such as p-nitro slow the rate of oxidation and electron-donating substituents speed the rate. Much more data than given here are available; for substituted cumenes the Hammett equation is obeyed, using σ^+, and the value of ρ is -0.4.† The peroxy radical is an electro-philic radical that attacks hydrocarbons at sites of relatively high electron density. The resonance structures for the transition state for reaction (18-2) include the polar form below.

$$\text{ROO}\bullet \ \text{H:R} \longleftrightarrow \text{ROO:}^- \ \overset{\bullet}{\text{H}} \ ^+\text{R}$$

Therefore, electron-donating groups in the R group would be expected to stabilize the transition state and speed the reaction, as is found.

Table 18-1 shows that the rate of oxidation decreases in the order cumene $>$ ethylbenzene $>$ toluene. Therefore, hydrogen abstraction

† G. A. Russell and R. C. Williamson, *J. Am. Chem. Soc.*, **86**, 2357 (1964). J. A. Howard and K. U. Ingold, *Can. J. Chem.*, **41**, 1750 (1963).

by the peroxy radical in reaction (18-2) occurs in the usual order: $3° > 2° > 1°$.

The absolute rate constants for the steps in the rate sequence can be obtained by rotating sector techniques and related methods. The rate constant for reaction (18-1) is of the order of 10^6, and the activation energy is less than 2 kcal/mole. The activation energy for reaction (18-2) is much higher, of the order of 8 to 12 kcal/mole. For example, for Tetralin at $25°C$, the rate constants for the reactions shown on page 292 are (in liter $mole^{-1} sec^{-1}$):[†]

$k_1 = 6.7 \times 10^7$
$k_2 = 13$
$k_t = 2 \times 10^7$

Sometimes interesting products can be produced by cooxidation of two substances. One particularly interesting example involves thiolacetic acid and indene.[‡] In the absence of oxygen, the addition of thiolacetic acid to indene is slow. However, when solutions of thiolacetic acid and indene are oxygenated, a cooxidation reaction occurs which is fast at room temperature. This chain process is shown below.

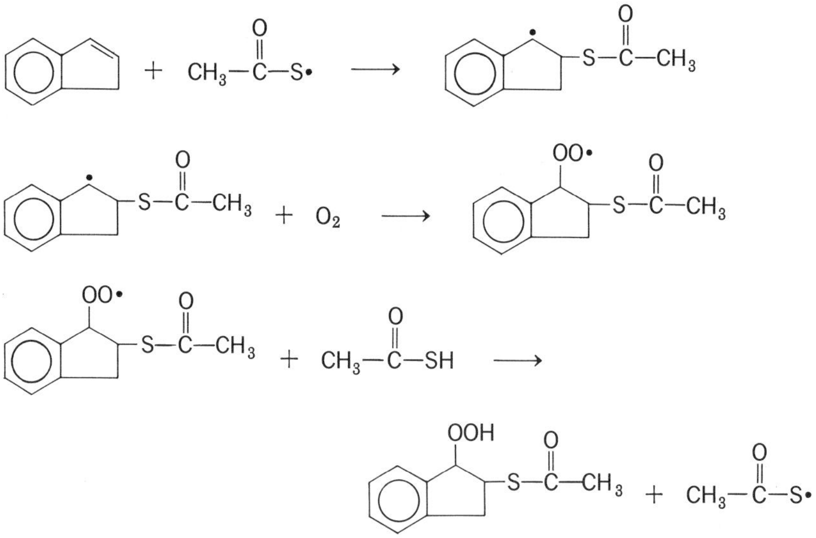

[†] C. H. Bamford and M. J. S. Dewar, *Proc. Roy. Soc. (London), Ser. A*, **198**, 252 (1949).

[‡] A. A. Oswald, K. Griesbaum, and W. Naegele, *J. Am. Chem. Soc.*, **86**, 3791 (1964).

PROBLEMS

18-1 In the autoxidation of isopropylbenzene (cumene), improved yields of the hydroperoxide are obtained if a base is present. Why? (Hint: The hydroperoxide undergoes an autocatalytic, acid-catalyzed, ionic reaction.)

18-2 Isobutane is stable in the presence of oxygen at 163°C. However, oxygen containing about 8% hydrogen bromide rapidly oxidizes isobutane to give a 70% yield of *t*-butyl hydroperoxide plus smaller amounts of *t*-butyl alcohol and *t*-butyl peroxide. Give the mechanism for this reaction.

SUGGESTIONS FOR FURTHER READING

Bateman, L.: *Quart. Rev. (London)*, **8**, 147 (1954).

Bolland, J. L.: *Quart. Rev. (London)*, **3**, 1 (1949).

Frank, C. E.: *Chem. Rev.*, **46**, 155 (1950).

Russell, G. A.: *J. Chem. Educ.*, **36**, 111 (1959).

Tipper, C. F. H.: *Quart. Rev. (London)*, **11**, 313 (1957).

Walling, C.: "Free Radicals in Solution," John Wiley & Sons, Inc., New York, 1957, chap. 9.

chapter nineteen Diradicals

Diradicals are species containing two unpaired electrons. As might be expected, these somewhat exotic species give unique reactions and often lead to products not easily synthesized by other means.

In this chapter we shall consider the reactions of species such as •CH_2—CH_2—CH_2—CH_2—CH_2• in which the locations of the two odd electrons are widely separated. These species are diradicals, and should have chemical properties much like monoradicals. Their spectra consist of two doublets, since each of the two odd electrons has a spin S of ½ and a multiplicity of $2S + 1 = 2$. We shall also consider the reactions of species in which the locations of the two odd electrons are close enough together so the electron spins are coupled. As was pointed out on p. 64, such species are triplets. The extent to which triplet species will have the properties of a diradical is somewhat complex, and we shall consider it further when we discuss the reactions of methylene.

Perhaps the most common triplet is the oxygen molecule, O_2. Oxygen is paramagnetic and has a pair of electrons with parallel spins:

(↑)   (↑)

:Ö—Ö:

It is a triplet because its highest-occupied electron orbital is degenerate (i.e., has two levels of equal energy), and Hund's rule of maximum multiplicity states that in this situation the electrons occupy different levels and have parallel spins.

A similar situation exists in methylene:†

CH_2:

The structure in which the lone pair of electrons have antiparallel spins is a singlet. It is of higher energy than the triplet and has the geometry

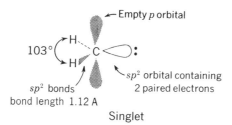

Singlet

† Derivatives of methylene are frequently called carbenes.

298

The ground state of methylene is a triplet state with the geometry

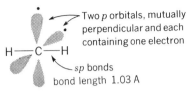

Triplet

As will be seen below, a common method of preparing methylene is by photolysis of diazomethane in the gas phase.

$$CH_2N_2 \xrightarrow{\text{Light}} CH_2\text{:} + N_2$$
(Singlet)

In this reaction, the methylene formed contains excess energy from the absorption of light, and the molecule is not in its ground state. This initially formed singlet methylene decays to its more stable triplet state provided there is a sufficiently high pressure of inert quenching gas present:

$$CH_2\text{:}(\text{Singlet}) + M(\text{Inert gas}) \longrightarrow \cdot CH_2\cdot(\text{Triplet}) + M \qquad (19\text{-}1)$$

SYNTHESIS OF METHYLENES

The formation of methylenes is extremely endothermic since two bonds must be broken. Several special synthetic methods are known, however. Dihalomethylenes can be synthesized by the ionic reaction of a base with a haloform. This is shown below, where B is a base.

$$B + X_3CH \longrightarrow BH^+ + X_3C^- \longrightarrow X^- + \text{:}CX_2$$

Depending on whether X is chlorine, bromine, or iodine, the removal of the proton and the loss of X either can be synchronous or can occur in two steps, as shown above. The dihalomethylenes from these ionic reactions are in singlet states.

Photolysis of ketene or diazomethane produces methylene:

$$CH_2{=}C{=}O \longrightarrow CH_2\text{:} + CO$$
$$CH_2{=}N{=}N \longrightarrow CH_2\text{:} + N_2$$

These photolyses are the most commonly used methods for the preparation of methylene or substituted methylenes in the gas phase.

Polymethylene compounds can be produced by the photolysis of cyclic ketones:

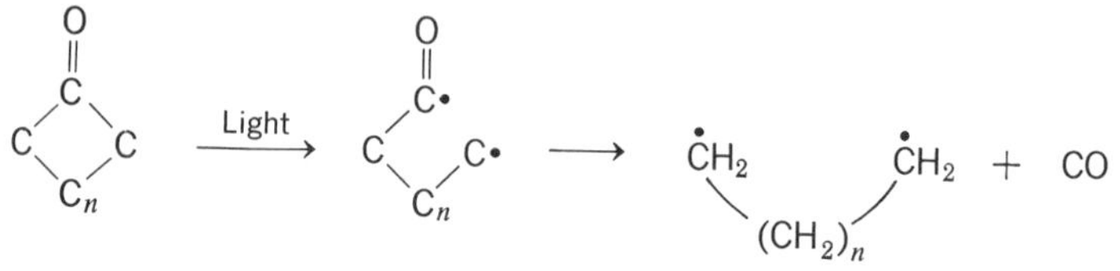

or by the reaction of dibromides with sodium vapor:

$BrCH_2-(CH_2)_n-CH_2Br + 2Na \longrightarrow 2NaBr + \cdot CH_2-(CH_2)_n-CH_2\cdot$

Pyrolysis of p-xylene produces p-xylylene.[†] If the pyrolysis products are trapped in a solvent held at $-78°C$, solutions of p-xylylene can be obtained.

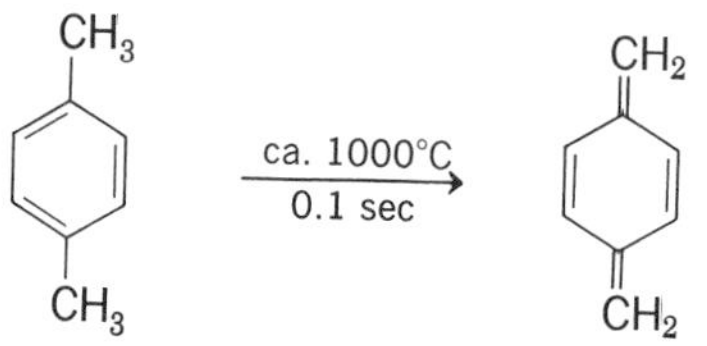

Calculations indicate that in this case the singlet state is 12 kcal/mole more stable than the triplet and that at room temperature all the material has the quinoidal structure shown above and is not a diradical. The mechanism of the pyrolysis, however, involves the formation of p-methyl-benzyl radicals as intermediates.

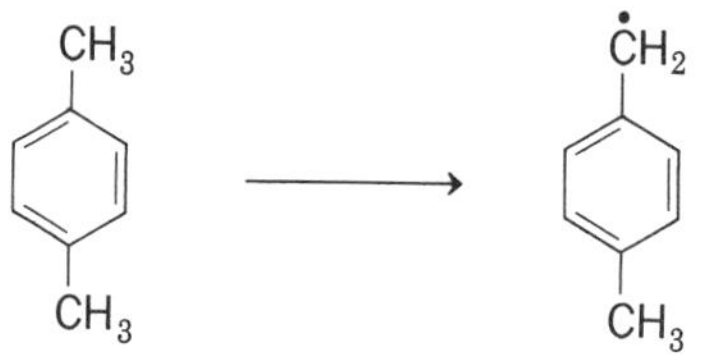

By the use of special fast-flow reaction techniques, these monoradical intermediates can be trapped.

† M. Szwarc, *Nature*, **160**, 403 (1947); L. A. Errede and B. F. Landrum, *J. Am. Chem. Soc.*, **79**, 4952 (1957).

REACTIONS OF METHYLENE

Perhaps the simplest reaction of methylene is that with metals to remove metallic mirrors. Interestingly, all metals are not removed, but tellurium, selenium, antimony, and arsenic mirrors are.

Methylene also can react by hydrogen abstraction. For example:

$$CH_2\colon + H_2 \longrightarrow CH_3\cdot + H\cdot$$

Methylene may also abstract halogen. An interesting but complex example is the reaction of methylene with carbon tetrachloride.† When diazomethane is irradiated in carbon tetrachloride, a 60% yield of the symmetrical tetrachloride (I) is obtained. The mechanism that has been suggested is

$$CH_2N_2 \xrightarrow{\ h\nu\ } \colon CH_2 + N_2$$

$$\colon CH_2 + CCl_4 \longrightarrow \cdot CH_2Cl + \cdot CCl_3$$

$$\cdot CCl_3 + CH_2N_2 \longrightarrow Cl_3C-CH_2\cdot + N_2$$

$$Cl_3C-CH_2\cdot \xrightarrow{\text{Rearranges}} Cl_2\overset{\bullet}{C}-CH_2Cl \xrightarrow{CH_2N_2} \overset{\overset{\bullet}{C}H_2}{\underset{}{\overset{|}{CCl_2}}-CH_2Cl}$$

$$\overset{\overset{\bullet}{C}H_2}{\underset{}{\overset{|}{CCl_2}}-CH_2Cl} \xrightarrow{\text{Rearranges}} \overset{CH_2Cl}{\underset{\bullet}{\overset{|}{CCl}}-CH_2Cl} \xrightarrow{CH_2N_2} \overset{CH_2Cl}{\cdot CH_2-\underset{Cl}{\overset{|}{C}}-CH_2Cl}$$

$$\overset{CH_2Cl}{\cdot CH_2-\underset{Cl}{\overset{|}{C}}-CH_2Cl} \xrightarrow{\text{Rearranges}} \overset{CH_2Cl}{ClCH_2-\underset{\bullet}{\overset{|}{C}}-CH_2Cl} \xrightarrow{CH_2N_2}$$

$$\overset{CH_2Cl}{ClCH_2-\underset{CH_2\cdot}{\overset{|}{C}}-CH_2Cl} \xrightarrow{CCl_4} \overset{CH_2Cl}{ClCH_2-\underset{CH_2Cl}{\overset{|}{C}}-CH_2Cl}$$

(I)

† W. H. Urry and J. R. Eiszner, *J. Am. Chem. Soc.*, **74**, 5822 (1952); W. H. Urry and N. Bilow, *ibid.*, **86**, 1815 (1964).

The mechanism postulates three 1,2-halogen migrations of the type described on page 274. Although this mechanism is unusual, it is difficult to suggest any other that explains the observed product.

In the gas phase, methylene is believed to react with methyl chloride predominantly by chlorine abstraction.

$$CH_2\!:\ +\ CH_3Cl \longrightarrow\ \cdot CH_2Cl\ +\ CH_3\cdot$$

The three combination reactions possible between these two radicals produce three products, $CH_2Cl\!-\!CH_2Cl$, $CH_3\!-\!CH_3$, and $CH_3\!-\!CH_2Cl$, in molar ratios of approximately $1:1:2$ as would be expected. Some hydrogen abstraction also occurs.[†]

Methylene also adds to double bonds. Direct addition occurs if the methylene is in an excited singlet state. For example,[‡] methylene from the photolysis of diazomethane adds to *cis*- and *trans*-2-butene to yield the two stereospecific products shown below.

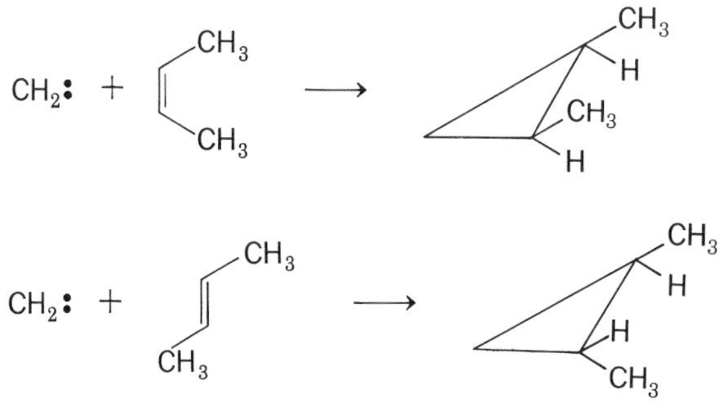

Since the addition is stereospecific, it probably is a one-step addition and does not involve a diradical as intermediate. However, in the gas phase in the presence of high concentrations of inert gases, the initially formed singlet methylene decays to the more stable triplet state before addition occurs. The triplet methylene then adds to olefins in a nonstereospecific reaction. For example, *cis*-2-butene produces both of the isomeric dimethylcyclopropanes:

[†] D. W. Setser, R. Littrell, and J. C. Hassler, *J. Am. Chem. Soc.*, **87**, 2062 (1965).
[‡] P. S. Skell and R. C. Woodworth, *J. Am. Chem. Soc.*, **81**, 3383 (1959); F. A. L. Anet, R. F. W. Bader, and A.-M. Van der Auwera, *ibid.*, **82**, 3217 (1960); H. M. Frey, *ibid.*, **82**, 5847 (1960).

$$CH_2\text{:} \text{ (singlet)} \; + \; M \; \longrightarrow \; \bullet CH_2 \bullet \text{ (triplet)} \; + \; M \qquad\qquad (19\text{-}1)$$

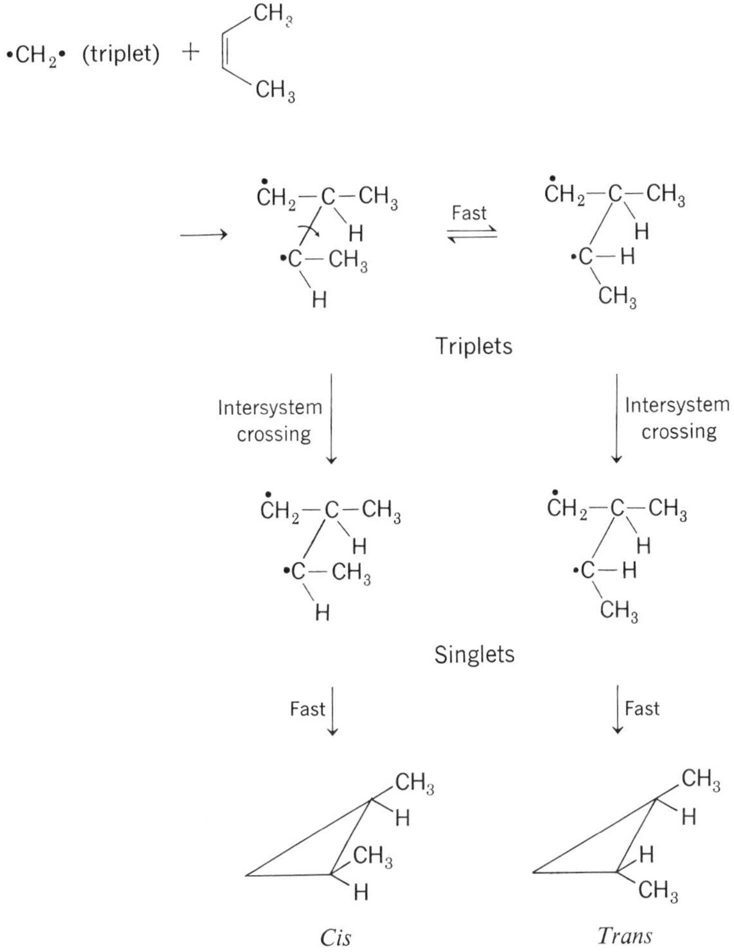

$$\bullet CH_2 \bullet \text{ (triplet)} \; + \; \underset{CH_3}{\overset{CH_3}{\diagdown\!\diagup}}$$

$$(19\text{-}2)$$

Triplets

Intersystem crossing

Intersystem crossing

Singlets

Fast

Fast

Cis

Trans

In the transition state for the addition of singlet methylene to the electron pair in a double bond, electrons of opposite spin can pair in one step. This is apparent in the equation below, where the directions of the electron spins are shown by arrows.

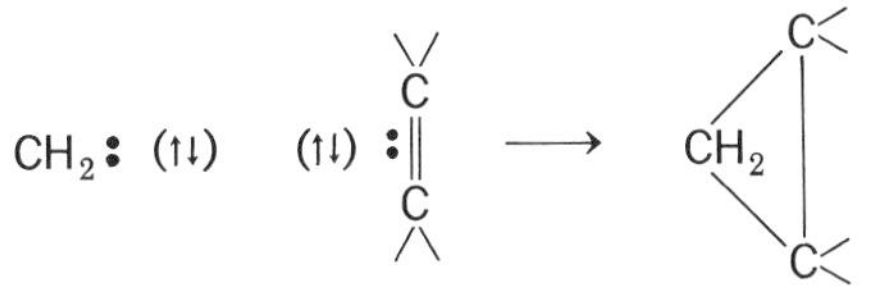

$$CH_2\text{:} \; (\uparrow\downarrow) \qquad (\uparrow\downarrow) \; \text{:}\overset{\diagup}{\underset{\diagdown}{\overset{C}{\underset{C}{\parallel}}}} \; \longrightarrow \; \overset{CH_2}{\underset{}{\triangle}}$$

The addition reaction of methylene in the triplet state must involve a diradical as an intermediate:

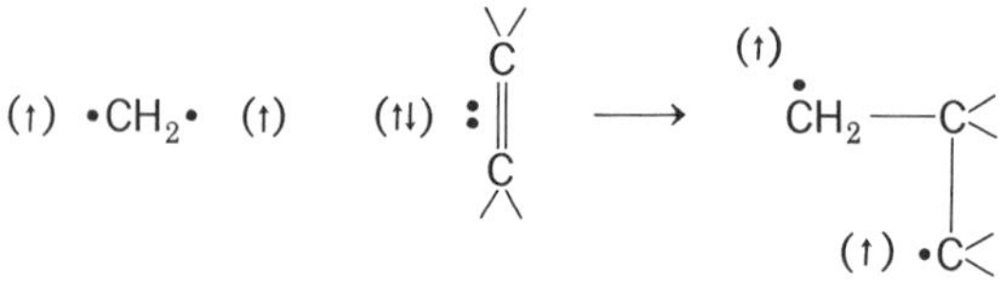

$$(\uparrow)\ \cdot CH_2\cdot\ (\uparrow)\qquad (\uparrow\downarrow)\ : \overset{\displaystyle \overset{\diagdown \diagup}{C}}{\underset{\displaystyle \underset{\diagup \diagdown}{C}}{\|}} \qquad \longrightarrow \qquad \overset{(\uparrow)}{\overset{\bullet}{C}H_2} - \overset{\textstyle |}{\underset{\textstyle |}{C\diagdown}}$$
$$(\uparrow)\ \cdot C\diagdown$$

This diradical must be converted to a singlet before ring closure can occur, and the time required for this change in multiplicity allows the two stereoisomeric forms to equilibrate, as is shown above in reaction (19-2).

The most characteristic reaction of methylene is the insertion reaction. In this reaction, the CH_2 group simply inserts itself into a C—H bond. Methylene produced by the photolysis of diazomethane is in an excited state and reacts almost completely randomly with C—H bonds. For example, the photolysis of diazomethane in liquid pentane gives the products shown below.†

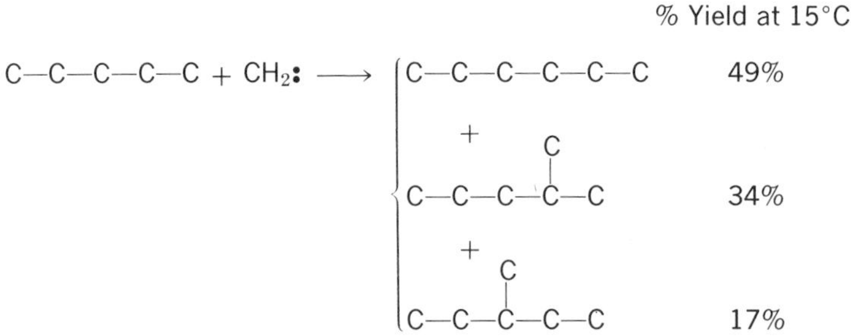

                                                                    % Yield at 15°C

$$C-C-C-C-C + CH_2: \longrightarrow \begin{cases} C-C-C-C-C-C & 49\% \\ \quad + \\ C-C-C-\overset{\displaystyle \overset{C}{|}}{C}-C & 34\% \\ \quad + \\ C-C-\overset{\displaystyle \overset{C}{|}}{C}-C-C & 17\% \end{cases}$$

The statistical yield of these products would be $6:4:2$, or $50:33:17$, very close to that observed. In the gas phase at high concentrations of inert diluents, collisional deactivation can occur before reaction, and a somewhat more selective reaction can sometimes be achieved.

Although the direct photolysis of diazomethane in the liquid phase leads to random reactions, more selective reactions can be obtained by an *indirect* photosensitized decomposition. If a solution containing benzophenone and diazomethane is irradiated with light of 3130 A wavelength, only the benzophenone is excited, since diazomethane does not absorb

† W. E. Doering, R. G. Buttery, R. G. Laughlin, and N. Chaudhuri, *J. Am. Chem. Soc.*, **78**, 3224 (1956).

light at that short a wavelength. The benzophenone decays to its triplet state, which then reacts with diazomethane to produce methylene in its triplet state.[†]

$\phi_2C{=}O \xrightarrow{\text{3130 A}} \phi_2C{=}O^*$ (Singlet)
$\phi_2C{=}O^*$ (Singlet) $\longrightarrow \phi_2C{=}O^*$ (Triplet)
$\phi_2C{=}O^*$ (Triplet) $+ CH_2N_2 \longrightarrow \phi_2C{=}O + CH_2N_2^*$ (Triplet)
$CH_2N_2^*$ (Triplet) $\longrightarrow CH_2\textbf{:}$ (Triplet) $+ N_2$

This triplet methylene is a much more selective reagent than is singlet methylene. For example, the different yields of products obtained using methylene from direct photolysis and from this photosensitized decomposition are shown below for the reaction with cyclohexene.

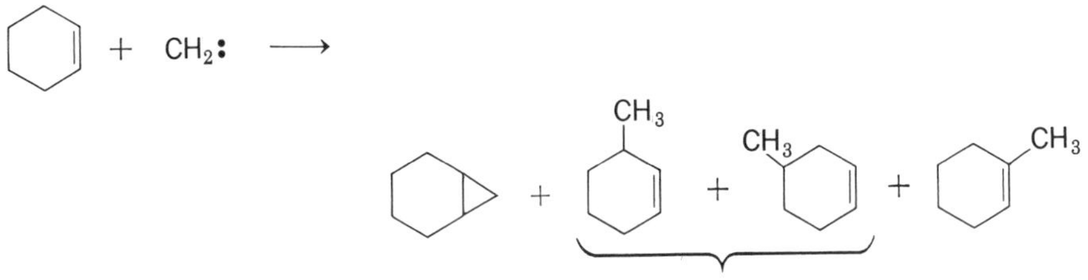

Direct photolysis:	0.7	1.0		0.18
Photosensitized decomposition:	2.5	1.0		0

The less energetic triplet methylene gives much less of the high-energy insertion and rearrangement reactions, and more simple addition to the double bond.

In this context, we should comment again on the chemical differences between singlet and triplet states. (See the discussion on p. 71.) When the locations of the two odd electrons in a species are widely separated, the spectrum shows two doublets and the species would be expected to react like a free radical. When the two odd electrons are closer together, the situation is less clear-cut. In the case of methylene, the two electronic states are well-characterized: one is a triplet with a considerable amount of diradical character, and the other is a singlet which is not a diradical. In this case, it is tempting to ascribe radical-like reactions (for example, non-stereospecific addition to olefins and hydrogen abstraction) solely to the

[†] K. R. Kopecky, G. S. Hammond, and P. A. Leermakers, *J. Am. Chem. Soc.*, **84**, 1015 (1962).

triplet state, and nonradical reactions (for example, the insertion reaction) to the singlet state. However, it is not known whether or not this is in fact correct. Nonstereospecific addition to olefins is commonly ascribed to the triplet state since, as discussed above, the products can be rationalized in terms of a diradical intermediate. However, it is not certain that singlet methylene may not also add nonstereospecifically. Similarly, certain singlet excited species may react by abstracting hydrogen atoms. These are areas which current research is probing.†

PROBLEMS

19-1 Distinguish between methylene in its singlet and triplet states on the basis of (a) energy; (b) hybridization of the nonbonded electron pair; (c) reactivity with double bonds; (d) reactivity with C—H bonds.

19-2 The photolysis of ketene in the gas phase in the presence of other gases has been studied as a function of the wavelength of the light used. By employing stereospecific addition to cis-2-butene as a diagnostic tool, the fraction α of methylene which is produced in its singlet versus its triplet state has been measured. At 2650 A, in the presence of inert gases, α is 0.98; at 3460 to 3820 A, α is less than 0.5. Suggest mechanisms for photolysis of ketene at long and at short wavelengths which account for this difference. Give particular attention to the species which undergoes intersystem crossing and the reaction which produces triplet methylene directly. [S. Ho, I. Unger, and W. A. Noyes, Jr., *J. Am. Chem. Soc.*, **87**, 2297 (1965).]

SUGGESTIONS FOR FURTHER READING

DeMore, W. B., and S. W. Benson: Preparation, Properties and Reactivity of Methylene, in W. A. Noyes, G. S. Hammond, and J. N. Pitts (eds.), "Advances

† For a more complete discussion of these ideas see W. B. DeMore and S. W. Benson, "Advances in Photochemistry," vol. 2, Interscience Publishers, Inc., New York, 1964, pp. 219–261; S. P. McGlynn, F. J. Smith, and G. Cilento, "Photochemistry and Photobiology," vol. 3, Pergamon Press, New York, 1964, pp. 269–294.

in Photochemistry," vol. 2, Interscience Publishers, Inc., New York, 1964, pp. 219–261.

Hine, J.: "Divalent Carbon," The Ronald Press Company, New York, 1964.

Hine, J.: "Physical Organic Chemistry," McGraw-Hill Book Company, New York, 2d ed., 1962, pp. 484–504.

Kirmse, W.: "Carbene Chemistry," Academic Press Inc., New York, 1964.

Parham, W. E., and E. E. Schweizer: in A. C. Cope (ed.), "Organic Reactions," vol. 13, John Wiley & Sons, Inc., New York, 1963, pp. 55–90.

part
four TERMINATION
REACTIONS

chapter twenty

Combination and Disproportionation Reactions

INTRODUCTION

Termination reactions occur in every radical system. In fact, one of the most characteristic features of radical species is that they react together in pairs; neither carbonium ions nor carbanions show this pairing reaction.

Alkyl radicals can terminate in two ways: by combination and by disproportionation. Combination is simply the reverse of dissociation:

$$2R\cdot \longrightarrow R{-}R$$

In disproportionation, a hydrogen atom that is beta to one radical center is transferred:

$$R\cdot \; + \; R_2\overset{H}{\underset{}{C}}{-}\overset{\bullet}{C}R_2 \quad \longrightarrow \quad R{-}H \; + \; R_2C{=}CR_2$$

There is some uncertainty about the structure of the transition state for disproportionation. It is known that a β hydrogen is transferred, since two $CH_3{-}CD_2\cdot$ radicals disproportionate as shown below.

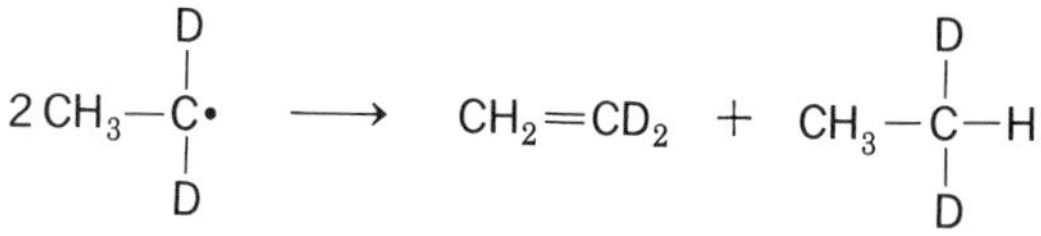

$$2\,CH_3{-}\overset{D}{\underset{D}{C}}\cdot \quad \longrightarrow \quad CH_2{=}CD_2 \; + \; CH_3{-}\overset{D}{\underset{D}{C}}{-}H$$

It might, therefore, be thought that disproportionation involves a simple head-to-tail transition state:

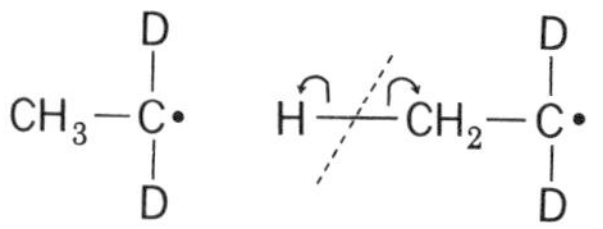

$$CH_3{-}\overset{D}{\underset{D}{C}}\cdot \qquad H{-}CH_2{-}\overset{D}{\underset{D}{C}}\cdot$$

However, if this were true, the Arrhenius A factor would be expected to be similar for disproportionations and for ordinary hydrogen abstraction reactions from alkanes. Actually, disproportionations have $A \cong 10^{10}$ sec^{-1}, whereas ordinary hydrogen abstractions have much lower A factors, near 10^8 sec^{-1}. Thus, the disproportionation transition state has a more favorable entropy than does an ordinary hydrogen abstraction. The A

312

factors for disproportionation and for combination are similar, and both types of termination reactions may involve similar transition states.†

Since bond making is exothermic, the combination of two radicals produces a molecule containing all the energy of the new covalent bond. For this molecule to become stable, it must dissipate this excess energy, either by spreading it throughout its vibrational modes or by collision with a wall or another molecule. Consider the combination of two radicals to form an initially excited species $XY°$:

$$X\bullet + Y\bullet \underset{k_2}{\overset{k_1}{\rightleftharpoons}} XY* \tag{20-1}$$

$$XY* + M \xrightarrow{k_3} XY + M \tag{20-2}$$

where M is an inert third body which deactivates $XY°$ by collision. At the steady state in the excited species $XY°$, the rate of formation of the stable molecule XY is

$$\frac{d(XY)}{dt} = \frac{k_1 k_3 (X\bullet)(Y\bullet)(M)}{k_2 + k_3(M)}$$

There are two cases: At low concentrations of M, $k_2 \gg k_3(M)$, and the rate of formation of XY equals $(k_1 k_3 / k_2)(X\bullet)(Y\bullet)(M)$. At high concentrations of M, $k_2 \ll k_3(M)$, and the rate reduces to $k_1(X\bullet)(Y\bullet)$ and becomes independent of the concentration of the third body. Experimental work has confirmed this "third-body" effect for methyl and ethyl radicals and iodine atoms, but larger radicals always follow second-order termination rate laws. An example is the combination of two ethyl radicals, which is third-order at very low pressures but above 1 mm becomes second-order. The rate of third-order combinations depends on the concentration of the third body and also on its structure. For example, the efficiency of various molecules to promote the combination of two iodine atoms has been found to increase as the size and complexity of the third body increases.

As we have just seen, termination reactions are usually bimolecular.

† One group of workers has argued that the transition state for combination and disproportionation must be very similar, and might be represented as a four-center reaction. For this viewpoint see J. N. Bradley and B. S. Rabinovitch, *J. Chem. Phys.*, **36**, 3498 (1962); and J. A. Kerr and A. F. Trotman-Dickenson, "Progress in Reaction Kinetics," vol. 1, Pergamon Press, New York, 1961, p. 113. It has also been argued that the two transition states are not similar, but that both involve a transition state with pronounced ionic character. For this view see S. W. Benson, "Advances in Photochemistry," vol. 2, John Wiley & Sons, Inc., New York, 1964, pp. 1–15.

The kinetic consequence of this is a rate dependence of the overall process on the square root of the rate of initiation. This results because the steady-state assumption equates the square of the radical concentration to the rate of initiation. For example, for the initiation and termination steps

Initiator $\xrightarrow{R_i}$ 2R•

2R• $\xrightarrow{k_t}$ Nonradical products

The steady-state hypothesis gives

$$R_i = 2k_t(\text{R}•)^2$$
$$(\text{R}•) = \left(\frac{R_i}{2k_t}\right)^{1/2}$$

The rate of the overall process observed usually is proportional to the concentration of radicals, and the total rate of the process therefore varies with the square root of the rate of initiation. For example, the rate of polymerization given in Eq. (15-8) on page 237 depends on the square root of the concentration of initiator.

ABSOLUTE VALUES OF RATE CONSTANTS

The measurement of the rate of combination of methyl radicals was discussed on page 48. The currently accepted rate constant is

$$k = 2 \times 10^{10} \qquad \text{liter mole}^{-1} \text{ sec}^{-1}$$

The energy of activation is zero with an uncertainty of ± 0.70 kcal/mole. This constant was first obtained by Gomer and Kistiakowsky in 1951. They used rotating-sector measurements and methyl radicals from the photolysis of acetone and from pyrolysis of dimethylmercury. Subsequently, the rate was measured by several other workers using rotating sector techniques, mass-spectrographic methods, and a sensitive manometric technique; the results are all in reasonable agreement.

The combination of ethyl radicals has been measured with somewhat less precision. The best value for the rate constant is probably

$$k = 1.6 \times 10^{11} \, e^{(-2,000 \pm 1,000)/RT} \qquad \text{liter mole}^{-1} \text{ sec}^{-1}$$

The activation energies have been measured for the combinations of the following radicals and found to be zero:

2CF$_3$•
2CCl$_3$•
2NO$_2$•
NO• + CH$_3$•

COMBINATION OF UNLIKE RADICALS

When two unlike radicals are present, three possible combination reactions can occur:

$$2A\cdot \xrightarrow{\ k_{aa}\ } AA$$

$$2B\cdot \xrightarrow{\ k_{bb}\ } BB$$

$$A\cdot + B\cdot \xrightarrow{\ k_{ab}\ } AB$$

As pointed out on page 14, the statistical expectation is that†

$$\phi = \frac{k_{ab}}{(k_{aa}k_{bb})^{1/2}} = 2$$

The value of ϕ has been measured for most of the simple aliphatic radicals in the gas phase, using gas chromatography, and ϕ is always found to be very close to 2. However, for polymeric radicals of differing charge types, ϕ is often 100-fold or larger. Values of ϕ very different from 2 are also found in autoxidation systems, where combinations between R• and ROO• are often favored over either homo-combination. These variations of ϕ from the expected value of 2 are due to a polar effect. Values of ϕ have been summarized in Table 20-1 for a number of radicals.

† Sometimes an alternative definition of ϕ is used in which $\phi = k_{ab}/2(k_{aa}k_{bb})^{1/2}$. In this definition, ϕ is statistically expected to be 1 rather than 2. This alternative definition is used, for example, by C. Walling, "Free Radicals in Solution," John Wiley & Sons, Inc., New York, 1957, pp. 145, 244, and 419. However, all the references cited in Table 20-1 employ the definition used here. The reader must be careful to determine which definition of ϕ is used if different authors' values are compared.

Table 20-1   Values of $\phi = k_{ab}/(k_{aa}k_{bb})^{1/2}$ for combination reactions of unlike radicals†

Radicals		
A	B	ϕ
Methyl	Ethyl	2.0
Methyl	Methoxy	1.9
Methyl	Acetyl	1.7
Methyl	Propyl	2.1
Ethyl	Propyl	1.9
Polystyryl	Poly(p-methoxystyryl)	1
Polystyryl	Poly(methyl methacrylyl)	14
Polystyryl	Poly(butyl acrylyl)	150

† A. F. Trotman-Dickenson, *Ann. Rept. Chem. Soc.*, **55**, 41 (1958); G. M. Burnett, "Mechanism of Polymer Reactions," Interscience Publishers, Inc., New York, 1954, p. 292; J. A. Kerr and A. F. Trotman-Dickenson, *Progr. Reaction Kinetics*, **1**, 108 (1961); J. Grotewold and J. A. Kerr, *J. Chem. Soc.*, 4337, 4342 (1963).

COMBINATION-DISPROPORTIONATION RATIOS

The ratio of combination to disproportionation can be studied by product analysis. Aliphatic radicals have usually been studied in the gas phase, using gas-phase chromatography as the analytical technique. Table 20-2 gives typical data; combination is favored for unbranched radicals, but disproportionation becomes more important as the radical becomes more branched. In general, radicals with larger numbers of β hydrogens have larger k_d/k_c ratios, where k_d is the rate constant for disproportionation and k_c that for combination. If the assumption is made that all the radicals listed in Table 20-2 have the same value of k_c, then the ratios of k_d/k_c represent the relative rates of disproportionation of the radicals listed. If the assumption is correct, much more disproportionation occurs in branched radicals than could be explained by a statistical effect. For example, the isopropyl radical has twice as many β hydrogens as the ethyl radical (i.e., six versus three) but has a five-fold larger k_d/k_c ratio. Similarly, t-butyl has nine β hydrogens and ethyl has three; statistically, therefore, t-butyl should have a threefold larger k_d/k_c ratio. Actually it is 46 times larger. The discrepancy in every case could be explained by assuming that the absolute rate constant for combination becomes smaller as the radical becomes more hindered. This would amount to postulating an F strain (strain from the front due to compression necessary to form a

Table 20-2   Disproportionation/combination ratios for radicals†

Radicals	°C	k_d/k_c
$CH_3 \cdot$ $C_2H_5 \cdot$	25–240	0.04
$CH_3 \cdot$ $CH_3CH_2CH_2 \cdot$	118–144	0.03
$2CH_3CH_2 \cdot$	25–350	0.1
$2CH_3CH_2CH_2 \cdot$	25–150	0.1
$2CH_3\overset{\bullet}{-}CH-CH_3$	20–200	0.5
$2(CH_3)_2CH-CH_2 \cdot$	100	0.4
$2CH_3-CH_2-\overset{\bullet}{C}H-CH_3$	100	2.3
$2(CH_3)_3C \cdot$	100	4.6

† A. F. Trotman-Dickenson, "Free Radicals," Methuen & Co., Ltd., London, 1959, p. 53; J. Grotewold and J. A. Kerr, *J. Chem. Soc.*, 4337, 4342 (1963).

bond) for the combination reaction. Unfortunately, data are not available to decide whether this variation in k_d/k_c is due to a change in the rate constant for combination or to a change in k_d that is much larger than statistical. However, as pointed out above, methyl radicals undergo termination with zero activation energy whereas ethyl radicals require about 2000 cal/mole. Thus, the values of k_c may very well decrease as the radical becomes more complex.

Most polymeric free radicals terminate predominantly or entirely by combination, and k_d/k_c is very small. The polymeric radical from methyl methacrylate, however, undergoes termination by both mechanisms. The activation energy for disproportionation is about 5 kcal/mole larger than for combination, and the fraction of termination by disproportionation therefore increases with increasing temperature. At 60°C, k_d/k_c is about 1.5.†

The rate constants for combination reactions are so large that the rate of termination in the liquid phase can become diffusion-controlled; that is, the diffusion of two radicals through the solution to meet each other is the slow process, and bond formation occurs as soon as the two meet. Under these conditions, termination rates vary with the nature of the solvent and especially with its viscosity. One very dramatic illustration of this is the so-called Trommsdorff effect: The rate of polymeriza-

† J. C. Bevington, "Radical Polymerization," Academic Press Inc., New York, 1961, p. 136.

Table 20-3 Absolute rate constants for the polymerization of vinyl acetate at 25°C†

Polymerization, %	Approx. τ, sec	k_p	k_t	$k_p/k_t^{1/2}$
23	2.5	1,290	126	0.37
46	10	1,280	90	0.42
57	15	555	6.7	0.67
65	23	87	1.1	0.26

† W. I. Bengough and H. W. Melville, *Proc. Roy. Soc.* (*London*), *Ser.* A, **230**, 429 (1955).

tion of certain monomers is observed to increase as the percent reaction increases. As the reaction solution contains more and more polymer, the viscosity increases and the rate of termination decreases. The rate of polymerization, which is proportional to $k_p/k_t^{1/2}$, therefore increases. The absolute values of the rate constants for the polymerization of vinyl acetate have been measured as a function of the extent of polymerization; these data are given in Table 20-3. As the percent conversion to polymer increases, the reaction solution becomes more viscous, and the lifetime τ of the growing polymeric radical increases. At moderate conversions, k_t decreases and k_p remains fairly constant; in these solutions, the monomer can diffuse to the polymeric radical at a nearly normal rate, but the termination between two polymeric radicals becomes diffusion-controlled. At high conversions, even k_p decreases. The result is that the polymerizability of the monomer, given by $k_p/k_t^{1/2}$, goes through a maximum.

PROBLEM

20-1 Two values of k_d/k_c can be measured for the reaction between ethyl and propyl radicals, since either ethylene or propylene can be formed in the disproportionation.

$$C_2H_5\bullet + C_3H_7\bullet \xrightarrow{k_c} C_5H_{12}$$

$$C_2H_5\bullet + C_3H_7\bullet \xrightarrow{k_e} H_2C{=}CH_2 + C_3H_8$$

$$C_2H_5\bullet + C_3H_7\bullet \xrightarrow{k_p} H_2C{=}CH{-}CH_3 + C_2H_6$$

It is found that $k_p/k_c = 0.081$.   Compare this value with others in Table 20-2.   Is it reasonable?   Predict an approximate value for k_e/k_c.   [J. Grotewold and J. A. Kerr, *J. Chem. Soc.*, 4337 (1963).]

SUGGESTIONS FOR FURTHER READING

Benson, S. W.: "Advances in Photochemistry," vol. 2, John Wiley & Sons, Inc., New York, 1964, pp. 1–24.
Lapporte, S. J.: *Angew. Chem.*, **72,** 759 (1960).
Trotman-Dickenson, A. F.: *Ann. Rept. Chem. Soc.*, **55,** 36 (1958).

chapter twenty-one Inhibition

It is appropriate that in this final chapter we turn to ways in which radical processes can be inhibited, retarded, and stopped. Most radical reactions are chain processes, and the introduction of relatively few radicals into the system produces many product molecules. For the same reason, the capture of the relatively few radicals that constitute the propagating chains can entirely stop product formation. Thus, inhibition is of particular importance and of dramatic consequence in chain reactions.

The controlled use of inhibitors is of great practical utility. For example, polymerization monomers are sold with an added inhibitor to reduce the amount of polymer formed during storage; this inhibitor is removed before using the monomer. The honored safety step of keeping an iron wire in bottles of ether is an example of inhibition; ethers autoxidize to form hydroperoxides. The ether hydroperoxides are dangerously explosive, and their formation is autocatalytic; however, in the presence of iron, peroxidic materials are reduced and their concentration is controlled.

Lubricating oils and gasolines are inhibited to prevent a buildup of "sludge" (i.e., undesirable polymers). Plastic window panels contain inhibitors to prevent sun damage (i.e., destructive photolysis). Literally hundreds of new compounds are tested each year in the continuing search for a better inhibitor for a particular industrial product or process.

The processes of initiation and inhibition are related. In the general radical chain process, the substrate S is converted to a species S$\cdot$ which takes part in a kinetic chain. Initiation can occur by the dissociation of an initiator to radical fragments:

$$\text{Initiator} \longrightarrow 2R\cdot \qquad (21\text{-}1)$$
$$R\cdot + S \longrightarrow S\cdot \qquad (21\text{-}2)$$

At low concentrations of initiators, radicals are formed in low concentrations, and R$\cdot$ radicals mainly initiate chains [reaction (21-2)]. However, if the radical concentration is high and if the radical R$\cdot$ is relatively stable and has a long lifetime, then termination reactions involving R$\cdot$ radicals can occur in addition to the usual termination between two S$\cdot$ radicals:

$$
\left.
\begin{array}{l}
2R\cdot \\
R\cdot + S\cdot \\
2S\cdot
\end{array}
\right\} \longrightarrow \text{Nonradical products}
\qquad
\begin{array}{l}
(21\text{-}3) \\
(21\text{-}4) \\
(21\text{-}5)
\end{array}
$$

As was observed in the preceding chapter, polar effects frequently make the cross-termination reaction (21-4) particularly favorable. Conse-

322

quently, moderately high concentrations of R• radicals may provide another termination path, in addition to reaction (21-5), and slow the rate of the overall process.

These phenomena are well known in radical polymerizations. At high initiator concentrations, radicals from the initiators (so-called primary radicals) terminate growing chains. This reaction is called primary radical termination, and it leads to decreased efficiencies of initiators and a polymer of lower molecular weight than would be formed by the combination of two polymeric radicals.†

Inhibitors need not be radicals themselves. They can be substances that react with radicals to produce another radical either too stable to enter into the kinetic chain or reactive in some new pathway. Phenols, amines, and other similar materials with active hydrogens are inhibitors:

$$S• + I—H \longrightarrow SH + I•$$ (21-6)

$$I• \longrightarrow \text{New reaction}$$

Quinones are inhibitors, and four different reactions can be envisioned to explain their action:

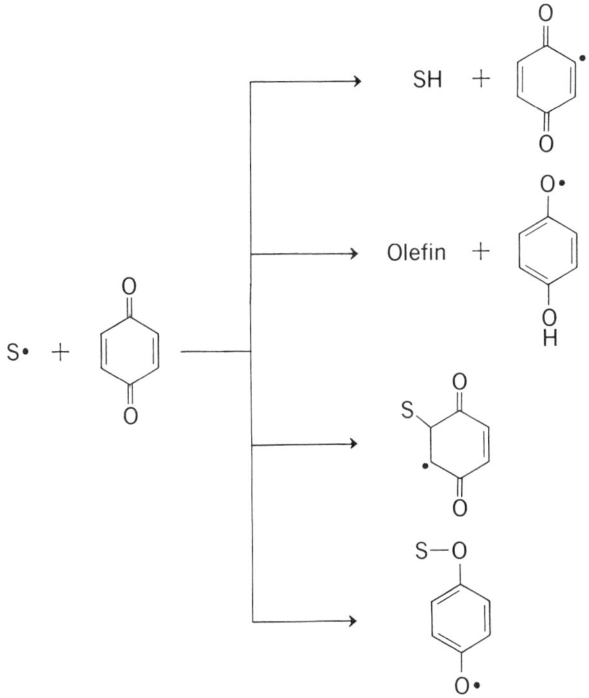

† C. H. Bamford, A. D. Jenkins, and R. Johnston, *Trans. Faraday Soc.*, **55**, 1451 (1959); G. Henrici-Olivé and S. Olivé, *Makromol. Chem.*, **37**, 71 (1960).

Reaction (21-7a) is hydrogen abstraction from the quinone by the radical R•. Reaction (21-7b) is hydrogen abstraction from the radical by the quinone Q:

$$\underset{H}{\overset{|}{\text{C}}}\text{--CH}_2\bullet \; + \; Q \; \longrightarrow \; \text{C}{=}\text{CH}_2 \; + \; (QH)\bullet$$

Reaction (21-7c) is addition of R• to the quinone carbon-carbon double bond, and reaction (21-7d) is addition of R• to the quinone oxygen.

Inorganic redox materials also can act as inhibitors; for example, ferric chloride inhibits the polymerization of styrene:

$$M_n\bullet + FeCl_3 \longrightarrow M_n\text{--Cl} + FeCl_2$$

This is an example of ligand transfer (see page 139).

The mechanisms of inhibitor action are complex and not entirely understood. Often, the variety of facts is, in itself, amazing. For example, benzoquinone inhibits the polymerization of vinyl acetate and terminates one kinetic chain per molecule; it also inhibits styrene but with a stoichiometry of two kinetic chains per molecule. On the other hand, tetrachloroquinone (chloranil) inhibits vinyl acetate but copolymerizes with styrene. All these facts apply to *initiated* polymerizations. In the *thermal* polymerization of styrene, both chloranil and benzoquinone are inhibitors but disappear at anomalously fast rates. This sometimes bewildering situation results from the fact that radical systems are generally complex to start with, and inhibitors may provide several additional reaction paths and several new products.

In general, three mechanisms for inhibition can be visualized:

1. *Inhibition by radicals.* An added free radical species will inhibit the process shown in Eqs. (21-1) and (21-2) if it scavenges S• but does not react with S to convert it to S•.

2. *Atom transfer.* Atom transfer is accompanied by inhibition if the transfer agent forms a stable radical that does not reinitiate. In radical polymerizations, this process is called degradative transfer, and the transfer agent can be considered an inhibitor. An example is transfer by diphenylpicrylhydrazine, which produces the very stable DPPH radical in the transfer step:

$$M_n\bullet + DPPH\text{--H} \xrightarrow{k_{tr}} M_n\text{--H} + DPPH\bullet$$

DPPH$\cdot$ + M $\xrightarrow{k_a}$ M$_n\cdot$

M$_n\cdot$ + M $\xrightarrow{k_p}$ M$_{n+1}^{\cdot}$

Inhibition results since k_a is small relative to k_p.

3. *Addition.* Some substances add radicals to form stabilized species that do not propagate the kinetic chain. An example is the inhibition of radical polymerization by oxygen:

M$_n\cdot$ + O$_2$ $\longrightarrow$ M$_n$OO$\cdot$

KINETICS

A generalized reaction system inhibited by the inhibitor I is

$$\text{Initiator} \xrightarrow{R_i} \text{S}\cdot \tag{21-8}$$

$$\text{S}\cdot + \text{S} \xrightarrow{k_p} \text{S}\cdot \tag{21-9}$$

$$\text{S}\cdot + \text{I} \xrightarrow{k_{10}} \text{SI}\cdot \quad (\text{or S} + \text{I}\cdot) \tag{21-10}$$

$$
\left.
\begin{aligned}
&2\text{I}\cdot \\
&\text{I}\cdot + \text{S}\cdot \\
&2\text{S}\cdot
\end{aligned}
\right\} \longrightarrow \text{Nonradical products}
$$

$$\tag{21-11}$$
$$\tag{21-12}$$
$$\tag{21-13}$$

If reaction (21-11) is the main termination mechanism, the usual square-root dependence of the state of initiation no longer holds; rather, the rate of the propagation process depends on the first power of the rate of initiation. If termination is by (21-12), then each inhibitor molecule stops two growing chains; if by (21-11) or (21-13), each inhibitor stops one chain. Generally, several processes compete simultaneously, and a stoichiometry between one and two is found.

The ratio of k_{10}/k_p is defined as the inhibitor constant, C_{inh}, and is analogous to the transfer constant as used in Eq. (15-21) on page 246.

$$C_{inh} = \frac{k_{10}}{k_p}$$

Values of these inhibitor constants are known for a variety of processes and inhibitors. For example, in the polymerization of vinyl acetate, duroquinone has an inhibitor constant of 90 at 45°C and stops one chain per molecule;[†] that is, the growing vinyl acetate polymeric radical reacts with the inhibitor 90 times faster than it adds another unit of vinyl acetate. The inhibitor constant for diphenylpicrylhydrazyl in the polymerization of methyl methacrylate at 45°C is 2,100.[‡]

The inhibitor constants of ferric chloride in dimethylformamide as solvent have been measured in the polymerization of a number of monomers.[¶] The constant has the value of 500 for styrene and 3 for acrylonitrile, both at 60°C. In the transfer

$$FeCl_2 \bullet \text{-----} \overset{\bullet}{Cl} \text{-----} \bullet M_n$$

the ionic resonance forms shown below are important:

$$FeCl_2 \bullet \, Cl\overset{\text{-}}{:} \, {}^+M_n \quad \longleftrightarrow \quad FeCl_2\overset{\text{-}}{:} \, \overset{\bullet}{Cl} \, {}^+M_n$$

This charge-separated resonance structure would lead to the prediction that styrene should have a larger transfer constant than acrylonitrile, as is observed.

Phenols and amines are particularly effective inhibitors of autoxidations. In the inhibition of the autoxidation of styrene, phenols function by a hydrogen transfer reaction to the styrylperoxy radical

$$ROO\bullet + ArOH \longrightarrow ROOH + ArO\bullet$$

The rate constants for this reaction have been found to obey the Hammett equation, using values of σ^+ and a value of ρ of -1.58. This negative ρ is in accord with the electrophilic nature of the peroxy radical and suggests the resonance structures for the transition state shown below.

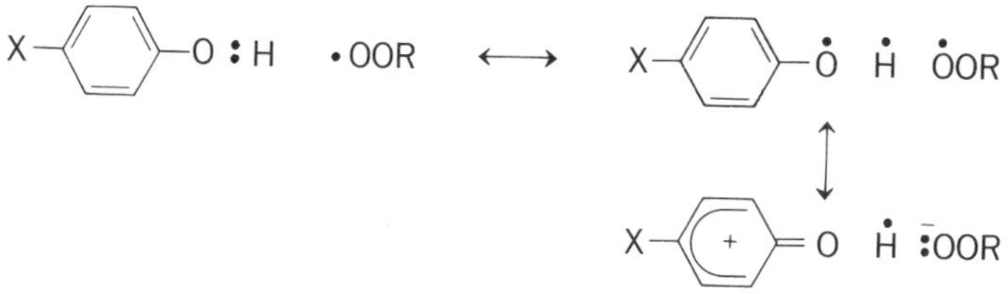

[†] P. D. Bartlett and H. Kwart, *J. Am. Chem. Soc.*, **72**, 1051 (1950).
[‡] J. Kice, *J. Am. Chem. Soc.*, **76**, 6274 (1954).
[¶] C. H. Bamford, A. D. Jenkins, and R. Johnston, *Proc. Roy. Soc.* (*London*), Ser. A, **239**, 214 (1957).

Electron-releasing X groups would be expected to stabilize this transition state and speed the reaction, as is observed.[†]

REACTIONS INVOLVING STABLE FREE RADICALS

Before concluding the discussion of inhibitors, the reactions of unusually stable radicals should be considered. Some radicals are sufficiently stable so that relatively concentrated solutions of them can be prepared. For example, DPPH is a stable radical, and its concentration can be measured by utilizing its intense light absorption at 350 to 520 mμ. If an initiator is decomposed in the presence of DPPH, the color of the DPPH is observed to fade. The reactions which occur can be written as shown below, where I is an initiator:

$$I \xrightarrow{k_{14}} 2R\bullet \qquad\qquad (21\text{-}14)$$

$$R\bullet + DPPH \xrightarrow{k_{15}} Nonradical\ products \qquad\qquad (21\text{-}15)$$

The rate of reaction (21-15) is

$$R_{15} = k_{15}(R\bullet)(DPPH)$$

However, the rate constant k_{15} cannot be calculated unless the concentration of R$\bullet$ is known. Radical concentrations usually are not known, but systems of this type can be utilized to calculate the rate of reaction (21-14).[‡] At the steady state in R$\bullet$ concentration

$$2k_{14}f(I) = k_{15}(R\bullet)(DPPH)$$

where f is the fraction of the radicals from I which become free. Therefore,

$$\frac{-d(DPPH)}{dt} = k_{15}(R\bullet)(DPPH)$$

$$= 2k_{14}f(I)$$

Thus, the rate of disappearance of the DPPH color can be related to k_{14}, but the rate constant for the radical reaction itself, k_{15}, is not obtainable.

[†] J. A. Howard and K. U. Ingold, *Can. J. Chem.*, **41**, 1744 (1963).
[‡] J. Osugi, M. Sato, and M. Sasaki, *Rev. Phys. Chem. Japan*, **33**, 53 (1963); R. C. Lamb and J. G. Pacifici, *J. Am. Chem. Soc.*, **86**, 914 (1964).

However, some radicals have been discovered which are stable enough so they can be prepared in concentrated solutions but reactive enough so they undergo ordinary halogen abstraction reactions. Zinc reduction in a high vacuum system of the pyridinium iodide shown below gives a solution of the dark emerald green pyridinyl radical.[†]

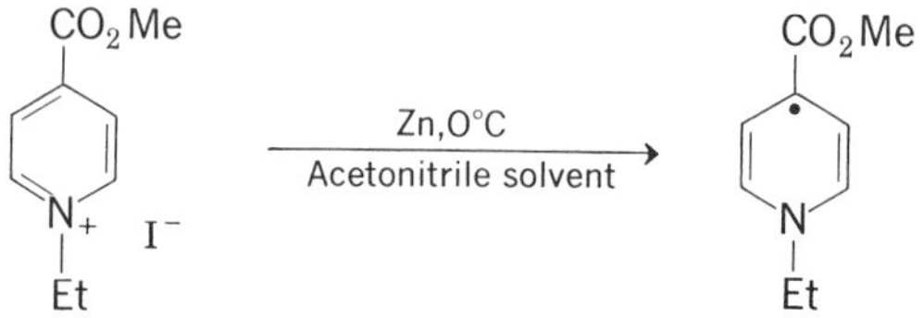

The radical can be extracted into hexane, the hexane removed, and the radical distilled under high vacuum. (It distills at $40°C$ at about 10^{-6} mm.) The radical reacts instantly with oxygen or carbon tetrachloride even at $-200°C$. However, the rate of its reaction with less reactive halocarbons can be measured by observing the slow fading of the color of the radical. For example, the reaction shown below has been studied.

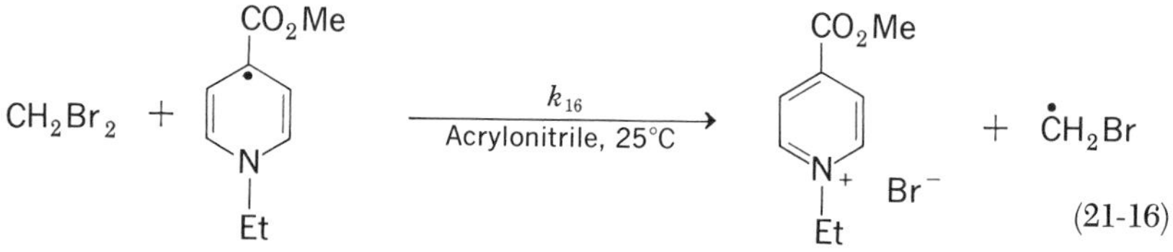

$$(21\text{-}16)$$

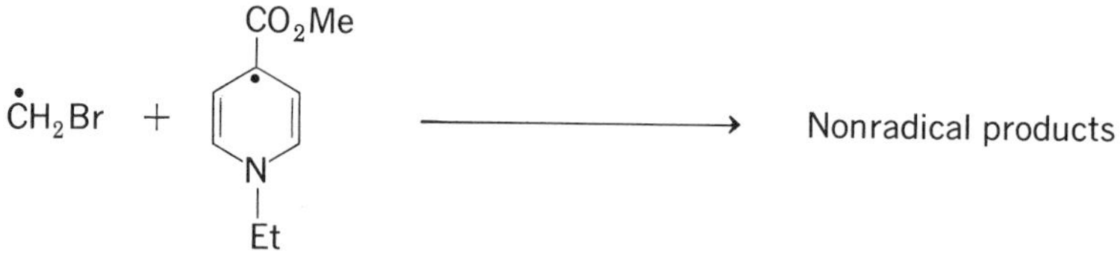

In this reaction of the unusually stable pyridinyl radical, the rate constant k_{16} can be calculated directly since the concentrations of both reactants are known.[‡] The rate of reaction (21-16) is given below, where $(P\bullet)$ is the concentration of the pyridinyl radical,

$$\frac{-d(P\bullet)}{dt} = k_{16}(CH_2Br_2)(P\bullet)$$

[†] E. M. Kosower and E. J. Poziomek, *J. Am. Chem. Soc.*, **85**, 2035 (1963).
[‡] E. M. Kosower and J. Schwager, *J. Am. Chem. Soc.*, **86**, 4493 (1964).

The value of k_{16} is found to be 2.0×10^{-4} liter mole^{-1} sec^{-1} for a solution which is 0.012 M in the pyridinyl radical and 0.84 M in dibromomethane in acetonitrile as solvent. The reaction rate is first order in the concentration of each reactant as expected. One unexpected feature is that the rate constant is almost identical in the solvents acetonitrile, isopropyl alcohol, and dichloromethane. It is surprising that this rate constant does not depend more on the nature of the solvent, since a charge-separated resonance structure can be written for the transition state which would appear to be energetically favorable.

Transition state

PROBLEM

21-1 Derive the rate law for a process $(-dS/dt)$ involving reactions (21-8) to (21-11). Give a system that might exemplify the first-order initiator dependence.

SUGGESTIONS FOR FURTHER READING

Bevington, J. C.: "Radical Polymerization," Academic Press Inc., New York, 1961, chap. 7. (Inhibition in polymerizations.)

Ingold, K. U.: *Chem. Rev.*, **61**, 563 (1961). (Inhibition in autoxidation.)

Walling, C.: "Free Radicals in Solution," John Wiley & Sons, Inc., New York, 1957, pp. 162–178, 430–436.

Name Index

Subject Index